2 DAY LOAN

Return to Learning Centre of issue
Fines are charged at £2 per day
No renewal

Oxford Studies in European Law

General Editors: Paul Craig and Gráinne de Búrca

ANTI-DISCRIMINATION LAW AND THE EUROPEAN UNION

Anti-Discrimination Law and the European Union

MARK BELL
Lecturer in Law, University of Leicester

OXFORD
UNIVERSITY PRESS

*This book has been printed digitally and produced in a standard specification
in order to ensure its continuing availability*

OXFORD
UNIVERSITY PRESS

Great Clarendon Street, Oxford OX2 6DP

Oxford University Press is a department of the University of Oxford.
It furthers the University's objective of excellence in research, scholarship,
and education by publishing worldwide in

Oxford New York

Auckland Bangkok Buenos Aires Cape Town Chennai
Dar es Salaam Delhi Hong Kong Istanbul Karachi Kolkata
Kuala Lumpur Madrid Melbourne Mexico City Mumbai Nairobi
São Paulo Shanghai Taipei Tokyo Toronto

Oxford is a registered trade mark of Oxford University Press
in the UK and in certain other countries

Published in the United States
by Oxford University Press Inc., New York

ISBN 0-19-924450-2

Cover illustration: DNA model. Photo: Photo Disc.

For my parents and in memory of John Hall

GENERAL EDITORS' PREFACE

The field of EU anti-discrimination law has provoked a great deal of scholarly and practical interest since the introduction of Article 13 EC by the Amsterdam Treaty. This book traces the legal changes which have occurred since then and analyzes the significance of the new Treaty provision, along with the relevant legislation and anti-discrimination policies which have been adopted since its enactment. Considering these changes also in the context of current constitutional events, the author assesses them against the background of the recently proclaimed EU Charter of Fundamental Rights.

More specifically, the book breaks new ground in placing the recent developments in historical context by providing a detailed account of the gradual emergence of EU anti-discrimination policy over time, with particular focus on two hitherto relatively neglected areas: those of racial discrimination and sexual orientation discrimination. While there are already many academic commentaries on EC sex discrimination law, as well as on the general legal principle of non-discrimination, and the principle of non-discrimination on grounds of nationality in the field of free movement, the primary focus of this book on the areas of race and sexual orientation is original and welcome. The comparative analysis of the differential evolution of EU equal treatment policy in these two respective policy fields is revealing and thought provoking.

Two models of European social policy are identified and contrasted in the book: the market integration model and the social citizenship model. While acknowledging certain significant developments towards the latter, the author demonstrates how the dynamics of market integration remain strongly persuasive in determining the direction of EU social policy. Attention is also paid to softer European legal initiatives and to the intersection of anti-discrimination norms within new fields of EU activity such as employment policy which use experimental instruments of governance. The national dimension of European anti-discrimination policy is also given careful attention, with a chapter outlining the diverse legal regimes and models of equality law to be found within member states, and an overview in the final chapter of the extent to which national legal traditions in this field may be converging.

This is an important and engaging work on a new and vibrant area of European law which will be relevant to all those interested in EC social law and policy, as well as to EU law academics and practitioners more generally.

Paul Craig
Gráinne de Búrca
February 2002

ACKNOWLEDGEMENTS

First and foremost, I wish to thank my parents for their constant and generous support in all ways, without which it would not have been possible for me to complete this book.

I want also to acknowledge the support I have found from my whole family, who have demonstrated interest and enthusiasm throughout, which has been a great source of encouragement.

This book is substantially based on the research conducted during my doctoral studies at the European University Institute, Florence. I am indebted to all the many people at the Institute who provided help and advice, ensuring that my time there was very rewarding. Specifically, I wish to acknowledge the constructive and enlightening discussions over the years with both my supervisor, Silvana Sciarra, and co-supervisor, Colin Crouch. Moreover, I want to thank Gráinne de Búrca for her generous support and advice in transforming this text from a thesis into a book.

I am also very grateful to the other members of my thesis examining jury. Barry Fitzpatrick kindly read this book from the earliest drafts and his guidance has greatly informed my ideas and understanding. I wish to thank also Elspeth Guild who provided me with perceptive and insightful comments that were very useful in shaping this book.

Beyond the Institute, I must acknowledge the assistance and encouragement I received from Andrea Subhan. I wish also to thank the many individual activists who provided so much help in my research, and in particular Kurt Krickler, Isabelle Chopin and Patrick Yu who gave me opportunities to participate in this valuable work.

I have been very fortunate to find myself at the University of Leicester since leaving Florence. As I worked towards the completion of this book, my colleagues have been constantly helpful and encouraging. I would like to acknowledge in particular the valuable guidance provided by Robin White. I wish also to take this opportunity to thank Pascale Lorber for our many labour law conservations that have been so useful when writing this text.

I am very grateful to John Louth and his colleagues at OUP—he has been supportive and understanding throughout the completion of this book.

There are so many friends who have helped me greatly in the long process of writing first the PhD and then the book—I cannot begin to name them all. I want to thank all those who provided such supportive friendship and the very happy memories shared together. Particular appreciation goes to those with whom I lived in Florence and the happy environment they always provided—Marie-Louise, Mishal, Mia, Nadia and Alexander. Finally, I wish to thank especially Maurice for all the time spent listening, advising and encouraging.

Chapter 5 is a modified version of the following article first published by the Maastricht Journal of European and Comparative Law and is reproduced with their kind permission:

M Bell, 'The new Article 13 EC Treaty: a sound basis for European anti-discrimination law?' (1999) 6 Maastricht J of Eur and Comparative L 5.

CONTENTS

ABBREVIATIONS

A-G	Advocate General
Art	Article
CEEP	European Centre of Enterprises with Public Participation and of Enterprises of General Economic Interest
CFI	Court of First Instance
CGB	Commissie Gelijke Behandeling
CRE	Commission for Racial Equality
CS	Coal and Steel Community Treaty
Dec	Decision
D-G	Directorate-General
Dir	Directive
DO	Discrimination Ombudsman
EC	European Community
ECHR	European Convention on Human Rights
ECJ	European Court of Justice
ECR	European Court Reports
ECRI	European Commission Against Racism and Intolerance
ECSC	European Coal and Steel Community
EEC	European Economic Community
ETUC	European Trade Union Confederation
EU	European Union
GU	Gazzetta Ufficiale
ICCPR	International Covenant on Civil and Political Rights
ICESCR	International Covenant on Economic, Social and Cultural Rights
IGC	Intergovernmental Conference
ILO	International Labour Organisation
MEP	Member of the European Parliament
NGO	Non-governmental organisation
OJ	Official Journal of the European Communities
OOPEC	Office for Official Publications of the European Communities
para	paragraph
Reg	Regulation
RRA	Race Relations Act
SEA	Single European Act
SWT	South-West Trains
TEU	Treaty on European Union
UNHCR	United Nations High Commission for Refugees
UNICE	Union of Industrial and Employers Confederations of Europe

TABLES

TABLE OF CASES

Court of First Instance

European Court of Human Rights

Other Jurisdictions

France

Germany

Ireland

UK

TABLE OF LEGISLATION

European Union Legislation

Decisions

Directives

National Legislation

Belgium

Denmark

Introduction

European social policy is traditionally one of the least satisfactory aspects of European integration. For some, it is a troublesome interference in a field best left to national discretion and only weakly related to the essentially economic vocation of the European Union.[1] For others, it seems a perpetual source of disappointment—a policy full of worthy objectives, but characterised by a failure to live up to the high expectations it self-generates.[2] Disagreement extends to the diagnosis of the fundamental problems in social policy. Certain authors have focused on the role played by the founding Treaties, and the limited legal competence provided for Community intervention.[3] Others have challenged this view, arguing that the Treaty base debate is only a means to disguise the Member States' basic equivocation on social legislation.[4]

Within this general debate on why social policy has not enjoyed the same fortune as economic integration, it is also possible to highlight uneven development inside social policy, where certain issues have progressed relatively fast, whilst others remain stagnant. Anti-discrimination is a very clear example of this phenomenon. A sharp contrast exists between the well-established body of EU law on gender and nationality discrimination and the relatively recent first steps of the Union in regulating other forms of discrimination.

This book aims to provide a better understanding of the forces influencing the direction and development of European social policy, through an analysis of the situation within anti-discrimination law. In particular, it is proposed that EU social policy is located between primarily two theoretical frameworks. On one side, there is the market integration model of social policy. This prescribes

[1] For further discussion of this 'liberal' outlook see B Hepple, 'Social Values and European Law' (1995) 48 CLP II: Collected Papers 39, 40.

[2] J Kenner, 'Citizenship and fundamental rights: reshaping the European social model' in J Kenner (ed), *Trends in European social policy. Essays in memory of Malcolm Mead* (Aldershot: Dartmouth, 1995) 83.

[3] D Collins, *The European Communities—the social policy of the first phase. Volume 2 The European Economic Community 1958–72* (London: Martin Robertson, 1975) 232.

[4] E Szyszczak, 'L'Espace Sociale Européenne: reality, dreams, or nightmares?' (1990) 33 German Ybk of Int L 284.

a very limited role for the Union in social policy; EU intervention in employment regulation is regarded as justified only where this is necessary to prevent unfair competition that could disrupt the smooth functioning of the internal market. On the other side, a social citizenship model of social policy foresees an expanded role for the Union in guaranteeing a range of fundamental social rights and hence building a sense of European citizenship amongst the beneficiaries of those rights. This book examines the extent to which these models can help explain the development of EU anti-discrimination law. Moreover, given the recent expansion of the Union's anti-discrimination law, the book considers whether this reveals a shift in the general nature of European social policy—in particular, whether this represents a move away from a social policy dependent on a market integration rationale and towards a more autonomous social policy based on the protection of fundamental rights.

To fulfil these objectives, this book takes two specific grounds of discrimination and examines their development within EU law and policy. First, the case of racial discrimination is considered. This emerges as an area where no binding EU rules previously existed, but a significant amount of non-binding, soft law instruments were already in place. However, this picture changed radically in June 2000 when the Council adopted the Racial Equality Directive.[5] This law forbids discrimination on the grounds of racial or ethnic origin in employment, social protection (including social security and healthcare), education, social advantages, and access to and the supply of goods and services, including housing.

The second form of discrimination studied is that based on sexual orientation.[5a] This immediately provides a useful contrast, as it is a subject previously little discussed at the European level, and an area where the Member States' views diverge sharply. Unlike racial discrimination, there is only a thin legacy of earlier soft law instruments. Indeed, pressure for change in this area has notably focused on strategic litigation at the Court of Justice.[6] Whilst these cases ultimately proved unsuccessful, significant legislative reform has occurred as a result of the adoption of the so-called Framework Directive in November 2000.[7] This law forbids discrimination in employment on the grounds of religion or belief, age, disability or sexual orientation.

---

[5] Council Dir (EC) 2000/43 of 29 June 2000 implementing the principle of equal treatment between persons irrespective of racial or ethnic origin [2000] OJ L180/22.

[5a] 'Sexual orientation' means heterosexual, homosexual or bisexual orientation.

[6] Case C–249/96 *Grant v South-West Trains* [1998] ECR I–621, Cases C–122/99P and C–125/99P *D and Sweden v Council* [2001] ECR I–4319.

[7] Council Dir (EC) 2000/78 of 27 November 2000 establishing a general framework for equal treatment in employment and occupation [2000] OJ L303/16.

In selecting the cases for comparison, a range of discriminatory grounds could have been studied. However, the new anti-discrimination law of the European Union is founded on an amendment of the EC Treaty in 1997 to add Article 13, which provides specific powers for the Union to combat discrimination on grounds of sex, racial or ethnic origin, religion or belief, age, disability or sexual orientation. Therefore, it is logical to make a comparison from within these grounds. Sex discrimination can be distinguished immediately because, although present in EC Treaty, Article 13, it is not a new ground of discrimination for EU law, but in fact it has been the subject of EU regulation from the outset of European integration. The decision of the EU legislator in 2000 to separate the remaining Article 13 grounds between racial discrimination (which is the subject of a specific Directive) and the other grounds (which are the subject of the general Framework Directive) indicates the need to compare discrimination on grounds of racial or ethnic origin with another ground of discrimination, because there is clearly a different approach by the EU in relation to race discrimination. Of the remaining grounds, disability discrimination has already been the subject of a comprehensive volume by Lisa Waddington, *Disability, Employment and the European Community*.[8] Whilst religion, age or sexual orientation could each make a potentially interesting comparison with racial discrimination, the advantage of choosing sexual orientation lies in the body of litigation that has surrounded this ground of discrimination in recent years in the EU courts—this is of particular interest and it has not occurred in respect of either religious or age discrimination.

Structure of the book

The book commences with an overview of the nature of European social policy and the location of anti-discrimination law therein. In particular, Chapter 1 develops the theoretical framework. Specifically, this chapter explores the two dominant, and alternative, models of European social policy: the market integration model and the social citizenship model. This discussion is placed in the context of the agreement of the EU Charter of Fundamental Rights in December 2000[9] and there is an exploration of the extent to which this may indicate a new phase in EU law and policy, particularly in the social field.

---

[8] L Waddington, *Disability, employment and the European Community* (Antwerpen: Maklu, 1995).
[9] [2000] OJ C364/1.

Chapter 2 proceeds to a more focused examination of the existing experience in EU anti-discrimination law. It analyses the state of play regarding law on nationality discrimination and gender discrimination. In particular, there is attention to the underlying factors that have allowed the Union to construct a well-developed role in the regulation of these forms of discrimination, notwithstanding the generally slow development of European social law.

Following on from the general and specific contexts provided in Chapters 1 and 2 respectively, Chapters 3 and 4 present the situations of racial and sexual orientation discrimination in EU law. These chapters pursue an essentially chronological structure in respect of the emergence of the policy debate, drawing some initial conclusions on the dynamics that have governed the pace of change. Emphasis is placed on understanding better the decision of the Member States to amend the EC Treaty in 1997 to insert a new legal competence for combating discrimination. Subsequent to this discussion, Chapter 3 analyses the content of the Racial Equality Directive, and Chapter 4 explores the provisions of the Framework Directive.

Chapter 5 examines the nature of the new EU anti-discrimination law since EC Treaty, Article 13 and the agreement of the Directives. In particular, there is an exploration of the character of these legal instruments with a view to understanding their location within the theoretical framework of European social policy introduced in Chapter 1. Does the new anti-discrimination law reflect an abandonment of the market-driven social policy in favour of a rights-based approach? To this end, the legal scope of EC Treaty, Article 13 and the Directives is interrogated, with a stress on exploring the capacity of the Union to regulate discrimination outside participation in the labour market.

Chapter 5 indicates the fuzzy boundaries of the new EU anti-discrimination law and the difficulty in finding the limits to the scope for EU intervention. Chapter 6 moves from an analysis of the legal parameters to EU anti-discrimination law and instead concentrates on understanding better the appropriate role for the Union in this field. To this end, there is an examination of national laws on discrimination on the grounds of race and sexual orientation in the area of employment. This legal survey is with a view to appreciating the different national legal traditions and practices that exist and how they have shaped the evolution of EU anti-discrimination law. Reflectively, this overview also permits an insight into the impact that the Directives will have on the current patterns of national anti-discrimination law.

Finally, Chapter 7 returns to the theoretical framework presented at the outset of the book. It considers the location of the EC Treaty, Article 13 laws within this framework and how these influence the overall nature of current

European social policy. Whilst progress has been made in building a set of basic labour law rights, social policy still remains linked to a market integration rationale. Nonetheless, the rise of new forms of EU regulation—specifically, the open method of co-ordination—have produced a shift away from the focus on market integration in favour of facilitating market participation. The emphasis on removing barriers to participation in the labour market has created new space for anti-discrimination law, albeit in a different context from a fundamental rights rationale.

This final chapter looks beyond the EC Treaty, Article 13 Directives and considers the overall anti-discrimination policy framework. It identifies the need for complementary, flanking measures in order to ensure the efficacy of the Directives, reflected in the growing attention to mainstreaming equality considerations in EU law and policy making. This section indicates the need to provide more coherence in the structures and processes for mainstreaming at the EU level. Finally, this chapter considers the potential for future EU anti-discrimination legislation. Whilst considerable progress has been made through the two EC Treaty, Article 13 Directives, the apparent hierarchy in the level of legislative protection against discrimination remains intact. In conclusion, this chapter highlights the need to address these disparities in order to realise fully the spirit behind Article 13.

European Social Policy: Between Market Integration and Social Citizenship

European integration has been concerned first and foremost with integration in the economic sphere. In 1951, the six founding Member States set about creating a common market in coal and steel,[1] and this was followed in 1957 by the agreement of the Treaty establishing the European Economic Community (EEC).[2] The very title of the Treaty, the European *Economic* Community, indicates the primary focus of the signatories. At the same time, much of the motivation for European integration drew on non-economic factors, and in particular a desire to preserve the post-war peace in Europe. Indeed, the preamble of the 1957 EEC Treaty states the resolve of the signatories 'to preserve and strengthen peace and liberty' through the pooling of their resources. Moreover, the Member States recognised that economic integration would inevitably have social effects, and thus the appropriate role for social policy was debated from the outset.

Two theoretical models of European social policy may be identified. First, there is the *market integration model*[3] which prescribes a limited social policy for the European Union. This is predicated on the assumption that the primary goal of the Union is to achieve economic integration. Therefore, the EU only intervenes in the social sphere when this is required to support and sustain the smooth functioning of the common market. Essentially this is a model for a social policy dependent on the economics of European integration. Alternatively, there is a model of social policy as an independent policy

---

[1] The 1951 Treaty establishing the European Coal and Steel Community (ECSC) was signed by Italy, France, the Federal Republic of Germany, Luxembourg, Belgium and The Netherlands.

[2] Also referred to as the Treaty of Rome. Simultaneously, a Treaty establishing the European Atomic Energy Community was also agreed.

[3] B Fitzpatrick, 'Straining the definition of health and safety?' (1997) 26 ILJ 115, 117.

objective for the EU, foreseeing a social policy as vibrant and autonomous as the Union's activities in the economic sphere. This is centred around a role for the Union as a guarantor of fundamental social rights and may be described as the *social citizenship model*.[4] It is within these policy frameworks that EU anti-discrimination law has developed.

This chapter aims to provide a theoretical context for the rest of the book through exploring the development of European social policy, with particular regard for anti-discrimination law therein. The discussion commences with an examination of the two models of social policy, followed by a consideration of the potential impact on social policy of the EU Charter of Fundamental Rights.

I. The market integration model

European integration has always possessed social objectives. Beyond the underlying aim of ensuring peace and stability in Europe, the EEC Treaty specified in Article 117 'the need to promote improved working conditions and an improved standard of living for workers'. Differences have arisen though in both the detailed elaboration of the overall objective of 'social progress' and in the means to the attainment of this objective. During the negotiation of the EEC Treaty, the six governments were divided between those who did not perceive a need for any significant social dimension and those, principally France, who took the view that a certain level of social intervention was necessary.[5] In particular, there was a fear that indigenous industry would not prove sufficiently competitive in a common market due to the higher levels of social protection which existed in France compared to the other prospective Member States.[6]

On one side, it was argued that it was neither necessary nor appropriate to develop an EEC social policy. First, competitiveness is a product of a complex mix of factors. Thus, whilst higher social charges undoubtedly raise production costs, these may be offset by other factors, such as national differences in

---

[4] B Fitzpatrick, 'The Community's social policy: recent developments and remaining problems' in S Konstadinidis (ed), *A People's Europe: turning a concept into content* (Aldershot: Dartmouth, 1999) 34.

[5] C Hoskyns, *Integrating Gender—Women, Law and Politics in the European Union* (London: Verso, 1996) 49.

[6] D Collins, *The European Communities—the social policy of the first phase. Volume 2 The European Economic Community 1958–72* (London: Martin Robertson, 1975) 7.

the skill level of the workforce, infrastructure and technological develop-ment. A Member State which possessed high social costs,[7] but nevertheless had a well-skilled, and therefore highly productive labour force, could prove more competitive than a state with low charges, but poor infrastructure and/or a weak educational system.[8] Second, it was by no means evident that social policies were readily amenable to a programme of supranational har-monisation.[9] An International Labour Office (ILO) committee of experts particularly stressed the role played by national traditions in shaping the development of national social policy provisions: 'international differences in wages and other labour conditions depend upon a complicated set of factors, including differences in national traditions and customs, differences in the strength of trades unions, the nature of the different jobs, the demand for and availability of particular skills and so on'.[10]

Nonetheless, it was ultimately accepted that whilst differences in social costs amongst the Member States would not generally be such as to cause dis-tortions in the operation of the common market, it was possible that, where these were especially marked, it could place certain Member States at a com-petitive disadvantage.[11] For example, the French delegation had identified differences in national legislation on equal pay for men and women as being likely to disturb the balance of trade in the common market.[12] The French argument was based on the premise that those countries which did not pos-sess legislation on equal pay between men and women could rely more heav-ily on cheap female labour as a means of reducing production costs *vis-à-vis* Member States which had already prohibited such wage discrimination.

The compromise which emerged out of these competing arguments can be referred to as the market integration model of European social policy, and this was institutionalised through the terms of the EEC Treaty. In principle, this model prescribes for the Community a supplementary social policy; it is not

---

[7] 'Social costs' have been defined by the Commission as the combination of labour costs which result from the social security contributions an employer must make for each employee, and costs arising from legislation governing working conditions, such as laws on holiday pay or redundancy entitlements (Commission, 'Explanatory Memorandum on the proposals for Directives concern-ing certain employment relationships' COM (90) 228, 28).

[8] International Labour Office (ILO), *Social Aspects of European Economic Cooperation—report by a group of experts* (London: Staples Press, 1956) 86.

[9] O Kahn-Freund, 'Labor law and social security' in E Stein and T Nicholson (eds), *American Enterprise in the European Common Market—A Legal Profile* Vol 1 (Michigan: Ann Arbor, 1960) 304.

[10] ILO (n 8 above) 64.

[11] Lord Wedderburn, *Labour Law and Freedom: Further Essays in Labour Law* (London: Lawrence and Wishart, 1995) 263.

[12] Collins (n 6 above) 7.

an autonomous endeavour, but rather the 'handmaiden to economic integration'.[13] It is based on the premise that the realisation of the common market would result in increased economic growth and employment within the Member States, and that this would ensure the Community achieved its goal of improving living and working conditions. However, the model also accepts that there may be certain circumstances where Community intervention is necessary in order to ensure the smooth functioning of the common market. Indeed, former EEC Treaty, Article 117 explicitly stated that social progress 'will ensue not only from the functioning of the common market . . . but also from the procedures laid down by law, regulation or administrative action'.

Nevertheless, common rules are adopted only where this appears *necessary* for the smooth operation of the common market; in the absence of such a market imperative, there is no provision for the elaboration of common social legislation. Kahn-Freund remarks that it was 'certainly not the policy of the Treaty to make supranational legislation easy'.[14] Indeed, the EEC Treaty did not contain any specific legal base for the adoption of social legislation. It did acknowledge French concerns through the inclusion of EEC Treaty, Article 119: 'each Member State shall during the first stage ensure and subsequently maintain the application of the principle that men and women should receive equal pay for equal work'.[15] Yet, this remained an ambiguous commitment as it was not anticipated that this provision was open to enforcement by individuals against national governments.[16]

Over time, shifts have been evident between a *minimalist* version of the market integration model and a *maximalist* version.[17] Therefore, in certain periods, such as the mid-1970s, the Member States enlarged their view of the degree of social policy necessary to maintain the smooth functioning of the common market. More concretely, such a shift in perspective occurred during the move from the common market to the internal market, through the 1986 Single European Act.

The drive to remove the remaining barriers to the free movement of goods, services, capital and persons by 31 December 1992[18] reawakened concerns about 'social dumping'. This has been summarised by the Commission as 'the

---

[13] P Davies, 'The Emergence of European Labour Law' in W McCarthy (ed), *Legal Interventions in Industrial Relations: Gains and Losses* (Oxford: Basil Blackwell, 1992) 343.

[14] Kahn-Freund (n 9 above) 309.

[15] This was accompanied by EEC Treaty, Art 120: 'Member States shall endeavour to maintain the existing equivalence between paid holiday schemes.'

[16] Kahn-Freund (n 9 above) 329.

[17] I am indebted to Barry Fitzpatrick for suggesting this dichotomy to me.

[18] EC Treaty, Art 14.

gaining of an unfair competitive advantage within the Community through unacceptably low social standards'.[19] Opinions differ as to the reality of social dumping. Collins points out that, despite higher social standards, French industry flourished within the common market and as a result the French government was not impelled to pursue further social policy harmonisation between the Member States.[20] At its most elemental, Mosley states that 'if labour costs alone determined international competitiveness there would be no industry in high-wage countries'.[21] Indeed, the social dumping argument may be criticised for often regarding labour regulations as simply barriers to competitiveness; costs without benefits. On the contrary, a positive conception of labour law is possible. Deakin and Wilkinson stress the constructive role labour standards can play as a bulwark against a slide into a low-wage, low-productivity economy.[22]

Nonetheless, the *perception* of social dumping as a genuine threat to competitiveness has proven very real.[23] High-profile cases serve to reinforce a public perception of jobs being lost to other Member States as a result of unacceptable reductions in social protection elsewhere.[24] Moreover, firms have an incentive to encourage the idea of footloose capital as a means to strengthen their bargaining power with national authorities in negotiating the appropriate level of social regulation.[25] In this respect, the most persuasive dimension of the social dumping argument may be that common minimum labour standards are needed to prevent damage to the integrity of the European Union.[26]

[19] Commission, 'Green Paper: European Social Policy—Options for the Union' COM (93) 551, 6.

[20] D Collins, *The European Communities—the social policy of the first phase. Volume 2 The European Economic Community 1958–72* (London: Martin Robertson, 1975) 24.

[21] H Mosley, 'The social dimension of European integration' (1990) 129 *Int Labour Rev* 147, 161.

[22] S Deakin and F Wilkinson, 'Rights vs Efficiency? The economic case for transnational labour standards' (1994) 23 ILJ 289, 308.

[23] B Fitzpatrick, 'The Community's social policy: recent developments and remaining problems' in S Konstadinidis (ed), *A People's Europe: turning a concept into content* (Aldershot: Dartmouth, 1999) 34. Hervey makes the same observation in respect of 'welfare dumping': T Hervey, 'Social solidarity: a buttress against internal market law?' in J Shaw (ed), *Social law and policy in an evolving European Union* (Oxford: Hart Publishing, 2000) 43.

[24] For example, the relocation of Hoover from France to Scotland: Editorial, 'Are European values being hoovered away?' (1993) 30 CML Rev 445.

[25] C Crouch, 'Introduction' in C Crouch (ed), *After the Euro: shaping institutions for governance in the wake of European monetary union* (Oxford: Oxford University Press, 2000) 7; C Barnard, 'Regulating competitive federalism in the European Union? The case of EU social policy' in J Shaw (ed), *Social law and policy in an evolving European Union* (Oxford: Hart Publishing, 2000) 63.

[26] See further: Council Resolution on certain aspects for a EU social policy: a contribution to economic and social convergence in the Union [1994] OJ C368/3.

In addition to the spillover pressures arising from debates on social dumping, there has also been increasing evidence—primarily at the Court of Justice—of internal market law being using to challenge established areas of national social policy, hitherto frequently unaffected by EU law.[27] For example, EU competition law has been deployed to confront state monopolies in the provision of employment placement services[28] and monopolies in the supply of labour.[29] Alternatively, national labour law regulations governing the keeping of employment records and minimum wage requirements have been challenged as restrictions on the free movement of services.[30] This expanding body of case law, where national social policies have been subjected to the deregulatory wind of EU internal market rules, inevitably produces pressure for fresh intervention at the European level in order to regain political control of the management of social policy. At the same time, the areas of social policy now being affected by internal market law—such as health care,[31] pension funds,[32] and social welfare provision[33]—touch on aspects of 'distributive' social policy previously excluded from EU intervention.[34] There is no firm evidence yet that the Member States are willing to respond to these cases by significantly expanding the remit of European social policy. Nonetheless, it demonstrates that, as market integration penetrates even further into national law and policy, this may produce a wider space for the management of social policy at the EU level.

The basic philosophy which underpins the post-internal market era in social policy has been summarised by the Commission as a commitment to

[27] See further: P Davies, 'Market integration and social policy in the Court of Justice' (1995) 24 ILJ 49; T Hervey (n 23 above); ch 6, E Szyszczak, *EC Labour Law* (Harlow: Longman, 2000); M Poiares Maduro, 'Striking the elusive balance between economic freedom and social rights in the EU' in P Alston, M Bustelo and J Heenan (eds), *The EU and human rights* (Oxford: Oxford University Press, 1999); S Leibfried and P Pierson, 'Social policy—left to courts and markets?' in H Wallace and W Wallace (eds), *Policy-making in the European Union* (Oxford: Oxford University Press, 2000).

[28] Case C–41/90 *Höfner and Elser v Macroton* [1991] ECR I–1979; Case C–55/96 *Job Centre* [1997] ECR I–7119; Case C–258/98 *Carra* [2000] ECR I–4217.

[29] Case C–179/90 *Merci convenzionali porto di Genova SpA v Siderurgico Gabrielli SpA* [1991] ECR I–5889; Case C–163/96 *Raso* [1998] ECR I–533.

[30] Cases C–369/96 and C–376/96 *Arblade* [1999] ECR I–8453.

[31] Case C–158/96 *Kohll v Union des Caisses de Maladie* [1998] ECR I–1931; Case C–120/95 *Decker v Caisse de Maladie des Employés Privés* [1998] ECR I–1831.

[32] *Inter alia*, Case C–67/96 *Albany International BV v Stichting Bedrijfspensioenfonds Textielindustrie* [1999] ECR I–5751.

[33] Case C–70/95 *Sodemare SA v Regione Lombardia* [1997] ECR I–3395.

[34] M Poiares Maduro, 'Europe's social self: "The sickness unto Death"' in J Shaw (ed), *Social law and policy in an evolving European Union* (Oxford: Hart Publishing, 2000) 330.

'the establishment of a framework of basic minimum standards . . . [as] a bulwark against using low social standards as an instrument of unfair economic competition and protection against reducing social standards to gain competitiveness'.[35] In this vein, there has been a series of initiatives designed to broaden the scope of European labour law. One can point to the 1989 *Community Charter of the Fundamental Social Rights of Workers*[36] (hereafter 'the Social Charter'), which generated a significant amount of new social legislation.[37] Moreover, the social provisions, as amended by the 1999 Treaty of Amsterdam, clearly represent a substantial expansion of EC competence in this sphere.[38] Nevertheless, as will be discussed in the following section, these initiatives remain closer to the model of a social policy based on the needs of market integration, than a perspective oriented towards the generation of a European social citizenship.

II. The social citizenship model

The social citizenship model can be defined initially as the inverse of certain aspects of the market integration model. Thus, it implies the rejection of a social policy based on supplementing economic integration. At its core, the model prescribes for the EU a role as a guarantor of fundamental human and social rights.[39] This implies that in some form or another there should be a comprehensive statement of rights at EU level, although there appears to be little consensus as to which rights should be included and how they should be enforced.[40] In particular, there are differing views on whether it is preferable to develop a wide-ranging guarantee of citizens' basic civil, political, social

---

[35] Commission, 'European Social Policy—a way forward for the Union: a White Paper' COM (94) 333, Introduction, para 19.

[36] Text appears in *Social Europe* 1/90, 46–50.

[37] Commission, 'Communication from the Commission concerning its action programme relating to the implementation of the Community Charter of Fundamental Social Rights for Workers' COM (89) 586.

[38] Arts 136–145 EC.

[39] Commission, *For a Europe of civic and social rights—Report by the Comité des Sages* (Luxembourg: OOPEC, 1996) 10.

[40] On the options for implementation of social rights, see B de Witte, 'Protection of fundamental social rights in the European Union—the choice of the appropriate legal instrument' in L Betten and D MacDevitt (eds), *The protection of fundamental social rights in the European Union* (London: Kluwer Law International, 1996).

and economic rights at the EU level,[41] or whether a narrow 'inner circle' of labour law rights would be a more effective venture.[42] To a certain extent, this debate has now been resolved with the adoption of the EU Charter of Fundamental Rights on 7 December 2000,[43] which opts for a wide-ranging list of rights. However, the Charter is not (yet) legally binding and its impact remains uncertain. This section will examine the social citizenship model and the extent to which it has already been integrated in European social policy. The following section specifically considers the contribution of the Charter.

The underlying aim of the social citizenship model is the generation of greater legitimacy for the Union and the cultivation of deeper support for European integration amongst the peoples of the Member States.[44] In this respect, the sense of citizenship nurtured through the role for the Union as a protector of fundamental rights addresses the profoundly political objective of winning the 'consent' and 'trust' of the citizens of the EU for the integration process.[45] EU law has, from the outset, conferred rights on citizens, however, these have been characterised by their connection to free movement and the internal market—for example, the right to work in another state or to receive services in another state. Everson characterises this as a form of 'market citizenship'; the rights conferred are dependent on participation in the market.[46] The difficulty with this model lies in the small proportion of the population of the Union who do exercise the right to work and live in other Member States. In contrast, guaranteeing general social rights—such as the right to maximum working hours and paid holidays[47]—has the potential to affect a much wider section of the public.

---

[41] A Cassese, C Lalumière, P Leuprecht and M Robinson, *Leading by example: a human rights agenda for the European Union for the Year 2000. Agenda of the Comité des Sages and final project report* (Florence: European University Institute, 1998).

[42] R Blanpain, B Hepple, S Sciarra and M Weiss, *Fundamental Social Rights: Proposals for the European Union* (Leuven: Peeters, 1996) 9.

[43] [2000] OJ C364/1.

[44] C Barnard, 'P v S: kite flying or a new constitutional approach?' in A Dashwood and S O'Leary (eds), *The principle of equal treatment in European Community law* (London: Sweet & Maxwell, 1997) 67.

[45] J Shaw, 'The interpretation of European Union citizenship' (1998) 61 MLR 293; B Bercusson, S Deakin, P Koistinen, Y Kravaritou, U Mückenberger, A Supiot and B Veneziani, *A Manifesto for a Social Europe* (Brussels: European Trade Union Institute, 1996) 10–11.

[46] M Everson, 'The legacy of the market citizen' in J Shaw and G More (eds), *New legal dynamics of European Union* (Oxford: Clarendon Press, 1995).

[47] Council Dir (EEC) 93/104 of 23 November 1993 concerning certain aspects of the organisation of working time [1993] OJ L307/18.

Moreover, there is an implication that a sense of shared rights will generate a perception of a shared identity, and as a result the social citizenship model will not only legitimise, but will also promote, further integration. Certain authors note, though, that the mere guaranteeing of rights by the EU will not in itself be sufficient to create a stronger democratic legitimacy for the integration process. Shaw identifies the 'top-down' nature of EU citizenship rights, which are delivered to a diverse body of citizens not sharing the traditional bonds of cohesion present in a nation-state.[48] She suggests that the provision of rights alone will have a 'limited capacity to generate citizen loyalty'.[49] De Búrca stresses the need for accompanying measures to strengthen the legitimacy of the Union—in particular, an enhancement of public participation in the debate on the future of the EU.[50]

Weiler also questions the ability of ever-increasing human rights guarantees to deliver popular support for the European Union. On one side, he notes the danger of 'rights saturation'.[51] If the rights concerned are already adequately protected through national or other European and international instruments, additional guarantees from the Union are unlikely to be perceptible to citizens, or regarded as conferring much added value. On the other side, there is potential for rights to be divisive.[52] Where rights are not based on shared values, then some sections of the public may regard the rights as damaging rather than liberating.[53] This is especially important to keep in mind when considering issues relating to sexual orientation discrimination. As will be explained, rights here are strongly contested and it is not evident that European Union intervention will necessarily result in a 'net gain' in public allegiance to the integration process.

Fears have also been expressed that the creation of a substantive role for the EU in the guaranteeing of rights would imply a significant extension of the

---

[48] J Shaw, 'The many pasts and futures of citizenship in the European Union' (1997) 22 ELR 554, 561.

[49] ibid 564.

[50] G de Búrca, 'The quest for legitimacy in the European Union' (1996) 59 MLR 349, 375. See also: K Armstrong, 'Legal integration: theorizing the legal dimension of European integration' (1998) 36 Journal of Common Market Studies 149.

[51] J Weiler, *The Constitution of Europe—'Do the new clothes have an emperor?' and other essays on European integration* (Cambridge: Cambridge University Press, 1999) 334.

[52] J Weiler, 'Fundamental rights and fundamental boundaries: on standards and values in the protection of human rights' in N Neuwahl and A Rosas (eds), *The European Union and human rights* (London: Martinus Nijhoff, 1995) 55.

[53] G de Búrca, 'The language of rights and European integration' in G More and J Shaw (eds), *New legal dynamics of European Union* (Oxford: Clarendon Press, 1995) 46.

competence of the Union.[54] However, the impact of any statement of rights could be limited through the principle of subsidiarity.[55] Whilst this is now defined in the EC Treaty,[56] it may be summarised as the notion that tasks should be undertaken by the level of government most appropriate for the achievement of the objectives of the action. Where there is discretion, then governance should be as close to the citizen as possible. Nonetheless, the breadth of the principle leaves it inherently flexible and open to varying interpretations. For instance, Bercusson *et al* argue that subsidiarity implies an obligation on the EU to intervene where national action proves insufficient to uphold respect for basic rights.[57] Alternatively, the EU's social rights *Comité des Sages* noted that subsidiarity requires that the 'leading role in social matters should belong to the Member States'.[58] Spicker suggests that subsidiarity be interpreted as devolving responsibility to the national level for matters in the 'private domain', which are sensitive to differences in national culture and morality.[59] Yet, this creates difficulties where rights in the public and private spheres coincide, such as where a woman seeks to exercise her right to free movement in order to terminate a pregnancy.[60]

Whilst the social citizenship model has evolved as a theoretical alternative to the market integration model, in practice it remains more an aspiration

[54] For example, the German Government's submission to the 1993 Green Paper on Social Policy stated: 'the Commission's suggestions on a "consolidated statement of citizen's rights" is a doubtful starter even as regards the basic idea of enshrining abstract, social citizens' rights. . . . Enshrining these rights would exceed the Community's statute and case-law would lead in practice to the "communitization" of important areas of social policy.' (Commission, 'Contributions to the preparatory work for the White Paper on European social policy' *Social Europe* 2/94, 46.)

[55] G de Búrca, 'Reappraising subsidiarity's significance after Amsterdam' (1999) Harvard Jean Monnet Working Papers 7/99: *http://www.law.harvard.edu/programs/JeanMonnet/papers/papers99. html*; R Dehousse, 'Community competences: are there limits to growth? in R Dehousse (ed), *Europe after Maastricht: an ever closer union?* (Munich: Law Books in Europe, 1994); G Lyon-Caen, 'Subsidiarity' in P Davies; A Lyon-Caen; S Sciarra; S Simitis, *European Community Labour Law: Principles and Perspectives. Liber Amicorum Lord Wedderburn* (Oxford: Clarendon Press, 1997).

[56] EC Treaty, Art 5 states: 'In areas which do not fall within its exclusive competence, the Community shall take action, in accordance with the principle of subsidiarity, only if and in so far as the objectives of the proposed action cannot be sufficiently achieved by the Member States and can therefore, by reason of the scale or effects of the proposed action, be better achieved by the Community.' See also, Treaty of Amsterdam, Protocol on the application of the principles of subsidiarity and proportionality.

[57] Bercusson *et al* (n 45 above) 13.

[58] Commission, *For a Europe of civic and social rights—Report by the Comité des Sages* (Luxembourg: OOPEC, 1996) 42.

[59] P Spicker, 'The Principle of Subsidiarity and the Social Policy of the European Community' (1991) 1 J of Eur Social Policy 3, 13.

[60] See further G de Búrca, 'Fundamental human rights and the reach of EC law' (1993) 13 OJLS 283.

than a reality. Some moves towards the development of a form of social citizenship have occurred though, through both legislative and judicial intervention. Looking first at the legislative measures, the notion of fundamental rights was introduced into social policy first through the 1989 Social Charter.[61] The Charter was a non-binding declaration of fundamental social rights. Nevertheless, it was built mainly on the existing legal competence of the Community at that time and the rights dealt with seemed determined more by a pragmatic assessment of what was politically possible than a thorough analysis of what were the *fundamental* social rights shared by the Member States.[62] As such, the substance of the Charter fits more into the *ad hoc* nature of the market integration model, notwithstanding its symbolic commitment to a rights-based social policy.

The Treaty of Amsterdam represented a more significant step in the direction of a social citizenship model.[63] On the one hand, the Amsterdam social provisions substantially enlarged the competence of the Community for social policy, well beyond that contained in the original EEC Treaty. Independent legal bases for the adoption of a broad range of social legislation were created,[64] thereby reducing the need to justify social policy measures on the ground that they are required for the smooth functioning of the internal

[61]   Text appears in *Social Europe* 1/90, 46–50.

[62]   For example, responsibility for combating racism was simply devolved to the Member States with no references to racial discrimination outside of the preamble of the Charter. See further, B Bercusson, 'The European Community's Charter of Fundamental Social Rights of Workers' (1990) 53 MLR 624; B Hepple, 'The Implementation of the Community Charter on Fundamental Social Rights' (1990) 53 MLR 643.

[63]   See generally, S Langrish, 'The Treaty of Amsterdam: Selected Highlights' (1998) 23 ELR 3. On the social provisions, C Barnard, 'The United Kingdom, the "Social Chapter" and the Amsterdam Treaty' (1997) 26 ILJ 275.

[64]   EC Treaty, Art 137 states: '1. With a view to achieving the objectives of Art 136, the Community shall support and complement the activities of the Member States in the following fields:–improvement in particular of the working environment to protect workers' health and safety; working conditions; the information and consultation of workers; the integration of persons excluded from the labour market . . ., equality between men and women with regard to labour market opportunities and treatment at work; the integration of persons excluded from the labour market . . .

2. To this end, the Council may adopt, by means of directives, minimum requirements for gradual implementation, having regard to the conditions and technical rules obtaining in each of the Member States.'

Art 137(3) also allows for the adoption of measures in the areas of:

'social security and social protection of workers; protection of workers where their employment contract is terminated; representation and collective defence of the interests of workers and employers, including co-determination . . .; conditions of employment for third-country nationals legally residing in Community territory; financial contributions for promotion of employment and job-creation'.

market. Moreover, EC Treaty, Article 136 states that when pursuing the objectives of social policy, the Community and the Member States shall have 'in mind fundamental social rights'. Nonetheless, these changes still fall short of an image of a European social policy based on a guarantee of fundamental social rights. In particular, there remain significant omissions in the scope of social policy. [65] Notable in this respect is the curtailment of the competences provided in EC Treaty, Article 137, by paragraph 6: 'the provisions of this Article shall not apply to pay, the right of association, the right to strike or the right to impose lock-outs'. In contrast, Wedderburn describes the rights to organise, bargain and strike as the 'three basic human rights of modern democratic labour law'.[66]

The Treaty of Nice, agreed in December 2000,[67] will not fundamentally alter the *status quo* in social policy. The Member States were unable to agree to any further extension of qualified-majority voting within the Council in this area, although for most areas of social policy a decision to move to qualified-majority voting and the co-decision procedure[68] can now be taken by a unanimous vote in the Council—thereby avoiding the need for this reform to wait for another intergovernmental conference.[69] Significantly, 'the combating of social exclusion' and the 'modernisation of social protection systems' have been added explicitly to the objectives of the Community in the social field. However, this is balanced by the specific exclusion of any harmonising measures in these areas.[70] Moreover, the exclusion of pay, association and the right to strike/impose lock-outs remains intact.

Outside of the specific developments in social policy, the emergence of a European social citizenship was most visibly enhanced by the 1993 Treaty on European Union, which created a chapter in the EC Treaty on 'citizenship of the Union'.[71] The distinctive quality of the rights conferred is the fact that they are all explicitly 'European' in flavour. For example, EC Treaty, Article 18 extends the right to free movement throughout the territory of the Member States, 'subject to the limitations and conditions laid down in this

---

[65] S Sciarra, 'European Social Policy and Labour Law—Challenges and Perspectives' (1995) IV(I) Collected Courses of the Academy of European Law 301, 323.

[66] Lord Wedderburn, *Labour Law and Freedom: Further Essays in Labour Law* (London: Lawrence and Wishart, 1995) 272.

[67] Signed 26 February 2001, [2001] OJ C80/1. For a critical assessment, see P Pescatore, 'Nice—Aftermath' (2001) 38 CML Rev 265.

[68] EC Treaty, Art 251.   [69] Treaty of Nice, Art 2(9).   [70] ibid.

[71] For a review of Union citizenship, see N Reich, 'Union citizenship—metaphor or source of rights?' (2001) 7 Eur LJ 4.

Treaty and by measures adopted to give it effect'.[72] Importantly, EC Treaty, Article 22 raises the possibility of a future extension of the provisions on citizenship, without the need for Treaty amendment. This in-built potential for the ongoing enlargement of the rights of Union citizens created some expectation that this could provide an alternative avenue through which to elaborate a set of basic human and social rights guaranteed at the EU level.[73] However, whilst this remains possible in theory, in practice the Member States have shown little enthusiasm for the augmentation of the rights contained in this chapter of the EC Treaty. The rights largely remain dependent on free movement, and as such the core of Union citizenship is still market citizenship.[74] The Treaty of Amsterdam merely reinforced the limited nature of Union citizenship through the addition to the EC Treaty, Article 17 of the sentence 'citizenship of the Union shall complement and not replace national citizenship'. The Treaty of Nice also fails to make any significant change to the provisions on citizenship.[75]

Overall, whilst the Member States have been increasingly prepared to incorporate the 'language of rights' within social policy,[76] there has been considerably less progress in the actual establishment of enforceable basic rights for EU citizens. The formal introduction of citizenship in the EC Treaty seems akin to a form of corporate rebranding;[77] a new logo for the same old product. The hesitancy of the Member States has, to some extent, been moderated by the influence of the Court of Justice. Its well-developed case law on respect for fundamental rights within Community law permits the identification of more concrete evidence of progress.

---

[72] Alternatively, EC Treaty, Art 19 grants European citizens the right to vote and stand in municipal and European elections in any of the Member States.

[73] J Monar and R Bieber, *Citizenship and the Union* European Parliament Directorate-General for Research Working Paper; Legal Series W-5, 6-1995. See also, J Kenner, 'Citizenship and fundamental rights: reshaping the European social model' in J Kenner (ed), *Trends in European social policy. Essays in memory of Malcolm Mead* (Aldershot: Dartmouth, 1995).

[74] M Everson, 'The legacy of the market citizen' in J Shaw and G More (eds), *New legal dynamics of European Union* (Oxford: Clarendon Press, 1995) 79.

[75] Treaty of Nice, Art 2(3) extends qualified-majority voting and the co-decision procedure to TEU, Art 18 on free movement of citizens, however, this will not apply in respect of 'passports, identity cards, residence permits or any other such document or to provisions on social security or social protection'. Therefore, on most of the key areas where qualified-majority voting would be valuable to facilitate progress, it remains excluded.

[76] G de Búrca, 'The language of rights and European integration' in G More and J Shaw (eds), *New legal dynamics of European Union* (Oxford: Clarendon Press, 1995).

[77] J Weiler, *The Constitution of Europe, 'Do the new clothes have an emperor?' and other essays on European integration* (Cambridge: Cambridge University Press, 1999) 333.

One of the first problems to arise in the Community legal order was the relationship between the provisions of EC law and those in national law. From the outset, the Court insisted that Community law must be regarded as superior to conflicting national legal provisions, as otherwise its basic nature and effectiveness would be 'called into question'.[78] However, concerns were raised at the consequences of this judgment, notably amongst the German and Italian judiciaries.[79] The fear expressed was that the protection of fundamental rights would be diminished by a situation where, on the one hand, Community measures could not be challenged on the ground of a breach of a fundamental right (given that there was no statement of rights in the EC Treaty), whilst on the other there remained no possibility of impugning Community legal provisions by reference to the rights enshrined in national constitutions, a point established by the Court in *Internationale Handelsgesellschaft*.[80] In response, the Court developed case law to the effect that fundamental rights were to be regarded 'as part of the general principles of law which the Community had to respect in its activities'.[81] The strength of this principle is that it allows challenges to the validity of EC legislation on the ground of a breach of fundamental rights. However, there are two principal limitations.

First, measures may be challenged only if they fall within the scope of Community law. [82] The fundamental rights principle essentially provides a procedural guarantee that when the Community (or a Member State under its authority) acts then such action must be in conformity with respect for human rights. It does not provide an independent legal competence for the EC.[83] Therefore, the mere fact that respect for freedom of religion is a

---

[78]   Case 6/64 *Costa v ENEL* [1964] ECR 585, 594.

[79]   B de Witte, 'Community law and national constitutional values' (1991/2) Legal issues of European Integration 1, 11.

[80]   'The validity of a Community measure or its effect within a Member State cannot be affected by allegations that it runs counter to either fundamental rights as formulated by the constitution of that State or the principles of a national constitutional structure': Case 11/70 *Internationale Handelsgesellschaft* [1970] ECR 1125, 1134.

[81]   de Witte (n 79 above). See also Case 4/73 *Nold v Commission* [1974] ECR 491, para 13.

[82]   K Lenaerts, 'Fundamental Rights to be included in a Community catalogue' (1991) 16 ELR 367, 372. See also E Guild, 'EC law and the means to combat racism and xenophobia' in A Dashwood and S O'Leary (eds), *The principle of equal treatment in European Community law* (London: Sweet & Maxwell, 1997).

[83]   The Court has stated that 'no Treaty provision confers on the Community institutions any general power to enact rules on human rights or to conclude international conventions in this field'; Opinion 2/94 (Accession by the Community to the European Convention for the Protection of Human Rights and Fundamental Freedoms) [1996] ECR I–1759, para 27. Moreover, in *Grant v South-West Trains*, the Court stated that 'although respect for the fundamental rights which form

condition of the legality of EC law[84] does not mean that the Community enjoys the power to adopt specific measures against religious discrimination in the absence of any independent legal authority in the EC Treaty.

Second, given the absence of any statement of rights in the founding Treaties, it is for the Court to determine the nature and extent of fundamental rights on a case-by-case basis. In defining what constitutes fundamental rights, TEU Article 6(2) is the primary source of guidance from the founding treaties: 'The Union shall respect fundamental rights, as guaranteed by the European Convention for the Protection of Human Rights and Fundamental Freedoms signed in Rome on 4 November 1950 and as they result from the constitutional traditions common to the Member States, as general principles of Community law.'

The Court also draws its inspiration from 'international treaties on which the Member States have collaborated or of which they are signatories'.[85] The inclusion of references to the Council of Europe's 1961 European Social Charter[86] in both the EU and EC Treaties[87] confirms that this is another important source for the Court to take into account. Nonetheless, the absence of an express reference to social rights in TEU, Article 6 underlines the weaker position these rights have generally been accorded in the Court's case law on fundamental rights.[88] The Court has consistently held that all the sources of fundamental rights support the existence of a strong principle of equality and non-discrimination.[89] This applies to all manner of interventions by the Community.[90] For example, in *Ruckdeschel*, the Court held that

an integral part of those general principles of law is a condition of the legality of Community acts, those rights cannot in themselves have the effect of extending the scope of the Treaty provisions beyond the competences of the Community': case C–249/96 [1998] ECR I–621, para 45.

[84]   Case 130/75 *Prais v Council* [1976] ECR 1589.

[85]   Case 136/79 *National Panasonic (UK) Ltd v Commission* [1980] ECR 2033, para 18.

[86]   For an overview, see: O Kahn-Freund, 'The European Social Charter' in F Jacobs (ed), *European law and the individual* (Oxford: North Holland Publishing, 1976).

[87]   TEU, Preamble; EC Treaty, Art 136.

[88]   B de Witte, 'Protection of fundamental social rights in the European Union—the choice of the appropriate legal instrument' in L Bettes and D MacDevitt (eds), *The protection of fundamental social rights in the European Union* (London: Kluwer Law International, 1996) 65; Commission, 'Affirming fundamental rights in the European Union—time to act' Report of the expert group on fundamental rights (Luxembourg: OOPEC, 1999) 13.

[89]   See C Docksey, 'The Principle of Equality between Men and Women as a Fundamental Right under Community Law' (1991) 20 ILJ 258, and B Hepple, 'Social Values and European Law' (1995) 48 Current Legal Problems II: Collected Papers 39.

[90]   See G More, 'The principle of equal treatment: from market unifier to fundamental right?' in P Craig and G de Búrca (eds), *The evolution of EU law* (2nd edn, Oxford: Oxford University Press, 1999).

the principle of non-discrimination applied to the activities of the Community in the common agricultural policy.[91] This general principle has been most obviously employed with respect to non-discrimination between men and women. In *Defrenne III*,[92] the Court drew on the provisions of the 1961 European Social Charter and ILO Convention No 111[93] in support of its view that: 'respect for fundamental personal human rights is one of the general principles of Community law, the observance of which it [the Court] has a duty to ensure. There can be no doubt that the elimination of discrimination based on sex forms part of those fundamental rights'.[94]

Whilst equality between women and men is thoroughly supported in the sources of law relied on by the Court, other aspects of the principle of equality present more difficulties. For example, there is a general consensus that discrimination on grounds of racial or ethnic origin is contrary to fundamental rights as guaranteed by the Court,[95] although the Court has yet to pronounce explicitly on this point. However, discrimination on grounds of third country nationality would raise more difficulties for the Court as there is no clear agreement in the legal sources. In many Member States' legal systems, extensive distinctions are made between citizens and third country nationals. Furthermore, the International Convention for the Elimination of Racial Discrimination, Article 1(2) provides that 'this Convention shall not apply to distinctions, exclusions, restrictions or preferences made by a State Party to this Convention between citizens and non-citizens'.[96] In contrast, in the European Convention on Human Rights (ECHR) Article 14 on non-discrimination includes 'national origin' and the European Court of Human Rights has held that only 'very weighty reasons' can justify discrimination on this ground.[97]

---

[91] Cases 117/76 and 16/77 *Ruckdeschel & Co and Hansa-Lagerhaus Ströh & Co v Hauptzollamt Hamburg-St Annen* [1977] ECR 1753, paras 16–17. For a general statement of the principle of equality, see Case T–10/93 *A v Commission* [1994] ECR II–179, para 42.

[92] Case 149/77 *Defrenne v SABENA (III)* [1978] ECR 1365.

[93] On discrimination in employment: ILO, *International Labour Conventions and Recommendations 1952–1976 Volume 2* (Geneva: ILO, 1996) 176.

[94] Case 149/77 *Defrenne v SABENA (III)* [1978] ECR 1365 paras 26–27.

[95] E Guild, 'Race Discrimination and Community Law' (1993) 1 Migrantenrecht 6; C Docksey (n 89 above) 262; D Curtin and M Geurts, 'Race discrimination and the European Union Anno 1996: from rhetoric to legal remedy?' (1996) 14 *Netherlands Q of Human Rights* 147, 152.

[96] It is also notable that 'nationality' was specifically deleted from the draft versions of ILO Convention No 111 due to objections from the signatory states (ILO, *Equality in employment and occupation: report of the Committee of Experts on the application of Conventions and Recommendations* (Geneva: ILO, 1996) para 240.

[97] *Gaygusuz v Austria* (1997) 23 EHRR 364.

Alternatively, no international human rights instrument or national constitution of a Member State explicitly refers to non-discrimination on the ground of sexual orientation.[98] Whilst the Court of Justice has recently recognised the principle of equal treatment irrespective of sexual orientation,[99] its application to discrimination against same-sex partnerships remains controversial. The case of *D and Sweden v Council* concerned the denial of employment benefits in respect of the registered partner (under Swedish law) of a gay man working for the EU Council, where the benefits were provided to 'married officials'.[100] The Court decided that the difference in treatment was not based on sexual orientation,[101] but on the legal distinction between a registered partnership and a marital partnership, even though Swedish law provided for these to have the 'same legal effects' subject to certain limited exceptions.[102] Advocate-General Mischo adopted an even more controversial approach, arguing that married and registered partners were not in a comparable situation because of the differences in 'nature' between a heterosexual and homosexual couple, irrespective of any differences in law.[103]

The decision in *D and Sweden v Council* confirms the vagaries of relying purely on the Courts to find and define fundamental rights principles. The Court can be criticised for its narrow interpretation of the scope of the principle of equal treatment irrespective of sexual orientation. There is no acknowledgement that distinctions based on marital status inherently discriminate against lesbians and gay men because same-sex marriage is not permitted in any Member State, with the exception of the Netherlands.

Both examples above demonstrate the sometimes ambiguous and unpredictable nature of the fundamental rights protected by the Court, given the absence of a clear statement of rights in the founding Treaties. Furthermore, they reveal the underlying difficulty in finding a consensus on what constitutes *fundamental* human and social rights. This is especially true where the rights in question are closely linked to different national perceptions of moral

---

[98] See generally, R Wintemute, *Sexual Orientation and Human Rights—the United States Constitution, the European Convention and the Canadian Charter* (Oxford: Clarendon Press, 1995); E Heinze, *Sexual Orientation: a human right—an essay on international human rights law* (Dordrecht: Martinus Nijhoff, 1995); L Helfer and A Miller, 'Sexual orientation and human rights: towards an United States and transnational jurisprudence' (1996) 9 *Harvard Human Rights J* 61; D Saunders, 'Getting lesbian and gay issues on the international human rights agenda' (1996) 18 *Human Rights Q* 67.

[99] Cases C–122/99P and C–125/99P *D and Sweden v Council* [2001] ECR I–4319, para 47.

[100] ibid para 2.   [101] ibid para 47.   [102] ibid para 3.

[103] Opinion of A-G Mischo, 22 February 2001, para 87.

or cultural values. The principle of subsidiarity recalls 'the importance to balance national traditions against the supranational construction of social rights'.[104] Indeed, the EU Treaty requires respect for the diverse national identities in the Union.[105] Striking the correct balance is further complicated by the lack of clarity in the EC Treaty on the application of subsidiarity to the proceedings of the Court.[106]

III. The Charter of Fundamental Rights

On 7 December 2000, the Council, Parliament and Commission solemnly proclaimed the Charter of Fundamental Rights of the European Union.[107] At first glance, the Charter might seem to be a comprehensive solution to any gaps in the protection of fundamental rights in the Union. The Charter sets out a wide range of rights, in contrast to the limited civil and political rights found in the citizenship provisions of the EC Treaty. Chapter IV on 'solidarity' establishes a range of social rights which move beyond the labour market rights found in the 1989 Social Charter.[108] Moreover, the Charter provides innovatory commitments to protect the integrity of the individual, such as 'the prohibition of the reproductive cloning of human beings'.[109] The diversity and breadth of these commitments suggest a genuine departure from the economic orientation of European integration. However, the Charter inevitably confronts the hard rocks of legal competence. Article 51 is crucial is this regard:

1. The provisions of this Charter are addressed to the institutions and bodies of the Union with due regard for the principle of subsidiarity and to the Member States

---

[104] S Sciarra, 'From Strasbourg to Amsterdam: prospects for the convergence of European social rights policy' in P Alston, M Bustelo and J Heenan (eds), *The EU and human rights* (Oxford: Oxford University Press, 1999) 477.

[105] TEU, Art 6 states that 'the Union shall respect the national identities of its Member States'.

[106] G de Búrca, 'The principle of subsidiarity and the Court of Justice as an institutional actor' (1998) 36 J of Common Market Studies 217.

[107] [2000] OJ C364/1. For a discussion on the background, drafting and content of the Charter, see G Braibant, 'La Charte des droits fondamentaux' (2001) 1 *Droit Social* 69; S Fredman, C McCrudden and M Freedland, 'An EU Charter of fundamental rights' (2000) Public L 178; G de Búrca, 'The drafting of the European Union Charter of Fundamental Rights' (2001) 26 ELR 126; Editorial, 'The EU Charter of Fundamental Rights still under discussion' (2001) 38 CML Rev 1.

[108] For example, Art 35 declares the 'right of access to preventive health care and the right to benefit from medical treatment'.

[109] Art 3(2).

only when they are implementing Union law. They shall therefore respect the rights, observe the principles and promote the application thereof in accordance with their respective powers.

2. This Charter does not establish any new power or task for the Community or the Union, or modify powers and tasks defined by the Treaties.

Article 51 indicates that the Charter is not a radical break with the past, but rather a logical progression from the existing fundamental rights case law of the Court. When the European Council decided to commission the drafting of a Charter, its stated objective was to make 'more visible to the Union's citizens' the fundamental rights protected within European Union law.[110] As discussed earlier, one of the primary weaknesses with the Court's case law is the difficulty for citizens to determine in advance which rights are protected under EU law. The Charter performs a useful role in this context, not least in the area of anti-discrimination. Article 21(1) provides an open-ended ban on all forms of discrimination, but specifies seventeen grounds in particular.[111] This clarifies that, *inter alia*, genetic features, disability, age and sexual orientation are prohibited grounds of discrimination—which is valuable given the weaker presence of these grounds in existing international and national human rights instruments.[112]

However, this clarifying function of the Charter is seriously compromised by its non-binding legal status. This means that the Court is not obliged to examine or to follow its provisions. In this light, it is possible that the Charter will even provide further confusion. Citizens are now faced with an instrument that appears to provide greater legal certainty as to their rights, but this certainty is then undermined by the dilemma surrounding the degree to which the Court will have cognisance of its provisions. For example, in *D and Sweden v Council*, the Court made no reference to the Charter despite the fact that Advocate-General Mischo had specifically raised its applicability.[113] His opinion is also significant because he chose to ignore Article 21(1) on non-discrimination and focused instead on Article 9 on the right to marry.[114] This

---

[110]   Presidency Conclusions, Cologne European Council, 3–4 June 1999, Annex IV, EU Bull, 6-1999.

[111]   'Any discrimination based on any ground such as sex, race, colour, ethnic or social origin, genetic features, language, religion or belief, political or other opinion, membership of a national minority, property, birth, disability, age or sexual orientation shall be prohibited.'

[112]   For example, none is mentioned in ECHR, Art 14.

[113]   Cases C–122/99P and C–125/99P *D and Sweden v Council*, A-G Opinion of 22 February, para 97.

[114]   ibid. Art 9 states: 'the right to marry and the right to found a family shall be guaranteed in accordance with the national law governing the exercise of these rights'.

approach was instrumental in supporting his conclusion that the Council's discrimination between married and registered partnerships was justified. Importantly, his opinion illustrates that even if the judicial authorities are prepared to examine the provisions of the Charter, it will not provide greater certainty for individuals in areas where rights remain contested.

In some areas, the strict constraints imposed by Community competence gives rise to the risk that the Charter will mislead citizens into believing that a certain level of protection is accorded, when in reality the issue currently falls outside the scope of Community law.[115] For example, Article 28 provides the right for workers and employers 'to take collective action to defend their interests, including strike action'. Yet, as has been highlighted, Article 137(6) excludes 'the right to strike' from the Community's competence in social policy.[116] By building a concrete axis between the existing Treaties and the Charter, Parmar argues that the market orientation of European integration is preserved.[117]

At this early stage, it would be rash to make any firm conclusions on the impact and effect of the Charter. Clearly, much will depend on the reaction from the Court,[118] and whether its legal status is enhanced in the future.[119] By itself, the Charter does not fundamentally shift European social policy in the direction of a social citizenship model. The experience of the 1989 Social Charter demonstrates that the mere incorporation of a rights discourse is not sufficient to ensure a rights-based social policy in substance. Nonetheless, the Charter usefully provides yet another source which encourages the Union to adopt a social citizenship perspective in the elaboration of social policy. An example of the considerable potential this contains is provided in

[115] K Lenaerts and E de Smijter, 'A "Bill of Rights" for the European Union' (2001) 38 CML Rev 273, 288; P Pescatore, 'Nice—Aftermath' (2001) 38 CML Rev 265, 268.

[116] The explanatory memorandum to the Charter confirms that even the question of parallel strikes across different Member States remains a matter for national law only: Praesidium, 'Text of the explanations relating to the complete text of the Charter as set out in CHARTE 4487/00 CONVENT 50' CHARTE 4473/00 CONVENT 49, 11 October 2000, 28.

[117] S Parmar, 'Human rights and the constitutional dimensions of the Charter of Fundamental Rights of the European Union' Paper presented at the 18th Annual Graduate Student Conference, The Institute for the Study of Europe, Columbia University, 29 March 2001, 13.

[118] In Case T–112/98 *Mannesmannröhren-Werke AG v Commission* [2001] ECR II–729, the Court of First Instance rejected an argument to apply the provisions of the Charter on the basis that the case before it concerned a review of the legality of a measure adopted prior to its proclamation (para 76).

[119] At Nice, the Member States committed themselves to convening another IGC in 2004. One of the key items on the agenda will be the 'status of the Charter'; Treaty of Nice, Declaration 23.

the Opinion of Advocate-General Tizzano in *BECTU*.[120] The case concerned access to the right to paid leave (conferred by the Working Time Directive[121]) by individuals who work on a series of short-term contracts—for example, make-up artists or camera operators. Under the UK regulations implementing the Directive, the paid leave entitlement only accrued following thirteen weeks' employment by the same employer. BECTU, a trade union whose members were adversely affected by this precondition, argued that this was in breach of the terms of the Directive. Importantly, Tizzano stated at the outset the need to place the Directive in the 'wider context of fundamental social rights'.[122] In this regard, he examined a variety of international sources dealing with the right to a period of paid leave, before then declaring 'even more significant, it seems to me, is the fact that right is now solemnly upheld in the Charter of Fundamental Rights . . . in proceedings concerned with the nature and scope of a fundamental right the relevant statements of the Charter cannot be ignored'.[123] Clearly, this statement is a salient contribution as the Court begins to grapple with the legal relevance and role for the Charter. However, in the context of this book, it is even more pertinent to look further into Tizzano's opinion. Later, he acknowledges the essential market integration aim of this Directive: 'the objective of ensuring a comparable minimum level of protection as between the various Member States also meets the requirement, dictated by the need to prevent distortion of competition, of avoiding any type of social dumping'[124].

Essentially, Tizzano relies on the Charter (and other international social rights instruments) to recast the Directive away from its market integration dimensions and to place it firmly in the arena of social citizenship. This approach can already be seen historically in the Court's identification of EEC Treaty, Article 119 as 'part of the social objectives of the Community'.[125] In fact, the Court has now even gone so far as to declare the economic objectives of the former EEC Treaty, Article 119, 'secondary' to its social goal.[126] Adopting such a perspective via the Charter not only permits the discovery of a stronger presence of social citizenship rights in EU law than perhaps previously imagined, but also supports a purposive interpretation of such rights. If the Charter supports a re-imagination of the foundations of European social

---

[120] Case C–173/99 *Broadcasting, Entertainment, Cinematographic and Theatre Union (BECTU) v Secretary of State for Trade and Industry*, [2001] ECR I–4881.

[121] Council Dir (EEC) 93/104 of 23 November 1993 concerning certain aspects of the organisation of working time [1993] OJ L307/18.

[122] Para 22.   [123] Paras 26 and 28.   [124] Para 45.

[125] Case 43/75 *Defrenne* (II) [1976] ECR 455, 472.

[126] Case C–50/96 *Deutsche Telekom AG v Lilli Schröder* [2000] ECR I–743, para 57.

policy, then it may yet make a positive contribution to creating space for European social citizenship.

The decision of the Court in *BECTU* is predictably more cautious, not making any explicit reference to the Charter of Fundamental Rights. Nonetheless, its influence is very present, most clearly reflected in the Court's readiness to adopt the language of social rights. In interpreting the scope of the right to paid leave, the Court explicitly draws attention to the right to paid annual leave in the 1989 Social Charter.[127] As a consequence, the Court declares 'it follows that the entitlement of every worker to paid annual leave must be regarded as a particularly important principle of Community social law from which there can be no derogations'.[128] Moreover, later it refers to the relevant provision of the Directive as conferring a 'social right' and an 'individual right'.[129] This fresh endorsement of the existence of fundamental social rights is also manifested in the Court's forthright rejection of the UK's argument based on the supposed problems the right would create for small and medium-sized undertakings: 'the improvement of workers' safety, hygiene and health at work is an objective which should not be subordinated to purely economic considerations.'[130] So whilst the judgment tells us little about the Court's ultimate attitude to the Charter, it indicates at least a new willingness to examine European labour law instruments though the lens of fundamental social rights.

IV. Understanding European social policy

Taking an overview of the current state of European social policy, it is difficult to describe it as neatly falling into either of the two models proposed. The market integration model is clearly evident as the original vision of the appropriate role for social policy. However, this model has mutated during certain periods, in the direction of a much broader social policy than that envisaged by the drafters of the Treaties; a social policy based around establishing common minimum labour law standards. At the same time, it is important to recognise that this process has not been unidirectional. It is quite evident that the Delors vision of social policy which underpinned the

---

[127] Case C–173/99 *Broadcasting, Entertainment, Cinematographic and Theatre Union (BECTU) v Secretary of State for Trade and Industry* [2001] ECR I–4881.

[128] ibid para 43.   [129] ibid paras 47–48.   [130] ibid para 59.

1989 Social Charter has since given way to a much more cautious assessment of the contribution the Union can make in this field.

The social citizenship model has also been subject to ebbs and flows. For instance, several authors have suggested that the EU should focus on the establishment of an inner circle of basic rights, those most closely linked to the labour market.[131] Sciarra recommends that labour lawyers focus on non-discrimination, non-dismissal 'without a just cause' and rights to information and consultation.[132] The Charter initially appears to conflict with an emphasis on guaranteeing a small number of core labour law rights. Yet, Article 51 makes it quite clear that the Charter is not intended to generate a new wave of legislation—social or otherwise. Within the confines of the current social policy competence, Sciarra's proposal remains a realistic assessment of how European social policy could be reoriented towards a social citizenship model.

This approach is strengthened by the international dimension to the social rights debate.[133] There has been increasing awareness that even if the perceived risk of social dumping is countered within the EU, there remains the very real possibility of the competitive reduction of labour standards by states outside the EU.[134] Moreover, Lo Faro suggests concerns surrounding social dumping will become reinvigorated as the prospect of EU enlargement draws closer.[135] In this vein, calls for the EU to legislate for a basic set of fundamental rights in the field of labour law coincide with attempts by the ILO to gain worldwide accord on the implementation of a limited number of social rights. Specifically, the ILO has argued for the global recognition of four fundamental social rights: freedom of association, the elimination of all forms of compulsory labour, the abolition of child labour and the 'elimination of discrimination in respect of employment and occupation'.[136]

---

[131] R Blanpain; B Hepple; S Sciarra; M Weiss, *Fundamental Social Rights: Proposals for the European Union* (Leuven: Peeters, 1996).

[132] S Sciarra, 'Social Values and the Multiple Sources of European Social Law' (1995) 1 Eur LJ 60, 81. Similarly, Simitis stresses the need to focus on the guarantee of a few key principles, such as non-discrimination, the right to privacy and freedom of association (S Simitis, 'Dismantling or strengthening labour law: the case of the European Court of Justice' (1996) 2 Eur LJ 156, 169).

[133] Organisation for Economic Co-operation and Development, *Trade, Employment and Labour Standards: A study of core workers rights and international trade* (Paris: OECD, 1996).

[134] On the impact of globalisation on labour standards, see: C Crouch, 'Un commento al saggio di Simitis' (1997) 76 *Giornale di diritto del lavoro e di relazioni industriali* 643.

[135] A Lo Faro, *Regulating Social Europe—reality and myth of collective bargaining in the EC legal order* (Oxford: Hart Publishing, 2000) 42. For example, 'Republic loses 1,000 jobs to Hungary' Irish Times, 13 December 2000.

[136] ILO Declaration on fundamental principles and rights at work, (1998) 37 Intl Legal Materials 1237.

In summary, the market integration model now accepts the need for some basic labour law standards to combat destructive competition within the internal market. To the extent that these basic standards can be approximated to agreement on a limited core of fundamental social rights, then the two models have a meeting place where progress may be possible.[137] Importantly, anti-discrimination law finds a location in both, whether as a tool against the gaining of unfair competitive advantages through cheap labour, or as a breach of the fundamental right to non-discrimination. As a result, this renders it an area fertile for an expanded EU role.

The theoretical models offer general explanations for the pattern of EU social policy. However, either model is limited when it comes to making sense of specifics in labour law. In explaining developments in a precise field, much of the literature focuses on the legal provisions of the founding Treaties and what scope they provided for social policy measures. Action or inaction is thus explained by reference to the social provisions. For instance, in 1992, Davies argued that 'plans to enact progressive and protective labour legislation will be exposed as mere naivety when they encounter the hard facts of the Community's actual legislative powers in the area of social policy'.[138]

Similarly, Collins submits that 'it was where the Treaties were precise and provided the institutions with the support of definite procedures and deadlines that social action was most successful'.[139] Certainly, it is true that the existence or non-existence of a legal authority for intervention is a potent factor in helping to understand the way in which labour law has developed. It is doubtful if gender equality law would have been so vibrant had it not been for the resolute terms of the original EEC Treaty, Article 119 and the opportunity this presented to the Court of Justice to generate an individual right to equal pay between women and men.[140]

Nonetheless, an alternative dynamic of labour law is found in the national legal systems. Indeed, it is precisely the relevance of national law which makes the integration process so challenging. For example, Kahn-Freund sounded a note of caution about the potential for a common social policy, when he remarked that in the Member States one finds 'differences in tradition, in

---

[137] M Poiares Maduro, 'Europe's social self: "The Sickness unto Death"' in J Shaw (ed), *Social law and policy in an evolving European Union* (Oxford: Hart Publishing, 2000) 343.

[138] P Davies, 'The Emergence of European Labour Law' in W McCarthy (ed), *Legal Interventions in Industrial Relations: Gains and Losses* (Oxford: Basil Blackwell, 1992) 317.

[139] D Collins, *The European Communities—the social policy of the first phase. Volume 2 The European Economic Community 1958–72* (London: Martin Robertson, 1975) 232.

[140] C Docksey, 'The Principle of Equality between Men and Women as a Fundamental Right under Community Law' (1991) 20 ILJ 258, 279.

political outlook, in social *mores*—differences which are deeply rooted in the political and social history of Europe and quite incapable of being eliminated by a stroke of the pen of a legislator or treaty maker'.[141]

A focus on the influence of the Member States' legal systems also helps understand the uneven nature of EU law. European labour law is less the outcome of an overall vision of the appropriate role for the EU, but more frequently the result of *ad hoc* political initiatives and compromises resulting from the interaction of fifteen different national viewpoints.[142] For example, had it not been for the insistence of the French Government on a commitment to equal pay between women and men, it is doubtful if gender equality would have evolved as one of the focal areas of EU social policy. EEC Treaty, Article 119 was therefore principally a by-product of an argument based on the national self-interest of one Member State concerned to protect its domestic enterprises. Similarly, the outcome of national self-interest helps explain the progress made on health and safety policy in the 1980s.[143] Whilst the UK pursued a general policy of blocking new social legislation, it was prepared to agree to a significant range of measures on health and safety, and also the creation of an important new legal competence.[144] Wedderburn attributes this to the historical tradition in the UK of legislating against occupational hazards and a fear that other states would gain a competitive advantage through lower standards in this field.[145]

Bercusson argues that a distinction may thus be identified between accounts of EU labour law based on the primacy of legal factors, and those founded on essentially political factors.[146] A *legal* approach to labour law focuses on the limits and opportunities that result from the founding

---

[141] O Kahn-Freund, 'Labor law and social security' in E Stein and T Nicholson (eds), *American Enterprise in the European Common Market—A Legal Profile* Vol 1 (Michigan: Ann Arbor, 1960) 304. See also, D Purdy and P Devine, 'Social Policy' in M Artis and N Lee (eds), *The Economics of the European Union—policy and analysis* (Oxford: Oxford University Press, 1994) 275–277; J Due, J Steen Madsen, C Strøby Jensen, 'The Social Dimension: convergence or diversification of industrial relations in the single European market?' (1991) 22 Industrial Relations J 85; P Teague and J Grahl, '1992 and the emergence of a European industrial relations area' (1990) XIII J of Eur Integration 167.

[142] Milward extends this argument to the history of European integration in general: A Milward, *The European rescue of the nation-state* (London: Routledge, 1992).

[143] P James, 'Occupational health and safety' in M Gold (ed), *The Social Dimension—Employment in the European Community* (2nd edn, London: Pinter Publishers, 1993).

[144] EEC Treaty, Art. 118a, as amended by the Single European Act 1986.

[145] Lord Wedderburn, 'Labour standards, global markets and labour laws in Europe' in W Sengenberger and D Campbell (eds), *International labour standards and economic interdependence* (Geneva: International Institute for Labour Studies, 1994) 258.

[146] B Bercusson, 'The conceptualization of European Labour Law' (1995) 24 ILJ 3, 8.

Treaties. A *political* approach emphasises factors external to the Treaties, such as the legal position in the Member States and the role played by non-state actors. Both approaches combine law and politics, but Bercusson argues that the former emphasises law as the dominant variable, and the latter politics: 'the question is whether one starts with a view of the law as setting the limits to EC labour law and social policy, or whether one starts with the view that the political will and ability of the actors involved determines its development'.[147]

Underlying this 'law versus politics' approach seems a choice between focusing more on *European Union* law factors, such as legal competence or the balance of powers between the institutions, and emphasising *national* law as the key to understanding European legal developments. Clearly, EU law reflects a combination of both changes in the national and European context. This seems especially true in respect of the origins of a European Union competence. Certainly, it is the case that EU law has an autonomous dynamic over which the Member States lack full control, principally as a result of the role played by the Court of Justice. The transformation of EEC Treaty, Article 119 into an enforceable right available to individuals is an example of this. However, it is arguably the Member States and national legal systems which hold the dominant influence on the initiation of a field of law at EU level, notably the decision on whether to create a new Treaty competence. As shall be seen, so far the Member States have been able to keep a strict limit on EU intervention in racial and sexual orientation discrimination, whereas EU law on gender and nationality discrimination has constantly evolved, often in directions neither foreseen nor intended by the Member States.[148] Therefore, in the analysis of the development of EU anti-discrimination law it is necessary to keep in mind not simply the EU level influences, but also the input of national variables.

Having established a broad overview of European social policy, and the various explanations for its development, it is necessary to turn now to the specific focus of this book: anti-discrimination law. In particular, the next chapter examines those areas of anti-discrimination law that are well developed, notwithstanding the dominance of the market integration model of social policy.

---

[147] ibid 9.

[148] For example, the decision of the Court that discrimination on grounds of sex also includes discrimination on grounds relating to gender reassignment (Case C–13/94 *P v S and Cornwall County Council* [1996] ECR I–2143).

Emerging Rights of Social Citizenship? Discrimination on Grounds of Nationality and Gender

Anti-discrimination law has been a central element of social policy from the earliest stages of European integration. In particular, a solid body of law governing discrimination on the grounds of nationality and gender has been constructed. This chapter aims to examine both these established areas of EU anti-discrimination law in the light of the alternative models of social policy proposed in Chapter 1. In both cases, the original impetus for European intervention lies comfortably within the market integration model. However, the gradual development of law on both grounds has strained the limits implied by a market integration approach, and increasingly anti-discrimination law in these fields is more characteristic of the social citizenship model. At the same time, the unco-ordinated nature of these initiatives has produced a *hierarchy of equality*,[1] where the right to non-discrimination is thorough and well established in these areas, but weak and fragmented in others.

Whilst the Union has not been inactive on other forms of discrimination, such as that based on grounds of race[2] or disability,[3] a clear legal hierarchy exists in anti-discrimination law, within which nationality and gender traditionally have been privileged categories. As a result, before proceeding to consider those forms of discrimination which were previously 'non-

---

[1] A Hegarty and C Keown, 'Hierarchies of discrimination: the political, legal and social prioritisation of the equality agenda in Northern Ireland' (1996) 15 *Equal Opportunities Intl* 1.

[2] M Bell, 'EU anti-discrimination policy: from equal opportunities between women and men to combating racism' LIBE 102 EN (Luxembourg: European Parliament, 1998).

[3] L Waddington, *Disability, employment and the European Community* (Antwerpen: Maklu, 1995).

privileged' in Union law, it seems logical to focus first on reaching an understanding of the fields where there has already been some success.

I. EU law on nationality discrimination

Freedom from discrimination on grounds of nationality is the most fundamental right conferred by the Treaty and must be seen as a basic ingredient of Union citizenship.[4]

From the outset, it was recognised by the founders of the Communities that a common market characterised by free movement would not be consistent with internal discrimination based on nationality. The ECSC Treaty includes a number of provisions forbidding nationality discrimination in the common market in coal and steel.[5] Whilst most of these concerned discrimination between consumers and suppliers, ECSC Treaty, Article 69 extended to individuals, forbidding discrimination in wages and working conditions against migrant coal and steel workers. The EEC Treaty also included prohibitions on nationality discrimination in areas as diverse as agriculture[6] and transport,[7] but went further through the inclusion of EC Treaty, Article 12[8] which provides: 'Within the scope of application of this Treaty, and without prejudice to any special provisions contained therein, any discrimination on grounds of nationality shall be prohibited.'

This Article is supplemented by more detailed provisions elsewhere in the Treaty and in secondary legislation, the most significant for individual EU citizens being EC Treaty, Article 39(2) which states that free movement of workers 'shall entail the abolition of any discrimination based on nationality between workers of the Member States as regards employment, remuneration and other conditions of work and employment'.

This is developed in Regulation (EEC) 1612/68 on free movement for workers within the Community,[9] Article 7(2) of which provides that EU migrant workers 'shall enjoy the same social and tax advantages as national workers'.

In contrast with most national anti-discrimination law instruments, EU law provides no definition of what constitutes 'nationality discrimination'.

---

[4] Opinion of A-G Jacobs, Case C–274/96 *Bickel and Franz* [1998] ECR I–7637, para 24.
[5] ECSC Treaty, Arts 4(b), 54, 60, 63, 66, 69 and 70. [6] Art 34(3). [7] Art 75.
[8] See further, N Bernard, 'What are the purposes of EC discrimination law?' in J Dine and B Watt (eds), *Discrimination Law—concepts, limitations, and justifications* (London: Longman, 1996).
[9] [1968] OJ Spec Ed (II) 475.

Therefore, the Court of Justice has been required to give the various legislative provisions more substance. The Court has consistently held that the ban on nationality discrimination covers both 'overt' and 'covert' forms of discrimination,[10] concepts which can be approximated to the more familiar notions of direct and indirect discrimination. Direct discrimination is normally easier to identify, as it concerns situations where distinctions are made explicitly on the grounds of nationality. For example, in *Commission v Greece*,[11] a variety of social benefits were granted to families which included three children or more. These were confined to Greek nationals, though, a rule which quite clearly constituted direct discrimination on grounds of nationality against other EU migrant families in Greece. More difficult to challenge is indirect discrimination, where apparently neutral criteria are used, but which in fact disproportionately disadvantage EU migrants. For example, in *Commission v Belgium*,[12] tideover allowances (a form of unemployment benefit) were provided by the Belgian state to young people who had completed their education and were seeking their first job. These were, however, conditional on having 'completed full-time secondary education or technical or vocational training at a centre run, recognized or subsidized by the state'.[13] The Commission argued that this placed young people from other Member States, but now resident in Belgium, at a particular disadvantage as they were likely to have completed their secondary education in an establishment not run, recognised or subsidised by the Belgian state. Belgium argued that there needed to be statistical evidence to support this proposition, but the Court rejected such an approach:

a provision of national law must be regarded as indirectly discriminatory if it is intrinsically liable to affect migrant workers more than national workers and if there is a consequent risk that it will place the former at a particular disadvantage. It is not necessary to find that the provision in question does in practice affect a substantially higher proportion of migrant workers.[14]

The strength of this definition of indirect discrimination lies in the fact that it impugns rules 'intrinsically liable' to disadvantage migrant workers, without

---

[10]   Case 15/69 *Württenbergische Milchverwertung-Sudmilch v Ugliola* [1969] ECR 363. See also, *inter alia*, Case C-187/96 *Commission v Greece* [1998] ECR I-1095, Case C-57/96 *H Meints v Minister van Landbouw, Natuurbeheer en Visserij* [1997] ECR I-6689.

[11]   Case C-185/96 [1998] ECR I-6601.   [12]   Case C-278/94 [1996] ECR I-4307.

[13]   ibid 4330.

[14]   ibid 4337. On the facts the Court held that the condition would be filled 'more easily' by Belgian young people than by nationals of other Member States and hence operated in an indirectly discriminatory fashion (4340). See also Case C-237/94 *John O'Flynn v Adjudication Officer* [1996] ECR I-2617, 2639; Case C-35/97 *Commission v France* [1998] ECR I-5325.

requiring statistical evidence to confirm that the provision or practice has had this disadvantageous effect.[15] This compares favourably with the definition of indirect discrimination in EU gender equality law which demands evidence that a provision or practice affects a 'substantially higher proportion' of women than men (or vice versa).[16] This stipulation normally requires statistical evidence and this has proven to be problematic in certain cases.[17]

The Court has been less clear on the permissible justifications for nationality discrimination.[18] First, there are the statutory justifications for discrimination, such as EC Treaty, Article 39(4) which provides that 'the provisions of this Article shall not apply to employment in the public service'. The Court has maintained that, as an exemption to a fundamental right, this must be interpreted narrowly, and it has confined this to posts involving the 'direct or indirect participation in the exercise of powers conferred by public law and duties designed to safeguard the general interests of the State of other public authorities'.[19] Therefore, a domestic nationality requirement for primary school teachers was held to be outside the scope of the exception in Article 39(4).[20]

In addition to the statutory exceptions, indirect discrimination is also open to 'objective justification'. Considerations such as the enforcement of judgments,[21] the prevention of fraud,[22] or the promotion of the official language of the state[23] have all been accepted as constituting potentially legitimate reasons for indirect nationality discrimination. Nonetheless, even such rules must still conform to the principle of proportionality; that is, the action in question must be 'appropriate and necessary to achieve the aim pursued,

---

[15] R Allen, 'Article 13 and the search for equality in Europe: an overview' in Europaforum Wien (eds), *Anti-discrimination: the way forward* (Wien: Europaforum, 1999) 18.

[16] Council Directive (EC) 97/80 on the burden of proof in cases of discrimination based on sex [1998] OJ L14/6, Art 2(2).

[17] See further Case C–167/97 *R v Secretary of State, ex p Seymour-Smith and Perez* [1999] ECR I–623; C Barnard and B Hepple, 'Indirect discrimination: interpreting *Seymour-Smith*' (1999) 58 CLJ 399.

[18] S Fries and J Shaw, 'Citizenship of the Union: first steps in the European Court of Justice' (1998) 4 Eur Public L 533, 544.

[19] Case C–473/93 *Commission v Luxembourg* [1996] ECR I–3207, 3258.

[20] ibid. See also Case C–173/94 *Commission v Belgium* [1996] ECR I–3265; Case C–290/94 *Commission v Greece* [1996] ECR I–3285; Case C–187/96 *Commission v Greece* [1998] I–1095; Case C–283/99 *Commission v Italy* [2001] ECR I–4363.

[21] Case C–29/95 *Pastoors and Trans-Cap GmbH v Belgian State* [1997] ECR I–285, 308.

[22] Case C–168/91 *Konstantinidis* [1993] ECR I–1191, 1206.

[23] Case C–378/87 *Groener v Minister for Education and City of Dublin Vocational Education Committee* [1989] ECR 3967.

without going beyond what is essential in order to attain it'.[24] For example, in *Clean Car*,[25] the Austrian Government sought to maintain that Austrian residence requirements for managers of undertakings were necessary, *inter alia*, to ensure that fines could be served on the business. The Court pointed out that there were less restrictive means of guaranteeing that fines could be served, such as serving them to the registered office of the firm, or relying on international conventions on the enforcement of judgments, if necessary.[26] It can be seen, therefore, that the Court will not easily accept wide-ranging justifications which are vulnerable to detailed examination.

Notwithstanding the relative strength of the Court's case law on the definition of 'discrimination', omissions and weakness in the basic principles governing EU law on nationality discrimination continue to betray its essentially market-driven nature. This can be demonstrated by reference to two issues: the permissibility of reverse discrimination; and the absence of any prohibition on discrimination against third country nationals.

Whilst nationality discrimination is forbidden against EU nationals living or working in another Member State, the situation is more ambiguous where the discrimination is by a Member State against its own nationals, in comparison with other EU migrants. In *Morsen and Jhanjan*,[27] the two plaintiffs were third country nationals who sought permission to join their daughter and son respectively in the Netherlands, their children both being Dutch nationals. They were refused permission to do so, but appealed against this decision on the ground that this was in breach of Regulation (EEC) 1612/68 Article 10(1).[28] On referral, the Court of Justice rejected the women's submission; it held that the free movement provisions of the EC Treaty, and secondary legislation thereto, could be relied upon only where the situation in question actually involved free movement between the Member States,[29] and this 'does not cover the position of dependent relatives of a worker who is a national of the Member State within whose territory he is employed'.[30] Consequently, nationals resident in their own Member State can find themselves in a weaker legal position *vis-à-vis* family reunion rights, than EU

[24] *Pastoors* (n 21 above) 308.

[25] Case C–350/96 *Clean Car Autoservice GmbH v Landeshauptmann von Wein* [1998] ECR I–2521.

[26] paras 35–37.

[27] Cases 35, 36/82 [1982] ECR 3723. See also Case 175/78 *R v Saunders* [1979] ECR 1129, para 10.

[28] Art 10(1) provides that EU migrant workers may be joined by their spouse, descendants who are under 21 or who are dependants, and dependent relatives in the ascending line of both the worker and their spouse, irrespective of their relatives' nationality.

[29] para 15.   [30] para 13.

migrants. In this respect, Regulation (EEC) 1612/68 produces a situation of reverse discrimination against domestic nationals.[31] The fact that EU law does not prevent discrimination on grounds of nationality by a Member State against its own nationals reveals its dependency on the establishment of a nexus with free movement.[32] In this sense, it may be argued that Article 12 has been less concerned with establishing a fundamental right to non-discrimination on grounds of nationality, but instead is focused mainly on facilitating free movement.[33]

The market-oriented view of EU law on nationality discrimination is further reinforced if one considers the position of third country nationals under EC Treaty, Article 12. On the one hand, Article 12 simply prohibits any 'discrimination on grounds of nationality'. It does not explicitly curtail this to EU citizens, but in practice it has not been interpreted as applying to discrimination against third country nationals.[34] Again this is linked to the rules regarding free movement. EC Treaty, Article 39(2) requires 'the abolition of any discrimination based on nationality between workers of the Member States'. It does not state with clarity whether 'workers of the Member States' must also be nationals of the Member States. Despite persuasive arguments that the drafters intended Article 39 to apply to all workers in the Community,[35] the Member States have worked on the basis that free movement is a right only

---

[31] Interestingly, the Commission aims to eliminate this example of reverse discrimination through its proposed Directive on the right to family reunification. This would extend the relevant provisions of Reg (EEC) 1612/68 to EU nationals residing in their Member State of nationality (COM (1999) 638, Art 4).

[32] The Court has recognised that nationals who exercise their right to free movement and then return to their Member State of origin continue to enjoy certain Community law rights, including rights of family reunion; Case C–370/90 *R v Immigration Appeal Tribunal & Surinder Singh, ex p Secretary of State for the Home Department* [1992] ECR I–4265. See also: Case 136/78 *Ministère Public v Auer* [1979] ECR 437; Case C–18/95 *Terhoeve v Inspecteur van de Belastingsdienst Particulieren/Ondermingen Buitenland* [1999] ECR I–345; Case C–90/97 *Swaddling v Adjudication Officer* [1999] ECR I–1075; Case C–281/98 *Roman Angonese v Cassa di Risparmio di Bolzano SpA* [2000] ECR I–4139.

[33] G de Búrca, 'The role of equality in European Community Law' in A Dashwood and S O'Leary (eds), *The principle of equal treatment in European Community law* (London: Sweet & Maxwell, 1997) 16. Cf N Bernard, 'What are the purposes of EC discrimination law?' in J Dine and B Watt (eds), *Discrimination Law—concepts, limitations, and justifications* (London: Longman, 1996) 90.

[34] See further Opinion of A-G Jacobs, Cases C–95/99 to C–98/99 and C–180/99 *Khalil, Chaaban and Osseili v Bundesanstalt für Arbeit, Nasser v Landeshauptstadt Stuttgart, Addou v Land Nordrhein-Westfalen* 30 November 2000.

[35] See A Evans, 'Third-country nationals and the Treaty on European Union' (1994) 5 Eur J of Int L 199, 200; R Plender, 'Competence, European Community law and nationals of non-member states' (1990) 39 ICLQ 599, 604.

enjoyed by EU citizens.[36] It has consequently been assumed that the prohibition on nationality discrimination in the EC Treaty must also be restricted to EU citizens. In this fashion, it is once again demonstrated that Article 12 was not included in the EC Treaty as a means to combat irrational prejudice against foreigners, but was strictly confined to ensuring that discrimination did not become a barrier to free movement.[37]

Interestingly, a similar logic underpins the evolving case law of the Court on rights to non-discrimination under agreements between the EU and third countries. Whilst there is a plethora of agreements with non-Member States,[38] the association and co-operation agreements made between the EEC and Turkey,[39] Morocco,[40] and Algeria[41] have been the greatest sources of litigation. The starting point lies in the decision of the Court to recognise the possibility for individuals to rely on the provisions in certain association or co-operation agreements (and acts adopted thereto), in a similar fashion to the provisions of the EC Treaty.[42] The acceptance of this principle opened the way to a significant level of litigation by individuals seeking to enforce rights conferred by these agreements, often in cases concerning residence and work permits.[43] More recently, a number of cases have touched directly on the legal effects of the non-discrimination clauses within these agreements. In this regard, the Court of Justice has upheld a directly effective right to non-discrimination in the area of social security for Turkish,[44]

---

[36]   Reg (EEC) 1612/68 Art 1(1), specified that the free movement rights were only available to 'any national of a Member State'.

[37]   G de Búrca (n 33 above).

[38]   S Peers, 'Towards Equality: Actual and Potential Rights of Third-Country Nationals in the European Union' (1996) 33 CML Rev 7, 8.

[39]   Association agreement between the EEC and Turkey, signed on 12 September 1963; concluded by the EEC through Council Decision 64/732 [1964] JO 217/3685. Also, Additional Protocol (addressing free movement of goods, services and persons) [1972] JO L293/1.

[40]   Co-operation agreement between the EEC and Morocco, signed on 27 April 1976, concluded by the EEC through Council Reg (EEC) 2211/78 [1978] OJ L264/1.

[41]   Co-operation agreement between the EEC and Algeria, signed on 26 April 1976, concluded by the EEC through Council Reg (EEC) 2210/78 [1978] OJ L263/1.

[42]   Case C–12/86 *Demirel v Stadt Schwäbisch Gmünd* [1987] ECR 3719.

[43]   See further, S O'Leary, 'Employment and residence for Turkish workers and their families: analogies with the case law of the Court of Justice on Art 48 EC' in Università di Bologna, Seminario Giuridico (ed), *Scritti in onore di Giuseppe Federico Mancini—Vol II. Diritto dell'Unione Europea* (Milano: Giuffrè, 1998).

[44]   Case C–262/96 *Sürül v Bundesanstalt für Arbeit* [1999] ECR I–2685. See further S Peers, 'Social security equality for Turkish nationals' (1999) 24 ELR 627. See also Cases C–102/98 and C–211/98 *Kocak v Landesversicherungsanstalt Oberfranken und Mittelfranken, Örs v Bundesknappschaft* [2000] ECR I–1287.

Moroccan,[45] and Algerian[46] workers. What is significant in the context of this discussion is how the Court has linked the strength of the right to non-discrimination to the free movement of persons. Therefore, in *El-Yassini*,[47] the Court held that the principle of equal treatment in working conditions, in the context of the EEC–Morocco agreement, was not such as to require a Member State to renew a residence permit where the initial reason for leave to remain no longer exists, notwithstanding the fact that the individual is engaged in ongoing lawful employment. This contrasts with the position of Turkish workers, where a Member State must renew a residence permit if the individual remains in lawful employment for more than one year, irrespective of whether the initial reason for the granting of leave to remain continues to exist.[48] In justifying its decision in *El-Yassini*, the Court noted that 'the EEC–Morocco Agreement, unlike the EEC–Turkey Agreement, is not intended progressively to secure freedom of movement for workers'.[49]

Given, then, the free movement orientation of the law on nationality discrimination, it is quite in keeping with the market integration model of social policy for the EU to have assumed responsibility for ensuring non-discrimination in this area. Whilst it is true that the market foundation for anti-discrimination law creates limitations, it has nonetheless provided a basis for an expansion in the direction of fundamental social rights. In respect of discrimination against EU nationals, this is occurring in two ways: first, through the transformation of non-discrimination into a right of EU citizenship, and second, through the extension of this free movement rationale to other forms of discrimination.

In the first instance, the right to non-discrimination on grounds of EU nationality seems to be in a process of transition from a free movement right to a fundamental right. Specifically, the Court is increasingly building links between EC Treaty, Article 12 on non-discrimination and Article 17 which creates EU citizenship. *Martínez Sala*[50] concerned the denial of a child-raising allowance to a Spanish woman legally resident in Germany, although not in possession of a residence permit. The Court held that the refusal to

---

[45] Case C–126/95 *Hallouzi-Choho v Bestuur van de Sociale Verzekeringsbank* [1996] ECR I–4807.

[46] Case C–113/97 *Babahenini v Belgium* [1998] ECR I–183.

[47] Case C–416/96 *El-Yassini v Secretary of State for the Home Department* [1999] ECR I–1209.

[48] Case C–237/91 *Kus v Landeshauptstadt Wiesbaden* [1992] ECR I–6781. See H Lichtenberg, 'The rights of Turkish workers in Community Law' (1995) 24 ILJ 90.

[49] para 58. See also Case C–179/98 *Belgium v Mesbah* [1999] ECR I–7955, para 36; Opinion of A-G Alber, Case C–63/99 *R v Secretary of State for the Home Department, ex p Gloszczuk and Gloszczuk*, 14 September 2000 on the rights of individuals under the EC–Poland Agreement.

[50] Case C–85/96 *Martínez Sala v Freistaat Bayern* [1998] ECR I–2691.

accord her the benefit on the basis that she did not have a residence permit was direct discrimination on grounds of nationality, as no comparable requirement applied to German nationals. However, a difficulty arose concerning whether Mrs Sala could be regarded as being in a situation governed by Community law, as required to allow her to rely on Article 12. Although she was consistently resident in Germany from 1968, she had not been employed since 1989, and as a result it was unclear if she was a 'worker' for the purposes of Community law, under either Regulation (EEC) 1612/68 or Regulation (EEC) 1408/71.[51] Significantly, the Court held that even if she was not a worker for the purposes of EC law, she could rely on her status as an EU citizen: 'a citizen of the European Union, such as the appellant in the main proceedings, lawfully resident in the territory of the host Member State, can rely on Article [12] of the Treaty in all situations which fall within the scope *ratione materiae* of Community law'.[52]

Therefore, provided that the benefit in question fell within the material scope of the Treaty, by the sole reason of being an EU citizen lawfully living in another Member State, she could require non-discrimination in its administration. The potential significance of this judgment is the decoupling of Article 12 from the need for an individual plaintiff to show that they personally are in a situation governed by EC law, thus providing a much more general right of non-discrimination to all EU citizens living in another Member State.[53] At the same time, this expansion in the application of Article 12 remains carefully balanced by the requirement that individuals be 'lawfully resident' in the host state.[54]

The judgment in *Sala* has been made more concrete through the subsequent decision of the Court in *Bickel and Franz*.[55] The case concerned a German and an Austrian plaintiff involved in criminal proceedings in the province of Bolzano, Italy. Whereas residents of Bolzano were entitled to opt for court proceedings to take place in German (as opposed to Italian),

---

[51] On the application of social security schemes to employed persons, to self-employed persons and to members of their families moving within the Community [1971] JO L149/2.

[52] para 61.

[53] S O'Leary, 'Putting flesh on the bones of European Union citizenship' (1999) 24 ELR 68, 78.

[54] Views differ as to the precise impact of the lawful residence requirement. For example, Fries and Shaw argue it is a very broad criterion and will not prove a major obstacle to claiming rights under Art 12 ('Citizenship of the Union: first steps in the European Court of Justice' (1998) 4 EPL 533, 547). Cf G Gori, 'Union citizenship and equal treatment: a way of improving Community educational rights?' (1999) 21 J of Social Welfare and Family L 405.

[55] Case C–274/96 *Bickel and Franz* [1998] ECR I–7637. See B Doherty, '*Bickel*—extending the boundaries of European citizenship' (1999) 8 Irish J of Eur L 70.

this right was not extended to either of the accused on the basis that they were not resident in Bolzano. Notwithstanding the fact that this rule also applied to Italian nationals not resident in Bolzano, the Court held it was indirect discrimination on grounds of nationality.[56] The significance of the judgment lies in its implications with regard to the scope of Community law. First, the Court once again relied (in part) on the citizenship provisions as a basis for bringing the individuals within the personal scope of EC law.[57] The judgment goes beyond *Sala* though in supporting a very broad definition of the material scope of Article 12. Advocate-General Jacobs freely admits that the action against Mr Bickel (for driving under the influence of alcohol) had no substantive link to Community law.[58] Nonetheless, the mere fact that he was exercising his Community rights at the same time is accepted as bringing the matter within the material scope of EC law.[59] Indeed, the decision raises the possibility that almost any policy, rule or practice must now place EU migrants 'entirely on an equal footing with nationals of the Member State',[60] unless this can be justified objectively or falls within a limited range of activities where 'the essential characteristics of nationality are at stake', such as certain political rights.[61] The underlying significance of these trends in the Court's case law is the lower emphasis on establishing a link with the effect of the measure on free movement, but rather a more generalised right to equal treatment for EU citizens lawfully present in other Member States.[62]

The second means through which the market-based right to non-discrimination on grounds of nationality is evolving is the extension of the same logic to other forms of discrimination. In particular, it has been argued that if discrimination on grounds of nationality is a barrier to free movement, then also discrimination on grounds such as race,[63] religion,[64] or disability,[65]

---

[56] paras 25–27.   [57] para 15.   [58] Opinion of A-G Jacobs, para 15.

[59] This is in apparent contradiction to the decision of the Court in Case C–291/96 *Martino Grado and Shahid Bashir* [1997] ECR I–5531 where an EU migrant charged with a traffic offence was deemed not to be in a situation governed by Community law.

[60] Court judgment, para 14.

[61] Opinion of A-G Jacobs, para 27. Cf Case C–356/98 *Kaba v Secretary of State for the Home Department* [2000] ECR I–2623.

[62] N Bernard, 'What are the purposes of EC discrimination law' in J Durie and B Watt (eds), *Discrimination Law—concepts, limitations, and justifications* (London: Longman, 1996) 95.

[63] A Dummett, 'Racial Equality and "1992"' (1991) 3 *Feminist Rev* 85.

[64] I Chopin and J Niessen (eds), *Proposals for legislative measures to combat racism and to promote equal rights in the European Union* (London: Commission for Racial Equality, 1998) 17.

[65] European Disability Forum, *Guide to the Amsterdam Treaty* (Brussels: EDF, 1998) 10–11.

may also constitute an obstacle to free movement.[66] Through constructing discrimination in this manner, it has proven less difficult to justify the need for EU intervention as this accords with the market integration model. Significantly, the anti-discrimination competence conferred by the Treaty of Amsterdam was inserted beside EC Treaty, Article 12, indicating the parallel.[67]

Taking an overview of EU law on nationality discrimination, there are a number of features of broader relevance. First, it may be noticed that the existence of a strong Treaty foundation has enabled the Court to develop the basic principle of non-discrimination into a wide-ranging requirement throughout the full ambit of Community law. This includes areas which anti-discrimination legislation could easily omit to address, such as access to criminal injuries compensation funds,[68] or linguistic requirements in judicial proceedings.[69] Second, the strong nexus between the rules on nationality discrimination and the right to free movement underpins the inherent legitimacy with which the Union's interventions here are regarded. Whilst some have argued that the Court has, on occasions, gone too far in this field,[70] in general, this is not an area which has aroused special controversy. This clearly flows from the fact that prohibiting nationality discrimination has a strong market integration rationale.

II. EU law on gender discrimination

The only other area of anti-discrimination law provided for in the EEC Treaty was gender discrimination in the workplace. Specifically, Article 119 required equal pay for women and men. Notwithstanding the solitary nature of this provision, the EU has gradually developed a significant body of law on gender equality, summed up by Wedderburn as a 'separate citadel in the fortress of Community law'.[71] Whilst constraints of space make it impossible

---

[66] Commission, 'European Social Policy—a way forward for the Union: a White Paper' COM (94) 333, 52.

[67] EC Treaty, Art 13.   [68] Case C–186/87 *Cowan v Trésor public* [1989] ECR 195.

[69] Case C–274/96 *Bickel and Franz* [1998] ECR I–7637.

[70] S O'Leary, 'The principle of equal treatment on grounds of nationality in Article 6 EC. A lucrative source of rights for Member State nationals?' in A Dashwood and S O'Leary, *The principle of equal treatment in European Community law* (London: Sweet & Maxwell, 1997); K Hailbronner and J Polakiewicz, 'Non-EC nationals in the European Community: the need for a coordinated approach' (1992) 3 Duke J of Intl L 49.

[71] Lord Wedderburn, *Labour Law and Freedom: Further Essays in Labour Law* (London: Lawrence and Wishart, 1995) 265.

to provide a truly comprehensive overview of EU gender equality law, this section will provide an introduction to the principal features of the law and, more importantly, will seek to identify some of the factors which have enabled the relatively successful evolution of social policy in this area.[72]

It was only following a combination of political and judicial interventions in the 1970s that EEC Treaty, Article 119 was finally transformed from a dormant Treaty provision into an active equal opportunities law. From the political standpoint, the early 1970s witnessed an increasing acknowledgement by the Member States that European integration could not be sustained if it did not develop more popular legitimacy.[73] To this end, strengthening the social dimension became a priority, with equal opportunities for women one of the central elements of the 1974 social action programme.[74] Various reasons have been proffered as to why the Member States decided to place such emphasis on gender equality. Hoskyns argues that there was a 'feeling among politicians that women were not a threat'.[75] Ellis also supports this line, suggesting that equal opportunities provides 'a relatively innocuous, even high-sounding platform by means of which the Communities can demonstrate their commitment to social progress'.[76]

Was gender equality really so innocuous, though? Underlying this area of law is an attempt to alter traditional conceptions of the role of women and men. These assumptions and stereotypes tend to be deeply rooted in cultural and even moral values which may be difficult to reconcile. Indeed, from this point of view, gender equality law can be seen as quite radical, profoundly affecting social and legal norms throughout the Member States. However, balanced against this is the predominantly economic orientation of EU gender equality legislation. Issues such as reproductive rights[77] and violence

---

[72] See generally S Prechal and N Burrows, *Gender discrimination law of the European Community* (Aldershot: Dartmouth, 1990); E Ellis, *European Community sex equality law* (2nd edn, Oxford: Oxford University Press, 1998); T Hervey and D O'Keeffe, *Sex Equality in the European Union* (Chichester, John Wiley and Sons, 1996); A Dashwood and S O'Leary, *The principle of equal treatment in European Community law* (London, Sweet & Maxwell, 1997); G Mancini and S O'Leary, 'The new frontiers of sex equality law in the European Union' (1999) 24 ELR 331.

[73] Popular scepticism about the benefits of the Community was demonstrated during the accession negotiations in the early 1970s, culminating in the rejection of membership by the citizens of Norway. See generally, M Shanks, *European Social Policy, Today and Tomorrow* (Oxford: Pergamon Press, 1977).

[74] Commission, 'Social Action Programme' EC Bull Supplement, 2/74.

[75] C Hoskyns, *Integrating Gender—Women, Law and Politics in the European Union* (London: Verso, 1996) 196.

[76] E Ellis, *European Community sexual equality law* (Oxford: Oxford University Press, 1991) 40.

[77] See further T Hervey, 'Buy baby: the European Union and the regulation of human reproduction' (1998) 18 OJLS 207.

against women have traditionally been eschewed by EU law, despite strong arguments that these issues are intrinsically linked to female disadvantage in the workplace.[78] For instance, the threat of sexual assault may diminish women's ability to accept nightwork, due to fears for personal security that are not comparable for men.[79] Nonetheless, in line with the market integration model, the Member States have consistently sought to limit gender equality law to issues concerned with:

the 'public' aspects of the position of women, the public being the realm of the workplace, regarded as the natural province of men, at the expense of the 'private' or 'domestic' arena, the world of the home and the family, where decisions regarding reproduction, childcare and morality are taken, often considered to be the traditional realm of women.[80]

In this way, the EU neutralises potential issues of high sensitivity, especially where moral or religious considerations come into play. The Court has also generally worked within this framework. Therefore, it has held that the Equal Treatment Directive is not concerned with the division of family responsibilities,[81] and it has avoided any intervention on abortion rights.[82]

Reference to national and international law also helps understand the willingness of the Member States to accept common standards in the area of employment discrimination. Hoskyns notes that several Member States had already enacted laws on equal pay for women and men by the early 1970s.[83] Moreover, equal pay was required by the 1951 ILO Convention No 100,[84] and non-discrimination on grounds of sex was also demanded by the 1958 ILO Convention No 111 on discrimination in employment.[85] Similar

---

[78] Parliament, 'Report of the Committee on Women's Rights on violence against women' A2-44/86. 'Violence towards women is the sexualized expression of the oppression of women, the difference in power between men and women. In other words, the sexual and economic dependence of women are related', 41.

[79] A Orloff, 'Gender and the social rights of citizenship: the comparative analysis of gender relations and welfare states' (1993) 58 *American Sociological Rev* 303, 309.

[80] C McGlynn, 'EC Sex Equality: towards a human rights foundation' in T Hervey and D O'Keeffe (eds), *Sex equality in the European Union* (Chichester: John Wiley and Sons, 1996) 244.

[81] Case 184/83 *Hofmann v Barmer Ersatzkasse* [1984] ECR 3047, para 24. See also Case C–218/98 *Abdoulaye v Régie Nationale des Usines Renault SA* [1999] ECR I–5723.

[82] See Case C–159/90, *Society for the protection of the unborn child v Grogan* [1991] ECR I–4685; G de Búrca, 'Fundamental human rights and the reach of EC law' (1993) 13 OJLS 283.

[83] These included the UK (1970), France (1972) and the Netherlands (1975); Hoskyns (n 75 above) 216–220.

[84] ILO, *International Labour Conventions and Recommendations 1919–1951 Volume 1* (Geneva: ILO, 1996) 649.

[85] ILO, *International Labour Conventions and Recommendations 1952–1976 Volume 2* (Geneva: ILO, 1996) 176.

obligations were imposed by the 1961 Social Charter.[86] As a result, equality for women in employment had already been accepted by many Member States in a variety of international legal instruments.

The political imperatives for action were complemented by the actions of the Court of Justice. In 1971, in its first decision in the *Defrenne* case,[87] the Court indicated that Article 119 was capable of being given 'direct effect'.[88] In other words, the Court indicated that it would henceforth be open to individuals to rely directly on this provision as a basis for a legally enforceable right to equal pay throughout the Member States.[89] The significance of this ruling should not be underestimated. First, it generated a genuinely individual right in Community law to non-discrimination, a right which the Court has been able to develop through further case law. Second, it provided the Commission with a strong mandate to create a broader gender equality policy and to submit legislative proposals in this field.

Coinciding with the decisions of the Court in *Defrenne*, the Council of Ministers adopted a series of Directives expanding on the basic principle of equal pay. The first was confined to adding more detail to the concept of equal pay,[90] but this was followed in 1976 by the Equal Treatment Directive which extended the ban on discrimination to cover all aspects of the employment relationship.[91] The significance of this Directive is found both in its immediate impact on gender equality law, but also more generally in the implicit move away from a social policy driven solely by the needs of the common market.[92] Moreover, it was complemented by the 1978 Social Security Directive,[93] which aimed to achieve the progressive implementation

---

[86] Art 4(3); see also the preamble.

[87] Case 80/70 *Defrenne v Belgian State* (I) [1971] ECR 445. The case concerned pay discrimination by the Belgian airline, SABENA, between male and female employees.

[88] The principle of direct effect was first developed by the Court in Case 26/62 *Van Gend en Loos v Nederlandse Administratie der Belastingen* [1963] ECR 1.

[89] This interpretation was subsequently confirmed in 1976 in the Court's second decision in *Defrenne*: Case 43/75 *Defrenne v SABENA (II)* [1976] ECR 455.

[90] Council Dir (EEC) 75/117 on the approximation of the laws of the Member States relating to the application of the principle of equal pay for men and women [1975] OJ L45/19.

[91] Council Dir (EEC) 76/207 on the implementation of the principle of equal treatment for men and women as regards access to employment, vocational training and promotion and working conditions [1976] OJ L39/40. Art 3(1) forbids discrimination in access to employment, and Art 5(1) forbids discrimination in working conditions and dismissal.

[92] Lord Wedderburn, *Labour Law and Freedom: Further Essays in Labour Law* (London: Lawrence and Wishart, 1995) 294.

[93] Council Dir (EEC) 79/7 on the progressive implementation of the principle of equal treatment for men and women in matters of social security [1979] OJ L6/24.

of non-discrimination between men and women 'in the field of social security and other elements of social protection'.[94]

The legislative pace of reform slowed dramatically after 1978. On the one hand, this reflected the completion of the core rules on labour market discrimination where agreement was easiest to attain. On the other, the general tide of European social policy slowed again until its relaunch through the 1989 Social Charter. The need for unanimity proved problematic as the UK Government was especially obdurate in this period when confronted with proposals for new social legislation.[95] What policy momentum there existed came primarily from the Commission and the Court. For its part, the Commission implemented a series of equal opportunities action programmes and employed the strategic use of non-binding or 'soft law' instruments at times when no agreement on the adoption of legislation was forthcoming.[96] The Court was more influential though, fleshing out the basic principles in the legislation, and often filling the gaps left by the intransigence in the Council. For example, the Court developed a clearer definition of 'indirect discrimination', with particular regard to discrimination against part-time workers who are predominantly female.[97] It also acted to allow for the shifting of the burden of proof where a plaintiff raises a *prima facie* case of discrimination.[98] It is demonstrative of how the Court has been a leader in this field, that these areas have now been the subject of specific legislation.[99]

More recently, renewed flexibility in the Council has allowed progress in the adoption of additional legislation on gender equality.[100] Alongside new

---

[94] Art 1.

[95] Only two pieces of binding legislation on gender equality were agreed by the Council in the whole of the 1980s: Council Dir (EEC) 86/378 on the implementation of the principle of equal treatment for men and women in occupational social security schemes [1986] OJ L225/40; and Council Dir (EEC) 86/613 on the application of the principle of equal treatment between men and women engaged in an activity, including agriculture, in a self-employed capacity, and on the protection of self-employed women during pregnancy and motherhood [1986] OJ L359/56.

[96] For example, Council Recommendation (EEC) 84/635 on the promotion of positive action for women [1984] OJ L331/34; Commission Recommendation on the dignity of women and men at work [1992] OJ L49/1.

[97] See Case 170/84 *Bilka-Kaufhaus GmbH v Weber Von Hartz* [1986] ECR 1607.

[98] Case 109/88 *Handels- og Kontorfunktionaerernes forbund i Danmark v Danfoss* [1989] ECR 3199; Case C–127/92 *Enderby v Frenchay Health Authority and Secretary of State for Health* [1993] ECR I–5535.

[99] Specifically, Council Dir (EC) 97/80 on the burden of proof in cases of discrimination based on sex [1998] OJ L14/6; Council Dir (EC) 97/81 concerning the framework agreement on part-time work concluded by UNICE, CEEP and the ETUC [1998] OJ L14/9.

[100] For example, Council Dir (EC) 96/34 concerning the framework agreement on parental leave concluded by UNICE, CEEP and the ETUC [1996] OJ L145/4.

legislation, there has been an attempt to tackle gender discrimination throughout all EU policies, principally through the concept of 'mainstreaming'. This has been defined as: 'the systematic consideration of the differences between the conditions, situations and needs of women and men in all Community policies, at the point of planning, implementing and evaluation'.[101] For instance, the EU has approved new initiatives on violence against women.[102] These developments have now been complemented by the insertion of a new paragraph in EC Treaty, Article 3 which requires that in all areas of policy, 'the Community shall aim to eliminate inequalities, and to promote equality, between men and women'.[103]

Remarkably similar factors to those present in the early 1970s again help explain these advances. First, the difficulties experienced by several Member States in ratifying the Treaty on European Union, principally Denmark, France and the UK, raised questions over the degree of popular support for further European integration.[104] Concerns about public alienation have been especially salient in a period where the EU is engaged in its most ambitious economic project to date, monetary union. Thus, there has been a determined effort to demonstrate that the EU is not purely focused on the needs of business, but that it is also acting on the priorities of the general public.[105] Within this general trend, employment policy has emerged as a central tenet of the Union's attempts to become closer to the citizen. The agreement of a common set of annual 'employment guidelines' has been pursued as a means to reducing the high levels of unemployment experienced in many Member States in the 1990s.[106] It is under this aegis that a commitment to gender equality has been rediscovered. Equal opportunities is one of the four pillars in the guidelines, and there has been a growing

[101] Commission, 'Annual Report from the Commission: Equal Opportunities for Women and Men in the European Union 1996' COM (96) 650, 2 (published 12 February 1997).

[102] Decision (EC) 293/2000 of the European Parliament and of the Council of 24 January 2000 adopting a programme of Community action (the Daphne programme) (2000 to 2003) on preventive measures to fight violence against children, young persons and women [2000] OJ L34/1.

[103] EC Treaty, Art 3(2).

[104] A Mattera, 'Civis europaeus sum—citoyenneté européenne, droit de circulation et de séjour, applicabilité directe de l'Art. 8A du traité CE' (1998) *Revue du marché unique européen* 5, 24.

[105] See Conclusions of UK Presidency, Cardiff 15–16 June 1998, para IV, EC Bull, 6/1998.

[106] Council Resolution of 15 December 1997 on the 1998 Employment Guidelines [1998] OJ C30/1; Council Resolution on the 1999 employment guidelines [1999] OJ C69/2; Council Decision (EC) 2000/228 of 13 March 2000 on guidelines for Member States' employment policies for the year 2000 [2000] OJ L72/15; Council Decision (EC) 2001/63 of 19 January 2001 on Guidelines for Member States' employment policies for the year 2001 [2001] OJ L22/18.

acknowledgement that enhancing female participation in the workforce will make a positive contribution to competitiveness.[107] This view has been further strengthened by the emergence in some Member States of short-term labour shortages,[108] and concerns related to the future impact on European labour markets and social protection systems of an ageing population profile.[109] Whilst national implementation of the equal opportunities strand has been criticised,[110] it has provided pressure for real movement in consolidating the basic legislative framework at the EU level. Although employment policy has been portrayed as one aspect of making Europe more relevant to its citizens, the strategy currently being pursued does not easily fit within the social citizenship model of social policy. No enforceable rights are conferred; indeed, Sciarra refers to the development of a 'new and vague category of non-rights'.[111] Yet, equally this new dimension in employment policy reaches into areas of labour law such as wages or social protection which have been traditionally reserved for the Member States,[112] making it difficult to categorise within the more narrow confines of market integration social policy.[113]

Second, as in the early 1970s,[114] the late 1990s witnessed a remarkable constellation of centre-left governments in the Member States. Whilst these governments possessed starkly different analyses of the necessary level of general social regulation, equal opportunities proved less divisive. Thus, whilst proposals in areas such as employees' information and consultation

---

[107] For example, Presidency Conclusions, Lisbon European Council, 23–24 March 2000, EU Bull, 3–2000 para 4.

[108] For example, Ireland: Council Opinion of 12 February 2001 on the 2000 update of Ireland's stability programme, 2001–2003 [2001] C77/7; Guideline 6, 2001 employment guidelines (n 106 above).

[109] For example, debate on safe and sustainable pensions and pension systems: Employment and Social Policy Council, Brussels, 6 March 2001, Press Release 62, No 6507/01. On demographic change in the European Union see, Commission, 'Towards a Europe for all Ages—promoting prosperity and intergenerational solidarity' COM (1999) 221.

[110] Commission, 'From guidelines to action: the national action plans for employment' (Luxembourg: OOPEC, 1998) 15.

[111] S Sciarra, 'The employment title in the Amsterdam Treaty. A multi-language legal discourse' in D O'Keeffe and P Twomey (eds), *Legal issues of the Amsterdam Treaty* (Oxford: Hart Publishing, 1999) 170.

[112] E Szyszczak, 'The evolving European employment strategy' in J Shaw (ed), *Social law and policy in an evolving European Union* (Oxford: Hart Publishing, 2000) 203.

[113] See further ch 7 below.

[114] S Fredman, *Women and the law* (Oxford: Clarendon Press, 1997) 165.

rights have proven difficult,[115] agreement was forthcoming on four different equality-related Directives over a period of two years (1996–97).[116]

Finally, gender equality not only meets the Union's economic objectives, but it also contributes to its social and political goals, most especially with regard to the enhancement of Union citizenship. As noted earlier, the formal EC Treaty provisions on citizenship deal with a rather limited range of rights, mainly in the civil and political sphere. Shaw argues that the contents of European citizenship should not be confined to those formal provisions, but that other elements of the Treaties, secondary legislation and Court case law must also be considered.[117] Given this broader perspective, the additional provisions on gender equality can be understood as part of the incremental construction of citizenship, in particular augmenting the 'social dimension of Union citizenship'.[118]

Notwithstanding these developments in gender equality law, significant weaknesses remain. For instance, unequal pay between women and men has endured.[119] Most fundamentally, there is the question of the *effectiveness* of the law. A recurring criticism is that the existing legal provisions rely too heavily on a system of 'individual justice'.[120] This critique focuses on the reality that individual litigation remains the primary mechanism for the enforcement of employment equality, with little provision for the institutional support of individual plaintiffs. It is argued that this tends to ignore the substantial barriers to successful litigation which exist in practice. Some of the most common problems experienced include the financial costs of litigation, difficulties in evidence gathering,[121] insufficient safeguards against the victimisation of those involved in the litigation process and a lack of institutional support for

---

[115] Commission, 'Proposal for a Council Directive establishing a general framework for informing and consulting employees in the European Community' COM (1998) 612. Political agreement on this proposal was reached in the Council in June 2001: Press Release, 2357th meeting of the Employment and Social Policy Council, Luxembourg, Doc 9397/01, Presse 225.

[116] Council Dir (EC) 96/97 amending Council Dir (EEC) 86/378 on the implementation of the principle of equal treatment for men and women in occupational social security schemes [1997] OJ L46/20. See also nn 99 and 100 above .

[117] J Shaw, 'The interpretation of European Union citizenship' (1998) 61 MLR 293, 298.

[118] C Barnard, 'The United Kingdom, the "Social Chapter" and the Amsterdam Treaty' (1997) 26 ILJ 275, 280.

[119] C Hoskyns, *Integrating Gender—Women, Law and Politics in the European Union* (London: Verso, 1996) 228–231.

[120] See J Blom, B Fitzpatrick, J Gregory, R Knegt and U O'Hare, *The Utilisation of Sex Equality Litigation in the Member States of the European Community* V/782/96-EN (Report to the Equal Opportunities Unit of DG V, 1995).

[121] S Prechal and N Burrows, *Gender discrimination law of the European Community* (Aldershot: Dartmouth, 1990) 296–297.

plaintiffs.[122] These problems are compounded by often inadequate and inappropriate remedies. Unsurprisingly, then, it has been observed that the current legislation is 'difficult to use, is little used, and used with limited success'.[123]

Moreover, it is the most vulnerable groups of women who will be least likely to have recourse to litigation.[124] Another side-effect of the problems with the judicial process is that litigation will tend to focus on the most blatant forms of discrimination, with structural forms of discrimination, such as indirect discrimination and equal pay for work of equal value, given less priority. Structural forms of discrimination are intrinsically cases of collective discrimination against a group of female employees and are thus least amenable to challenge through the 'individual justice' model.[125] Ironically, though, it is these cases of structural discrimination that may be of the most consequence to realising gender equality, as these are the main vehicles for sustaining unequal pay in the workforce.

Gender equality law has demonstrated the ability of the EU to make a positive contribution to combating discrimination, even where this is not intrinsically linked to the free movement of persons. Moreover, equality between women and men has been seen as both consistent with the economic and the social goals of the Union. This interweaving of objectives has been strengthened by a general value consensus as to the impermissibility of gender discrimination, reflected in both national and international law. The shared nature of these values is assisted by the fact that the demographic position of women inevitably provides them with a certain amount of political power. Nonetheless, there remain constraints. Consistent with the market integration model, agreement on EU action has been progressively more difficult to attain, the further the Union has moved from employment-related discrimination. The other main obstacle occurs where underlying values remain divergent. Sexual harassment in the workplace is particularly interesting here, as there are both strong social and economic justifications for action,[126]

---

[122] Blom *et al* (n 120 above) 58–59. Some of these issues are addressed in the pending proposal to amend the Equal Treatment Directive. Political agreement on this proposal was reached in Council in June 2001: Press Release, 2357th meeting of the Employment and Social Policy Council, Luxembourg, Doc 9397/01, Presse 225.

[123] L Dickens, 'Anti-discrimination Legislation: exploring and explaining the impact on women's employment' in W McCarthy (ed), *Legal Interventions in Industrial Relations: Gains and Losses* (Oxford: Basil Blackwell, 1992) 134.

[124] Blom *et al* (n 120 above) 11.   [125] ibid 21–22.

[126] M Rubenstein, *Report on the Problem of Sexual Harassment in the Member States of the European Community* (Luxembourg: OOPEC, 1988).

and the EU undoubtedly has the competence to intervene.[127] However, the value differences in respect of what is or is not appropriate workplace behaviour blocked progress for many years.[128] The amendment to the Equal Treatment Directive agreed by the Council in June 2001 would specifically forbid sexual harassment for the first time.[129] The earlier productive application of non-binding rules here may contain lessons for other 'sensitive' areas of anti-discrimination law.[130]

III. Conclusion

Despite the weaknesses in European social policy identified in Chapter 1, anti-discrimination law has emerged from within this uncertain picture. Even in the periods where the Community was most focused on economic integration, combating discrimination persisted as one of the few concrete areas of social policy. The persuasive economic rationale in terms of enhancing competitiveness, coincides with a market integration justification of removing barriers to free movement and preventing the accumulation of unfair competitive advantages through the exploitation of cheap forms of labour. On the other side of the coin, equal treatment is consistently acknowledged to be one of the most fundamental social rights.[131] Non-discrimination is not only a central social right, but is also one of the core human rights.[132] The overlapping nature of equality as both a human and a social right is reflected in the fact that both the International Covenant on

[127] EC Treaty, Art 137(1) includes the *treatment* of women at work.

[128] Interview: Evelyn Collins, Belfast, 20 December 1996. For example, Valiente identifies a difference between Anglo-Saxon and Mediterranean concepts of acceptable workplace behaviour: C Valiente, 'Sexual harassment in the workplace—equality policies in post-authoritarian Spain' in T Carver and V Mottier (eds), *The politics of sexuality—identity, gender, citizenship* (London, Routledge/ECPR Studies in European political science, 1998) 171.

[129] See, Press Release, 2357th meeting of the Employment and Social Policy Council, Luxembourg, Doc 9397/01, Presse 225.

[130] Commission Recommendation on the dignity of women and men at work [1992] OJ L49/1. This is discussed at more length in ch 3 below.

[131] This has been reaffirmed most recently by the ILO in its Declaration on fundamental principles and rights at work (1998) 37 Intl Legal Materials 1237. See also B Hepple, 'Social Values and European Law' (1995) 48 CLP II: Collected Papers 39.

[132] For example, note the prominence of equality and non-discrimination in the agenda agreed by the EU human rights Comité des Sages: A Cassese, C Lalumière, P Leuprecht and M Robinson, *Leading by example: a human rights agenda for the European Union for the Year 2000. Agenda of the Comité des Sages and final project report* (Florence: European University Institute, 1998) 4–5.

Civil and Political Rights (ICCPR) and the International Covenant on Economic, Social and Cultural Rights (ICESCR) share provisions on guaranteeing the rights contained in the Covenants 'without discrimination of any kind as to race, colour, sex, language, religion, political or other opinion, national or social origin, property, birth or other status'.[133]

Yet, whilst there is this identifiable space in the EU legal order for anti-discrimination law, the actual provisions have traditionally only dealt with two forms of discrimination; nationality and gender. In contrast, as can be seen in the terms of the ICCPR and the ICESCR, discrimination occurs across a much wider range of social groups. Moreover, when one explores further, it is not simply that the EU acted against these two forms of discrimination and remained silent on all other equality issues; on the contrary there emerges a 'hierarchy of equality',[134] where different groups enjoyed a different standard of legal protection.

Looking beyond the cases of nationality and gender discrimination, certain other grounds were previously the subject of non-binding legislative instruments. Specifically, a number of soft law measures were addressed to discrimination on grounds of race or ethnicity,[135] and discrimination on grounds of disability.[136] A further level down, other grounds were the target of EU programmes, without this actually leading to any legislative instruments, binding or non-binding. For instance, age discrimination was tackled through various schemes for young and older people, since the 1974 social action programme.[137] Finally, there are those groups which were not previously the subject of any legislative intervention, or even the beneficiaries of a specific support programme. Principally, this may be said to apply to lesbians and gay men, and also to religious minorities, although the needs of the latter have at times been addressed within the context of measures against racism. Recent legislative developments have radically altered this equality hierarchy. However, it has been reconstructed, rather than deconstructed.

---

[133]   ICESCR, Art 2(2); ICCPR, Art 2(1).

[134]   A Hegarty and C Keown, 'Hierarchies of discrimination: the political, legal and social prioritisation of the equality agenda in Northern Ireland' (1996) 15 Equal Opportunities Intl 1.

[135]   Council Resolution on the fight against racism and xenophobia [1990] OJ C157/1; Council Resolution on the Fight against Racism and Xenophobia in the fields of Employment and Social Affairs [1995] OJ C296/13.

[136]   Council Recommendation (EEC) 86/379 of 27 July 1986 on the employment of disabled people in the Community [1986] OJ L225/43. See generally L Waddington, *Disability, employment and the European Community* (Antwerpen: Maklu, 1995).

[137]   Commission, 'Social Action Programme' EC Bull Supplement, 2/74, 17–18. See also, Commission, 'Towards a Europe for all ages—promoting prosperity and intergenerational solidarity' COM (1999) 221.

It is this equality hierarchy which forms the principal subject of this book. Why have some groups enjoyed (and continue to enjoy) much greater protection in EU law than others? The examination of EU law on nationality and gender discrimination demonstrates that the Union has already a well-established competence in the area of anti-discrimination, so it is justifiable to ask why certain grounds of discrimination have attracted greater protection from EU law than others. The significance of this investigation lies not only in an attempt to establish a better historical understanding of EU anti-discrimination law, but also its relationship to the future of this field of law. Two issues have been chosen to be the focus of this book: racial and sexual orientation discrimination. The first is an example of an area which EU law initially dealt with through non-binding legal instruments, but where now wide-ranging anti-discrimination law applies.[138] Sexual orientation discrimination provides a useful contrast, as an issue on the margins of EU law, not previously given even the quasi-acceptance enjoyed by the fight against racism. Whilst new legal measures have also been adopted in this area,[139] these remain considerably more limited than those pertaining to racism. Thus, there are crucial links and differences between the two issues. The next two chapters will take each issue in turn and examine its specific development within the EU legal order.

---

[138] Council Dir (EC) 2000/43 of 29 June 2000 implementing the principle of equal treatment between persons irrespective of racial or ethnic origin [2000] OJ L180/22.

[139] Council Dir (EC) 2000/78 of 27 November 2000 establishing a general framework for equal treatment in employment and occupation [2000] OJ L303/16.

Racial Discrimination

Discrimination on the grounds of racial or ethnic origin is an everyday real-ity for millions of people living in the European Union. At one end of the spectrum, there are extreme instances of racially motivated crime. For exam-ple, in the UK, during 1999/2000 the police recorded 47,814 racist incidents, most involving damage to property or verbal harassment.[1] Alternatively, in Italy, in 1996, on average one immigrant was murdered every three days; two-thirds of these incidents were estimated to be racially motivated.[2] Less extreme, but also disturbing, is the evidence of systematic discrimination uncovered by the ILO in an ongoing research project.[3] Discrimination test-ing revealed that in Germany 20 per cent of Turkish job applicants were dis-criminated against.[4] Finally, if any doubts remained about the widespread nature of racism in the EU, these have been dispelled by the results of various Eurostat surveys. In 1997, 33 per cent of EU respondents admitted to being quite or very racist, rising to 55 per cent of Belgian respondents, and 48 per cent in France.[5] In a 2001 survey, one in five EU respondents agreed that all immigrants, whether legal or illegal, from outside the EU and their children, even those born in the EU, should be sent back to their country of origin.[6]

[1] Home Office, 'Statistics on race and the criminal justice system' (London: Home Office, 2000) 49.

[2] La Repubblica (11.6.97) 'Immigrati in Italia—un' aggressione al giorno'.

[3] ILO, 'Combatting discrimination against (im)migrant workers and ethnic minorities in the world of work' Information Bulletin No 5 (Geneva: ILO, 1998).

[4] Migration News Sheet, May 1996, 13. Discrimination testing is the process whereby two equivalent applications are submitted to an employer, but with it being evident that in one applica-tion the candidate is a member of an ethnic minority community.

[5] Commission, 'Racism and xenophobia in Europe, Eurobarometer Opinion Poll No 47.1' (Luxembourg: OOPEC, 1998) 6.

[6] E Thalhammer, V Zucha, E Enzenhofer, B Salfinger and G Ogris, 'Attitudes towards minor-ity groups in the European Union' (Vienna: European Monitoring Centre on Racism and Xenophobia, 2001) 47.

It is difficult to estimate the precise numbers of individuals affected by these phenomena. In 1995, 5 per cent of the EU's population did not hold the citizenship of the country in which they resided. Of these, at least two-thirds, or approximately 12–13 million persons, were nationals of non-EU states, that is, third country nationals.[7] In addition, there are of course several million people with EU citizenship, but not of western European ethnic origin.

The response of the European Union to this evidence of persistent racism has been the subject of a growing debate since the mid-1980s. This eventually gave way to the amendment of the EC Treaty, in the form of Article 13, to create a specific competence for the Community to take 'appropriate action to combat discrimination based on . . . racial or ethnic origin'. Based on this provision, the Racial Equality Directive was adopted in June 2000, forbidding discrimination on grounds of racial or ethnic origin in a wide range of areas.[8] This chapter aims to chart the evolution of EU law and policy on racism with a view to identifying the factors which led the Member States to extend the Union's role in this field. In particular, it is necessary to consider how, given the market integration model of European social policy, anti-racism policy has been able to progress. The analysis will be divided into four periods: immigrants and the EEC, 1957–84; the origins of an EC policy on combating racism, 1985–90; towards the Treaty of Amsterdam, 1991–99; and the Racial Equality Directive.

I. Immigrants and the EEC, 1957–84

It is not surprising that the 1957 EEC Treaty is silent on the issue of racism. As seen in Chapter 1, the Treaty of Rome ascribed the EEC only a minimal role in social policy. Nonetheless, it might have been expected that the founding Treaties would mention the fight against racial and religious intolerance, given European integration's historical motivation as a legacy of the Second World War. The other explanation for the silence of the Treaties lies in the prevailing domestic situation. It is important to recall that migration from outside the Community was only just beginning to accelerate. The pace of the post-war economic recovery in western Europe began to create labour

---

[7] Commission, 'Employment in Europe 1997—analysis of key issues' (Luxembourg: OOPEC, 1998) 33.

[8] Council Dir (EC) 2000/43 of 29 June 2000 implementing the principle of equal treatment between persons irrespective of racial or ethnic origin [2000] OJ L180/22. See Annex 1.

shortages in the 1950s, which led northern European states to recruit labour from southern Europe and beyond.[9] An indication of the rapid increases in migrant labour can be gathered from the following figures. In 1959, three-quarters of all migrants were EC nationals living in another Member State, but by 1973, two-thirds of migrants were non-EC nationals, comprising 5 per cent of the EC labour force.[10] This dramatic shift in the composition of the migrant labour force helps illustrate why nationality discrimination, that is, discrimination against other EC nationals, as opposed to racial discrimination was the dominant concern during the drafting of the EEC Treaty. This was underpinned by the overriding perception and expectation that immigrant labour was a purely temporary phenomenon.[11] Thus, even when the levels of immigration had risen considerably, there was still little thought given to the need to adopt measures for the integration of immigrant workers and their families.

The absence of any explicit provisions on racial discrimination did not mean that the foundation of the EEC was without consequence for immigrant communities. Whilst the EEC Treaty was rather ambiguous as to its application to third country nationals, the Council of Ministers determined in 1968 that free movement was a right only available to nationals of the Member States.[12] Moreover, Regulation (EEC) 1612/68 also enshrined the principle of *Community preference* in EC law; that is, the objective of ensuring that EC nationals enjoy priority when filling employment vacancies in the Member States.[13] These were crucial decisions for the future development of anti-racism policy. Being excluded from free movement rights, there was no obvious market integration justification for the Community to become involved in matters relating to third country nationals, including racial discrimination.

The turning point in the Community's blindness to the issue of third country nationals came in the mid-1970s. First, the situation at the national level changed abruptly. Within several years, most states in western Europe acted to curtail legal avenues of labour migration. The primary impetus for this policy reversal was the changing economic climate. As growth slowed and unemployment began to reappear, the economic utility of immigrant work-

---

[9] D Thränhardt, *Europe—a new immigration continent. Policies and Politics in Comparative Perspective* (Hamburg: Lit, 1992) 25.

[10] M Shanks, *European Social Policy, Today and Tomorrow* (Oxford: Pergamon Press, 1977) 31.

[11] M Baldwin-Edwards, 'Immigration after 1992' (1991) 19 *Policy and Politics* 199.

[12] Reg (EEC) 1612/68, Art 1(1) on free movement for workers [1968] OJ Spec Ed (II) 475.

[13] Art 19.

ers was brought into question. This trend was catapulted forward with the 1973 oil crisis.[14] The economic consequences were severe and at 'the first alarming signs of rapidly rising unemployment'[15] the Member States acted in concert to block any additional intake of immigrant labour. As well as the economic factors, it is important to note that there was also rising concern over the integration of immigrant populations.[16]

In this context, the Commission launched its 1974 social action programme. Significantly, this included a number of proposals for common action on immigration policy, and it was followed in 1976 by a specific action programme for migrant workers and members of their families.[17] The proposals made were basically in two directions: immigration control and the better integration of existing immigrants. In this vein, the Commission sought to enhance control of immigration with a view to protecting the principle of Community preference in employment.[18] With regard to immigrant integration, as a first step, the rules governing the European Social Fund were amended, so as to allow third country nationals to have access to this source of support.[19]

Initially, the Council seemed to support the Commission in pursuing these initiatives. Indeed, in its Resolution on the 1974 action programme, the Council specified, as an objective of EC policy, the achievement of 'equality of treatment for Community and non-Community workers and members of their families in respect of living and working conditions, wages and economic rights, taking into account the Community provisions in force'.[20] However, it quickly emerged that there were deep divisions between the Member States as to the competence of the Community for third country nationals. In 1978, the Commission submitted a draft Directive on illegal immigration,[21] based on former EEC Treaty, Article 100, which is concerned with the approximation of provisions to ensure the proper functioning of the common market.[22] Some Member States rejected this legal base and argued

---

[14] Baldwin-Edwards (n 11 above) 199.

[15] Commission, 'Guidelines for a Community Policy on Migration' COM (85) 48, 5.

[16] T Hammar, *European immigration policy—a comparative study* (Cambridge: Cambridge University Press, 1985) 275.

[17] Council Resolution on an action programme for migrant workers and members of their families [1976] OJ C34/2.

[18] Commission, 'Social Action Programme' EC Bull Supplement 2/74, 21.

[19] Shanks (n 10 above) 15.   [20] Commission (n 18 above) 8.

[21] Proposal for a Council Directive concerning the approximation of the legislation of the Member States in order to combat illegal migration and illegal employment [1978] OJ C97/9.

[22] EEC Treaty, Art 100 (now EC Treaty, Art 94) states: 'the Council shall, acting unanimously on a proposal from the Commission and after consulting the European Parliament and the

that former EEC Treaty, Article 235 was the only possibility, as this allows for action where the Treaty has not otherwise provided the Community with the necessary competence, providing the action is consistent with the objectives of the common market.[23] However, both Articles 100 and 235 require evidence that the proposed measure was connected to the construction of the common market. For other Member States the link was not evident and the proposal floundered for want of a consensus in the Council.[24] In a similar fashion, competence objections blocked the inclusion of third country nationals in Directive (EEC) 77/486 on the education of the children of migrant workers.[25]

The failure of attempts by the Commission to carve out a role for the Community in immigration policy contrasts sharply with the progress made in gender equality law in the same period. George argues that, far from improving migrants' rights, Member States 'were anxious to make migrant workers less welcome in order to reserve jobs for their own nationals, who had the inestimable bargaining advantage of possessing votes in that state which they could cast against the government if they felt aggrieved'.[26] Whereas women enjoy the advantage of constituting more than half of the Community's population and electorate, immigrant communities are a varying fraction of the Member States' populations, and their political rights also fluctuate.[27]

Furthermore, it was only in the course of the 1970s that most Member States moved to forbid racial discrimination in national legislation.[28]

Economic and Social Committee, issue directives for the approximation of such laws, regulations or administrative provisions of the Member States as directly effect the establishment or functioning of the common market'.

[23] EEC Treaty, Art 235 (now EC Treaty, Art 308) states: 'if action by the Community should prove necessary to attain, in the course of the operation of the common market, one of the objectives of the Community and this Treaty has not provided the necessary powers, the Council shall, acting unanimously on a proposal from the Commission and after consulting the European Parliament, take the appropriate measures'.

[24] E Szyszczak, 'Race Discrimination: the limits of market equality?' in B Hepple and E Syzszczak (eds), *Discrimination: the limits of the law* (London: Mansell, 1992) 137.

[25] [1977] OJ L199/32. The Council did issue a non-binding Declaration stating that the Directive was intended to apply to children of all migrant workers, including third country nationals, but there is little evidence that this was enforced in practice (Commission, 'Report on the implementation in the Member States of Directive 77/486/EEC on the education of the children of migrant workers' COM (88) 787, 5).

[26] S George, *Politics and Policy in the European Community* (Oxford: Oxford University Press, 1991) 208.

[27] A Dummett, 'Racial equality and 1992' (1991) 3 *Feminist Rev* 85, 89.

[28] F Webber, 'From ethnocentrism to Euro-racism' (1991) 32 *Race and Class* 11, 13.

Following the agreement of the International Convention on the Elimination of Racial Discrimination in 1965,[29] and its entry into force in 1969, many European states moved gradually to ratify the Convention and to bring their national statutes into line with its requirements.[30] For example, new provisions on racism were introduced in Denmark[31] and the Netherlands[32] in 1971, and in France[33] and Germany[34] in 1972. This process continued during the second half of the decade, with new legislation against racism in the UK,[35] Ireland,[36] and Italy.[37] It is in this context that one can understand better the emergence of racial discrimination as a Community law issue in the 1980s.

II. The origins of an EC policy on combating racism, 1985–90

The Commission returned to immigration policy in the mid-1980s. The principal factor was undoubtedly the internal market programme, as foreseen in the 1986 Single European Act. In particular, the 1985 White Paper on the internal market noted that the realisation of a 'frontier-free' European Community would necessitate a much greater co-ordination of immigration policies, as the abolition of border controls would 'make it much easier for nationals of non-Community countries to move from one Member State to another'.[38] In the same year, the Commission submitted a communication on 'Guidelines for a Community policy on Migration'.[39] As in the 1970s, this

---

[29] Council of Europe Press, *Human Rights in International Law—basic texts* (Strasbourg: Council of Europe, 1992) 66.

[30] Ireland was the final EU state to ratify the Convention, which entered into force there on 28 January 2001: Department of Justice, Equality and Law Reform, 'UN International Convention on the Elimination of All Forms of Racial Discrimination enters into force', Press Release, 29 January 2001.

[31] Race Discrimination Act 1971; see M MacEwan, *Tackling racism in Europe: an examination of anti-discrimination law in practice* (Oxford: Berg Publishers, 1995) 100.

[32] Amendment of the Labour (Collective Agreements) Act: ibid 136.

[33] Law against racism 1972: ibid 124.   [34] Works Constitution Act 1972, Art 75.

[35] Race Relations Act 1976.   [36] Unfair Dismissals Act 1977, s 6(1).

[37] L 9 dicembre 1977, n 903, Art 13—Parità di trattomento tra uomini e donne in materia di lavoro.

[38] Commission, 'Completing the Internal Market' COM (85) 310, quoted in R Plender, 'Competence, European Community law and nationals of non-member states' (1990) 39 ICLQ 599.

[39] COM (85) 48.

proposed a policy with two dimensions: immigration control and the integration of existing immigrants. Moreover, the guidelines included proposals for a set of measures to combat racism.

The Commission took its first step in co-ordinating immigration policy through the adoption of Decision (EEC) 85/381 setting up a prior communication and consultation procedure on migration policies in relation to non-member countries.[40] Specifically, the Decision sought to oblige the Member States to notify the Commission in advance of any proposed changes to policies on third country workers and members of their families, with a view to ensuring that such measures would be 'in conformity with, and do not compromise the results of, Community policies and actions in these fields'.[41] However, Germany, Denmark, the UK, France, and the Netherlands proceeded to seek its annulment at the Court of Justice. Contrary to the arguments of the Member States, the Court accepted that there did exist a sufficient connection between migration policies and the EC labour market to bring the former within the scope of the 'social field' referred to in EEC Treaty, Article 118.[42] Nonetheless, this was 'only to the extent to which it [migration policy] concerns the situation of workers from non-member countries as regards their impact on the Community employment market and on working conditions'.[43] Therefore, the Court ruled invalid those provisions of the Decision relating to the cultural integration of immigrants. The judgment highlighted the dependency of initiatives on establishing a sufficient connection with the internal market. Measures based purely on ethnic and racial integration objectives were unable to find a position in the market-driven state of European social policy, thereby presenting a major obstacle to the development of a comprehensive anti-racism policy.

In the same period, the European Parliament began to focus on EC policy on racism. Following the surprising progress made by the parties of the

---

[40] [1985] OJ L217/25.　　　　　　　　　[41] Art 3.

[42] EEC Treaty, Art 118 was the legal base for the decision. It provided that: 'the Commission shall have the task of promoting close cooperation between Member States in the social field, particularly in matters relating to: employment; labour law and working conditions; basic and advanced vocational training; social security; prevention of occupational accidents and diseases; occupational hygiene; the right of association and collective bargaining between employers and workers.

To this end, the Commission shall act in close contact with Member States by making studies, delivering opinions and arranging consultations both on problems arising at national level and on those of concern to international organizations.'

[43] Cases C–281, 283, 284, 285 and 287/85 *Federal Republic of Germany v Commission* [1987] ECR 3203, para 23. See further, K Simmonds, 'The Concertation of Community Migration Policy' (1988) 25 CML Rev 177.

extreme right in the 1984 European Parliamentary elections,[44] the Parliament established a temporary committee of inquiry into the rise of fascism and racism in Europe. The *Evrigenis* report[45] identified serious problems of racism and xenophobia in the Member States and recommended action by the Community to supplement national measures, including a new EC Treaty competence on racial discrimination. In response, the Council agreed to sign, with the Parliament and Commission, a Joint Declaration against racism and xenophobia.[46] Its importance lay in its symbolic value as the first high-level acknowledgement that racism was a matter of EC concern. However, the Council insisted that this was not 'a starting point for concrete action'[47] as desired by the Parliament, but rather an end in itself.[48] As a result, the immediate momentum following the Declaration dissipated amidst interinstitutional deadlock.[49]

The subsequent adoption in 1989 of the EC Social Charter initially appeared to promise a new 'rights-based' era in European social policy. Consequently, the Parliament was keen to ensure that racism should be on this agenda. The Council raised by now familiar opposition on the basis of EC legal competence.[50] Ultimately, the Parliament threatened to reject the Charter over, *inter alia*, the weakness of the text with respect to racism,[51] but a compromise was reached whereby the importance of combating all forms of discrimination was mentioned in the preamble,[52] alongside a statement reaffirming that the treatment of third country nationals was a matter for the Member States.[53] The weak mandate thus provided by the Charter was

[44] Notably in France where the *Front National* received 11.1% of the vote and won 10 seats: N Mayer, 'Ethnocentrism and the *Front National* vote in the 1988 French Presidential election' in A Hargreaves and J Leaman (eds), *Racism, Ethnicity and Politics in Contemporary Europe* (Aldershot: Edward Elgar, 1995) 101.

[45] European Parliament, 'Committee of Inquiry into the Rise of Fascism and Racism in Europe' (Luxembourg: OOPEC, 1985).

[46] [1986] OJ C158/1.

[47] Formigioni, Debates of the European Parliament No 2-340/107, 11 June 1986.

[48] Adam-Schwaetzer, Debates of the European Parliament No 2-366/66, 14 June 1988.

[49] European Parliament, 'Report of the Political Affairs Committee on the Joint Declaration against Racism and Xenophobia and an action programme by the Council of Ministers' A2-261/88, 11.

[50] Papandreou, Debates of the European Parliament No 3-391/181, 13 June 1990.

[51] S George, *Politics and Policy in the European Community* (Oxford: Oxford University Press, 1991) 204.

[52] 'In order to ensure equal treatment, it is important to combat every form of discrimination, including discrimination on grounds of sex, colour, race, opinions and belief': Text appears in *Social Europe* 1/90, 46–50.

[53] 'It is for the Member States to guarantee that workers from non-member countries and members of their families who are legally resident in a Member State of the European Community are

reflected in the Commission's decision not to submit any legislative proposals on racism.[54]

Despite this, racism remained on the Council's agenda by virtue of an outstanding proposal from 1988 for a Resolution on combating racism.[55] Predictably, the Council was seriously divided on the precise terms of the Resolution. The final recital in the preamble of the draft Resolution proved especially controversial. This stated that 'any measure taken in this connection must protect all persons on Community territory, whether they are nationals of Member States or of non-member countries, foreigners in a Member State or nationals who are perceived or who perceive themselves as belonging to a foreign minority'.

Several Member States, in particular the UK, objected to this clause on the basis that it would imply a competence for the Community vis-à-vis third country nationals. These objections ultimately required the clause to be deleted.[56]

This dilution of the Resolution infuriated both the Parliament[57] and the Commission; the latter taking the 'unusual step of publicly distancing itself from [the Resolution] . . . on the grounds that the text had been so watered down as to be almost meaningless'.[58] For its part, the Parliament issued the *Ford report,*[59] the result of its second committee of inquiry into racism in Europe. Whilst full of recommendations for further action, it too ran up against the opposition of the Council, which simply reaffirmed that this was a matter for national legislation and not for the Community.[60]

Whilst racism entered into EC policy debate during the period 1985–90, primarily through the efforts of the Parliament, the opposition in the Council prevented any significant progress. Symbolic statements of commitment were

able to enjoy, as regards their living and working conditions, treatment comparable to that enjoyed by workers who are nationals of the Member State concerned': ibid.

[54] Commission, 'Communication from the Commission concerning its action programme relating to the implementation of the Community Charter of Fundamental Social Rights for Workers' COM (89) 586, Pt I, para 5.

[55] Commission, 'Communication from the Commission to the Council on the fight against racism and xenophobia' [1988] OJ C214/32.

[56] Council Resolution on the fight against racism and xenophobia [1990] OJ C157/1.

[57] Parliament Resolution on measures to combat racism and xenophobia [1990] OJ C175/179, para A.

[58] Financial Times, 30 May 1990 'Commission dismay at watering down of anti-racism measure', 3.

[59] European Parliament, 'Report of the Committee of Inquiry on Racism and Xenophobia' (Luxembourg: OOPEC, 1991).

[60] Vitalone, Debates of the European Parliament No 3-394/49, 9 October 1990.

not underpinned by a genuine desire to develop common measures against racial discrimination. The Council relied on the absence of any specific EC Treaty provision on racism to insist that this was not within the Community's legal competence. In this way, the question of competence became a kind of filter mechanism, a device to keep off the agenda issues the Council did not wish to address. It was of course open to the Member States to amend the EC Treaty, but no such amendment was included in either the Single European Act or its successor, the 1993 Treaty on European Union. Crucially, debates on combating racism were tied up with the legal situation of third country nationals in EC law.[61] As the latter did not enjoy free movement rights, they were not perceived to be internal market actors. Consequently, for most Member States 'immigrants' issues', which included racism, attracted no justification for EC intervention. Moreover, whilst there was pressure from the Commission and the Parliament, there was no significant evidence of an ethnic minority lobby supporting their calls for new EC legal instruments. Hence, there was very little reason for the Council to give way to their demands in the absence of any strong popular mobilisation in this direction.

III. Towards the Treaty of Amsterdam, 1991–99

One of the most surprising aspects of EC policy on racism is how quickly the opposition in the Council gave way to support for an amendment of the EC Treaty to provide the Community with a broad competence to forbid discrimination on grounds of racial or ethnic origin. Three principal reasons can be identified for this change in attitude: the development of cross-border racism; spillover effects from EU immigration and asylum policies; and the establishment of an effective EU lobby against racism.

(i)   The development of cross-border racism

During the 1990s, it became more evident that racism might affect the functioning of the internal market, and as a consequence, the case in favour of EC intervention strengthened considerably. In this period, racism, and especially violent racism, is perceived to have increased.[62] This was closely linked with

---

[61] Lord Wedderburn, *Labour Law and Freedom: Further Essays in Labour Law* (London: Lawrence and Wishart, 1995) 264.

[62] R Eatwell, 'Why are fascism and racism reviving in Western Europe?' (1994) 65 *Political Q* 313.

the rising fortunes of the parties of the extreme right who made electoral progress across Europe, with results unprecedented in the post-war period.[63] In addition, there has been growing evidence of cross-border co-operation between racist groups and the exploitation of differences in national laws to evade prosecution.[64] Perhaps the most manifest example of this has been the cross-border dissemination of racist propaganda.[65] For instance, prior to 1989, Ireland did not have any legislation prohibiting incitement to racial hatred. This contrasted with several other Member States which had such laws already in place. The Irish police then discovered that this divergence in law was being exploited by groups from the extreme right to produce racist material in Ireland, where it was not an offence to do so, which would then be exported to other Member States where it was prohibited.[66] Such a manipulation of the differences in national law created a classic justification for EU intervention. Moreover, the emergence of the Internet as another medium through which to disseminate racist propaganda/co-ordinate racist groups has served to reinforce the necessity of co-operation between the Member States.[67] Therefore, it is no coincidence that the first binding measure adopted by the Union specifically on racism sought to address the issue of cross-border dissemination of racist material and transnational co-operation between racist groups.[68] The 1996 Joint Action[69] requires Member States to 'ensure effective judicial co-operation' with respect to criminalising incitement to discrimination, Holocaust denial, racist material and racist organisations.[70]

[63] For example, in the 1994 elections to the European Parliament, the extreme right received in excess of 8 million votes, winning more than 10% of the vote in France and Belgium. In Germany, the Republicaner Party received well over 1 million votes (R Morgan (ed), *The Times Guide to the European Parliament* (London: Times Newspapers, 1994) 65).

[64] Commission, 'Report on the activities of the European Monitoring Centre on Racism and Xenophobia' COM (2000) 265, 5.

[65] See Ford, Debates of the European Parliament No 4-452/122, 26.10.94; Commission, 'Communication on illegal and harmful content on the Internet' COM (96) 487.

[66] To remedy the problem, the Irish Government was compelled to enact the Prohibition of Incitement to Hatred Act on 29 November 1989, which made the production of such material a criminal offence. See, European Parliament (n 59 above) 65.

[67] Commission, 'Creating a safer information society by improving the security of information infrastructures and combating computer-related crime' COM (2000) 890, 15.

[68] It should also be noted that already in 1989 the cross-border transmission of racist television broadcasts was prohibited in the 'Television without Frontiers' Directive. Art 22 requires Member States to 'ensure that broadcasts do not contain any incitement to hatred on grounds of race, sex, religion or nationality': Council Dir (EEC) 89/552 on the co-ordination of certain provisions laid down by law, regulation or administrative action in Member States concerning the pursuit of television broadcasting activities [1989] OJ L298/23.

[69] Joint Action concerning action to combat racism and xenophobia [1996] OJ L185/5.

[70] Title 1, Art A.

Alongside the new pressure to co-ordinate national laws on racist offences, there has been more explicit recognition that racism can act as an obstacle to the free movement of persons. This occurs in two ways:

[1] in the single market, unjust discrimination will interfere with the free movement of persons and services by preventing persons likely to suffer it from obtaining the jobs, housing or service they seek. . . . [2] variations between national levels of protection will discourage persons likely to suffer discrimination from moving to those states where protection is small or non-existent.[71]

There is little empirical evidence demonstrating the extent to which the risk of racism in other states deters free movement by individuals. Nonetheless, the same logic which regards nationality discrimination as an obstacle to free movement can easily be extended to other grounds of discrimination, including racial or ethnic origin. For example, research into the experience of ethnic minority professionals in the UK revealed that:

ethnic minority employees, whilst welcoming opportunities for assignments in North America . . . were much less enthusiastic about the prospects of working in European Union Member States outside the UK. Because of media images of violence and hostility towards ethnic minorities, most concerns were expressed about Germany and Austria, and, to a lesser extent, France.[72]

Alternatively, there are reported cases of ethnic minority students experiencing racism while in other Member States as part of exchange programmes.[73]

The relevance of combating racism to the internal market has also been reinforced by the decisions of the Court of Justice that, in certain limited circumstances, third country nationals may exercise free movement rights. In 1990, the Court held that the free movement of services included the right of firms to send third country nationals to another Member State as temporary posted workers.[74] This was reaffirmed by the Court in 1994.[75] The Commission subsequently proposed to facilitate these rulings through the

---

[71] A Dummett, 'The Starting Line: A proposal for a draft Council Directive concerning the elimination of racial discrimination' (1994) 20 *New Community* 530, 532.

[72] S Sanglin-Grant and R Schneider, *Moving on up? Racial equality and the corporate agenda. A study of FTSE 100 companies*, (London: The Runnymede Trust, 2000) para 1.3.2.

[73] 'Unwelcome guests', The Guardian, 20 October 1999.

[74] Case C–113/89 *Rush Portuguesa Lda v Office national d'immigration* [1990] ECR I–1439. The case concerned the right of a Portuguese firm to send Portuguese workers to perform a contract in France during the transitional period following Portugal's accession to the EC when full free movement rights were not in place. The firm successfully challenged a French law which stipulated that only the *Office national d'immigration* could recruit labour from outside the Community.

[75] Case C–43/93 *Vander Elst v Office des migrations internationales* [1994] ECR I–3803.

introduction of an 'EC service provision card' to allow the posting of third country national workers to other Member States without visa requirements.[76] The right of free movement includes third country nationals who are members of the family of an EU migrant worker.[77] However, the Commission has identified problems where these family members face racism at border crossings, despite exercising Community law rights in this context.[78]

(ii) Spillover effects from EU immigration and asylum policies

Also connected with the exercise of free movement rights is the impact of EU immigration policies on racial and ethnic relations. It is impossible to provide a complete overview here of the complex history of these policies, and in any case, this is already thoroughly documented.[79] It is worth noting, though, that, since the early 1990s, immigration co-operation has been significantly intensified. At the same time as the majority of Member States were seeking to dismantle all internal border controls,[80] migratory pressures from outside the Union increased significantly. The end of the Cold War created new sources of migration from central and eastern Europe. In addition, following the refugee crisis triggered by the war in the former Yugoslavia, the number of asylum-seekers in the EU more than doubled, from 170,650 in 1988 to 420,150 in 1991.[81] In response to these developments, the Member States moved to provide stronger structures for policy co-ordination. The 1993 Treaty on European Union transformed immigration co-operation by

[76] Commission, 'Proposal for a Directive of the European Parliament and of the Council on the posting of workers who are third country nationals for the provision of cross-border services; proposal for a Council Directive extending the freedom to provide cross-border services to third country nationals established within the Community' COM (1999) 3.

[77] Reg (EEC) 1612/68 on free movement for workers [1968] OJ Spec Ed (II) 475.

[78] Commission, 'Commission report on the implementation of the action plan on racism—mainstreaming the fight against racism', January 2000, 35. Available at: http://europa.eu.int/comm/employment_social/fundamri/eu_racism/main_en.htm

[79] See the comprehensive volume by E Guild with J Niessen, *The developing immigration and asylum policies of the European Union—adopted Conventions, Resolutions, Recommendations, Decisions and Conclusions* (London: Kluwer Law International, 1996). See also A Geddes, *Immigration and European integration—towards Fortress Europe?* (Manchester: Manchester University Press, 2000); E Guild, *Immigration Law in the European Community* (London: Kluwer Law International, 2001).

[80] In 1995, seven Member States removed internal border controls under the aegis of the Schengen Agreements. These states are France, Germany, Luxembourg, Belgium, the Netherlands, Spain and Portugal. In 1998, border controls were also removed with Italy and Austria, and in 2000 with Greece. In 2001, Norway, Iceland, Denmark, Sweden and Finland all became full participants in the Schengen Agreements.

[81] UNHCR Regional Office for European Institutions (1992) in A Butt-Philip, 'EU Immigration Policy: Phantom, Fantasy or Fact?' (1994) 17 *West European Politics* 168, 182.

placing it within an explicit legal framework, known as the 'third pillar'. This specified as areas of 'common interest'[82] 'immigration policy and policy regarding nationals of third countries', and allowed for the adoption of binding 'joint actions' by the Council.[83]

The measures which resulted were primarily targeted at reducing new forms of immigration; in doing so they have often raised concerns in respect of the treatment accorded to ethnic minorities already present in the EU.[84] In particular, by focusing heavily on immigration control, the direction of policy became unbalanced, verging on the repressive. This perspective has been summed up in the notion of 'Fortress Europe'.[85] A concrete example of the potential for immigration control measures to provoke discrimination is the issue of 'employer sanctions'. In 1996, the Council adopted a Recommendation stating that, *inter alia*, where an employer hires someone who does not possess the necessary work permit, the employer 'should be made subject to appropriate penalties'.[86] This creates a direct risk that employers, unfamiliar with which groups of people are entitled to work and which are not, will simply avoid employing third country nationals, or ethnic minorities in general. Indeed, research in the UK uncovered numerous instances where the introduction of precisely these rules led to the unequal treatment of both ethnic minority EU citizens and third country nationals.[87]

Paradoxically, the restrictive trend of EU immigration policies acted as a catalyst for EU policy on combating racism. The perception of 'Fortress Europe' galvanised national and European civil society into transnational action for anti-racism measures at the EU level, so as to ameliorate the effects of immigration policies.[88] Moreover, the EU institutions, in particular the Council, came under pressure to 'legitimise' immigration policies through greater attention to promoting integration.

---

[82] TEU, Art K.1.　　　　　　　　　　　[83] TEU, Art K.3.

[84] JCWI, *Annual report and policy review* (London: JCWI, 1996) 10.

[85] See, *inter alia*, S Ogata, 'Refugees and asylum-seekers: a challenge to European immigration policy' in S Ogata; D Cohn-Bendit; A Fortescue; R Haddawi and I Khalevinski, *Towards a European Immigration Policy* (Brussels: Philip Morris Institute for Public Policy Research, 1993); J King, 'Ethnic minorities and multilateral European institutions' in A Hargreaves and J Leaman (eds), *Racism, Ethnicity and Politics in Contemporary Europe* (Aldershot: Edward Elgar, 1995); A Geddes, 'Immigrants, ethnic minorities and the European Union's democratic deficit' (1995) 33 JCMS 197, 207.

[86] Council Recommendation on harmonizing means of combating illegal immigration and illegal employment and improving the relevant means of control, 22 December 1995 [1996] OJ C5/1.

[87] M Dustin and S d'Orey, *A culture of suspicion—the impact of internal immigration controls* (London: Joint Council for the Welfare of Immigrants, Commission for Racial Equality and the Refugee Council, 1998).

[88] A Dummett, 'Racial Equality and 1992' (1991) 3 *Feminist Rev* 85, 86.

(iii) *The establishment of an effective EU lobby against racism*

Hoskyns speaks vividly of a 'groundswell of opposition' emerging to European immigration policies in this period, comprising a range of migrants' rights groups, churches, human rights organisations,[89] UNHCR,[90] and the European Parliament.[91] The diversity of this lobby found a certain coherence through a 1991 initiative by the British Commission for Racial Equality, the Churches Committee for Migrants in Europe and the Dutch National Bureau against Racism. These groups, acting as 'the Starting Line Group', organised a number of legal experts from across the Union to produce a draft EC Directive, presented in December 1992.[92] The 'Starting Line Directive' proposed the prohibition of discrimination based on 'race, colour, descent, nationality, or national or ethnic origin' across a wide range of fields.[93] The proposal received the explicit backing of the European Parliament in December 1993,[94] and won the support of over 250 NGOs throughout the Member States, thus giving it a genuine mandate from European civil society. Nonetheless, the Commission concluded that the necessary legal competence for the Directive did not exist, and the proposal was not accepted. Pragmatically, the Starting Line Group then moved to submit the 'Starting Point', a proposal for an amendment of the EC Treaty to give the Community specific legal powers to adopt such legislation. Again this received the backing of almost 300 non-governmental and quasi-governmental actors, and the initiative was supported by the Commission[95] and the Parliament.[96]

Therefore, by the mid-1990s, a strong cross-border lobby had been constructed against racism, which carefully tailored its proposals to the decision-

[89] See, J van der Klaauw, 'Amnesty Lobbies for Refugees' in R H Pedler and M van Schendelen (eds), *Lobbying in the European Union—Companies, Trades Associations and Issue Groups* (Aldershot: Dartmouth Publishing, 1994).

[90] United Nations High Commission for Refugees (UNHCR), *An overview of protection issues in Western Europe: legislative trends and positions taken* (Geneva: UNHCR, 1994).

[91] C Hoskyns, *Integrating Gender—Women, Law and Politics in the European Union* (London: Verso, 1996) 175.

[92] Interview: Isabelle Chopin, Starting Line Group, Brussels, 12 December 1996. See also C Gearty, 'The internal and external "Other" in the Union legal order: racism, religious intolerance and xenophobia in Europe' in P Alston with M Bustelo and J Heenan, *The EU and human rights* (Oxford: Oxford University Press, 1999) 350–355.

[93] For the text of the proposal, see A Dummett, 'The Starting Line: A proposal for a draft Council Directive concerning the elimination of racial discrimination' (1994) 20 *New Community* 530, 534.

[94] Paragraph 4, Parliament Resolution on racism and xenophobia [1993] OJ C342/19.

[95] Commission, 'Communication on racism, xenophobia and anti-semitism' COM (95) 653, 19.

[96] [1995] OJ C151/56.

makers in the Commission and the Council. Alongside this lobby, there was a general pressure on the Council to improve the image of EU immigration policies and to deal with the growing phenomenon of cross-border racist crime. In this context, the shift in opinion within the Council becomes more understandable, and this is described in the next section.

(iv) Changing views in the Council

Evidence of the increasing prominence of racism on the Council's agenda is provided in the frequent references made to this subject in the Conclusions of the European Council meetings from 1990 onwards. The importance of combating racism was recorded at the 1990 Dublin Council,[97] the 1991 Maastricht Council,[98] the 1992 Edinburgh Council,[99] the 1993 Copenhagen Council,[100] and the 1994 Corfu[101] and Essen[102] Councils.[103] Moreover, in November 1993, the Justice and Home Affairs Council agreed a set of Council Conclusions on racism and xenophobia.[104] Nonetheless, fundamental disagreements on the appropriate role for the EU in this field prevented the Council going beyond this long series of non-binding statements of good intent.[105] In an apparent attempt to break the log-jam, in May 1994, the governments of France and Germany (both facing serious domestic electoral pressures from the extreme right) proposed the establishment of a 'Consultative Commission on racism and xenophobia'. This was endorsed the following month at the Corfu European Council. The Consultative Commission mainly comprised representatives of each of the Member

---

[97] Annex III, Declaration on anti-semitism, racism and xenophobia, EC Bull, 6-1990.

[98] Annex III, Declaration on racism and xenophobia, EC Bull, 12-1991.

[99] Annex 5, Declaration on principles of [sic] governing external aspects of migration policy, EC Bull, 12-1992.

[100] Point I.24, EC Bull, 6-1993.   [101] Point I.23, EC Bull, 6-1994.

[102] Point I.33, EC Bull, 12-1994.

[103] The Member States also were party to the Vienna Declaration of the Council of Europe which relauched its fight against racism in 1993; see R Cholewinski, *Migrant workers in international human rights law—their protection in countries of employment* (Oxford: Clarendon Press, 1997) 275.

[104] Annex 1, Press Release 10550/93, Presse 209. 1710th Council Meeting (Justice and Home Affairs) Brussels, 29–30 November 1993.

[105] Indeed, Weiler concludes that the anti-racism declarations were often outweighed by the anti-immigration rhetoric of the Council in this period: J Weiler, 'Thou shalt not oppress a stranger: on the judicial protection of the human rights of non-EC nationals—a critique' (1992) 3 Eur J of Intl L 65, 67.

States, and was charged with formulating 'recommendations, geared to national and local circumstances, on cooperation between governments'.[106]

In retrospect, the Kahn Commission[107] marked a decisive turning point in EU policy on racism. Its report, issued in spring 1995, concluded that there was a strong case for enhanced EU level action against racism. In particular, it stated that 'amendment of the Treaty to provide explicitly for Community competence must be regarded as an essential element in any serious European strategy aimed at combating racism and xenophobia'.[108] Furthermore, utilising the opportunities that such an amendment would provide, the Kahn Commission endorsed EU legislation on racial discrimination: 'the Community has already shown how effective it can be in combating discrimination on the basis of sex; it is appropriate that it should be given a similar mandate, and that it should adopt similar measures, to combating [sic] discrimination on grounds of race, religion or ethnic or national origins'.[109]

The strength of the report lay in the fact that it emerged from the representatives of the Member States themselves and was founded on a comparison of existing national laws on racism. Only one representative (that of the UK) was unable to accept the prevailing consensus on the basis that the best means to tackle racism varied depending on the national context.[110] Notwithstanding this dissenting voice, the report provoked the adoption of a range of new EU instruments against racism. Therefore, in October 1995, the Social Partners agreed a declaration on racism in the workplace,[111] alongside the adoption of two new Council Resolutions on racism, in the fields of employment and education.[112] In December 1995, the

---

[106] EU Bull 6-1994, point I.29. In a concession to the Parliament, two MEPs were permitted on the Commission, alongside a representative of the European Commission and an observer from the Council of Europe. The two MEPs in question were Glyn Ford of the Socialist Group, and Arie Oostlander of the European People's Party (Christian Democrats).

[107] The chair of the Commission was Jean Kahn.

[108] Consultative Commission on Racism and Xenophobia, 'Final Report' Ref 6906/1/95 Rev 1 Limite RAXEN 24 (Brussels: General Secretariat of the Council of the European Union, 1995) 57.

[109] ibid 59.   [110] ibid 63–64, statement by Baroness Flather, representative from the UK.

[111] Reproduced in Commission, *The European institutions in the fight against racism: selected texts* (Luxembourg: OOPEC, 1997).

[112] Council Resolution of 5 October 1995 on the fight against racism and xenophobia in the fields of employment and social affairs [1995] OJ C296/13; Council Resolution of 23 October 1995 on the response of educational systems to the problems of racism and xenophobia [1995] OJ C312/1.

Commission proposed the designation of 1997 as 'European year against racism',[113] an initiative which was duly approved by the Council.[114]

Whilst these soft law measures[115] demonstrated the much greater acceptance in the Council of racism as an issue relevant to the Union, agreement remained difficult in areas where more binding instruments were required. For example, Greece, France, the UK and Denmark, contrary to the wishes of Belgium and Germany, only agreed the 1996 Joint Action on racism following the acceptance of reservations to the main text.[116] Problems were also experienced with the implementation of another of the Kahn Commission's proposals, the creation of a European Monitoring Centre on racism and xenophobia. The Centre was designed, *inter alia*, to improve the co-ordination of European research on racism, to keep under review developments in national law and to formulate 'conclusions and opinions' for the Union and the Member States.[117] Given the absence of any specific Treaty provision on racism, the Commission proposal relied on former EC Treaty, Article 235.[118] However, this was initially opposed by Germany, Denmark and the UK.[119] Although the difficulties with the Monitoring Centre proposal were eventually resolved through agreement on a combination of Articles 235 and 213,[120] it reinforced the difficulties of operating within the existing EC Treaty.

In December 1995, the Council's intergovernmental conference reflection group noted 'majority support' for the inclusion of a general prohibition on

[113] Commission, 'Communication from the Commission on racism, xenophobia and anti-semitism and Proposal for a Council Decision designating 1997 European Year against Racism' COM (95) 653.

[114] Resolution of the Council and the representatives of the governments of the Member States, meeting within the Council concerning the European Year against Racism (1997) [1996] OJ C237/1.

[115] Further examples include Council Declaration of 24 November 1997 on the fight against racism, xenophobia and anti-semitism in the youth field [1997] OJ C368/1; Council Declaration of 16 December 1997 on respecting diversity and combating racism and xenophobia [1998] OJ C1/1.

[116] European Report, 20 March 1996, no 2117, section IV, 14.

[117] Reg 1035/97 establishing a European Monitoring Centre for Racism and Xenophobia [1997] OJ L151, Art 2.

[118] Now Art 308. Commission, 'Proposal for a Council Regulation (EC) establishing a European Monitoring Centre for Racism and Xenophobia' COM (96) 615.

[119] European Report, 2 December 1996, 'Racism and xenophobia—proposal to set up a monitoring centre'. Similarly, Germany and the UK objected to the use of Art 308 in the Commission's proposal for making 1997 European year against racism, and in the end the Council adopted only a Resolution on the subject, not a Decision, so as to circumvent having to specify a legal base for the act (European Report, No 2093, 16.12.95, section IV, 13).

[120] Now Art 284, which states that 'the Commission may, within the limits and under the conditions laid down by the Council in accordance with the provisions of this Treaty, collect any information and carry out any checks required for the performance of the tasks entrusted to it'.

discrimination in the EC Treaty, including discrimination based on race or religion. The main objections continued to come from the UK, which argued that 'problems of discrimination (particularly on such sensitive questions of race and religion) are best dealt with . . . through national legislation'.[121] The election of a Labour Government in the UK, less than two months before the Amsterdam Treaty was concluded, removed this final obstacle and there was common accord on the inclusion of two new provisions providing the Union with specific powers to combat racism. First, EC Treaty, Article 13:

Without prejudice to the other provisions of this Treaty and within the limits of the powers conferred by it upon the Community, the Council, acting unanimously on a proposal from the Commission and after consulting the European Parliament, may take appropriate action to combat discrimination based on sex, racial or ethnic origin, religion or belief, disability, age or sexual orientation.

Second, TEU, Article 29:

Without prejudice to the powers of the European Community, the Union's objective shall be to provide citizens with a high level of safety within an area of freedom, security and justice by developing common action among Member States in the fields of police and judicial cooperation in criminal matters and by preventing and combating racism and xenophobia.

Chapter 5 will consider the scope and significance of both these Treaty provisions in detail. The most obvious consequence of Article 13 has been the subsequent agreement in June 2000 of the Racial Equality Directive.

IV. The Racial Equality Directive

This section provides an overview of the background to and key elements of the Racial Equality Directive.[122] It does not give a 'clause-by-clause' analysis of the precise terms of the Directive,[123] but it identifies the key themes that will be taken forward in the subsequent chapters.

---

[121] Foreign and Commonwealth Office, *A Partnership of Nations* (London: HMSO, 1997) para 57.

[122] Council Directive (EC) 2000/43 of 29 June 2000 implementing the principle of equal treatment between persons irrespective of racial or ethnic origin [2000] OJ L180/22. See Annex 1.

[123] For more detailed examination, see L Waddington and M Bell, 'More Equal than Others: Distinguishing European Union Equality Directives' (2001) 38 CML Rev 587; M Bell, 'Meeting the challenge? A comparison between the EU Racial Equality Directive and the Starting Line' in I Chopin and J Niessen (eds), *The Starting Line and the incorporation of the Racial Equality Directive into the national laws of the EU Member States and accession states* (London: Migration Policy Group and Commission for Racial Equality, 2001).

Although the creation of Article 13 was clearly a turning point in policy development, it is worth recalling that the provision itself specifies no time frame for implementation, nor even generates any obligation to take further steps. Nonetheless, just over one year after Article 13 came into force, the Council adopted the Racial Equality Directive. Given the normally slow process of European law making, and the long history of incrementalism in this policy field, the speed with which the Directive was agreed is remarkable.[124] This section will examine further the factors that help explain this progress.

The Commission opened a debate on implementing Article 13 before the Treaty of Amsterdam was even ratified. In March 1998, 'an action plan against racism' was presented in which the Commission committed itself to 'presenting a legislative proposal to combat racial discrimination' before the end of 1999.[125] Responding to the call for a debate, the Starting Line Group revised its earlier proposal for a Directive. Again, the Group recommended a specific Directive on racial and religious discrimination with a wide material scope.[126] This received particular support from the European Parliament, which endorsed 'specific rules which precisely cover specific forms of discrimination, rather than general provisions'.[127] This emphasis is reflected in the final proposals. On 25 November 1999, the Commission proposed a three-strand package of measures to implement Article 13:

—a Directive forbidding discrimination on grounds of racial or ethnic origin, religion or belief, age, disability and sexual orientation in employment;[128]
—a Directive forbidding discrimination on grounds of racial or ethnic origin in employment, education, social protection, social advantages and access to goods and services;[129]
—an Action Programme against discrimination on all Article 13 grounds except sex.[130]

---

[124] E Guild, 'The EC Directive on race discrimination: surprises, possibilities and limitations' (2000) 29 ILJ 416.

[125] Commission, 'An action plan against racism' COM (1998) 183, 10.

[126] I Chopin and J Niessen (eds), *Proposals for legislative measures to combat racism and to promote equal rights in the European Union* (London: CRE, 1998).

[127] Resolution on the communication from the Commission 'An action plan against racism' [1999] OJ C98/491.

[128] Commission, 'Proposal for a Council Directive establishing a general framework for equal treatment in employment and occupation' COM (1999) 565.

[129] Commission, 'Proposal for a Council Directive implementing the principle of equal treatment between persons irrespective of racial or ethnic origin' COM (1999) 566.

[130] Commission, 'Proposal for a Council Decision establishing a Community Action Programme to combat discrimination 2001–2006', COM (1999) 567.

In justifying the decision to treat racial and ethnic discrimination differently, the Commission emphasised 'the strong political will which exists to take action to combat as many aspects as possible of racial discrimination'.[131] This preference for a combination of ground-specific (vertical) and general (horizontal) instruments was shared in the Council where only Italy argued in favour of amalgamating the two proposed Directives.[132]

Within weeks of the proposals from the Commission, an unexpected political event intervened with major significance for the Racial Equality Directive.[133] In February 2000, a change in the governing coalition in Austria was agreed, with the entry into government of Jorg Haider's Freedom Party. The presence in a European Union national government of a party from the extreme right produced protests from other Member States, leading to the imposition of bilateral diplomatic sanctions.[134] One consequence was an initiative from the Portuguese Presidency to fast-track the proposed Racial Equality Directive,[135] as a sign of the EU's commitment to combating racism. Specifically, the Portuguese Presidency aimed to complete the Directive by the end of June 2000, which in turn required the Parliament to deliver its opinion in an unusually quick period.[136] This gave the Parliament a useful bargaining power in negotiations with the Council. As a result, the Council was compelled to agree to a number of amendments strengthening the Directive by the Parliament in return for the early delivery of its opinion.[137] The resulting momentum also pressured individual Member States to be more flexible in their negotiating positions—with presumably no state wishing to be regarded as blocking new laws combating racism. Ultimately, the Council adopted the Racial Equality Directive on 6 June 2000, 'after a flurry of activity'.[138]

---

[131] Commission, 'Communication on certain Community measures to combat discrimination' COM (1999) 564, 8.

[132] EU Council, 'Outcome of Proceedings of the Social Questions Working Party on 21/22 February 2000' No 6435/00, Brussels, 1 March 2000, n 7.

[133] G de Búrca, 'The drafting of the European Union Charter of Fundamental Rights' (2001) 26 ELR 126, 136.

[134] Statement of the Portuguese Presidency, Lisbon, 31 January 2000.

[135] Baroness Blackstone, *Hansard*, HL (series 5) vol 614, col 1233 (30 June 2000).

[136] 'EU fights far right with laws on racism', The Guardian, 18 May 2000.

[137] *Inter alia*, the addition of instruction to discriminate in the definition of discrimination, and the addition of healthcare and housing to the material scope of the Directive: see Parliament amendments to the Proposal for a Council Directive on implementing the principle of equal treatment between persons irrespective of racial or ethnic origin [2001] OJ C59/263.

[138] Blackstone (n 135 above).

The Directive forbids four forms of discrimination on grounds of racial or ethnic origin: direct,[139] indirect,[140] harassment[141] and instruction to discriminate.[142] 'Direct discrimination' is defined as 'where one person is treated less favourably than another is, has been or would be treated in a comparable situation on grounds of racial or ethnic origin'. The explicit inclusion of possible recourse to hypothetical comparators marks a step forward from the Equal Treatment Directive,[143] and may be particularly valuable in areas where the ethnic minority population is relatively small. The definition of indirect discrimination builds on that applicable to nationality discrimination in EU law,[144] and thereby avoids a dependency on the production of statistical data.[145] Thus, there is no requirement to show that a practice affects a significantly higher proportion of persons of a particular racial or ethnic origin, but it is sufficient to demonstrate that 'an apparently neutral provision, criterion or practice would put persons of a racial or ethnic origin at a particular disadvantage compared with other persons'. Once again, this is likely to be especially valuable in places where the ethnic minority population is small and/or there is little statistical information on ethnic minorities.

'Harassment' is defined broadly as any 'unwanted conduct . . . with the purpose or effect of violating the dignity of a person and of creating an intimidating, hostile, degrading, humiliating or offensive environment'. Therefore, it should cover a range of actions, by a range of actors—such as students, landlords, patients or clients. However, the Directive leaves open questions surrounding the liability of employers or service-providers for harassment they did not directly initiate. For example, is an employer liable for unlawful harassment against one of his or her employees by another worker or a customer? Article 2(3) states that 'the concept of harassment may be defined in accordance with the national laws and practice of the Member States'. This appears to provide national authorities with a wide discretion to make their own decisions on the full scope of the ban on harassment. Nonetheless, in *BECTU*, the Court had to interpret a comparable provision

---

[139] Art 2(2)(a).   [140] Art 2(2)(b).   [141] Art 2(3).   [142] Art 2(4).

[143] R Whittle, 'The concept of disability discrimination and its legal construction', Paper presented at the workshop *Discrimination and affirmative action in the labour market—legal perspectives*, organised by Swedish National Institute for Working Life, 6–7 November 2000, Brussels.

[144] See ch 2 above.

[145] L Waddington, 'Tweede-generatie richtlijnen Gelijke Behandeling: de nieuwe Richtlijn inzake gelijke behandeling ongeacht ras of etnische afstamming en de Kaderrichtlijn gelijke behandeling in arbeid en beroep' (2000) 12 Sociaal Recht 357.

in the Working Time Directive.[146] In that context, the Court emphasised that national discretion could not undermine the substance of the right altogether.[147]

Finally, the ban on instructions to discriminate is especially valuable, given evidence in some Member States that employers have placed pressure on employment agencies not to send them workers of a particular ethnic origin.[148]

The material scope of the Directive is wide. It covers all aspects of employment,[149] as well as 'membership of and involvement in an organisation of workers or employers'.[150] Outside the employment arena, the Directive applies to 'social protection, including social security and healthcare; social advantages; education; access to and supply of goods and services which are available to the public, including housing'.[151] However, this is all subject to the proviso 'within the limits of the powers conferred upon the Community'. This problematic expression is also found in Article 13 and it has generated considerable debate.[152] Not only is it crucial to the scope of Article 13, it is now crucial to the scope of the Racial Equality Directive. This is examined in detail in Chapter 5.

There are three principal exceptions to the ban on discrimination. The first, and most significant, is found in Article 3(2), which provides that:

This Directive does not cover difference of treatment based on nationality and is without prejudice to provisions and conditions relating to the entry into and residence of third-country nationals and stateless persons on the territory of Member States, and to any treatment which arises from the legal status of the third-country nationals and stateless persons concerned.

The impact of the Directive on third country nationals was one of the most sensitive issues within the Council. Several Member States, in particular Denmark, Germany, Luxembourg and the UK,[153] were concerned at the

---

[146] Case C–173/99 *Broadcasting, Entertainment, Cinematographic and Theatre Union (BECTU) v Secretary of State for Trade and Industry* [2001] ECR I–4881. The Court was interpreting Art 7(1) which states: 'Member States shall take the measures necessary to ensure that every worker is entitled to paid leave of at least four weeks in accordance with the conditions for entitlement to, and granting of, such leave laid down by national legislation and/or practice.'

[147] ibid para 53.

[148] J Wrench, *European Compendium of Good Practice for the Prevention of Racism at the Workplace* (Luxembourg: OOPEC, 1997) 78.

[149] Art 3(1)(a)–(c).   [150] Art 3(1)(d).   [151] Art 3(1)(e)–(h).

[152] Cf, L Waddington, 'Testing the limits of the EC Treaty Article on Non-discrimination' (1999) 28 ILJ 133, 136; R Whittle, 'Disability rights after Amsterdam: the way forward' (2000) Eur Human Rights L Rev 33, 40–42.

[153] EU Council, 'Outcome of proceedings of the Social Questions Working Party on 10 May 2000' Doc 8454/00, Brussels, 16 May 2000, n 21.

relationship between existing work permit schemes and the Directive. Presumably, their worries were based on the possibility of measures restricting third country nationals' access to the labour market being challenged as indirect discrimination. Article 3(2) was the final compromise on this issue, and it seeks to protect rules and practices that treat less favourably third country nationals (in comparison with EU nationals) from complaints of unlawful discrimination. However, the breadth of this exception can be criticised. Specifically, it is not clear if it may be relied on by private sector firms or service providers. For example, where an employer pays third country nationals less than domestic nationals for equal work, or where third country nationals are denied benefits such as paid holidays, this is a difference of treatment based on nationality, but it is often also indirect racial discrimination.[154] As an exception to the principle of equal treatment, Article 3(2) should be interpreted narrowly,[155] and it will lie with the Court to determine the full scope of this provision.

The other exceptions are found in Article 4 (genuine and determining occupational requirements)[156] and Article 5 (positive action). The latter is likely to be the most controversial based on the experience of gender equality law.[157] Article 5 follows the pattern of EU gender equality law by facilitating positive action, without placing any obligation on Member States to avail of this possibility. Nonetheless, in its case law on positive action for women, the Court has excluded schemes involving automatic preferential treatment at the point of employment selection.[158] Chapter 6 identifies several states where this may affect existing positive action measures (principally in the UK and the Netherlands), assuming the Court of Justice applies a similar approach in interpreting the Racial Equality Directive. It also should be noted that the wider material scope of the Racial Equality Directive opens

---

[154] There is growing evidence of such discrimination against immigrant workers in Ireland: see '108 cases under scrutiny for breaches of labour laws', Irish Times, 8 June 2001.

[155] Case 222/84 *Johnston v Chief Constable of the RUC* [1986] ECR I–1651, 1686.

[156] For example, racial or ethnic origin might be a justifiable consideration in the delivery of certain social welfare and health services targeted at specific ethnic communities.

[157] See further, G Mancini and S O'Leary, 'The new frontiers of sex equality law in the European Union' (1999) 24 ELR 331; S Fredman, 'Affirmative action and the Court of Justice: a critical analysis' in J Shaw (ed), *Social law and policy in an evolving European Union* (Oxford: Hart Publishing, 2000).

[158] Case C–450/93 *Kalanke v Freie Hansestadt Bremen* [1995] ECR I–3069; Case C–409/95 *Marschall v Land Nordrhein-Westfalen* [1997] ECR I–6363; Case C–158/97 *Badeck v Hessischer Ministerpräsident* [2000] ECR I–1875; Case C–407/98 *Abrahamsson and Anderson v Fogelqvist* [2000] ECR I–5539.

new questions about how the Court will regard positive action in areas such as education or housing.

One of the most innovative aspects of the Directive is its focus on remedies and enforcement. This dimension clearly builds on the experience of the gender equality legislation where enforcement has proven challenging.[159] A variety of measures are taken to facilitate practical use of the Directive. First, organisations with a 'legitimate interest' may bring enforcement actions 'either on behalf or in support of the complainant, with his or her approval'.[160] Second, the burden of proof will shift to the respondent where 'facts from which it may be presumed that there has been direct or indirect discrimination' are established.[161] Third, 'any adverse treatment or consequence as a reaction to a complaint' is prohibited.[162] Fourth, 'sanctions, which may comprise the payment of compensation to the victim, must be effective, proportionate and dissuasive'.[163] Finally, and most significantly, Member States are obliged to designate 'a body or bodies for the promotion of equal treatment'. This institution will have a duty to 'provide independent assistance to victims of discrimination', as well as producing independent surveys and reports into discrimination.[164]

The recognition that enforcement issues cannot be completely devolved to the Member States is a welcome development in the Directive. Moreover, it takes into account many of the principles that the Court of Justice has been required to invent in order to provide effective remedies for gender equality rights.[165] Nonetheless, one of the core weaknesses in EU gender equality legislation—the dependency on *individual* litigation—remains intact. The Directive does not provide an autonomous right of action for trade unions or other relevant organisations to bring discrimination cases in their own name. Neither does the Directive clearly provide the equal treatment bodies with a right to start investigations into specific cases or patterns of discrimination or to initiate litigation. This can be particularly valuable in tackling institutional forms of discrimination that do not lend themselves to individual complaints. For example, if an employer has a predominantly white workforce and recruits only through 'word of mouth'—for example, via friends and family of the existing workforce—this is likely to disadvantage non-white

---

[159] J Blom, B Fitzpatrick, J Gregory, R Knegt and U O'Hare, *The Utilisation of Sex Equality Litigation in the Member States of the European Community* V/782/96-EN (Report to the Equal Opportunities Unit of DG V, 1995).

[160] Art 7(2).   [161] Art 8(1).   [162] Art 9.   [163] Art 15.   [164] Art 13.

[165] For example, Art 9 on victimisation reflects a principle established by the Court in Case C–185/97 *Coote v Granada Hospitality* [1998] ECR I–5199. See further, M Dougan, 'The Equal Treatment Directive: retaliation, remedies and direct effect' (1999) 24 ELR 664.

workers who may never have an opportunity to learn of vacancies.[166] Such practices tend to perpetuate ethnic inequality in the workforce, but the subtle nature of the discrimination poses barriers to individual litigation.

In addition to the specific enforcement provisions, there are also a number of measures in the Directive designed to enhance the implementation process. Member States are obliged to promote implementation through dialogue with the Social Partners—with a view to collective agreements on anti-discrimination rules,[167] as well as encouraging 'dialogue with appropriate non-governmental organisations'.[168] Finally, every five years Member States are required to submit evidence to the Commission which, taking into account information from NGOs and the EU Monitoring Centre, will compile a report on the application of the Directive. Although infrequent, this periodic reporting obligation will provide a useful opportunity to scrutinise the effectiveness of the Directive. Transposition into national law must be completed no later than 19 July 2003, with Member States obliged to report on their implementation of the Directive by 19 July 2005.

Given the slow progress in developing anti-racism policy, the strength and scope of the Racial Equality Directive mark a dramatic step forward. The Directive establishes a relatively high benchmark for national legislation and genuinely addresses the need to turn law into action. In particular, the equal treatment bodies should provide an important focus within each Member State for developing anti-discrimination law and putting into practice the Directive's principles. Surprisingly, the Member States did not choose simply to mirror the Equal Treatment Directive, but instead provided a new model for EU anti-discrimination law. The widespread implications of the Directive will be explored in the following chapters. Chapter 5 examines the lessons from the Directive for the scope and meaning of Article 13 EC. Chapter 6 considers in a reflective manner both the impact of existing national law and practice on the shaping of the Directive, as well as how the Directive will now in turn influence the development of national legal traditions. Finally, Chapter 7 considers the position of the Directive within the overall framework of EU anti-discrimination law, and the reordering of the equality hierarchy that it implies.

---

[166] Fair Employment Commission, *Fair Employment in Northern Ireland—Code of Practice* (Belfast: Department of Economic Development, 1989) 12.

[167] Art 11.   [168] Art 12.

V. Anti-racism policy: from the periphery to the centre

With the adoption of the Racial Equality Directive it is now certain that combating racism will be one of the primary facets of European social policy in
the years ahead. Looking back, the difficulties experienced in developing EU
policy on racism pre-Amsterdam can be clearly linked to the market integration model of social policy. The fact that one of the main groups affected by
racism—third country nationals—is an invisible actor in the internal market
underlined the weak nexus between initiatives to combat racism and market
integration. Moreover, Member States carefully protected national control
over immigration policies, which reinforced the marginal status of racial discrimination in the EU polity.

The transformation of anti-racism policy can be connected to the gradual
emergence of a market rationale for EU intervention. On the one hand, there
has been a growing appreciation that all forms of discrimination can create
barriers to free movement.[169] On the other, spillover pressures from the
internal market programme have compelled Member States to enter into
ever closer co-operation on immigration policies. This process reached a
new stage in the Treaty of Amsterdam with the creation of a specific chapter
in the EC Treaty on 'visas, asylum, immigration . . .'.[170]

The aim of this new Community competence is to create an Area of
Freedom, Security and Justice by 2004,[171] which includes the removal of all
internal border controls both for EU citizens and third country nationals.[172]
In 1999, the Tampere European Council agreed an agenda for implementing
these provisions, which included a reinforced emphasis on 'fair treatment of
third country nationals'.[173] The Commission has indicated that one dimension to the 'Freedom' aspect of the Area is freedom 'from any form of discrimination'.[174] Therefore, Article 13 measures, and especially anti-racism

---

[169] Commission, 'European Social Policy. A way forward for the Union—a White Paper' COM
(94) 333, ch VI, para 27.

[170] Arts 61–68. See further J Monar, 'Justice and Home Affairs in the Treaty of Amsterdam:
reform at the price of fragmentation' (1998) 23 ELR 320; H Bribosia, 'Liberté, sécurité et justice'
(1998) *Revue du Marché Unique Européen* 27; N Fennelly, 'The Area of "Freedom, Security and
Justice" and the European Court of Justice—a personal view' (2000) 49 ICLQ 1. It should be noted
that the UK, Ireland and Denmark have specific 'opt-outs' from these provisions: Treaty of
Amsterdam, Protocols B(4) and B(5).

[171] Art 61.   [172] Art 62.

[173] EU Bull, 10-1999, Presidency Conclusions, Tampere European Council, 15–16 October
1999.

[174] Commission, 'Towards an Area of Freedom, Security and Justice' COM (98) 459, 5.

instruments, have found a particular location in this new aspect of market integration.

Hervey highlights the inherent contradiction, however, in founding anti-racism initiatives on a need to guarantee the right to free movement for EU citizens—a right which enshrines indirect racial discrimination as a result of the exclusion of third country nationals.[175] Certainly, the free movement impetus will be more central if and when the Area of Freedom, Security and Justice is completed, as third country nationals would then also be internal market actors. The Commission has indicated the potential economic benefits this would generate; third country nationals could travel to consume services (for example as tourists) within the internal market.[176] Similarly, the Court has already identified the internal market logic in allowing third country nationals to move as service providers. Racial discrimination is an obvious deterrent to such movement (and market integration); hence, the logic behind shared market rules on such discrimination is becoming more concrete.

A further market-related factor that has been pushing the priority attached to combating racial discrimination is the European Employment Strategy. As mentioned in Chapter 2, the strategy is most visible in the agreement of the annual EU employment guidelines. The core aim of the strategy might be summarised as the removal of barriers to participating in the employment market leading to an increase in employment participation rates in the Union.[177] From the outset, the strategy acknowledged the need to address equal opportunities for women in order to improve female employability rates. As the strategy has evolved, there has been an extension of this rationale to other grounds of discrimination, including discrimination against ethnic minorities.[178] The importance of guaranteeing equal access for ethnic minorities to the labour market is reinforced by the growing realisation that one consequence of the shrinking working age population in the Union may be a new openness to further primary immigration.[179] In this context, it is

---

[175] T Hervey, 'Putting Europe's house in order: racism, race discrimination and xenophobia after the Treaty of Amsterdam' in D O'Keeffe and P Twomey (eds), *Legal issues of the Amsterdam Treaty* (Oxford: Hart Publishing, 1999) 341.

[176] Commission, 'Proposal for a Council Directive on the right of third country nationals to travel in the Community' COM (95) 346, 7.

[177] See further, Presidency Conclusions, Stockholm European Council, 23–24 March 2001, para 8 ('Towards full employment').

[178] Reference to ethnic minorities' participation in the labour market was first made in Guideline 9, Council Resolution on the 1999 employment guidelines [1999] OJ C69/2.

[179] Annex 1, Commission, 'Communication on a Community immigration policy' COM (2000) 757.

possible to understand why combating racism has grown in priority within the employment guidelines. Although the underlying function of this policy is not market integration in the traditional sense of removing obstacles to free movement, it is very much focused on the functioning of the economy of the internal market and falls within the new forms of European economic governance emerging alongside monetary union.[180]

It would be shortsighted though to see market imperatives as the only reason behind the Racial Equality Directive. In particular, the scope of the Directive cannot be comfortably reconciled with a market integration view of social policy. Gender equality law has largely remained tied to the employment market and workers, but the Racial Equality Directive extends into areas such as health, education and housing. It is striking that these are the traditional areas of social policy that dominate at the national level, but which have been highly limited at the EU level—precisely because of their weak link to the functioning of the internal market.[181] Indeed, although there may be aspects of the Racial Equality Directive that meet internal market objectives, it is not primarily based on the needs of the market.

Barnard describes Article 13 as part of the social dimension of EU citizenship.[182] In the same vein, the Racial Equality Directive seems to represent a social citizenship model of European social policy. The Directive is a concrete addition to the otherwise thin list of citizens' rights that the Union protects. Moreover, unlike most of the rights found in EC Treaty, Articles 17–22, the Directive's protection is not dependent on the prior exercise of the right to free movement. Therefore, it builds a more direct link between the Union and individual citizens. The Directive also performs an important function in creating a bond between the European Union and ethnic minority communities—a counter-balance to the impact of 'Fortress Europe' policies.[183]

Identifying the vision of citizenship that underpins the Directive is more complex. Shaw distinguishes two approaches to Union citizenship—one based on the idea of a European social model, and the other based on the Area

---

[180] E Szyszczak, 'Social Policy' (2001) 50 ICLQ 175, 179.

[181] M Poiares Maduro, 'Europe's social self: "the sickness unto death"' in J Shaw (ed), *Social law and policy in an evolving European Union* (Oxford: Hart Publishing, 2000) 330.

[182] C Barnard, 'P v S: kite flying or a new constitutional approach' in A Dashwood and S O'Leary (eds), *The principle of equal treatment in European Community law* (London: Sweet & Maxwell, 1997) 280.

[183] King argues that confidence in the European Union amongst ethnic minority communities has been weakened in the past as a result of restrictive immigration policies: J King, 'Ethnic minorities and multilateral European institutions' in A Hargreaves and J Leaman (eds), *Racism, Ethnicity and Politics in Contemporary Europe* (Aldershot: Edward Elgar, 1995).

of Freedom, Security and Justice.[184] The former can be characterised by an emphasis on social solidarity and cohesion, whereas in the latter 'the identity of the citizen is constructed through the "Other", the foreigner who needs to be excluded to make the citizen "secure"'.[185] Barnard suggests that the application of Article 13 to third country nationals reflects a European social model vision of citizenship: 'Article 13 therefore helps to create a bridge between a statist notion of citizenship towards a post-national construction, where rights are universal and given to all individuals.'[186]

The Racial Equality Directive does not clearly articulate one view of citizenship or the other. Its protective shield applies to third country nationals; therefore it performs a vital role in conferring rights under the aegis of post-national citizenship. Yet, the broad exception for nationality discrimination undermines the protective value of the Directive for third country nationals. There is a very thin line between not being able to reject someone for employment because they have a North African ethnic origin, whilst still being able to refuse employment because someone holds an Algerian passport and not one from a Member State of the European Union—irrespective of how long that person has been resident in the Union. The reluctance of the Member States to engage with such issues indicates a continuing tendency towards forms of citizenship centred on rights acquired by virtue of nationality.

Any citizenship is of course based on the extension of rights to a limited category of persons, namely the citizens. Therefore, by definition it requires the creation of insiders and outsiders.[187] The post-national model of citizenship proposed by Barnard would permit a wider circle of 'insiders', recognising the reality of different categories of non-nationals. Currently, Union law assimilates the non-national who passes through a state on a purely temporary basis with a non-national who has been continually resident in the state all their life. It is this latter category of persons, long-term residents, into which the majority of the EU's ethnic minorities fall, and it is in respect of these persons that the denial of legal equality is difficult to justify.

In recent years, the Commission has produced various legislative proposals that would extend certain rights to third country nationals resident in the

---

[184] J Shaw, 'The many pasts and futures of citizenship of the Union' (1997) 22 ELR 554, 564.

[185] ibid 571.

[186] C Barnard, 'Article 13: through the looking glass of Union citizenship' in D O'Keeffe and P Twomey (eds), *Legal issues of the Amsterdam Treaty* (Oxford: Hart Publishing, 1999) 384.

[187] T Hervey, 'Migrant workers and their families in the European Union: the pervasive market ideology of Community law' in J Shaw and G More, *New Legal Dynamics of European Union* (Oxford: Clarendon Press, 1995) 98.

Union.[188] Most significantly, it has now proposed a Directive to create a 'long-term resident' status for most third country nationals with five years' lawful residence.[189] This would confer the right to move and establish residence in another EU Member State,[190] as well as wide-ranging rights to equal treatment with EU nationals, including in employment, education, housing and healthcare.[191] The adoption of this instrument would certainly be a vital complement to the Racial Equality Directive. Moreover, it would indicate a model of social citizenship based on inclusion and solidarity.

Mapping EU anti-racism policy

Stocktaking developments in this area, there appear to be three key strands to the present policy on racism: legislative, institutional and mainstreaming.

The Racial Equality Directive naturally forms the cornerstone of the legislative strategy against racism, and the prospect of any further EC Treaty, Article 13 legislation on racism is quite remote for now. However, TEU, Article 29 on combating racism through police and judicial co-operation remains untested. The Commission has suggested a number of measures could be adopted here, including a Framework Decision on harmonising definitions and penalties for racist offences,[192] or the common penalisation of racist offences conducted through the Internet.[193] The 1996 Joint Action is still the only Justice and Home Affairs instrument on racism,[194] but it is difficult to ascertain its precise impact on national law. A Council report in 1998 identified only two Member States which had taken specific measures to

---

[188] Commission, 'Proposal for a Council Act establishing the Convention on rules for the admission of third country nationals to the Member States' COM (97) 387; Commission, 'Proposal for a Council Regulation (EC) amending Regulation (EEC) 1408/71 as regards its extension to nationals of third countries' COM (97) 561; Commission, 'Proposal for a Directive of the European Parliament and of the Council on the posting of workers who are third country nationals for the provision of cross-border services; proposal for a Council directive extending the freedom to provide cross-border services to third country nationals established within the Community' COM (1999) 3.

[189] Commission, 'Proposal for a Council Directive concerning the status of third country nationals who are long-term residents' COM (2001) 127.

[190] ibid Art 15.   [191] ibid Art 12.

[192] Commission, 'Scoreboard to review progress on the creation of an Area of "Freedom, Security and Justice" in the European Union' COM (2000) 167 final/2, 24.

[193] Commission, 'Creating a safer information society by improving the security of information infrastructures and combating computer-related crime' COM (2000) 890, 15. The Commission proposed a Framework Decision on racist offences on 28 November 2001. See COM (2001) 664.

[194] Joint Action concerning action to combat racism and xenophobia [1996] OJ L185/5.

implement the Joint Action, although the report also concluded that national law in most Member States already conformed with many of the key elements of the instrument.[195] If nothing else, it seems evident that the Union has yet to define a clear role for itself in combating racism through the criminal law.

The institutional dimension to policy on racism is represented by the construction of the EU Monitoring Centre on Racism and Xenophobia, as well as support for several relevant NGO networks. The Monitoring Centre was a key step forward in policy development because it institutionalised the intervention of the Union in policies on racism. Unfortunately, early experience of the Centre has not been promising. Various bureaucratic barriers delayed progress in its creation, so that despite the adoption of the Regulation establishing the Centre on 2 June 1997,[196] the official opening only took place on 7 April 2000.[197] Moreover, the Centre under-spent its budget in 1998 and 1999 by around €2 million.[198] Above all, the specific role for the Centre remains ambiguous. This contrasts with the European Commission on Racism and Intolerance (ECRI), at the Council of Europe, which has carved out a distinct role for itself through periodic review of each state party's national law and policy, and issuing general policy recommendations.[199] However, ECRI was formally created already in 1993, therefore it may be that the Monitoring Centre will develop a more defined contribution over time.

A different form of capacity building can be identified in the support from the EU for various networks on racism. A European Union Migrant's Forum was established in 1991, but it failed to emerge as a central actor in policy on racism. In particular, it has experienced problems with internal disputes and organisational difficulties.[200] In 1998, €602,866 was provided by the Union to support the creation of a European Network Against Racism (ENAR). This was increased to €1,320,432 for a period of eighteen months from 1 January 2000.[201] ENAR's role has been described by the Commission as 'to

---

[195] UE Conseil, 'Note de Comité K.4 au Coreper' Doc 7808/1/98 REV 1, Brussels, 29 April 1998. Austria and Luxembourg had taken specific implementing measures.

[196] Reg (EC) 1035/97 establishing a European Monitoring Centre for Racism and Xenophobia [1997] OJ L151.

[197] Commission, 'Report on the activities of the European Monitoring Centre on Racism and Xenophobia' COM (2000) 625, 10.

[198] ibid 9.   [199] See further: *www.ecri.coe.int*

[200] A Geddes, *Immigration and European integration—towards Fortress Europe?* (Manchester: Manchester University Press, 2000) 145.

[201] Joint Answer to Written Questions E–2072/00, E–2073/00, E–2074/00 and E–2075/00 given by Ms Diamantopoulou on behalf of the Commission [2001] OJ C81E/139.

keep a check on anti-racism policy in order to influence the decision-making process'.[202] Therefore, if the Monitoring Centre is intended to provide an 'official' contribution to policy development, this is complemented by ENAR's role as an 'independent' critic. The difficult relationship that exists between such networks and the institutions that fund them is explored further in Chapter 7.

The final strand of policy on racism can identified as mainstreaming. Borrowing from gender equality policy, the Commission's 1998 action plan on racism promised to complement the proposed Directive with measures to integrate racial equality objectives into all areas of EU policy-making.[203] For example, combating discrimination has received a greater priority with European Social Funds.[204] Alternatively, the record of the EU applicant countries on combating racism has been raised within the enlargement process.[205] EU immigration and asylum policies seem the obvious area where the need for mainstreaming is most pressing, however, Commission analysis of the racial impact of these policies remains rather superficial. A review in 2000 of the progress in mainstreaming racial equality simply notes that several funding programmes in Justice and Home Affairs provide a 'possibility' to support projects to raise awareness of racial equality issues with professionals in the justice system.[206] More fundamental questions can be raised though about the overall impact on ethnic minorities of pursuing restrictive policies on immigration and asylum.[207] The negative discourse that surrounds, in particular, asylum applicants, and the constant focus on ever-tougher measures to prevent the arrival of such individuals tends to reinforce in the public mind a sense of insecurity. Community immigration policies have typically been based on a 'firm but fair' rationale: the integration of existing migrant communities depends on public confidence in firm state

---

[202] Commission, 'Report on the implementation of the action plan against racism—mainstreaming the fight against racism', January 2000, 16. Available at: http://europa.eu.int/comm/employment_social/fundamri/eu_racism/main_en.htm

[203] Commission, 'An action plan against racism' COM (1998) 183, 3.

[204] The most significant commitment is the new EQUAL programme which has a budget of €2,847 million for 2000–2006: Commission, 'Communication establishing the guidelines for the Community initiative Equal concerning transnational cooperation to promote new forms of combating all forms of discrimination and inequalities in connection with the labour market' [2000] OJ C127/2.

[205] Commission, 'Countering racism, xenophobia and anti-semitism in the candidate countries' COM (1999) 256.

[206] Commission (n 202 above) 35.

[207] M Bell, 'Mainstreaming equality norms into European Union asylum law' (2001) 26 ELR 20.

control over any future migration.[208] Yet, this hypothesis is frequently contested:

Minorities have often argued that far from being inter-dependent, strict control and good integration contradict each other; if the government sends out a public message that certain kinds of people should be stopped from coming, those in the category who have already arrived will be the object of dislike and discrimination.[209]

Interrogating European immigration and asylum policies and their relationship to promoting racial equality remains highly sensitive. Meaningful mainstreaming requires that greater scrutiny must be addressed to this dynamic. Given the significant EU commitment in the form of the Racial Equality Directive, it would be disappointing to see its objectives compromised by contradictory messages from other EU policies.

---

[208] Commission, 'Communication on immigration and asylum policy' COM (94) 23, 32.

[209] Paragraph 8, Commission for Racial Equality, 'Submission on the European Commission's Green Paper on social policy together with comments on the communication on immigration and asylum', March 1994. Held at the library of the European Foundation for the Improvement of Living and Working Conditions, Dublin.

Sexual Orientation Discrimination

In February 1998, the Court of Justice held that 'Community law as it stands at present does not cover discrimination based on sexual orientation'.[1] In the light of this assessment, one might conclude that the history of EU law in this area would be brief and abrupt. On the contrary; the bare statement above conceals the slow evolution of the law and policy here, stretching back to a debate ignited by the European Parliament in the early 1980s. This incremental development stands in the face of repeated evidence of entrenched social and, in most instances, legal discrimination against lesbians and gay men across the Member States. Social research reveals that this form of discrimination operates on two levels; the overt discrimination faced by those who are open about their sexual orientation, and the more covert phenomenon of 'discrimination avoidance' by those who feel compelled to keep secret their sexual orientation.[2] Few statistical studies of lesbians and gay men in the workplace exist, but those that do paint a disturbing picture. In a 1997 Swedish survey of 650 gay/lesbian persons, 36 per cent stated that they had been discriminated against in work.[3] In Ireland, in a survey with over 100 respondents, 23 per cent claimed to have experienced discrimination at work, and 39 per cent stated that they had avoided certain job categories for fear of discrimination.[4] Finally, in the UK, a 1993 survey with 1,873 respondents recorded that 48 per cent had experienced harassment in the workplace, with 89 per cent stating that at some stage they had felt compelled to conceal their sexual orientation at work.[5]

[1] Case C–249/96 *Grant v South-West Trains* [1998] ECR I–621, 651.

[2] GLEN and NEXUS Research Cooperative, *Poverty—lesbians and gay men. The economic and social effects of discrimination* (Dublin: Combat Poverty Agency, 1995) 54.

[3] B Skolander, 'Sweden' in N Beger, K Krickler, J Lewis and M Wuch (eds), *Equality for lesbians and gay men: a relevant issue in the civil and social dialogue* (Brussels: ILGA-Europe, 1998) 87.

[4] GLEN (n 2 above) 55–59.

[5] A Palmer, *Less equal than others—a survey of lesbians and gay men at work* (London: Stonewall, 1993) 10.

The European Union has been generally wary of intervening in law and policy issues affecting gay men and lesbians. This reflects the great disparities that continue to exist between national laws in this area. Moreover, the divergence of state measures coincides with differing societal attitudes and responses to questions of sexual orientation. Variations in cultural, moral and religious beliefs make this a highly contested area. Nonetheless, the decision of the Council in November 2000 to prohibit sexual orientation discrimination in employment[6] ensures that this is, and will remain, a matter of shared responsibility between the Union and the Member States.

This chapter examines the approach of the EU institutions to sexual orientation discrimination. It traces the growth of a debate on the appropriate role for the Union,[7] through to the adoption of the Framework Directive on Equal Treatment in Employment and Occupation. Attention is also paid to the expanding litigation on this issue since 1996; in particular, the cases of *Grant v South-West Trains*[8] and *D and Sweden v Council*.[9]

I. Early debates in the EU institutions

Discrimination against lesbians and gay men has a long history, but the construction of their maltreatment as *discrimination*, and therefore unacceptable behaviour, is more recent. Indeed, it was 1985 before the first anti-discrimination provisions addressing sexual orientation were adopted in an EU Member State.[10] In this context, it is quite understandable that sexual orientation was not an issue debated in the drafting of the Treaty of Rome in 1957. In fact, the issue first found its way onto the EU policy agenda only as a spillover from a debate occurring within the Council of Europe.[11]

---

[6] Council Dir (EC) 2000/78 of 27 November 2000 establishing a general framework for equal treatment in employment and occupation [2000] OJ L303/16. See Annex 2.

[7] For more detail on the development of EC policy on sexual orientation during the 1980s and early 1990s, see M Bell, 'Sexual Orientation and Anti-Discrimination Policy: the European Community' in T Carver and V Mottier (eds), *The Politics of Sexuality* (London: Routledge, 1998).

[8] Case C–249/96 [1998] ECR I–621.

[9] Case T–264/97 *D v Council* [1999] Reports of European Community Staff Cases (ECR-SC) II-1; Cases C–122/99P and C–125/99P *D and Sweden v Council* [2001] ECR I–4319.

[10] See R Lalement, 'France' in N Beger, K Krickler, J Lewis and M Wuch (eds), *Equality for lesbians and gay men: a relevant issue in the civil and social dialogue* (Brussels: ILGA-Europe, 1998) 46.

[11] For more information on the Council of Europe and sexual orientation, see D Borrillo, 'Sexual orientation and human rights in Europe' in G Bhatia, J O'Neill, G Gael and P Bendin (eds), *Peace, justice and freedom—human rights challenges in the new millennium* (Alberta: University of Alberta Press, 2000).

In 1976, Jeffrey Dudgeon filed a complaint against the UK Government for a breach of ECHR, Article 8[12] alleging that his right to privacy was being contravened by the fact that consenting sexual relations between males remained a criminal offence in Northern Ireland. The Court of Human Rights agreed and held that a total prohibition on consenting male sexual relations was a breach of the Convention.[13]

The decision seems to have been the spur for MEPs to raise the issue in the European Parliament.[14] Following several motions from inside and outside the Parliament,[15] a report on the situation of lesbians and gay men was prepared.[16] In the ensuing debate, the rapporteur, Vera Squarcialupi, acknowledged that the study had been difficult, with 'very heated' debates founded on 'cultural and moral attitudes not easy to overcome'.[17] Indeed, there was strong opposition from a significant minority of Christian Democrats and UK Conservatives. For example, the Irish party, *Fine Gael*, abstained from voting on the Resolution on the basis that it exceeded Community competence: 'the Irish people are entitled to observe their own moral code and this Parliament has no right to dictate otherwise. [. . .] The EEC has no competence to decide the moral attitudes of society or the pattern of the criminal laws in the Member States.'[18]

Despite the objections, the Resolution was passed with 114 votes for, and 45 against.[19] It called on the Commission to submit proposals to ensure that

---

[12] '1. Everyone has the right to respect for his private and family life, his home and his correspondence.

2. There shall be no interference by a public authority with the exercise of this right except such as is in accordance with the law and is necessary in a democratic society in the interests of national security, public safety or the economic well-being of the country, for the prevention of disorder or crime, for the protection of health or morals, or for the protection of the rights and freedoms of others.'

[13] *Dudgeon v UK* (1981) Series A No 45.

[14] Homosexuality appears to have been mentioned only twice in the Parliament prior to 1984. First, in 1980, questions were placed concerning the refusal of visas by the US immigration authorities on the ground of homosexuality. The Council declared this matter was not 'within the Council's jurisdiction' (Written Question 1580/79; [1980] OJ C86/53). Second, in 1982, the treatment of homosexuals in the Soviet Union was discussed within the framework of a general debate on human rights in the USSR. See, Parliament, 'Report of the Committee on Political Affairs on human rights in the Soviet Union' [Bethell] A1-1364/82.

[15] EP Documents 1-172/82; 1-1072/82. A petition from the Dutch Labour Party's movement for gay and lesbian rights, PvdA Homogroep, was also submitted (Petition No 14/83; PE 85.093).

[16] Parliament, 'Report for the Committee on Social Affairs and Employment on sexual discrimination at the workplace' [Squarcialupi] A1-1358/83.

[17] Debates of the European Parliament No 1-311/12, 13 March 1984.

[18] Ryan, Debates of the European Parliament No 1-311/71, 13 March 1984.

[19] [1984] OJ C104/46.

'no cases arise in the Member States of discrimination against homosexuals with regard to access to employment and dismissals'.[20] On the whole, the report met with a favourable response from former Social Affairs Commissioner, Iver Richard. Yet, 'as a matter of practical politics', he could not foresee such a measure being acceptable to the Council of Ministers 'at least in the immediate future'.[21]

The Parliament again raised the issue in 1989, during the negotiations over the terms of the Social Charter.[22] In particular, it amended the Commission proposal to include a statement that priority should be given to 'the right of all workers to equal protection regardless of their nationality, race, religion, age, sex, *sexual preference* or legal status'.[23] The Commission rejected this proposal and replaced it with a more ambiguous text in the preamble, stating 'in order to ensure equal treatment, it is important to combat every form of discrimination, including discrimination on grounds of sex, colour, race, opinion and beliefs'.[24]

In reality, there was little prospect of the Parliament's various recommendations being accepted. It is worth recalling that consenting adult male sexual relations were still a criminal offence in one Member State (Ireland), whilst only one Member State (France) had taken the step of forbidding this type of discrimination in employment. With so little consensus at the national level, it was very unlikely that common measures at the Community level were going to find favour. Moreover, in a period when social policy as a whole made little progress, Spencer seems correct in his assessment that 'the Commission evidently decided that the issue was one on which it was fruitless to draw up proposals for legislation that would be rejected outright by the Council'.[25]

II. Incremental advances and competence expansion

With hindsight, the period of social activism that followed in the wake of the 1989 Social Charter marked the first genuine occasion when the Community,

---

[20] ibid para 5b.   [21] Debates of the European Parliament No 1–311/17, 13 March 1984.

[22] Calls for action against sexual orientation discrimination had also been included in two Parliamentary Resolutions from 1986. See Resolution on the rise of fascism and racism in Europe, para 2 [1986] OJ C141/462; Resolution on violence against women, para 12 [1986] OJ C176/73.

[23] Emphasis added, Parliament Resolution: [1989] OJ C323/44.

[24] *Social Europe* 1/90, 46.

[25] M Spencer, *States of Injustice—a guide to human rights and civil liberties in the European Union* (London: Pluto Press, 1995) 142.

principally through the Commission, actively engaged itself with sexual orientation issues. Three principal reasons for this turning point may be suggested; a coalition of common interests, spillover from policy on the fight against AIDS, and changes in national legislation.

First, in the early 1990s, a coincidence of forces supporting Community action on sexual orientation discrimination emerged unexpectedly. In the NGO sector, the UK lesbian and gay rights lobbying group, Stonewall, turned its attention to developments at the Community level, given the harsh domestic climate it faced under the Thatcher Government. Together with a number of other European groups, under the aegis of the International Lesbian and Gay Association (ILGA), it attempted the first systematic lobbying of the Commission, and held a number of meetings with officials from DGV[26] during the course of 1990.[27] Importantly, Stonewall sought to draw out an internal market dimension, by arguing that differences in the criminal law treatment of lesbians and gay men were creating barriers to free movement.[28] The approaches made by ILGA and Stonewall found a sympathetic ear; in the context of a general promotion of European social policy, the Commission seems to have been keen to encourage these examples of national organisations reorienting towards European-level lobbying. Therefore, a number of research projects dealing with lesbian and gay issues were authorised,[29] and recognition of harassment on grounds of sexual orientation was included in the 1991 Code of Practice on sexual harassment.[30]

A second factor of growing influence on the treatment of homosexuals, but especially gay men, was policy against AIDS. Undoubtedly the emergence of AIDS had very many negative effects on the gay rights movement.[31]

---

[26] Former Directorate-General for Employment, Industrial Relations and Social Affairs.

[27] 'Profile: Tim Barnett', *Equal Opportunities Rev* (1991) No 39, 32.

[28] ILGA and Stonewall, 'Harmonisation within the European Community—the reality for lesbians and gay men' (unpublished advice note prepared for the Commission, submitted 14 April 1990).

[29] In 1990, the Danish Gay and Lesbian Union received a grant of ECU 40,000 for research into the visibility of lesbians, with specific reference to lesbians in the labour market (D Saunders, 'Getting lesbian and gay issues on the international human rights agenda' (1996) 18 *Human Rights Q* 67, 87). This was followed up in 1993 with the publication of the Commission-funded report *Homosexuality: a European Community issue—essays on lesbian and gay rights in European law and policy* (A Clapham and K Waaldijk (eds) Dordrecht: Martinus Nijhoff, 1993).

[30] Commission Recommendation on the dignity of women and men at work, adopted 27 November 1991 [1992] OJ L49/1.

[31] For example, personnel were lost to the illness and scarce resources had to be redirected from law reform campaigning to meeting more immediate social needs in the gay community. Moreover, the initial hysteria provoked by the epidemic unleashed a further wave of discrimination, in new areas such as access to life insurance or mortgages. See U Vaid, *Virtual equality: the mainstreaming of gay and lesbian liberation* (New York: Anchor Books, 1996) 339.

Nonetheless, it also acted as a kind of catalyst for the mobilisation of gays and lesbians, and thus generated a much higher level of social visibility for their interests. As governments, and especially health departments, had to deal directly with gay groups, they became more sensitised to the problems they faced through discrimination. The connection between this trend and Community anti-discrimination initiatives lies in the role assumed by the Community in policies on AIDS from the mid-1980s onwards.[32] In particular, the emerging Community policy recognised the need to combat discrimination against seropositive persons.[33] For example, in 1990, the Council called on the Member States to 'extend the commitment to non-discrimination and social acceptance to those living with seropositive persons and people suffering from HIV/AIDS or to those who have contact with such persons'.[34] Whilst the impact of the various Resolutions adopted, or subsequent action programmes,[35] is difficult to quantify, it seems reasonable to assume that they gradually strengthened the arguments in favour of combating sexual orientation discrimination.[36]

Finally, the 1990s witnessed a steady transformation in the treatment of homosexuality by national law. This reflected the perception of a general increase in public acceptance of lesbians and gay men. Better organised lesbian and gay rights groups have increasingly sought the extension of existing anti-discrimination law provisions to cover sexual orientation discrimination. The success of this agenda is evidenced by the definitive trend in national law towards the inclusion of sexual orientation within anti-discrimination statutes (See Table 4.1). Clearly, the greater acceptance of homosexuality within national law has inevitably led to the creation of new opportunities for Community law to innovate in this field. The certainty of Member State hostility that prevented all progress in the 1980s has gradually been eroded, and as a result the Commission has been increasingly willing to test the limits of acceptability in the Council.

---

[32] Council Resolution of 29 May 1986 on AIDS [1986] OJ C184/21.

[33] Council Resolution of 22 December 1989 on the fight against AIDS [1990] OJ C10/3, para 1.

[34] Council conclusions of 3 December 1990 on AIDS [1990] OJ C329/21, para 2.

[35] For example, Decision (EC) 647/96 of the European Parliament and the Council of 29 March 1996 adopting a programme of Community action on the prevention of AIDS and certain other communicable diseases within the framework for action in the field of public health (1996–2000) [1996] OJ L95/16.

[36] See further R Bennet, C Erin and J Harris, *Research on bioethics: AIDS—ethics, justice and European policy* (Luxembourg: OOPEC, 1998).

Table 4.1 Legislation penalising sexual orientation discrimination in the Member States

Year in which legislation entered into force	Legislation on sexual orientation discrimination in employment[a]
1991	
1992	Netherlands
1993	Ireland
1994	Netherlands
1995	Spain, Finland
1996	Denmark
1997	Luxembourg
1998	
1999	Ireland, Sweden

[a] The Netherlands and Ireland appear twice due to subsequent extensions in the scope of the relevant legislation.

Legal and policy innovation by the Commission

Whilst the factors outlined above generated a more favourable environment, this is not to deny the reality that any discussion of sexual orientation issues remained highly sensitive. There was no sudden turnaround in policy development, but rather a gradualist evolution, often through rather subtle techniques of competency expansion on the part of the Commission.[37] Aside from the underlying political opposition that persisted in the Council of Ministers, the absence of an explicit reference to sexual orientation in the founding Treaties naturally constrained the freedom of the Commission to take initiatives in this area. Nonetheless, it pursued a number of minor measures that allowed the appearance of progress, if little changed in substance.

First, it is possible to identify a range of 'policy initiatives' that were taken to construct networks of interested actors. The Commission promoted various gay and lesbian community development programmes through small-scale financial subsidies.[38] In addition, the Commission also supported the

[37] L Cram, 'The European Commission as a multi-organization: social policy and IT policy in the European Union' (1994) 1 *J of Eur Public Policy* 195, 209.

[38] In Ireland, a 'Lesbian Education and Awareness' programme was funded under the aegis of the New Opportunities for Women programme. In April 1996, UK £90,000 was awarded to Foyle Friend, a gay and lesbian support service that operates in both Northern Ireland and the Republic

development of stronger structures for European lobbying on lesbian and gay issues. The activity in the early 1990s by Stonewall and ILGA was not sustained, mainly due to resource and organisational constraints within ILGA.[39] In 1997, a regional branch of ILGA, called ILGA-Europe, was established and there is no doubt that this has resulted in a significant enhancement in EU lobbying capacity. To support this, the Commission part-funded some preliminary research and networking activities.[40]

Alongside policy initiatives, the Commission also developed some minor legal innovations, namely soft law measures and non-discrimination clauses. Together with the binding legislative instruments (Regulations, Directives and Decisions), the EC Treaty also provides for non-binding legislative options.[41] These measures can play a role in gently promoting common legal norms. Sciarra argues that 'soft law can be used as a fulcrum against the standstill of European Social Policies, when hard law seems to be a far away achievement. It can anticipate future developments'.[42] Certainly, soft law has proven a relatively useful tool in this area. For example, in 1990 the Commission prepared a Code of Practice on sexual harassment. As mentioned earlier, this coincided with the lobbying efforts of Stonewall, and as a result[43] it contains the statement:

lesbians and women from racial minorities are disproportionately at risk. Gay men and young men are also vulnerable to harassment. It is undeniable that harassment on grounds of sexual orientation undermines the dignity of those affected and it is impossible to regard such harassment as appropriate workplace behaviour.[44]

---

of Ireland. The grant was provided under the EU Peace and Reconciliation Fund for Northern Ireland (Belfast Telegraph, 23 April 1996).

[39] Interview: Angela Mason, Stonewall, London, 10 January 1997; Interview: Suzy Byrne, GLEN, Dublin, 18 December 1996.

[40] See N Beger, K Krickler, J Lewis and M Wuch (eds), *Equality for lesbians and gay men: a relevant issue in the civil and social dialogue* (Brussels: ILGA-Europe, 1998).

[41] EC Treaty, Article 249 states: 'in order to carry out their tasks and in accordance with the provisions of this Treaty, the European Parliament acting jointly with the Council, the Council and the Commission shall make regulations and issue directives, take decisions, make recommendations or deliver opinions. . . . Recommendations and Opinions shall have no binding force.'

[42] S Sciarra, 'European Social Policy and Labour Law—Challenges and Perspectives' (1995) IV Collected Courses of the Academy of European Law 301, 340.

[43] Interview: Evelyn Collins, Belfast, 20 December 1996. E Collins, 'EU Sexual Harassment Policy' in R Elman (ed), *Sexual Politics and the European Union: the new Feminist Challenge* (Oxford: Berghahn Books, 1996) 31.

[44] Introduction, para 5, Commission Recommendation on the dignity of women and men at work, adopted 27 November 1991 [1992] OJ L49/1.

In general, the Code has been a productive instrument in terms of contributing to a variety of national-level actions against harassment.[45] Against this, the inherent limitation of non-binding measures is, of course, the discretion accorded to less committed Member States.[46] Certainly, there remain very few legal instruments on sexual orientation harassment at the national level. In the judicial context, there was an attempt in the UK to rely on the terms of the Code. In *Smith v Gardner Merchant Ltd*,[47] a gay barman taunted by a fellow employee because of his sexual orientation claimed that he had been subject to sexual harassment in contravention of the British Sex Discrimination Act 1975. In support of his application, the Code of Practice was cited. However, the Employment Appeal Tribunal felt that this, by itself, was not a sufficient basis for interpreting the statute as also forbidding sexual orientation harassment.[48]

In parallel to this soft law initiative, the Commission moved towards a more systematic recognition of non-discrimination requirements throughout EC legislation. The foundation for the Commission's approach was the case law of the Court of Justice concerning fundamental rights. As discussed in Chapter 1, a condition of the legality of Community law is respect for fundamental human rights, including the principle of non-discrimination. By inserting non-discrimination clauses into legislation, the Commission sought to provide a more express recognition of this principle, as well as clarifying the grounds to which non-discrimination requirements apply.

The first successful example of a non-discrimination clause can be found in the 'Television Without Frontiers' Directive from 1989.[49] Article 22 requires Member States to 'ensure that broadcasts do not contain any incitement to hatred on grounds of race, sex, religion or nationality'. A more systematic attempt to introduce such clauses was initiated in 1996 with a proposal in the Parental Leave Directive 'when Member States adopt the provisions to implement this Directive, they shall prohibit any discrimination based on

---

[45] Commission, 'Consultation of management and labour on the prevention of sexual harassment at work' COM (96) 373.

[46] J Gregory, 'Sexual Harassment—making the best use of European law' (1995) 2 *Eur J of Women's Studies* 421, 429.

[47] [1996] IRLR 342.

[48] The decision of the European Court of Justice in *Grant*, discussed later in this chapter, meant that the plaintiff did not pursue this line of reasoning at the Court of Appeal. Nonetheless, the English Court of Appeal ([1998] 3 All ER 852) ultimately held that harassment based on sexual orientation could be sex discrimination, but only if a male homosexual was the subject of harassment that would not also have been visited upon a female homosexual (Ward LJ, 868).

[49] Council Dir (EEC) 89/522 on the co-ordination of certain provisions laid down by law, regulation or administrative action in Member States concerning the pursuit of television broadcasting activities [1989] OJ L298/23.

race, sex, sexual orientation, colour, religion or nationality'.[50] However, the Council substituted this proposal with a clause in the preamble stating 'whereas the Community Charter on the Fundamental Social Rights of Workers recognizes the importance of the fight against all forms of discrimination, especially based on sex, colour, race, opinions and creeds'.[51] A similar pattern of events occurred in relation to the 1997 Part-Time Workers Directive,[52] and the 1998 Transfers of Undertakings Directive.[53] In both cases, the Council rejected the proposed non-discrimination clause and replaced it with a statement in the preamble referring to the Social Charter. No anti-discrimination clause was proposed for the 1999 Fixed-Term Workers Directive[54] and this strategy now appears to have been quietly dropped.

III. Free movement and same-sex partners

The Commission's various initiatives undoubtedly helped in sensitising EU policy-makers to sexual orientation issues, but little substantive progress can be identified. This reflects the weak location of sexual orientation discrimination within the market-driven character of European social policy. Stonewall and ILGA attempted to highlight an internal market dimension in their 1990 submission to the Commission. However, the differences in criminal law identified did not facilitate Community intervention as criminal law

[50] Article 2(3), Commission, 'Proposal for a Council Directive on the framework agreement on parental leave concluded by UNICE, CEEP, and the ETUC' COM (96) 26.

[51] Recital 17; Council Dir (EC) 96/34 of 3 June 1996 on the framework agreement on parental leave concluded by UNICE, CEEP and the ETUC [1996] OJ L145/4. For an account of the Council proceedings see, M Biagi, 'Fortune smiles on the Italian EU Presidency: talking half-seriously about the posted workers and parental leave directives' (1996) 12 Intl J of Comparative Labour L and Industrial Relations 97.

[52] Council Dir (EC) 97/81 on the framework agreement on part-time work concluded by UNICE, CEEP and the ETUC [1998] OJ L14/9.

[53] Council Dir (EC) 98/50 amending Dir (EEC) 77/187 on the approximation of the laws of Member States relating to the safeguarding of employees' rights in the event of transfers of undertakings, businesses or parts of businesses [1998] OJ L201/88. It should be noted that, in this case, the non-discrimination clause originated in an amendment by the Parliament ([1997] OJ C33/85).

[54] COM (99) 203: adopted without any anti-discrimination clause [1999] OJ L175/43. The Commission also omitted to propose an anti-discrimination clause in its draft Directive on the information and consultation rights of workers: Commission, 'Proposal for a Council Directive establishing a general framework for informing and consulting employees in the European Community' COM (1998) 612.

provisions were, at that time, firmly outside EC competence. A more direct link to the internal market has gradually revealed itself in relation to the legal recognition of same-sex partners.

The 1986 case of *Netherlands v Reed*[55] brought the issue into sharp focus. A British man moved to the Netherlands to take up an offer of work. His unmarried female partner came with him but, having failed to find any employment, she applied to the Dutch authorities for residence as his 'companion'. The case was eventually referred to the Court of Justice for clarification on the scope of Regulation (EEC) 1612/68, Article 10(1),[56] which, *inter alia*, entitles the migrant worker to be joined by his or her 'spouse' in the host state. The Court rejected the argument that an unmarried partner could be brought within the category of 'spouse':

The Community legislature used the word 'spouse' in the sense given to that word in family law. When, in support of a dynamic interpretation, reference is made to developments in social and legal conceptions, these developments must be visible in the whole of the Community; such an argument cannot be based on social and legal developments in only one or a few Member States. [. . .] As it now stands, it is impossible to speak of any consensus that unmarried companions should be treated as spouses.[57]

Nonetheless, the Court also held that the right to bring an unmarried partner into the state was capable of falling within the concept of a 'social advantage' for the purposes of Regulation (EEC) 1612/68, Article 7(2). As there must be no nationality discrimination in access to social advantages, any Member State which recognises unmarried partners for the purposes of its own domestic immigration law is consequently obliged to allow EU migrant workers to be accompanied by unmarried partners.[58]

Following the decision in *Reed*, the Commission proposed certain amendments to Regulation (EEC) 1612/68,[59] in order to bring the legislation into line with the Court judgment. The Parliament sought to amplify the proposal, and amended the draft text to extend residence rights to any person 'with whom the worker lives in a de facto union, recognised as such for administrative and legal purposes'.[60] Predictably, this was rejected by the Commission:

---

[55] Case 59/85 [1986] ECR 1283.   [56] [1968] OJ Spec Ed (II) 475.

[57] ibid paras 10–11.

[58] It should be noted that Art 7(2) is not found in other free movement legislation governing the free movement rights of students, retired persons or persons of independent means. Therefore, these individuals would have to rely on the general right to non-discrimination on grounds of nationality in EC Treaty, Art 12.

[59] Proposal for a Council Regulation (EEC) amending Reg (EEC) 1612/68 on free movement for workers within the Community [1989] OJ C100/6.

[60] [1990] OJ C68/88.

'We are reluctant to impinge on the traditional moral values and precepts, and often deeply-held religious perceptions, which exist in the various Member States in relation to this matter. [. . .] It is a fact that two Member States are prepared to accept such a provision. Equally, others are not.'[61]

Notwithstanding the Commission's caution, even its limited proposals failed to find a consensus in the Council and the amendment to Regulation (EEC) 1612/68 was never adopted.

In practice, it must be acknowledged that the presence of EU nationals in another Member State, even where they do not clearly enjoy a legal right to be present, is generally tolerated, unless there are public security reasons for the State to seek expulsion.[62] Such migrants remain though in an invidious state of quasi-legality. Their presence is tolerated precisely because it is assumed that they cannot make any claims on the state, such as welfare entitlements. Greater obstacles face unmarried couples where one partner is a third country national. In this instance, there is no right for the partner to join the EU migrant worker in another Member State (unless this is accepted for domestic nationals), and it may be very difficult in practice for the partner to enter and remain on the territory of the host state in the absence of express authorisation to do so.

In 1998, the Commission returned to this issue once again and it issued a new proposal to amend Regulation (EEC) 1612/68.[63] This aimed to reflect more expressly the judgment of the Court in *Reed*, by altering Article 10(1) to state that the worker is entitled to be joined by 'his spouse or any person corresponding to a spouse under the legislation of the host Member State'. A similar formulation has been adopted in the Commission's proposal for a Directive on family reunion rights, which would apply to refugees and legally resident third country immigrants (subject to certain restrictions). Family members are defined as 'the applicant's spouse, or an unmarried partner living in a durable relationship with the applicant, if the legislation of the Member State concerned treats the situation of unmarried couples as corresponding to that of married couples'.[64] These two proposals reflect the changes that have occurred at the national level where non-marital partnerships are increasingly accorded various forms of legal recognition.

[61] Vasso Papandreou, Debates of the European Parliament No 3-386/59, 13 February 1990.

[62] S Fries and J Shaw, 'Citizenship of the Union: first steps in the European Court of Justice' (1998) 4 Eur Public L 533, 547.

[63] Proposal for a European Parliament and Council Regulation amending Council Reg (EEC) 1612/68 on freedom of movement for workers within the Community [1998] OJ C344/9.

[64] Commission, 'Proposal for a Council Directive on the right to family reunification' COM (1999) 638, Art 5(1)(a).

Denmark (1989), Sweden (1995), the Netherlands (1998) and Finland (2001) have all adopted registered partnership laws that allow same-sex couples to enjoy almost all of the rights conferred by marriage.[65] Moreover, France,[66] Belgium,[67] Germany,[68] Portugal[69] and some regions of Spain[70] have adopted laws providing certain rights to same-sex couples, albeit considerably short of marriage. Most significantly though, since 1 April 2001, same-sex couples have been able to marry in the Netherlands.[71] The emergence of these new forms of partnership in law, together with the variety in the rights they confer, creates real challenges for EU free movement law. The proposals of the Commission aim to guarantee non-discrimination for EU and non-EU migrant workers in the spirit of the decision in *Reed*.[72] They fail to address the legal limbo facing registered partners who wish to move to another Member State where no form of recognition of same-sex couples exists in national law, or where this confers considerably less rights.[73] Previously the issue has been less pressing because only a small number of states possessed such laws and the number of individuals affected was

[65] See generally, R Wintemute and M Andenaes (eds), *Legal recognition of same sex partnerships—a study of national, European and international law* (Oxford: Hart Publishing, 2001). Also, S Jensen, 'La reconnaissance des préférences sexuelles: le modèle scandinave' in D Borrillo (ed), *Homosexualités et droit* (Paris: PUF, 1998). The new law in Finland is expected to enter into force in March 2002. See Euroletter, No 93, November 2001, available at: http://www.steff.suite.dk/eurolet.htm

[66] See further, D Borrillo, 'Le Pacte civil de solidarité: une reconnaissance timide des unions de même sexe' (2001) 3 Aktuelle Juristische Praxis 299.

[67] See O de Schutter and A Weyembergh, 'Statutory cohabitation under Belgian law: a step towards same-sex marriage?' in R Wintemute and M Andenaes (eds), *Legal recognition of same sex partnerships—a study of national, European and international law* (Oxford: Hart Publishing, 2001).

[68] See R Schimmel and S Heur, 'The legal situation of same-sex partnerships in Germany: an overview' in R Wintemute and M Andenaes (eds), *Legal recognition of same-sex partnership—a study of national, European and international law* (Oxford: Hart Publishing, 2001).

[69] Euroletter No 88, May 2001, ibid.

[70] F Salas, 'The stable unions law in Catalonia' in R Wintemute and M Andenaes (eds), *Legal recognition of same sex partnerships—a study of national, European and international law* (Oxford: Hart Publishing, 2001).

[71] Law of 21 December 2000 (Staatsblad 2001, no 9) on the opening up of marriage for same-sex partners: see further, K Waaldijk, 'Latest news about same-sex marriage in the Netherlands (and what it implies for foreigners)', available at: http://ruljis.leidenuniv.nl/user/cwaaldij/www/NHR/news.htm

[72] For example, an Italian gay man moving to work in the UK would be entitled to family reunion with his Brazilian partner as family reunion for same-sex couples is afforded to UK nationals under British immigration law (subject to various criteria).

[73] For example, a Dutch lesbian who enjoys a registered partnership with an Australian woman would not be entitled, under Community law, to be joined by her registered partner if she moves to work in Ireland, where same-sex couples are not recognised for immigration purposes.

relatively low. The spread of partnership laws, combined with a rapid increase in the number of persons participating, means that this is no longer a marginal phenomenon. For example, in France 29,855 couples registered under the 'Pacs' law during its first year.[74] In the Netherlands, 10,804 couples have registered their partnerships since 1998, of which 6,371 are same-sex couples.[75]

Inevitably the invisibility of these partnerships in EU law will provoke future litigation. To some extent, this has already been initiated from within EU institutions and agencies where various staff cases are pending.[76] Of these cases, the first to be concluded is *D and Sweden v Council*.[77] As mentioned in Chapter 1, a Swedish man challenged the denial by the EU Council (his employer) of family benefits in respect of his male partner. Before moving to Brussels, he had registered his partnership under Swedish law and enjoyed many of the rights of a married couple. Nonetheless, the Council regarded him as single for the purposes of the Staff Regulations. The Court of First Instance rejected his challenge to the denial of the benefit mainly by relying on the decision of the Court of Justice in *Grant v South-West Trains*, discussed later in this chapter. Therefore, it maintained that there was no breach of fundamental rights, as same-sex partnerships were not required to be accorded equal treatment with married couples under the European Convention on Human Rights.[78] Moreover, there was no sex discrimination as the rule in question applied equally to male and female homosexuals.[79] The term 'spouse' in the Staff Regulations was regarded as having a Community law definition, and this did not include registered partners. This aspect of the decision is particularly surprising given that 'spouse' is a status

[74] 'Le premier bilan du nombre de pacs signés est sensiblement inférieur aux prévisions', Le Monde, 29 January 2001.

[75] K Waaldijk, 'Latest news about same-sex marriage in the Netherlands (and what it implies for foreigners)' 30 March 2001, available at: http://ruljis.leidenuniv.nl/user/cwaaldij/www/NHR/InfoL&H.html

[76] Case T–102/99 *L v Commission* (Dutch registered partnership) [1999] OJ C188/29; Case T–167/00 *D v Commission* (same-sex stable union registered in Catalonia, Spain) [2000] OJ C247/35. Many thanks to Robert Wintemute for bringing these cases to my attention.

[77] Similar issues were raised in Case T–96/99 *Fleurbaay v Banque européenne d'investissement* [2000] OJ C233/28. This case concerned the non-recognition of a Dutch registered partnership by the European Investment Bank. However, the Court of First Instance held the complaint to be inadmissible because the act being challenged (a letter from the Bank to the applicant) was not capable of producing legal effects and consequently it was not a reviewable act.

[78] Case T–264/97 *D v Council* [1999] Reports of European Community Staff Cases (ECR-SC) II–1, para 39.

[79] para 43.

that can only be conferred through national law.[80] Scappucci also points out that under Swedish law someone in a registered partnership cannot legally marry another person, therefore it was disingenuous of the Court of First Instance to regard D as unmarried.[81]

D and Sweden appealed the decision to the Court of Justice.[82] At this stage, the free movement dimension to the case was stressed, given the lack of success at the Court of First Instance in a discrimination or human rights-based argument. D and Sweden argued that the failure of the Council to recognise the registered partnership created an unlawful obstacle to free movement.[83] This argument is founded on the principle most famously enounced in the *Bosman* decision: 'Provisions which preclude or deter a national of a Member State from leaving his country of origin in order to exercise his right to freedom of movement therefore constitute an obstacle to that freedom even if they apply without regard to the nationality of the workers concerned.'[84]

The facts of D appear to fall comfortably within the definition of an obstacle given by the Court in *Bosman*.[85] Ultimately, the Court of Justice held this argument to be inadmissible because it was not raised during the initial legal proceedings before the CFI.[86]

With regard to D's marital status, the Court decided that it was not possible to assimilate such a partnership to marriage. Whilst the Court acknowledged the growth in national laws giving legal recognition to same-sex partnerships, it concluded that 'the fact that, in a limited number of Member States, a registered partnership is assimilated, although incompletely, to marriage cannot have the consequence that, by mere interpretation, persons whose legal status is distinct from that of marriage can be covered by the term "married official" as used in the Staff Regulations'.[87]

This aspect of the decision suggests that registered partners will also face difficulties in trying to rely on Regulation (EEC) 1612/68 before the Court. More testing will be the response of the Court to Dutch *married* same-sex partners. Although these couples are unequivocally spouses within their

---

[80] C Denys, 'Homosexuality: A Non-Issue in Community Law?' (1999) 24 ELR 419, 421.

[81] G Scappucci, 'Court of First Instance refuses to recognize Swedish "Registered Partnership" rights and duties' (2000) 6 Eur Public L 355, 361.

[82] Cases C–122/99P and C–125/99P [2001] ECR I–4319.   [83] ibid para 53.

[84] Case C–415/93 *Union Royale Belge des Sociétés de Football Association ASBL v Bosman* [1995] ECR I–4921, 5069.

[85] See further, E Guild, 'Free movement and same-sex relationships: existing EC law and Article 13 EC' in R Wintemute and M Andenaes (eds), *Legal recognition of same sex partnerships—a study of national, European and international law* (Oxford: Hart Publishing, 2001).

[86] paras 55–56.   [87] para 39.

national legal system, the Court's approach in *D and Sweden v Council* was to impose a European definition on what constitutes marriage, independent of the situation in any individual or group of states. Therefore, even married same-sex partners cannot be sure of recognition as spouses for the purposes of Community law.

The free movement rationale for Community intervention is crucial from the perspective of the market integration model. It was also identified in Chapter 3 as important in pushing forward policy development on racism. In relation to sexual orientation discrimination, the market integration logic would suggest the EU should first act to harmonise rules on same-sex partnerships or to introduce some form of mutual recognition,[88] as this is the area where the most obvious barriers to free movement exist.[89] Yet, this touches on issues of particular cultural and religious sensitivity, as well as family law, which is mainly a national law competence. The adoption of national laws on the recognition of same-sex partnerships has been occasionally accompanied by highly divisive debates,[90] and it is unsurprising that the Union is reluctant to intervene. This provides a clear example of the limitations in a purely market integration-based social policy. One might also argue that the general differences in the level of protection against sexual orientation discrimination create barriers to free movement—for example a Dutch lesbian might be reluctant to work in Greece where the legal situation is likely to be less favourable. Nonetheless, it is simultaneously true that sexual orientation discrimination can perversely encourage the exercise of free movement rights—with some lesbians and gays migrating from states with limited public space for homosexuality to those states (or more often the large cities therein) where the social and legal situation is more favourable.[91] Therefore, an internal market perspective does not, by itself, provide a convincing rationale for EU intervention in sexual orientation discrimination. This weak nexus to the market helps understand the slow progress experienced in this policy area.

---

[88] In 1995, Denmark, Norway and Sweden concluded a treaty obliging the mutual recognition of registered partnerships made in any of the signatory states: K Waaldijk, 'Free Movement of Same-Sex Partners' (1996) 3 Maastricht J of Eur and Comparative L 271.

[89] See also R Elman, 'The limits of citizenship: migration, sex discrimination and same-sex partners in EU law' (2000) 38 J of Common Market Studies 729.

[90] D Borrillo, 'L'homophobie dans le discours des jurists autour du débat sur l'union entre personnes de même sexe' in L-G Tin and G Pastre (eds), *Homosexualités, expression/repression* (Paris: Stock, 1999).

[91] See further, G Valentine, 'An equal place to work? Anti-lesbian discrimination and sexual citizenship in the European Union' in M García-Ramon and J Monk (eds) *Woman of the European Union—the politics of work and daily life* (London: Routledge, 1996); J Binnie, 'Invisible Europeans: sexual citizenship in the New Europe' (1997) 29 *Environment and Planning* A 237.

IV. Amending the EC Treaty

It seems fair to remark that the inclusion of sexual orientation in EC Treaty, Article 13 was rather unexpected.[92] Unlike the race or disability lobbies, there had not been a very extensive lobbying effort by lesbian and gay NGOs to support such a Treaty amendment, nor had the amendment received specific backing from the European Commission. Therefore, it is of some importance to identify how such a significant step forward was accomplished. In particular, it is possible to highlight the role of the European Parliament and the 'bandwagon effect'.

(a) The role of the European Parliament

In contrast to the hesitant approach of the Commission, the Parliament attempted to kick-start EU policy on sexual orientation through the 1994 *Roth report*. The own-initiative report proposed sweeping legal reforms to provide 'at least' for an end to 'any discrimination in criminal, civil, contract and commercial law' and 'all forms of discrimination in labour and public service law'.[93] It also demanded the creation of a European 'equivalent legal framework' to marriage for same-sex couples and the extension of adoption rights to same-sex couples.[94] Unsurprisingly, the report proved deeply divisive within the Parliament. Support was strongest amongst MEPs from the Green and the Socialist groups, and correspondingly, support was weakest amongst the Christian Democrats and other right-wing factions. Alongside the normal party political divisions were discernible differences based on MEPs' national background. For example, Dutch Christian Democrats proved largely supportive of the Resolution, despite the formal opposition of their group. This illustrates the impact of national cultural traditions in shaping attitudes to issues of sexual orientation.

Significant opposition was based on arguments surrounding Community legal competence, and respect for the principle of subsidiarity.[95] Underlying

---

[92]   K Berthou and A Masselot, 'La CJCE et les couples homosexuels' (1998) 12 Droit Social 1034.

[93]   Parliament, 'Report for the Committee on Internal Affairs and Citizens Rights on Equal Rights for Homosexuals and Lesbians in the European Community' [Roth] A3-28/94, Art 14.

[94]   ibid.

[95]   'there are going to be difficulties in terms of subsidiarity in many of our countries where laws relating to such issues as adoption and marriage would make it impossible to accept those elements in her [the Rapporteur] report': M Banotti (Ireland) Debates of the European Parliament No 3-442/43, 7 February 1994.

this debate was the reality that many MEPs also objected to the substance of the proposals. The justifications presented for this opposition drew on a mixture of cultural and religious arguments. For example, several speakers criticised same-sex partnership rights as being contrary to the traditional notion of the family in their national culture. Other speakers explicitly sought to advance religious reasons for their opposition.[96] These twin arguments were neatly summarised by Deputy Guidolin: 'it is unacceptable to claim the right to marriage and adoption. Such claims upset the foundation of such essential institutions as the family . . . it is inconceivable that during the International Year of the Family, the European Parliament, which represents peoples stemming from a Christian background, should devote its time to legitimizing false families.'[97]

The extreme sensitivity of this issue was further demonstrated by the intervention of Pope John Paul II, who criticised the Resolution in a public address at the Vatican. On the one hand, the Pope reaffirmed the opposition of the Church to 'unjust discrimination' against homosexuals, but, on the other, he stated that by adopting the Resolution, the Parliament was requesting the legitimisation of a moral disorder.[98] This intervention by the religious authorities was also evident in Ireland, where one MEP who voted for the Resolution was heavily criticised and subject to an organised attempt to defeat her at the European elections, which followed four months after the debate.[99]

Ultimately, the Resolution was adopted.[100] Clearly, it stands open to the criticism that by being so ambitious it made it easier for the Commission to dismiss the Resolution as well beyond any competence it enjoyed and politically unsustainable.[101] Nevertheless, it provided a degree of acceptance for the full agenda of lesbian and gay rights not previously demonstrated by any European legislative institution. As such it was an important symbolic statement in favour of equality, and its central elements have since been regularly reaffirmed by the

---

[96] 'It is antiscriptural and is severely denounced in the Bible which is the Word of God.', I Paisley (Northern Ireland) Debates of the European Parliament No 3-442/72, 8 February 1994.

[97] Guidolin (Italy) Debates of the European Parliament No 3-442/43, 7 February 1994.

[98] 'In essa non si sono semplicemente prese le difese delle persona con tendenze omosessuali, rifiutando ingiuste discriminazioni nei loro confronti. Su questo anche la Chiesa è d'accordo . . . ma si deve dire che con la risoluzione del Parlamento europeo si è chiesto di legittimare un disordine morale', comments reproduced in G Perico, 'Il Parlamento Europeo e i diritti degli omosessuali' (1994) 9/10 *Aggiornamenti Sociali* 593, 601.

[99] Interview: Mary Banotti MEP, Dublin, 19 December 1996.

[100] 159 votes for, 96 against; Resolution on equal rights for homosexuals and lesbians in the EC [1994] OJ C61/40.

[101] Commissioner Bruce Millan, Debates of the European Parliament No 3-442/43, 7 February 1994.

Parliament in the context of its annual report on human rights in the EU.[102]

(b) The bandwagon effect

The most lasting effect of the Roth report is probably the raised profile it generated for sexual orientation discrimination in the Treaty reform negotiations. As discussed in Chapter 3, after 1993, the Starting Line Group and others were campaigning actively for an amendment of the EC Treaty to create a specific competence for measures against racial discrimination. Similarly, in 1993, the European Disabled People's Parliament called for the insertion of a general anti-discrimination clause in the EC Treaty.[103] Following the Roth report, it was clear that, at least for the European Parliament, sexual orientation was also on the agenda.[104] This was further confirmed by the conclusions of the European Council's Reflection Group on the reform of the Treaties, which stated: 'many of us think it important that the Treaty should clearly proclaim European values such as equality between men and women, non-discrimination on grounds of race, religion, sexual orientation, age or disability'.[105]

By the stage of the December 1996 'Dublin draft' of the amending Treaty, it was evident that there would be an anti-discrimination amendment. A strong campaign by NGOs, together with the support of the Parliament, Commission and many Member States had made this inevitable. However, at no stage in the negotiations was it certain that sexual orientation would definitely be included in the amendment. Indeed, there were clear reservations on the part of some Member States, specifically pertaining to this ground.

First, in spring 1996, the Italian Presidency deleted sexual orientation from the drafts of the new Treaty, but this was reinstated following the change in government in Italy to the Ulivo coalition.[106] The Irish Presidency, backed by

---

[102] See Parliament, 'Annual report of the Committee on Civil Liberties and Internal Affairs on respect for human rights in the European Union in 1994' [Esteban Martin] A4-223/96; Parliament, 'Annual report on respect for human rights in the European Union (1995)' [Roth] A4-112/97; Parliament, 'Report of the Committee on Civil Liberties and Internal Affairs on respect for human rights in the European Union (1996)' [Pailler] A4-34/98; Parliament, 'Report of the Committee on Civil Liberties and Internal Affairs on respect for human rights in the European Union (1997)' [Schaffner] A4-468/98; Resolution on respect for human rights in the European Union (1998–1999) [2000] OJ C377/344.

[103] M Bell and L Waddington, 'The 1996 Intergovernmental conference and the prospects of a non-discrimination Treaty article' (1996) 25 ILJ 320, 328.

[104] [1994] OJ C61/40, para 3.

[105] EU Council, 'Reflection Group report and other references for documentary purposes' (Brussels: General Secretariat of the Council of the European Union, 1995) 22.

Italy and Austria,[107] proved supportive to the inclusion of sexual orientation following concerted domestic lobbying,[108] but the Dublin draft noted the caution of some Member States.[109] As an attempted compromise, in March 1997, the Dutch Presidency tried to focus the new article through the deletion of social origin, disability, age and sexual orientation. However, this decision was publicised by Green MEP Nel van Dijk, and following protests by the Parliament and NGOs, the Dutch Government decided to reinstate all the deleted categories, bar social origin.[110]

Therefore, by the time of the Amsterdam European Council in June 1997, a kind of 'bandwagon' had been set in train, with no state apparently wishing to be seen as openly objecting to anti-discrimination measures for any of the grounds in the draft Article. It may be that some states were secretly hoping the UK would provide an obstructive veto,[111] but the change of government in May 1997 removed the final dangers to the agreement of the full Article 13. So it was that, despite the lack of a strong lobby or widespread governmental support, sexual orientation entered into the EC Treaty.

V. Equality litigation and the EU courts

The Treaty of Amsterdam entered into force on 1 May 1999, and eighteen months later the Framework Directive was adopted. In the intervening period, sexual orientation discrimination grew in prominence within EU law, mainly due to two key test cases on the subject. Lesbian and gay rights groups have generally employed two techniques to promote law reform; lobbying parliamentarians and governments for legislative change, and bringing test cases to challenge the validity and scope of existing laws in a range of judicial

[106] Bell and Waddington (n 103 above) 336.

[107] 'Dutch government rules out European equality for older people, lesbians and gay men and disabled people', Euroletter No 49, April 1997. Available at: http://www.steff.suite.dk/eurolet.htm

[108] Interview: Suzy Byrne, GLEN, Dublin, 16 December 1996.

[109] 'With regard to the categories of discrimination against which action could be taken by the Community, further detailed examination by the Conference will be required in order to agree a definitive list and precise definitions', Art 6a, Comment 1; Conference of the Representatives of the Governments of the Member States, 'European Union Today and Tomorrow—adapting the European Union for the benefit of its peoples and preparing it for the future. A general outline for a draft revision of the Treaties' European Report (Supplement) No 2183, 14 December 1996.

[110] For a detailed account of these proceedings, see generally, Euroletter No 49, April 1997: http://www.steff.suite.dk/eurolet.htm

[111] European Disability Forum, *Guide to the Amsterdam Treaty* (Brussels: EDF, 1998) 20.

forums.[112] The former seems the most satisfactory means of proceeding as it relies on achieving law reform through persuading the legislature of the merits of anti-discrimination laws. Nonetheless, where the legislature has set its face firmly against law reform, then it has become common for interest groups of all hues to turn to the courts, as a means of short-circuiting an intransigent policy process.[113]

The history of legislative intransigence at the EU level pre-Amsterdam encouraged some organisations to promote change through a European litigation strategy. In particular, in the UK, Stonewall sought to promote European litigation as a means to challenge the reluctance of successive UK Governments to forbid (or repeal) sexual orientation discrimination. Until 1996, this litigation focused on domestic courts and the European Court of Human Rights.[114] However, the decision of the Court of Justice in *P v S and Cornwall County Council*[115] caused attention to turn to the prospects at Luxembourg.

(a) P v S and Cornwall County Council

P v S concerned the dismissal of a transsexual woman following a decision to undergo gender reassignment to change her physical sex from male to female. Subsequently, an English industrial tribunal decided to stay the proceedings and referred the case to the Court of Justice, for a determination as to whether discrimination on the basis of gender reassignment was discrimination on the ground of sex, contrary to the Equal Treatment Directive. The Court issued its judgment on 30 April 1996, finding that Article 5(1)[116] of the Directive precluded the dismissal of a person for a reason related to gender

---

[112]   N Bamforth, *Sexuality, Morals and Justice* (London: Cassell, 1997) 23.

[113]   For example, the British Equal Opportunities Commission has frequently employed a test case strategy to push back the frontiers of sexual discrimination law. See, C Barnard, 'A European litigation strategy: the case of the Equal Opportunities Commission' in J Shaw and G More (eds), *New Legal Dynamics of European Union* (Oxford: Clarendon Press, 1995).

[114]   The principal case concerned a challenge to the ban on homosexual persons serving in the UK military, which was ultimately referred to the Court of Human Rights: *R v Ministry of Defence, ex p Smith* [1995] All ER 427 QBD, 7 June 1995; [1996] 1 All ER 257 CA, 3 November 1995. See, P Skidmore, 'No gays in the military, Lawrence of Arabia need not apply' (1995) 24 ILJ 363; P Skidmore, 'Homosexuals have human rights too' (1996) 25 ILJ 63.

[115]   Case C–13/94 ECR [1996] I–2143. See further: P Skidmore, 'Can transsexuals suffer sex discrimination?' (1997) 19 JSWFL 105, A Campbell and H Lardy, 'Discrimination against transsexuals in employment' (1996) 21 ELR 412, C Barnard, 'P v S: kite flying or Constitutional Charter' in A Dashwood and S O'Leary (eds), *The principle of equal treatment in European Community law* (London: Sweet & Maxwell, 1997).

[116]   'Application of the principle of equal treatment with regard to working conditions, including the conditions governing dismissal, means that men and women shall be guaranteed the same conditions without discrimination on grounds of sex.'

reassignment. In particular, the Court noted that the discrimination was 'based, essentially if not exclusively, on the sex of the person concerned'.[117] Moreover, 'to tolerate such discrimination would be tantamount, as regards such a person, to a failure to respect the dignity and freedom to which he or she is entitled, and which the Court has a duty to safeguard.'[118]

The open-ended nature of the decision in *P v S* suggested that the Court could see fit to extend this logic to sexual orientation discrimination, as another instance of discrimination which was based 'essentially if not exclusively' on sex. So, when this argument was raised in legal proceedings in July 1996, an English industrial tribunal decided to refer the question to the Court of Justice. Ironically, this referral came within weeks of the agreement of the Treaty of Amsterdam, and EC Treaty, Article 13.

(b) Grant v South-West Trains

Employees of South-West Trains (SWT) were entitled to free travel for their partners, married or unmarried. This was though subject to the condition that the partner is of the opposite sex, and on this ground Lisa Grant was refused free travel for her female partner, a loss of benefits equivalent to approximately €1500 per annum.[119] Lisa Grant subsequently brought a case against SWT, alleging that its refusal to supply the travel concession in respect of her partner was in breach of the former EC Treaty, Article 119. The cornerstone of her sex discrimination claim rested on the argument that if a man living with a woman in a non-marital relationship is entitled to the free travel benefit, then it is sexual discrimination to refuse the benefit in respect of a woman living with a woman in a non-marital relationship. On 17 February 1998, the Court of Justice held that the refusal to supply travel concessions to the same-sex partner of an employee, where such concessions were provided for opposite-sex partners, whether married or unmarried, was not discrimination prohibited under Article 119:

travel concessions are refused to a male worker if he is living with a person of the same sex, just as they are to a female worker if she is living with a person of the same sex. Since the condition imposed by the undertaking's regulations applies in the same way to male and female workers it cannot be regarded as constituting discrimination directly based on sex.[120]

The decision in *Grant* generated a large volume of academic comment.[121]

---

[117] [1996] ECR I–2143, para 21.   [118] ibid para 22.
[119] Case C–249/96 [1998] ECR I–621, 629.   [120] ibid 646.

At this juncture, it is useful to consider the significance of the case in retrospect. The adoption of the Framework Directive (see later in this chapter) might suggest that *Grant* is historically interesting, but not so important in the long run. Admittedly, the heated debates over whether sexual orientation could be squeezed within the framework of gender discrimination laws could be expected to fade now that specific and separate protection against sexual orientation discrimination exists in Community law. Nonetheless, there are a number of implications from *Grant* that continue to be relevant.

First, *Grant* was crucial in creating a separation in Community law between 'sex' and 'sexual orientation'. *P v S* moved Community law in the direction of a broader concept of gender discrimination, but *Grant* emphasised the limits to this approach. As a consequence, sexual orientation has received specific recognition in the Framework Directive and the EU Charter of Fundamental Rights.[122] In contrast, discrimination by reason of gender reassignment has been submerged within the general category of 'sex'.[123] *Grant* encouraged the Union to address sexual orientation issues in an overt and direct fashion that may prove to be ultimately more beneficial than covert inclusion in the gender equality legal framework. Although ini-

---

[121] See, *inter alia*, K Armstrong, 'Tales of the Community: sexual orientation discrimination and EU law' (1998) 20 JSWFL 455; N Bamforth, 'Sexual orientation discrimination after *Grant v South-West Trains*' (2000) 63 MLR 694; C Barnard, 'Some are more equal than others: the decision of the Court of Justice in *Grant v South-West Trains*' (1998) 1 Cambridge Yrbk of Legal Studies 147; N Beger, 'Queer readings of Europe: gender identity, sexual orientation and the (im)potency of rights politics at the European Court of Justice' (2000) 9 Social and Legal Studies 249; M Bell, 'Shifting conceptions of sexual discrimination at the Court of Justice: from *P v S* to *Grant v SWT*' (1999) 5 ELJ 63; K Berthou and A Masselot, 'La CJCE et les couples homosexuels' (1998) 12 *Droit Social* 1034; N Burrows, 'Sex and sexuality in the European Court' (1998) 14 Intl J of Comparative Labour L and Industrial Relations 153; P Cabral, 'Arrêt Grant' (1998) *Revue du Marché Unique Européen* 254; I Canor, 'Equality for lesbians and gay men in the European Community legal order' (2000) 7 Maastricht J of Eur and Comparative L 273; T Connor, 'Community discrimination law: no right to equal treatment in employment in respect of same sex partner' (1998) 23 ELR 378; S Greco, 'Nuovi sviluppi in materia di tutela dei diritti fondamentali' (1999) Rivista italiana di diritto pubblico comunitario 1369; B Guiguet, 'Le droit communautaire et la reconnaissance des partenaires de même sexe' (1999) Cahiers de droit européen 537; L Idot, 'Homosexualité, droit communautaire, et Traité d'Amsterdam' (1998) 4 (April) Europe 3; C Stychin, '*Grant*-ing rights: the politics of rights, sexuality and European Union' (2000) 51 Northern Ireland Legal Q 281; S Terrett, 'A bridge too far? Non-discrimination and homosexuality in European Community law' (1998) 4 EPL 487; C Tobler, 'Europe: same-sex couples under the law of the EU' (2001) 3 Aktuelle Juristische Praxis 269.

[122] EU Charter, Art 21(1).

[123] ILGA-Europe sought to add 'gender identity' to the list of prohibited grounds of discrimination in the EU Charter of Fundamental Rights as an explicit reference to discrimination related to gender reassignment, however this proposal was not adopted: Doc CHARTE 4246/00, CONTRIB 119, Brussels 19 April 2000.

tially it seemed that the failure of the *Grant* case might alienate lesbian and gay rights organisations from engaging in EU law and policy debates, *Grant* reinforced the reasons why legislation implementing EC Treaty, Article 13 was essential.[124] The swift steps to adopt the Framework Directive should restore the relevance of the Union for national NGOs in this area.

Second, *Grant* has proven influential in setting standards for the treatment of same-sex partners by Community law. Crucially, in its decision the Court rejected the argument that discrimination against same-sex partners was in breach of the general principle of respect for fundamental rights: 'in the present state of law within the Community, stable relationships between two persons of the same sex are not regarded as equivalent to marriages or stable relationships outside marriage between two persons of the opposite sex'.[125] The significance of this statement was revealed by the decision of the Court of First Instance (CFI) in *D v Council*.[126] The CFI relied on the principle in *Grant* to reject D's argument that his fundamental rights had been infringed.[127] Advocate-General Mischo took this argument a stage further in his opinion on the appeal of the decision in *D v Council* to the Court of Justice. He concluded that the statements in *Grant* reflected a general principle in Community law that same-sex and opposite-sex partnerships are not equivalent.[128] Moreover, this was not by reason of differences in the legal status of such relationships, but by virtue of differences 'in nature' between homosexual and heterosexual couples.[129]

In its judgment in *D and Sweden v Council*, the Court rejected the approach of the Advocate-General, making it clear that *Grant* could not be simply extended to the situation of D because there was a legal recognition of his relationship, whereas in *Grant* it was purely a *de facto* union.[130] Nonetheless, the Court still held the general principle of equal treatment to be inapplicable where the differential treatment was between a registered partnership and a married partnership. Crucially, the Court held that this was not a comparable situation:

The existing situation in the Member States of the Community as regards recogni-

---

[124] D Borrillo, 'L'orientation sexuelle en Europe—esquisse d'une politique publique antidiscriminatoire' (July/August 2000) *Le Temps Modernes* 263, 273.

[125] [1998] ECR I–621, 648.

[126] Case T–264/97 *D v Council* [1999] Reports of European Community Staff Cases (ECR-SC) II–1.

[127] ibid para 28.

[128] Cases C–122/99P and C–125/99P *D and Sweden v Council* [2001] ECR I–4319, para 86.

[129] ibid para 87.

[130] Cases C–122/99P and C–125/99P *D and Sweden v Council* [2001] ECR I–4319, para 33.

tion of partnerships between persons of the same sex or of the opposite sex reflects a great diversity of laws and the absence of any general assimilation of marriage and other forms of statutory union . . . In those circumstances, the situation of an official who has registered a partnership in Sweden cannot be held to be comparable, for the purposes of applying the Staff Regulations, to that of a married official.[131]

The entrenchment of this principle of inequality marks a worrying trend in Community law. Whilst it remains true that the majority of Member States do not legally recognise same-sex partnerships, as noted earlier, this is a situation that is changing rapidly. The Court's statement refers to the 'existing situation' in the Community and hence leaves open the door for a revision of this approach at a later stage. Nonetheless, it would be optimistic to expect such a change in the near future.

The blindness of the EU Courts to same-sex partnerships appears to be an institutional legacy of *Grant*.[132] Their caution confirms the observation by Harrison that in diverse fields, they tend to 'avoid making far-reaching decisions which challenge important institutions such as marriage and the family'.[133] This conservatism must be borne in mind when analysing the possibilities under the Framework Directive and how the Court of Justice can be expected to interpret areas of ambiguity.

VI. The Framework Directive

In its decision in *Grant*, the Court drew attention to EC Treaty, Article 13 (not then ratified) as an indication that should the Union wish to prohibit sexual orientation discrimination, it would shortly enjoy the legal powers to do so.[134]

---

[131]   C–125/99P *D and Sweden v Council* [2001] ECR I–4319, paras 50–51.

[132]   In contrast, the Court was prepared to make an exception for an unmarried opposite-sex couple in Case C–65/98 *Eyüp v Landesgeschäftsstelle des Arbeitsmarktservice Vorarlberg* [2000] ECR I–4747. In that case, a Turkish national sought to rely on the family reunion provisions of Decision 1/80 made pursuant to the EEC–Turkey Association Agreement. Mrs Eyüp was authorised to reside in Austria with her husband, but they subsequently divorced. However, they remained living together and eventually remarried. Mrs Eyüp sought to rely on the period when they lived together (although unmarried) in order to establish certain rights under the Agreement. The Court emphasised that the objective of the family reunion provisions was 'de facto family unity in the host Member State' and as a result 'the Eyüps' period of extra-marital cohabitation . . . cannot be regarded as an interruption of their joint family life in Austria' (paras 34 and 36).

[133]   V Harrison, 'Using EC law to challenge sexual orientation discrimination at work' in T Hervey and D O'Keeffe (eds), *Sexual Equality in the European Union* (Chichester: John Wiley and Sons, 1996) 280.

As already described in Chapter 3, in 1999 the Commission proposed a package of anti-discrimination initiatives for the initial implementation of Article 13. Whereas racial discrimination was the subject of a specific proposed Directive,[135] sexual orientation discrimination was to be addressed through the proposal for a general 'Framework Directive' forbidding discrimination in employment on a range of grounds.[136] In retrospect, the package of measures was a type of 'each-way' bet from the Commission—there was no declared priority or order for the proposals, although it was recognised that whichever was adopted first would significantly determine the content of the other.[137]

Events in Austria secured the primacy of the Racial Equality Directive, but this also conferred indirect benefits for the Framework Directive. Most of the key definitions and features of the Racial Equality Directive were subsequently transported into the Framework Directive, reducing the outstanding points of contention. Moreover, the French Presidency in the second half of 2000 immediately sought to build on the momentum from the Racial Equality Directive, and political agreement on the Framework Directive was reached in Council on 17 October 2000.[138]

At its core, the Directive forbids discrimination on the grounds of religion or belief, age, disability and sexual orientation in employment.[139] In respect of religion or belief and sexual orientation, national implementing measures must be in place by 2 December 2003.[140] For age and disability, there is the possibility for Member States to extend this period by a further three years. In many aspects, the Directive mirrors the Racial Equality Directive. For example, 'unlawful discrimination' is defined as direct and indirect discrimination, harassment and an instruction to discriminate.[141] There is provision for positive action and various enforcement mechanisms, all very similar to the Racial Equality Directive. However, the wider grounds covered by the Framework Directive raised a diverse range of sensitive questions where

---

[134] [1998] ECR I–621, 651.

[135] Commission, 'Proposal for a Council Directive implementing the principle of equal treatment between persons irrespective of racial or ethnic origin' COM (1999) 566.

[136] Commission, 'Proposal for a Council Directive establishing a general framework for equal treatment in employment and occupation' COM (1999) 565. See further, L Waddington, 'Article 13 EC: setting priorities in the proposal for a horizontal employment Directive' (2000) 20 ILJ 176.

[137] COM (1999) 564, 8.

[138] See further, P Skidmore, 'The EC Framework Directive on Equal Treatment in Employment: towards a comprehensive Community anti-discrimination policy?' (2001) 30 ILJ 126.

[139] Council Dir (EC) 2000/78 of 27 November 2000 establishing a general framework for equal treatment in employment and occupation [2000] OJ L303/16, Art 2. See Annex 2 below.

[140] Art 18.   [141] Art 2.

the Member States had strong differences of opinion. In order to allow for the swift agreement of the Directive, many of these detailed concerns were accommodated through a variety of exceptions and derogations, which have resulted in a more complex and ambivalent text than the Racial Equality Directive. The points of divergence between the two Directives can be divided between general exceptions and omissions in the Framework Directive and measures related to specific grounds of discrimination therein.

(a) General exceptions and omissions

The most fundamental difference between the two Directives lies in their material scope. The Framework Directive only applies to employment.[142] Moreover, it expressly precludes application to 'payments of any kind made by state schemes or similar, including state social security or social protection schemes'.[143] The strict contours of the Directive are reinforced in the preamble. Recital 13 states that it does not apply to 'any kind of payment by the State aimed at providing access to employment or maintaining employment'. This suggests that state employment schemes to facilitate access or a return to the labour market might not fall within the scope of the Framework Directive. This is a problematic exception given the growth in such forms of employment, especially as the provision of such programmes is promoted under the aegis of the European Employment Strategy.[144]

The second key difference between the Directives is the absence in the Framework Directive of any requirement to establish a body for the promotion of equal treatment. Therefore, Member States are free to establish a body that is only competent to deal with claims of racial discrimination. This difference between the texts of the two Directives is particularly difficult to justify. There is no obvious reason why the quality of the enforcement mechanisms should vary according to the ground of discrimination. Moreover, the differences thereby drawn between the Directives ignore situations of multiple discrimination. For example, where an Asian woman faces harassment at work it may be quite difficult in practice to separate cleanly the harassment between that which is based on sex or race or religion. Yet, the legislative framework created by the Union contains only a right to assistance in respect

---

[142] Art 3.   [143] Art 3(3).

[144] Guideline 1, Council Decision of 19 January 2001 on Guidelines for Member States' employment policies for the year 2001 [2001] OJ L22/18.

of those aspects of harassment based on racial or ethnic origin.[145]

A further distinction is created in relation to the application of the burden of proof provisions. The specific articles on the burden of proof in the two Directives are identical. However, the Framework Directive, Recital 31 adds that 'it is not for the respondent to prove that the plaintiff adheres to a particular religion or belief, has a particular disability, is of a particular age or has a particular sexual orientation'. This suggests that there may be situations where individuals are required to 'prove' their sexual orientation. This is quite disturbing as it creates an obvious conflict with privacy rights and it could deter many individuals from litigating. A better view would be that sexual orientation discrimination occurs where the employer or any other person discriminates on the basis of an assumption regarding a person's sexual orientation. For example, an employer might refuse to employ a man because he or she thinks that the man in question is gay. For discrimination law, it seems irrelevant whether the man actually is gay or not; in either case, he has suffered discrimination based on (perceived) sexual orientation and the detriment is no less real. The Framework Directive does not explicitly deal with this issue, but Article 2(1) states that any discrimination 'whatsoever' on grounds of sexual orientation is prohibited.[146] This formulation appears sufficiently broad to include discrimination based on perceived sexual orientation.

The final general difference between the two Directives is the addition in the Framework Directive of an open-ended justification for any form of discrimination in Article 2(5): 'This Directive shall be without prejudice to measures laid down by law which, in a democratic society, are necessary for public security, for maintenance of public order and the prevention of criminal offences, for health protection and for the protection of the rights and freedoms of others.'

This provision was only inserted in the Directive late in its negotiation and its intended purpose is not immediately apparent. From the perspective of sexual orientation, it may be aimed at reassuring national law makers (and the general public) that a ban on sexual orientation discrimination cannot be interpreted as according protection to paedophiles or other persons engaging in unlawful sexual behaviour.[147] However, the breadth of the exception raises the possibility of an extended application. For example, it is conceiv-

---

[145] It should be noted that the proposed amendments to the Equal Treatment Directive would require Member States to establish also an equal treatment body to assist individuals with complaints of gender discrimination: COM (2000) 334, 17.

[146] Art 2(1).   [147] Cf Ireland's Employment Equality Act, s 16(5).

able that certain Member States might attempt to rely on this provision to defend restrictions on the expression of homosexuality within the armed forces.[148] The scope of Article 2(5) will be ultimately a matter for the Court of Justice to determine, but it introduces an unwelcome area of ambiguity.

(b) Ground-specific exceptions

Exceptions that apply to one or several of the grounds in the Framework Directive also exist alongside the general provisions mentioned above. For example, Member States may decide not to apply the age and disability provisions to their armed forces.[149] In the context of this chapter, it is appropriate to focus on the exceptions of special relevance to sexual orientation discrimination. Essentially, there are two provisions to consider here relating to marital benefits and religious organisations respectively.

As demonstrated by *Grant* and *D v Council*, benefits provided by employers in respect of the members of an individual worker's family are frequently a source of discrimination against lesbian and gay workers. This discrimination takes mainly two forms; denial of benefits to unmarried partners irrespective of sex (*D v Council*), and denial of benefits specifically to same-sex couples (*Grant*). The latter is the most straightforward to challenge as it is direct discrimination on the basis of sexual orientation and the Directive prohibits this. Nonetheless, in many cases—like *D v Council*—benefits are limited to married couples, thereby creating indirect discrimination on the ground of sexual orientation as lesbians and gay men are placed at a particular disadvantage because they are unable to marry their partners (with the exception of in the Netherlands).

Although indirectly discriminatory measures are also prohibited by the Directive, they can be 'objectively justified' where there is 'a legitimate aim and the means of achieving that aim are appropriate and necessary'.[150] In respect of benefits available only to married couples, the Member States have strongly indicated that these are to be regarded as objectively justified. Recital 22 in the preamble states 'this Directive is without prejudice to national laws on marital status and the benefits dependent thereon'. As part of the preamble, this is not binding on the Court of Justice.[151] Nonetheless, it is unlikely the Court would disregard such a clear direction in the Directive, especially in the light of its general caution in matters pertaining to

---

[148] Skidmore (n 138 above) 130.   [149] Art 3(4).   [150] Art 2(2)(b)(i).

[151] Opinion of A-G Tizzano, Case C–173/99 *BECTU v Secretary of State for Trade and Industry* [2001] ECR I–4881, para 41.

marriage and the family.

The other provision most directly related to sexual orientation discrimination is an exception in the Directive for employment in 'churches or other public or private organisations the ethos of which is based on religion or belief'.[152] This was the site of intense debate during the negotiation of the Directive, with an active campaign by certain religious lobby groups to have an open-ended exception for religious organisations, or even the deletion of sexual orientation and religion from the Directive altogether.[153] The terms of this exception shifted considerably during the legislative process, and the final text is a complex and cumbersome compromise. Essentially there are three key elements. First, it is important to note that this is not, strictly speaking, an exception to the ban on sexual orientation discrimination. In fact, this is an exception to the prohibition on discrimination on grounds of religion or belief, and Article 4(2) expressly states that it 'should not justify discrimination on another ground'. At the same time, the reluctance of certain organisations with a religious ethos to employ lesbians and gay men is one of the key reasons why this provision is present in the Directive, and therefore it would be naïve to ignore the connections between these two issues. The Directive does not, however, permit a religious organisation to simply (and overtly) exclude all lesbians and gay men from access to employment.[154]

Second, where it is already permitted in national law or practice, religious organisations will continue to be able to take into account religion or belief in making recruitment decisions, but only if this is necessary to maintain the ethos of the organisation. In deciding whether or not such a difference in treatment is necessary, regard must be had to the specific occupation in question. For example, in selecting a teacher for a religious school, it will be easy to justify taking the religion of a candidate into account if the position in question is a religious education teacher. In contrast, if the position was in, say, maths or chemistry, then the school would need to establish more closely why the teacher needs to share the religion of the organisation. If all teachers were required to undertake certain religious activities—such as prayers with a class at the start of the day or religious counselling with a teacher's individual year group of students—then this might be sufficient to justify religion being a

---

[152] Art 4(2).

[153] Christian Institute, 'European threat to religious freedom—a response to the European Union's Employment Directive' (London: Christian Institute, 2000).

[154] Equal Opportunities Review, 'EU Employment Framework Directive: an EOR guide' (Jan/Feb 2001) No 95, 32, 36.

relevant characteristic of teachers in general.

Finally, in respect of existing employees, religious bodies can 'require individuals working for them to act in good faith and with loyalty to the organisation's ethos',[155] although this is subject to compliance with the other provisions of the Directive.[156] The extent of these 'good faith' obligations is not explained elsewhere in the Directive, and as this provision resulted from an amendment late in the negotiations, there is no other source to account for its meaning. A delicate issue would be the degree to which a religious organisation could require a lesbian or gay employee to keep secret their sexual orientation, or alternatively to refrain from making statements contrary to the official teaching of the religion in question on homosexuality.

The intersection of rights to religious freedom and equal treatment is one of the most difficult areas of the Directive to negotiate. The provisions of the Directive provide some guidance, but equally leave much to be determined by the courts based on the facts of any specific dispute.[157] Both parties to such a case will evidently take the view that their own fundamental right should 'trump' that of the other. However, as the spirit of the Directive indicates, a careful balancing act will be necessary on a case-by-case basis.

VII. An evolving framework: sexual orientation and the EU

In taking an overview of EU law and policy on sexual orientation issues, it is considerably easier to explain why there was a long period of inaction, than to account for the recent reversal in fortunes. Yet, as Borrillo highlights, there has been a fundamental shift from the 'declaratory' phase of this policy in the 1980s, to the adoption on binding legal norms in December 2000.[158]

The weak case for Union intervention in sexual orientation discrimination can be easily traced to the market foundations of European social policy. Sexual orientation discrimination (in employment) has not been regarded as a major public policy issue. There is comparatively little empirical data demonstrating the existence of this problem and its invisibility is reinforced by the capacity for lesbians and gay men to avoid discrimination through con-

---

[155] Art 4(2).   [156] Many thanks to Robin Allen for highlighting this point.

[157] P Skidmore, 'The EC Framework Directive on Equal Treatment in Employment: towards a comprehensive Community anti-discrimination policy?' (2001) 30 ILJ 126, 131.

[158] D Borrillo, 'L'orientation sexuelle en Europe—esquisse d'une politique publique antidiscriminatoire' (July–August 2000) *Le Temps Modernes* 263, 264.

cealment of their sexual orientation at work. The Commission took the view that this was, at most, a question of privacy rights and best dealt with through the Council of Europe mechanisms.[159] Moreover, the sensitive moral debates connected with sexual orientation issues undoubtedly reinforced the perception that this was not a matter appropriate for Union intervention. Clapham and Weiler acknowledge that EU action risked being perceived as a classical example of 'Community legislative excess' and an intrusion into matters best left to national discretion.[160]

Evidence of the low 'market profile' of sexual orientation discrimination can be found in the EU employment guidelines. Discrimination on the grounds of gender, racial or ethnic origin, disability and age have been explicitly recognised as creating barriers to participation in the European labour market and undermining overall economic competitiveness. Many of the same arguments could be applied to sexual orientation discrimination—for example, the importance of a diverse workforce for accessing diverse parts of the consumer market. Nonetheless, sexual orientation remains an invisible category in the employment strategy.

The internal market rationale for combating sexual orientation discrimination is greatest in respect of same-sex partnership rights, as the divergence between national legislation on this topic is giving rise to new barriers to free movement. Stychin suggests this is strong terrain for Union intervention: 'the advantage of deploying EC law for gays and lesbians is that the economic paradigm of rights abstracts them from an obviously moral underpinning, making it easier to make claims in a morally "neutral", economically grounded language'.[161] Although this is an initially persuasive argument, it is not clear that morally charged debates are less prevalent at the Union level. Where direct conflict has taken place—for example the Parliament's endorsement of same-sex unions in the 1994 Roth Resolution—an intense debate ensued. Alternatively, the position of religious employers under the Framework Directive generated considerable attention, at least in the UK. The dominant impression emerging is that the Union seeks to avoid moral controversies before they arise. Therefore, great caution has been exercised in respecting national diversity on the (non-) recognition of same-sex part-

[159] For example, Peter Sutherland, Debates of the European Parliament No 2-328/164, 11 July 1985.

[160] A Clapham and J Weiler, 'Human dignity shall be inviolable: the human rights of gays and lesbians in the EC legal order' (1992) III(2) Collected Courses in the Academy of European Law 237, 264.

[161] C Stychin, '*Grant*-ing rights: the politics of rights, sexuality and European Union' (2000) 51 Northern Ireland Legal Q 281, 290.

nerships. This is perhaps best described as a form of 'moral subsidiarity', which regards issues of cultural or moral sensitivity as best left to national discretion.[162]

Nonetheless, sexual orientation issues are beginning to be confronted by EU law, especially since Article 13 and most visibly in the Framework Directive. Both instruments demonstrate the potential for progress as part of a wider equality agenda. The 'general' character of the Framework Directive (or Article 13) diluted attention from any single ground of discrimination therein, and encouraged a collective analysis of the issues. Sexual orientation has been nested within wider discourses on developing Union citizenship and removing barriers to participation in the employment market. Taken alone, it is doubtful if sexual orientation could have garnered sufficient support to permit EU intervention—unlike issues of race and ethnicity which have been dealt with specifically and separately. Whilst the broad equality and citizenship agenda has been a source of strength for policy development, the absence of targeted measures for gay men and lesbians remains a core weakness of EU interventions here.

Borrillo concludes that an EU policy framework on sexual orientation remains to be completed.[163] EU policy on racism goes beyond the Racial Equality Directive and is complemented by wider measures—notably the mainstreaming approach. In contrast, the Commission has yet to publish any communication solely examining sexual orientation issues in EU law and policy, and there is little evidence of any scheme to integrate equal treatment for lesbians and gay men throughout EU policies. Nonetheless, the spillover pressures from the Framework Directive will inevitably emerge—in particular around the question of partnership rights with its nexus to free movement law. The Framework Directive provides a platform for action, but it remains a more lonely intervention than the panoply of actions to combat racism.

---

[162]   P Spicker, 'The Principle of Subsidiarity and the Social Policy of the European Community' (1991) 1 J of Eur Social Policy 3, 13.

[163]   Borrillo (n 158 above) 278.

Exploring Article 13 EC

Chapters 2, 3 and 4 have provided a detailed overview of both the traditional contours of EU anti-discrimination law, and two examples from the evolving body of law post-Amsterdam. As already indicated, EC Treaty, Article 13 forms both the legal and political bedrock of the new anti-discrimination law initiatives. The strength of this provision undoubtedly lies in its broad scope. Placed at the outset of the EC Treaty, in the chapter on 'principles', the impression generated is that Article 13 now forms a core component of the essential social objectives of the Union. Its proximity to EC Treaty, Article 12 on nationality discrimination also encourages a view of Article 13 as a key element of the rights of Union citizens. Although not formally within the Treaty chapter on citizenship, Shaw has argued that the rights of Union citizens are scattered throughout the EC Treaty—Article 12 being an obvious example, to which Article 13 now represents an important complement.[1]

In this light, Article 13 might be seen as concrete evidence of the social citizenship model of social policy in action. This is not a Treaty provision that depends on the establishment of an economic rationale in terms of market integration, but one that allows for the independent pursuit by the Union of specific social objectives. Moreover, the overlapping nature of equality as both a goal of European social policy, and at the same time the protection of a fundamental right, rests comfortably with the rights-based model of social policy that the social citizenship approach proposes.

Nonetheless, closer examination of Article 13 calls into question the extent to which it is truly free of market dependency. As discussed in Chapter 2, gender equality has already emerged as an autonomous objective of European social policy. However, this has been moderated by an emphasis on gender equality in the marketplace—most notably at work. Expanding beyond the

---

[1] J Shaw, 'The interpretation of European Union citizenship' (1998) 61 MLR 293, 298.

rights of market citizens has proven problematic.[2] As Article 13 is not found in the social chapter of the Treaty, this suggests that it is a transversal policy objective, rather than a purely labour market instrument. Yet, crucially its remit remains subject to the 'limits of the powers conferred by it [the Treaty] upon the Community'. This chapter explores the character of Article 13 through an examination of its legal scope. The ability of this provision to provide a foundation for the extension of rights beyond those traditionally associated with market citizenship is analysed, with particular reference to aspects of social policy which have normally remained areas of national discretion—such as health, education and social welfare provision.[3] In scrutinising Article 13, the Directives already adopted form vital evidence from which a better understanding of this provision may be gleaned. The chapter begins with a short review of the basic principles governing the exercise of Community competences, followed by sections on the content of Article 13, and the limits to its scope.[4]

I. Basic principles governing EC legislative powers

The European Community is a body of limited powers. It enjoys powers only in those areas where the Member States have agreed to pool their national sovereignty. This principle is expressed in the EC Treaty, in particular, the first paragraph of Article 5: 'the Community shall act within the limits of the powers conferred upon it by this Treaty and of the objectives assigned to it therein.' The Court has consistently upheld this basic principle of limited powers. Indeed, it insists that respect for these delimitations must be ensured throughout the full range of Community actions. For instance, the Court accepted as admissible an action from France for the annulment of a Communication of the Commission. The Commission argued that as a Communication did not impose any binding obligations on the Member States then it was not possible to challenge this on the ground of a lack of legal

---

[2] M Everson, 'The legacy of the market citizen' in J Shaw and G More (eds), *New legal dynamics of the European Union* (Oxford: Clarendon Press, 1995) 79.

[3] M Poiares Maduro, 'Europe's Social Self: "The sickness unto death"' in J Shaw (ed), *Social law and policy in an evolving European Union* (Oxford: Hart Publishing, 2000) 330.

[4] This chapter is a modified version of an article first published by the Maastricht J of Eur and Comparative L and this material is used with its publishers' permission: M Bell, 'The new Article 13 EC Treaty: a sound basis for European anti-discrimination law?' (1999) 6 Maastricht J of Eur and Comparative L 5.

competence. On the contrary, the Court held that 'an action for annulment is available in the case of all measures adopted by the institutions, whatever their nature or form, which are intended to have legal effects'.[5]

A further expression of this principle is the requirement that all binding legislation must cite the authority that enables the Community to act. EC Treaty, Article 253 states that 'Regulations, Directives and Decisions adopted jointly by the European Parliament and the Council, and such acts adopted by the Council or the Commission, shall state the reasons on which they are based'. The Court has interpreted this as obliging a reference to a precise Treaty article(s) when enacting legislation. In the *Generalized Tariff Preferences*[6] case, the measure under challenge stated only that it was based on the EEC Treaty, without identifying any particular provision therein. The Court held that this would:

not necessarily constitute an infringement of essential procedural requirements when the legal basis for the measure may be determined from other parts of the measure. However, such explicit reference is indispensable where, in its absence, the parties concerned and the Court are left uncertain as to the precise legal basis.[7]

The difficulties with Treaty bases tend to arise in the borderline areas, where no specific competence is conferred, but it may be possible to bring the matter within the scope of the Treaties through generous interpretation of their provisions. There are limits, though, to how far these provisions may be stretched. The Court maintains that 'the choice of legal basis for a measure must be made on objective factors which are amenable to judicial review. Those factors include in particular the aim and content of the measure'.[8] The realities of the limits to Community competence were most visibly demonstrated by the Court's decision in October 2000 to annul the Tobacco Advertising Directive on the ground of a lack of competence.[9] Advocate-General Fennelly emphasised the duty on the Court 'as a repository of the trust and confidence of the Community institutions, the Member States and the citizens of the Union, to perform this difficult function of upholding the constitutional division of powers between the Community and the Member States on the basis of objective criteria'.[10]

---

[5] Case C–57/95 *French Republic v Commission* [1997] ECR I–1627.

[6] Case 45/86 *Commission v Council* [1987] ECR 1493.　　　[7] ibid 1519–1520.

[8] Case C–22/96 *Parliament v Council* [1998] ECR I–3231, para 23. See also Case C–350/92 *Spain v Council* [1995] ECR I–1985.

[9] Case C–376/98 *Germany v Parliament and Council* [2000] ECR I–8419.

[10] ibid para 4.

European labour lawyers have been especially adept in finding innovative Treaty bases, as a consequence of the historically weak position of social policy in the EC Treaty.[11] This inevitably resulted in 'interpretative acrobatics',[12] and at times the legal foundations of social legislation verged on the edge of credibility.[13] The EC Treaty now provides a much firmer foundation for social law since the amendments introduced by the Treaty of Amsterdam. The new Social Chapter, derived from the Agreement on Social Policy, provides a more straightforward source of Community competence, although again not without its limitations.[14] The fact that clearer legal competences are now provided for in the EC Treaty may help explain the willingness of the Court in the Tobacco Advertising case to compel the Community to respect the limits of these competences.

II. EC Treaty, Article 13: the final wording

Chapter 4 noted the rather bumpy ride Article 13 experienced on its journey to inclusion in the EC Treaty. The December 1996 draft version provided:

Within the scope of application of this Treaty and without prejudice to any special provisions contained therein, the Council, acting unanimously on a proposal from the Commission and after consulting the European Parliament, may take appropriate action to prohibit discrimination based on sex, racial, ethnic or social origin, religious belief, disability, age or sexual orientation.[15]

The final text differs subtly, but significantly:

Without prejudice to the other provisions of this Treaty and within the limits of the powers conferred by it upon the Community, the Council, acting unanimously on a

---

[11] See, *inter alia*, E Vogel-Polsky, 'What future is there for a Social Europe after the Strasbourg summit?' (1990) 19 ILJ 65; B Hepple, 'The Implementation of the Community Charter on Fundamental Social Rights' (1990) 53 MLR 643.

[12] S Sciarra, 'European Social Policy and Labour Law—Challenges and Perspectives' (1995) IV(I) Collected Courses of the Academy of European Law 301, 317.

[13] For example, Davies calls into question the nexus between the functioning of the internal market and the 1977 Collective Redundancies Directive: P Davies, 'The Emergence of European Labour Law' in W McCarthy (ed), *Legal Interventions in Industrial Relations: Gains and Losses* (Oxford: Basil Blackwell, 1992) 330.

[14] Notably, EC Treaty, Article 137(6).

[15] Conference of the representatives of governments of the Member States, 'European Union Today and Tomorrow—adapting the European Union for the benefit of its peoples and preparing it for the future', CONF/2500/96, 5 December 1996.

proposal from the Commission and after consulting the European Parliament, may take appropriate action to combat discrimination based on sex, racial or ethnic origin, religion or belief, disability, age or sexual orientation.

(a) Direct effect

A number of initial points may be made about the final text. Contrary to the wishes of the European Parliament,[16] the Article does not possess direct effect. There has been some argument in German literature that Article 13 could be construed as obliging Member States to forbid discrimination, through a linkage with EC Treaty, Article 10.[17] This requires that 'Member States take all appropriate measures, whether general or particular, to ensure fulfilment of the obligations arising out of this Treaty'. Yet, the central element of Article 13 is that there are no obligations as such—it is merely an enabling clause, as indicated by the phrase 'the Council . . . *may* take appropriate action' (emphasis added).

(b) Decision-making procedures

Second, with regard to the decision-making process, the European Parliament is assigned a marginal role in the legislative process, with only the right to consultation. This is especially significant, given that it was one of the main proponents of a greater commitment from the EU to combating discrimination. Nonetheless, the Court has affirmed elsewhere that whilst this may provide a rather constrained role, it is still a prerogative that must be fully respected by the other institutions.[18] Indeed the obligation on the Council to await the Parliament's opinion proved a valuable negotiating chip during the adoption of the Racial Equality Directive.[19] More importantly, Article 13 requires unanimity in the Council. Thus, just one recalcitrant state may block progress in anti-discrimination law. Fears concerning the levelling-down

---

[16] Paragraph 4, Parliament Resolution on racism, xenophobia and anti-semitism and on the results of the European Year against racism (1997) [1998] OJ C56/13.

[17] J Cirkel, 'Gleichheitsrechte im Gemeinschaftsrecht' (1998) 51 Neue Juristische Wochenschrift 3332. Many thanks to Dagmar Schiek for bringing this to my attention.

[18] For example, Case C–392/95 *Parliament v Council* [1997] ECR I–3213, where the Court annulled a Council Regulation on third country nationals who must be in possession of a visa when crossing external borders. The Court held that as the essence of the proposal had been changed as a result of substantial amendments by the Council after the Parliament had given its initial opinion, the Council was under a duty to re-consult the Parliament and its failure to do so was a breach of essential procedural requirements.

[19] See further ch 3 above.

impact of this voting procedure have been slightly allayed by the strength of the Racial Equality Directive. However, the tyranny of the veto was more clearly in evidence in the Framework Directive where various provisions reflect very specific concerns of individual Member States.[20]

It had been thought that the unanimity requirement could be removed in the context of the Treaty of Nice reforms. In the event, the Member States opted for a halfway house. If ratified, the Treaty of Nice will add a second paragraph to Article 13:

By way of derogation from paragraph 1, when the Council adopts Community incentive measures, excluding any harmonisation of the laws and regulations of the Member States, to support action taken by the Member States in order to contribute to the achievement of the objectives referred to in paragraph 1, it shall act in accordance with the procedure referred to in Article 251.

The effects of this amendment are two-fold. On one side, Article 13(2) will introduce not only qualified-majority voting in the Council, but also the 'co-decision' legislative procedure. This gives the Parliament a considerably enhanced role, with the ultimate power to veto any proposed measure.[21] On the other side, this decision-making procedure is carefully circumscribed to exclude its application to binding legislative instruments. For example, future Action Programmes presumably can be adopted on the basis of this paragraph, whereas future Directives cannot. The strongest instruments that seem feasible under paragraph 2 might be Codes of Practice. Whilst these are non-binding, they are often useful in guiding courts as to the correct interpretation and application of binding legislative norms.[22] Clearly, the area where qualified-majority voting and co-decision could really produce a difference is in relation to binding instruments. The opportunity to achieve further change to Article 13 will next occur during the intergovernmental conference to be held in 2004.[23]

(c) Grounds of discrimination

Article 13 applies to eight different grounds of discrimination, of which religion and belief, and racial or ethnic origin, are linked together. In contrast,

---

[20] The most notable is Art 15, which provides specific exceptions for Northern Ireland with respect to recruitment for policing and teaching.

[21] For more detail on the co-decision procedure, see P Craig and G de Búrca, *EU law—text, cases and materials* (2nd edn, Oxford: Oxford University Press, 1998) 135.

[22] For example, Commission Recommendation on the dignity of women and men at work, adopted 27 November 1991 [1992] OJ L49/1.

[23] Declaration 23 on the future of the Union, Treaty of Nice [2001] OJ C80/1.

the EU Charter of Fundamental Rights, Article 21(1) contains no less than seventeen grounds of prohibited discrimination, and this list is non-exhaustive. The European Convention on Human Rights, Article 14 is also open-ended, but lists twelve specific grounds where discrimination is prohibited. The closed list found in Article 13 is not entirely surprising: the Member States are protective of national prerogatives and extensions of Community competence have been carefully controlled, especially since the 1993 Treaty on European Union. Nonetheless, this produces inflexibility within Article 13 that overlooks the dynamic nature of anti-discrimination law. For example, the Charter is innovative in its reference to discrimination on the ground of 'genetic features'. This is an attempt to respond to the growing evidence that progress in genetic testing, and the predictive effect of such tests, might produce discrimination against certain groups of people based on their genes. This is already an issue in relation to access to insurance policies for those individuals where genetic testing reveals a disposition towards certain illnesses.[24]

Other categories of discrimination excluded from Article 13 include language, political opinion, national origin, and family status.[25] 'Language' is present in other international legal instruments as a prohibited ground of discrimination[26] and such discrimination can be based on the same kinds of prejudice as inspire racism. For example, in the Netherlands, the Equal Treatment Commission held linguistic discrimination to be essentially racial discrimination in a case where an employer refused to hire a Surinamese woman on the basis of her accent in Dutch, although her fluency was evident.[27] Discrimination on linguistic grounds can also be a significant problem for many national minorities in Europe.

Alternatively, ILO Convention No 111 on discrimination in employment includes reference to 'political opinion, national extraction and social origin', none of which is explicitly included in Article 13.[28] National extraction, also referred to as national origin, could be useful in addressing discrimination between citizens of the same country, where distinctions are made on the

---

[24] On genetic testing in the workplace, see J Craig, *Privacy and employment law* (Oxford: Hart Publishing, 1999).

[25] Family status can be broadly described as being with or without dependants and/or caring responsibilities.

[26] ECHR, Art 14; International Covenant on Civil and Political Rights, Art 26.

[27] Commissie Gelijke Behandeling, *Annual Report 1997* (Utrecht: Commissie Gelijke Behandeling, 1998) 15.

[28] ILO, *International Labour Conventions and Recommendations 1952–1976 Volume 2* (Geneva: ILO, 1996) 176.

basis of 'a person's place of birth, ancestry or foreign origin'.[29] Whilst it must be hoped that this is generally covered under the aegis of 'racial or ethnic origin' in Article 13, an explicit reference would have been beneficial for situations such as discrimination against persons from Northern Ireland in England.[30]

Notwithstanding the remarks above, Article 13 does cover a relatively wide range of forms of discrimination. The decision-making procedures may be difficult, but these did not stand in the way of the two Directives adopted in 2000. Greater difficulty arises in respect of the legal scope of the provision, and in particular, the meaning of the proviso that it only applies 'within the limits of the powers' of the Community.

III. The limits of the powers

The application of Article 13 is subject to the following qualification: 'without prejudice to the other provisions of this Treaty and within the limits of the powers conferred by it upon the Community'. This can be broken into two elements.

(a) *Without prejudice to the other provisions of this Treaty*

This phrase implies that nothing within Article 13 should be taken as constraining the scope or effects of any other provision of the EC Treaty.[31] In other words, Article 13 shall not act to the detriment of other Treaty articles. Article 12 EC on nationality discrimination contains a similar (but not identical) phrase, 'without prejudice to any special provisions contained [in the Treaty]'. In *Cowan v Trésor public*,[32] concerning access of a British tourist mugged in Paris to a French criminal injuries compensation fund, the Court stated that this phrase in Article 12 referred to:

other provisions of the Treaty in which the application of the general principle set out in that article is given concrete form in respect of specific situations. Examples of that

---

[29]   ILO, *Equality in employment and occupation*, Report of the Committee of Experts on the application of conventions and recommendations (Geneva: ILO, 1996) para 33.

[30]   On 'national origin' as a ground of discrimination in UK law, see A McColgan, *Discrimination Law—text, cases and materials* (Oxford: Hart Publishing, 2000) 428.

[31]   Many thanks to Ann Dummett for assistance on this point.

[32]   Case 186/87 *Cowan v Trésor public* [1989] ECR 195.

are the provisions concerning free movement of workers, the right of establishment and the freedom to provide services.[33]

Similarly, in Article 13, the phrase 'without prejudice to the other provisions of the Treaty' should be interpreted as referring to other Treaty articles where discrimination is dealt with in respect of a specific situation. In particular, Article 137(1) EC, and Article 141 EC, both provide express powers to adopt measures for combating sexual discrimination in employment. Therefore, the proviso in Article 13 would suggest that measures concerning sexual equality in employment are to be dealt with under either of these more specific provisions. Indeed, the Commission's proposed amendments to the Equal Treatment Directive are based on Article 141(3).[34]

Where Article 13 differs from Article 12 is in the reference to 'without prejudice to the *other* provisions' rather than 'without prejudice to any *special* provisions'. Waddington proposes that implies a broader application for the Article 13 proviso than is the case in Article 12.[35] Whereas Article 12 is without prejudice to any other Treaty provision which *specifically* deals with nationality discrimination (such as Article 39 EC), Article 13 is without prejudice to any other Treaty provision which deals with discrimination, *whether specific or not*. An example of the potential importance of this lies in relation to the social provisions.[36] A number of these provide powers for the Community to act which seem to overlap with Article 13, albeit not explicitly. EC Treaty, Article 137(2) provides for the adoption of Directives on matters such as 'working conditions', improving the 'working environment' and 'the integration of persons excluded from the labour market'. Whilst not specifically mentioned, discrimination in the workplace would appear to fall within all of these headings. This is especially true of the 'working environment', given the holistic definition the Court of Justice has attributed to this term.[37]

The significance of this point relates to the different decision-making procedures available under different Treaty articles.[38] Whereas Article 13

---

[33] para 14. [34] COM (2000) 334, 13.

[35] L Waddington, 'Testing the limits of the EC Treaty article on non-discrimination' (1999) 28 ILJ 133, 135; See also L Flynn, 'The implications of Article 13 EC—after Amsterdam, will some forms of discrimination be more equal than others?' (1999) 36 CML Rev 1127, 1133.

[36] EC Treaty, Arts 136–141.

[37] The Court has described health and safety as 'embracing all factors, physical or otherwise, capable of affecting the health and safety of the worker in his working environment': Case C–84/94 *UK v Council* [1996] ECR I–5755, para 15.

[38] See also, R Whittle, 'Disability rights after Amsterdam: the way forward' (2000) 5 Eur Human Rights L Rev 33.

requires unanimity in the Council and ascribes only a minimal role to the Parliament, Article 137(2) allows for the adoption of Directives by qualified-majority voting in the Council, and assigns the Parliament a much more influential role through the co-decision procedure.[39] Moreover, measures adopted in respect of Article 137 must first be subject to the social dialogue procedure, pursuant to Article 139. Together with the initial proviso in Article 13, it should be noted that a more general rule of law augurs in favour of the use of the social provisions, if at all possible. In *Commission v Council (Titanium Dioxide)*,[40] the Court held that where more than one legal base is available, but these have conflicting decision-making procedures, then that which accords the maximum role to the Parliament must be deployed.

Nonetheless, Article 13 formed the legal base for the Framework Directive (which only addresses employment discrimination). The Commission gave two reasons for this choice. First, the scope of the Framework Directive extended to self-employed persons and 'the liberal professions' by virtue of Article 3(1)(d) of the Directive,[41] whereas EC Treaty, Article 137(2) only applies to 'workers'. Second, the personal scope of the Directive went beyond those 'excluded from the labour market' and included measures for individuals already participating in the labour market, therefore Article 137(2), indent 4 (the integration of persons excluded from the labour market) was inapplicable.[42] Both of these reasons are based on a rather strict, literal reading of the relevant Treaty provisions. Measures to integrate persons excluded from the labour market can surely also encompass measures to *prevent* exclusion—consequently embracing those already in the labour market, but at risk of exclusion because of discrimination. Moreover, the Court has given varying interpretations of the term 'worker'. In the context of Article 42 (co-ordination of social security schemes), the Court has defined 'worker' as extending to the self-employed,[43] therefore questions remain as to whether Article 137(2) really does not cover measures applying to the self-employed.

---

[39]   EC Treaty, Art 251.

[40]   Case C–300/89 [1991] ECR I–2867. See M O'Neill, 'The choice of a legal basis: more than a number' (1994) 1 Irish J of Eur L 44; L Waddington, 'Throwing some light on Article 13 EC Treaty' (1999) 6 Maastricht J of Eur and Comparative L 1.

[41]   Commission, 'Proposal for a Council Directive establishing a general framework for equal treatment in employment and occupation' COM (1999) 565, 7.

[42]   Many thanks to Richard Whittle for bringing these points to my attention.

[43]   For an overview, see Opinion of A-G Jacobs, Cases C–95/99 to 98/99 and C–180/99, *Khalil, Chaaban and Osseili v Bundesanstalt für Arbeit*; *Nasser v Landeshauptstadt Stuttgart*; *Addou v Land Nordrhein-Westfalen*, 30 November 2000.

Ultimately, the reasons for using Article 13 in preference to Article 137(2) may be more political than legal. Article 13 allowed the Member States to keep control of the legislative process through the unanimity requirement, whereas Article 137(2) could have opened the door to legislating via the social dialogue procedure, as well as qualified-majority voting. Moreover, the use of Article 13 placed less emphasis on the Framework Directive as an instrument of labour law, but reinforced the impression that this was part of a framework of basic rights of Union citizens.

(b) Within the limits of the powers conferred by the Treaty on the Community

In this proviso, the definition of the term 'powers' is crucial to understanding the precise ambit of Article 13. If 'powers' is interpreted in a narrow fashion, then Article 13 will be curtailed in its potential effects. If, on the other hand, 'powers' is read in a broad sense, then Article 13 may be relied upon for the creation of far-reaching anti-discrimination law. Interpreting the meaning of 'powers' in Article 13 has provoked considerable academic debate.[44] The significance of the term is most obvious when contrasted with EC Treaty, Article 12: 'Within the scope of application of this Treaty, and without prejudice to any special provisions contained therein, any discrimination on grounds of nationality shall be prohibited'.

Article 12 differs from Article 13, as it possesses direct effect. Therefore, even in the absence of any implementing legislation, Article 12 prohibits nationality discrimination. However, this is subject to the proviso, 'within the scope of application of this Treaty'. Thus, it is not sufficient solely for a plaintiff to demonstrate that there has been discrimination on the basis of nationality, but they must also satisfy the Court that this has occurred within the field of application of Community law.

The 'scope of application' of the EC Treaty has two dimensions: its personal scope and its material scope. An individual litigant needs to establish both that they are 'in a situation governed by EC law',[45] and that the law or

---

[44] For example, R Whittle, 'Disability rights after Amsterdam: the way forward' (2000) 5 Eur Human Rights L Rev 33; L Flynn, 'The implications of Article 13 EC—after Amsterdam, will some forms of discrimination be more equal than others? (1999) 36 CML Rev 1127, 1135; L Waddington, 'Testing the limits of the EC Treaty article on non-discrimination' (1999) 28 ILJ 133, 136.

[45] Case C–122/96 *Saldanha and MTS Securities Corporation v Hiross Holding AG* [1997] ECR I–5325, para 25.

practice under challenge falls within 'the Treaty's area of application'.[46] The material scope of the EC Treaty is most easily understood by reference to the competences of the Community, as expressed through the provisions of the Treaty.[47] Yet, the Court has gradually expounded the notion that the scope of the Treaty and its competences are not contiguous.

This is especially evident in the judgment of the Court in *Forcheri*.[48] The case concerned the wife of an official at the Commission who challenged a requirement to pay the Minerval, an additional enrolment fee for foreign students in Belgium. The Court had to determine whether 'access to educational courses, in particular those concerning vocational training, falls within the scope of application of the Treaty'.[49] The Court concluded that whereas: 'educational and vocational training policy is not as such part of the areas which the Treaty has allotted to the competence of the Community institutions, the opportunity for such kinds of instruction falls within the scope of the Treaty'.[50]

This distinction between competence and scope is reinforced by the decision in *Bickel and Franz*.[51] The case concerned the right to have criminal proceedings in Bolzano, Italy, conducted in the German language for two Austrian nationals. In the case of Mr Bickel, Advocate-General Jacobs candidly stated: 'There appear to be no provisions in the Treaty or in Community legislation which, as such, might bear on the substance of the charge brought against Mr Bickel, namely driving under the influence of alcohol.'[52]

Nonetheless, he still reached the conclusion that Article 12 required equal treatment within the proceedings relating to this offence, a conclusion accepted by the Court. Implicit in the reasoning of both the Court and the Advocate-General, is the argument that whilst criminal law proceedings may not fall within the competences of the Community, they may, nonetheless, fall with the scope of application of the Treaty.[53]

---

[46] Case C–291/96 *Grado and Bashir* [1997] ECR I–5531, para 13.

[47] For instance, Case C–122/96 *Saldanha* [1997] ECR I–5325, para 20.

[48] Case C–152/82 *Forcheri and his wife Marisa Forcheri, née Marino, v Belgian State and asbl Institut Supérieur de Sciences Humaines Appliquées—École Ouvrière Supérieure* [1983] ECR 2323.

[49] ibid para 13.

[50] ibid para 17. This finding was based principally on former EC Treaty, Article 128 which provided the Council with the powers to lay down general principles for implementing a common vocational training policy.

[51] Case C–274/96 *Bickel and Franz* [1998] ECR I–7637. See further ch 2 above.

[52] ibid para 15.

[53] 'Such a conclusion does not of course entail a transfer of Member States' competence in criminal matters to the Community. It merely recognises the fact that, as the Court noted in *Cowan*, Member States must exercise their powers in this area in conformity with the fundamental

How does this relate to Article 13? Importantly, Article 13 is not prefixed by the phrase 'within the scope of application of this Treaty', but refers instead to 'within the limits of the powers' conferred on the Community by the Treaty. Logically, the choice of a different expression would incline towards the conclusion that the Member States intended the two articles to have a different effect. This is reinforced when one considers that Article 13 in the Dublin draft did have the same form as Article 12, but this was amended in the final version of the Treaty.[54] Whilst this may lead one to the conclusion that Articles 12 and 13 are not identical in scope, it does not assist in determining the nature of this difference. On the one hand, it could be that Article 13 is of broader application. This rests on the assumption that the term 'powers' is less restrictive than the term 'scope'. 'Powers' could be read as a reference to the fundamental limits to the powers of the Community, such as the requirement that the prerogatives of each institution are respected, or the delineation of powers between the European Community and the European Union.[55] For instance, given that there is also a competence for action against racism under the provisions of the Treaty on European Union,[56] 'powers' in Article 13 could be a reference to ensuring that Community action does not infringe upon the powers assigned to the Union on racism. This reading of the term 'powers' would make it slightly less restrictive than the reference to 'scope' in Article 12.

Yet, it is also possible that 'powers' may be a more restrictive term than 'scope'. As established above, the scope of the Treaty is considerably broader than its competences. Therefore, if powers was interpreted as equivalent to competences, this would render Article 13 more limited in effect than Article 12, as, unlike the latter, Article 13 would be closely linked in its application to the existing competences of the Treaty. In this fashion, subject matter, such as criminal law proceedings, which fall outside the competences of the Community, but inside the scope of the Treaty, would not be within the remit of measures adopted pursuant to Article 13. In other words, by referring to powers rather than scope, the Member States may have been trying to avoid

principle of equal treatment'; para 25, Opinion of the A-G. See also Case C–168/91 *Konstantinidis* [1993] ECR I–1191, 1204.

[54] Conference of the representatives of governments of the Member States, 'European Union Today and Tomorrow—adapting the European Union for the benefit of its peoples and preparing it for the future', CONF/2500/96, 5 December 1996.

[55] I Chopin and J Niessen (eds), *Proposals for legislative measures to combat racism and to promote equal rights in the European Union* (London: Migration Policy Group and Commission for Racial Equality, 1998) 21.

[56] TEU, Art 29.

the expansive application of the Article, as has occurred with Article 12. This of course depends on the assumption that powers in Article 13 means in essence competences.

Evidence to support this view is found in the other language versions of the Treaty. For example, the French,[57] Italian,[58] Portuguese[59] and German[60] texts do not use the expression 'powers' in Article 13, but explicitly state within the limits of the *competences* of the Treaty. If anything, this indicates that Article 13 is less broad in its field than Article 12. The implication is that Article 13 may only be relied upon to prohibit discrimination within those areas for which the Community already has competence.[61]

Material scope and the Directives

Article 3(1) of both Directives provides detail on the scope of the instruments. This also proves instructive with regard to interpreting EC Treaty, Article 13. Regarding the Racial Equality Directive, the English version simply reproduces the wording of EC Treaty, Article 13; the Directive applies 'within the limits of the powers conferred upon the Community'. Similarly, the French version of the Racial Equality Directive reproduces the relevant part of EC Treaty, Article 13 ('dans les limites des compétences conférées à la Communauté'), thus perpetuating the interchangeable use of 'powers' and 'competences' in different language versions. However, the waters are muddied by the Italian version of the Racial Equality Directive which abandons the reference to competences in the Italian version of EC Treaty, Article 13, but instead states that the Directive applies 'nei limiti dei poteri conferiti alla Comunità' (within the limits of the powers conferred on the Community). Therefore, whilst 'powers' is used consistently in English, and 'competence' in French, these are interchangeable in the Italian texts.

---

[57] Sans préjudice des autres dispositions du présent traité et dans les limites des *compétences* que celui-ci confère à la Communauté.

[58] Fatte salve le altre disposizioni del presente trattato e nell'ambito delle *competenze* da esso conferite alla Comunità.

[59] Sem prejuízo das demais disposições do presente Tratado e dentro dos limites das *competências* que este confere à Comunidade.

[60] Unbeschadet der sonstigen Bestimmungen dieses Vertrags kann der Rat im Rahmen der durch den Vertrag auf die Gemeinschaft übertragenen *Zuständigkeiten*.

[61] This view is also taken in R Whittle, 'Disability discrimination and the Amsterdam Treaty' (1998) 23 ELR 50, 53; L Flynn, 'The implications of Article 13 EC—after Amsterdam, will some forms of discrimination be more equal than others? (1999) 36 CML Rev 1127, 1135; L Waddington, 'Testing the limits of the EC Treaty article on non-discrimination' (1999) 28 ILJ 133, 136.

Unfortunately, the Framework Directive creates further difficulties. Regarding the material scope of that Directive, the French text reproduces the exact wording of Article 13 and the Racial Equality Directive. The Italian version is consistent with the Racial Equality Directive, but not—as seen above—with the original EC Treaty, Article 13 in that language. Surprisingly, the English version of the Framework Directive is inconsistent with both the English versions of Article 13 and the Racial Equality Directive. In reference to the material scope of the Framework Directive, the English text declares that it applies 'within the limits of the areas of competence conferred on the Community'—abandoning the use of the term 'powers'. Ultimately, these semantics must lead one to the conclusion that 'powers' and 'competences' are interchangeable in Community legal terminology.[62] The importance of this discussion is in establishing that Article 13 EC is not a truly autonomous competence for anti-discrimination law. On the contrary, it is subject to the existing (and evolving) limits of Community competence throughout the Treaty. In turn, this raises further questions concerning its ability to deliver a social citizenship-based social policy. As the competences of the Community largely reflect its economic origins and objectives, then Article 13 may be still twinned with market integration. In particular, fundamental doubts exist as to the ability of the Community to tackle discrimination in certain areas of social policy—such as healthcare, social welfare and education—when these have been traditionally at the margins of Community competence.[63] If Article 13 then remains tied to marketplace discrimination, most notably the labour market, its capacity to contribute to the construction of European social citizenship is diminished. The next section examines these issues in greater depth, with particular reference to the Racial Equality Directive, which does address itself to wider areas of social policy.

---

[62] Lenaerts and Van Nuffel suggest a subtle distinction exists between powers and competences in some Community languages, but not all. Powers, in some languages, refers to the means available to exercise a competence, whereas in other languages (such as Dutch) there is simply one word for both the competence and the means to exercise it: K Lenaerts and P Van Nuffel, *Constitutional law of the European Union* (London: Sweet & Maxwell, 1999) 88. See also, A Gil Ibáñez, *The administrative supervision and enforcement of EC law: powers, procedures and limits* (Oxford: Hart Publishing, 1999) 52.

[63] Lord Dholakia, *Hansard*, HL (Series 5) vol 614, col 1227 (30 June 2000).

IV. Moving beyond employment discrimination?

Even a cursory examination of the Racial Equality Directive confirms a departure from the traditional labour market focus of European social policy. Discrimination in employment is thoroughly regulated by the Directive,[64] but it also applies to a number of areas wholly outside the employment sphere: 'social protection, including social security and healthcare; social advantages; education; access to and supply of goods and services which are available to the public, including housing.'[65] The importance of understanding the true scope of these provisions lies not only in the need to identify the obligations imposed on Member States by the Racial Equality Directive, but also to appreciate the scope for future measures to regulate discrimination in the non-employment sphere on the other grounds in Article 13. This is likely to become a pressing issue since commitments have already been made to submit such proposals in respect of gender discrimination[66] and disability discrimination.[67] De Búrca even raises questions over the legal foundations of the Racial Equality Directive in respect of its application to 'public sector healthcare and housing' given the need to respect the limits to Community competence.[68] This section of the chapter will examine three aspects of the material scope of the Directive further: goods and services, housing and healthcare.

(a) Goods and services

The application of the Directive to goods and services is a novelty in Community law, but not one that radically departs from the market integration model. Indeed, the internal market is fundamentally based on removing barriers to the supply (and consumption) of goods on the one hand,[69] and the provision and receipt of services on the other.[70] Article 12 already prohibits nationality discrimination, which can act as an obstacle to access to goods and services. For example, in *Commission v Greece*,[71] nationality restrictions on the

---

[64] Art 3(1)(a)–(d).   [65] Art 3(1)(e)–(h).

[66] European Social Agenda approved by the Nice European Council meeting on 7, 8 and 9 December 2000 [2001] OJ C157/4.

[67] L Waddington, 'Article 13 EC: setting priorities in the proposal for a horizontal employment Directive' (2000) 29 ILJ 176, 181.

[68] G de Búrca, 'The drafting of the European Union Charter of Fundamental Rights' (2001) 26 ELR 126, 135.

[69] EC Treaty, Arts 23–31.   [70] EC Treaty, Arts 49–55.

[71] Case C–62/96 [1997] ECR I–6725.

right to be inscribed in the Greek shipping register were held to be contrary to Article 12. This applied equally to non-economic shipping, as the Court held that migrant workers also required equal 'access to leisure activities available in that State'.[72] This may be instructive as frequent sites of racial discrimination are in access to leisure services—such as bars, clubs, restaurants and hotels.[73] Nonetheless, existing Community competence to regulate goods and services frequently depends on a connection with free movement. Specifically, EC Treaty, Article 12 does not usually affect nationality discrimination within a Member State, between its own nationals in access to goods and services, as it does not apply to purely internal situations.[74] In this light, the Racial Equality Directive considerably extends the penetration of Community law in the national legal order, as its application does not depend on establishing a cross-border dimension to the case.

Such harmonisation is far from unique, however. EC Treaty, Article 95 permits the adoption of harmonising measures 'which have as their object the establishment and functioning of the internal market'. Measures adopted under Article 95 may have as their objective the working of the internal market, but the consequences frequently extend into purely domestic legal affairs. For example, the Unfair Terms in Consumer Contracts Directive[75] naturally regulates both cross-border and domestic contracts.[76] There has been a temptation for the Community institutions to rely on Article 95 as a general power for market regulation. If this was true in the past, in the Tobacco Advertising judgment the Court of Justice laid down clear markers to prevent 'abuse' of this competence in the future. In reference to Article 95, the Court declared:

To construe that article as meaning that it vests in the Community legislature a general power to regulate the internal market would . . . be incompatible with the principle embodied in Article 3b of the EC Treaty (now Article 5 EC) that the powers of the Community are limited to those specifically conferred on it.

Moreover, a measure adopted on the basis of Article 100a [now 95] of the Treaty must genuinely have as its object the improvement of the conditions for the establishment and functioning of the internal market. If a mere finding of disparities

---

[72] ibid para 19.

[73] For an example from Irish equality law: *Ward and Ward v Quigley*, DEC-S2001-001, 16 March 2001 (refusal to serve Irish Travellers in a bar), available at: *http://www.odei.ie*

[74] A Arnull, *The European Union and its Court of Justice* (Oxford: Oxford University Press, 1999) 337.

[75] Council Dir (EEC) 93/13 of 5 April 1993 on unfair terms in consumer contracts; [1993] OJ L95/29.

[76] See further, S Weatherill, *EC Consumer law and policy* (London: Longman, 1997).

between national rules and of the abstract risk of obstacles to the exercise of fundamental freedoms or of distortions of competition liable to result therefrom were sufficient to justify the choice of Article 100a [now 95] as a legal basis, judicial review of compliance with the proper legal basis might be rendered nugatory.[77]

The importance of this case to understanding the scope of Article 13 and the Racial Equality Directive is twofold. First, the Court is clearly indicating that the limits to Community competence must be respected, and that it is willing to enforce those limits to the point of annulling a prominent piece of legislation supported by a clear majority of Member States. Second, the scope of Article 95 is not unlimited and it cannot be relied upon to regulate obstacles to the functioning of the internal market whose existence has not been substantiated. Therefore, given that Article 13 only applies within the limits of the competences of the Community, does this include the power to regulate generally access to and the supply of goods and services? The hypothetical justification is not difficult to explain. For example, if a British national, of Indian origin, travels to Italy on vacation and is refused a hotel room or entry to a bar on the grounds of his racial or ethnic origin, then there is an undeniable barrier to free movement for the purposes of receiving services. Whilst it seems probable that such a scenario has occurred in practice, there is little empirical evidence beyond the anecdotal. This sits uneasily with the Court's emphasis in Tobacco Advertising on the need for genuine evidence of obstacles within the internal market to activate Community competence.

(b) Housing

The explicit reference to housing in the Racial Equality Directive, Article 3(1) is notable because this was not included in the original Commission proposal.[78] It stems instead from an amendment by the Parliament, later accepted by the Commission.[79] Housing is not mentioned in the EC Treaty, but Article 44(e) permits the Community to adopt legislation 'enabling a national of one Member State to acquire and use land and buildings situated in the territory of another Member State'.[80] Nonetheless, this is subject to EC Treaty, Article 295, which states: 'this Treaty shall in no way prejudice the

[77] Case C–376/98 *Germany v Parliament and Council* [2000] ECR I–8419, paras 83–84. See further, T Hervey, 'Up in smoke? Community (anti) tobacco law and policy' (2001) 26 ELR 101.

[78] Commission, 'Proposal for a Council Directive establishing a general framework for equal treatment in employment and occupation' COM (1999) 565.

[79] Commission, 'Amended proposal for a Council Directive implementing the principle of equal treatment between persons irrespective racial or ethnic origin' COM (2000) 328.

[80] See also EC Treaty, Art 57(2) on investment in real estate.

rules in the Member States governing the system of property ownership.' The Court considered the relationship between these provisions further in *Konle*, which concerned the legality of an Austrian law requiring prior authorisation for the acquisition of land.[81] The Court held that 'although the system of property ownership continues to be a matter for each Member State under Article 295 EC, that provision does not have the effect of exempting such a system from the fundamental rules of the Treaty'.[82]

Housing has been also addressed in the context of the free movement of workers. Regulation (EEC) 1612/68 states in the preamble the need for the Community to combat discrimination in housing: 'the right of freedom of movement, in order that it may be exercised, by objective standards, in freedom and dignity, requires that equality of treatment shall be ensured in fact and in law in respect of all matters relating to the actual pursuit of activities as employed persons and to eligibility for housing'.[83]

Furthermore, Article 9(1) specifically provides that EU migrant workers 'shall enjoy all the rights and benefits accorded to national workers in matters of housing, including ownership of the housing he needs'. The Court has also stressed the importance of combating discrimination in housing to securing an effective right to free movement. In *Commission v Greece*,[84] the Court was called upon to consider the legality of certain rules in Greek legislation that prohibited the ownership of property by non-Greek citizens in border regions, which accounted for approximately 55 per cent of Greek territory. The Court held that such rules were incompatible with the prohibition on nationality discrimination in Article 12:

it follows that access to housing and ownership of property, provided for in Article 9 of Regulation No. 1612/68, is the corollary of freedom of movement for workers and is for that reason covered by the prohibition of discrimination against a national of a Member State who wishes to take employment in another Member State, laid now in Article 48 [now 39] of the Treaty.[85]

The situation with regard to housing is comparable to that for goods and services. On the one hand, housing is not an express Community competence. On the other, Community law provisions that have as their main objective securing free movement and the functioning of the internal market have affected housing matters. *Konle* is perhaps an instructive case in this light.[86] The authorities in the Tyrol argued that a prior authorisation

---

[81] Case C–302/97 *Konle v Republic of Austria* [1999] ECR I–3099. [82] ibid para 38.
[83] [1968] OJ Spec Ed (II) 475. [84] Case 305/87 [1989] ECR 1461.
[85] ibid para 18. [86] Also, Case 68/86 *Commission v Italy* [1988] ECR 29.

requirement for property purchase was necessary to ensure the maintenance of a permanently resident population in the region and economic activities independent of tourism. Whilst the Court implicitly accepted that this was a legitimate aim for the region to pursue, the procedure deployed revealed 'the intention of using the means of assessment offered by the authorisation procedure in order to subject applications from foreigners, including nationals of the Member States of the Community, to a more thorough check than applications from Austrian nationals'.[87] In other words, the Tyrolean authorities were free to adopt their own town and country planning policies, so long as these did not discriminate against other EU citizens. Similarly, the Racial Equality Directive will leave housing policies to the Member States, so long as these do not involve racial discrimination. The issue is certainly not academic. Planning policies in the west of Ireland, not dissimilar to those at stake in *Konle*, have been accused of masking covert racial discrimination.[88]

(c) Healthcare

The application of the Directive to healthcare poses greater difficulties— ironically precisely because health policy is specifically provided for in the EC Treaty, Article 152 which details the competence of the Community for the regulation of 'public health'. Paragraph 4 of this Article lists the areas where the Community can adopt binding instruments:

(a) measures setting high standards of quality and safety of organs and substances of human origin, blood and blood derivatives;

(b) . . . measures in the veterinary and phytosanitary fields which have as their direct object the protection of public health.

Far more significant are the limitations placed on the Community role in health regulation. First, aside from sub-paragraphs (a) and (b) mentioned above, the Community is competent to take 'incentive measures designed to protect and improve human health, *excluding any harmonisation* of the laws and regulations of the Member States'.[89] Second, sub-paragraph (a) is subject to the condition that it 'shall not affect national provisions on the donation or medical use of organs and blood'.[90] Finally, 'Community action in the field of public health shall fully respect the responsibilities of the Member States for the organisation and delivery of health services and medical care'.[91]

---

[87] Case C–302/97 *Konle v Republic of Austria* [1999] ECR I–3099, para 41.

[88] 'Councils risking "racism" in policies to save countryside', 'Locals-only building code raises a cry of racism', Irish Times, 29 April 2000.

[89] Emphasis added, Art 152(4)(c).   [90] Art 152(5).   [91] ibid.

Advocate-General Fennelly has described this competence as 'relatively minor',[92] whilst Craig and de Búrca argue that it is circumscribed to such an extent that it is 'rendered almost exhortatory'.[93]

The strict limits imposed by EC Treaty, Article 152 do not tell the whole story of EU healthcare law. Many instruments with a relevance to health regulation have in fact been adopted on the basis of EC Treaty, Article 95 as internal market harmonisation measures—for instance, laws on the advertising of medicinal products,[94] the regulation of pharmaceuticals,[95] standards in clinical trials[96] or tobacco labelling.[97] However, the use of Article 95 as a source of health law competence has recently been called into question. In the Tobacco Advertising case, the Court was confronted with a legal challenge from Germany to a Directive aimed at forbidding most forms of tobacco advertising and sponsorship.[98] The Directive was based on Article 95, but Germany argued that it was really a health policy measure rather than an internal market instrument. Moreover, as Article 152(4)(c) excludes any harmonisation of Member States' laws in the health field (save for the two narrow exceptions), then there would have been no competence to adopt the Directive based on Article 152.

The Court of Justice develops two principles directly relevant to understanding the scope of Community competence to regulate health policy. First, 'other articles of the Treaty may not, however, be used as a legal basis in order to circumvent the express exclusion of harmonisation laid down in Article [152(4)] of the Treaty'.[99] Second, Article 152(4) 'does not mean that harmonising measures adopted on the basis of other provisions of the Treaty cannot have any impact on the protection of human health. Indeed, the third

---

[92] Case C–376/98 *Germany v Parliament and Council* [2000] ECR I–8419, para 92.

[93] P Craig and G de Búrca, *EU law—text, cases and materials* (2nd edn, Oxford: Oxford University Press, 1998) 25.

[94] Dir (EEC) 92/28 on the advertising of medicinal products for human use [1992] OJ L113/13.

[95] Reg (EEC) 1768/92 concerning the creation of a supplementary protection certificate for medicinal products [1992] OJ L182/1.

[96] Dir (EC) 2001/20 on the approximation of the laws, regulations and administrative provisions of the Member States relating to the implementation of good clinical practice in the conduct of clinical trials on medicinal products for human use [2001] OJ L121/34.

[97] Dir (EEC) 92/41 amending Dir (EEC) 89/622 on the approximation of the laws, regulations and administrative provisions of the Member States concerning the labelling of tobacco products [1992] OJ L158/30.

[98] Dir (EC) 98/43 on the approximation of the laws, regulations and administrative provisions of the Member States relating to the advertising and sponsorship of tobacco products [1998] OJ L213/9.

[99] Case C–376/98 *Germany v Parliament and Council* [2000] ECR I–8419, para 79.

paragraph of [Article 152(1)] provides that health requirements are to form a constituent part of the Community's other policies'.[100] In respect of Article 95, this was interpreted to mean that simply because public health protection is an integral aspect of a particular instrument, this does not prevent it being adopted as an internal market measure, providing it is genuinely designed to address a barrier to the functioning of the internal market.[101]

Looking at this from the perspective of Article 13, it is clear that measures adopted on this legal basis cannot be a covert means to circumvent the exclusion of health law harmonisation in Article 152(4)(c). Nonetheless, the fact that measures adopted on the basis of Article 13 may contribute to improvements in public health is not an obstacle. The difficulty that arises is that Article 13, unlike Article 95, does not possess its own autonomous competence. On the contrary, the terms of Article 13 create a symbiotic relationship with the other provisions of the Treaty, as it is subject to their limits. Therefore, can harmonisation in healthcare be achieved via Article 13, when this is expressly excluded in Article 152(4)(c)?

The real significance of this technical legal discussion is revealed when one considers the implementation of the Racial Equality Directive's provisions on healthcare. Discrimination in healthcare can arise in a wide variety of forms. At the macro level, it can refer to inequality in resource allocation— for example, if ethnic minorities live mainly in the north of a particular city, and this part of the city is under-resourced in terms of doctors and clinical facilities (in comparison with the rest of the city), then there is indirect discrimination in healthcare resources against ethnic minorities. At the micro level, racial discrimination can occur in individual treatment decisions, for example the priority accorded to a particular patient, or their place on a waiting list for treatment. Racism can also occur by virtue of racist behaviour by doctors, nurses or other patients. It does not seem clear if the Racial Equality Directive will require individual Member States to forbid all of these diverse forms of discrimination, as this depends on whether they all fall 'within the limits of the powers of the Community'.[102] For instance, in 1998 a family in the UK gave instructions that their relative's organs were to be donated to a white recipient only.[103] This is an obvious example of overt racial discrimination, yet Article 152(5) excludes binding Community measures affecting 'national provisions on the donation or medical use of organs and blood'.

---

[100]   Case C–376/98 *Germany v Parliament and Council* [2000] ECR I–8419, para 78.
[101]   ibid para 98.   [102]   Racial Equality Directive, Art 3(1).
[103]   Department of Health, 'An investigation into conditional organ donation', 22 February 2000: available at: *http://www.doh.gov.uk/organdonation/*

The core problem that underpins this discussion is the fuzzy boundaries to Community competence that sometimes exist.[104] The dilemmas in health law are also true for education where the Treaty only foresees 'incentive measures, excluding any harmonisation of the laws and regulations of the Member States'.[105] The aim of the Member States in writing Article 13 (and the Racial Equality Directive) seems to have been to avoid the extensive application which the Court has given to EC Treaty, Article 12, and broadly to keep Article 13's remit within the existing policy competences of the Community. However, translating this idea into law has thrown up many difficulties, as there is no agreed definition of what are the Community's competences. De Búrca argues that in a fluid and dynamic system of multi-level governance it is unrealistic to expect to be able to draw red lines between national and Community competences.[106] Nonetheless, the Court ultimately has to perform this task, such as in the Tobacco Advertising case. More pressing is how the Member States will interpret the Racial Equality Directive in their national implementing legislation. This may provide a clearer guide to the states' understanding of the scope of the Directive. In the meantime, there is an unsatisfactory ambiguity that does not assist individuals to identify the rights conferred on them by the Directive.

V. EC Treaty, Article 13: post-market integration?

Article 13 clearly marks a turning point in EU anti-discrimination law. Whilst most attention has focused on the extension of Community law into new grounds of discrimination, equally significant is the intervention in new areas of discrimination—such as education, housing, social welfare and healthcare. When one considers social policy within the national polity, these are the classical sites of state intervention. However, the European Union's market integration model of social policy produced a myopic focus on the labour market. This is particularly problematic for anti-discrimination law. Discrimination cuts across many different aspects of public policy, making

---

[104] S Parmar, 'Human rights and the constitutional dimensions of the Charter of Fundamental Rights of the European Union' Paper presented at the 18th Annual Graduate Student Conference, The Institute for the Study of Europe, Columbia University, 29 March 2001, 12.

[105] EC Treaty, Art 149(4).

[106] G de Búrca, 'Reappraising subsidiarity's significance after Amsterdam' (1999) Harvard Jean Monnet Working Papers, No 7/99, available at: *http://www.law.harvard.edu/programs/ JeanMonnet/papers/papers99.html*

the effectiveness of policy in one area at least partially dependent on policies pursued elsewhere. For instance, equal treatment and opportunity in education is an obvious precondition to equal participation in the labour market.

EU gender equality law is often cited as one area of European social policy that has escaped from the market integration model.[107] Whilst it has developed an autonomous dynamic, it remains tied to a concept of citizenship within the market; the rights conferred largely can only be enjoyed by participating in the labour market. This creates particular problems for certain categories of discrimination where labour market participation is naturally not the sole objective. In particular, some people with severe disabilities may not be able to take up employment, and some older people may no longer wish to work. A meaningful sense of European citizenship for these individuals demands attention to equal treatment outside the marketplace.

Article 13 provides a step in this direction. Nonetheless, the link with the market is diminished rather than broken altogether. The dependency of Article 13 on the limits of the competences of the Community draws it back towards a market focus, because Community competences are strongest and most clear in those areas directly connected to the functioning of the internal market. Indeed, if the Member States (and the Court) take a very restrictive interpretation of the competences of the Community, then Article 13's contribution to combating discrimination in areas such as health and education could remain more symbolic than substantive. Ultimately, the reference to powers or competences generates more confusion than clarity, and it is regrettable that the approach taken in Article 12 was not transposed to Article 13.

The very openness and ambiguity of Article 13 means that it provides little explanation for the legislative choices finally made by the Council. Article 13 extends a broad legal space for EU anti-discrimination law, but other influences and factors must be examined in order to understand how the Directives were shaped. Chapter 6 turns to the national legal and political context in an attempt to explain further the initial implementation of Article 13.

---

[107] Lord Wedderburn, *Labour law and Freedom: Further essays in labour law* (London: Lawrence and Wishart, 1995) 265.

6

Reconciling Diverse Legal Traditions: Anti-Discrimination Law in the Member States

The difficulty involved in deciphering the limits to the Community's competences ultimately creates a barrier to using legal scope as a means of revealing the role for Article 13. In a different context, Gil Ibáñez suggests 'given the present confusion on the division of competencies and powers, it is advisable rather to focus on the level of procedures and means'.[1] Applying this to Article 13, a more instructive analysis of the role for the EU in anti-discrimination law may spring from a focus on understanding better the *appropriate* areas for Union intervention. In other words, if reference to legal competence cannot provide many answers on the role for the Union in regulating discrimination, then it may be more useful to consider in terms of practical policy how the Union can most effectively make a contribution in this area. This is echoed in de Búrca's analysis of the principle of subsidiarity:

it is no longer possible to say with any certainty that an area of policy falls entirely outside the sphere of Community competence . . . This is not by any means an argument for unlimited Community competence. Rather it is an acknowledgment of something that is increasingly hard to deny: that there are in fact no clear boundaries to the Community's potential competence and that any formal legalistic boundaries we may try to erect will be constantly changing and shifting; and that it would be more realistic and more sensible to consider openly the cluster of 'appropriateness' issues which underlie the subsidiarity question.[2]

---

[1] A Gil Ibáñez, *The administrative supervision and enforcement of EC law: powers, procedures and limits* (Oxford: Hart Publishing, 1999) 53.

[2] Section II (3)(b), G de Búrca, 'Reappraising subsidiarity's significance after Amsterdam' (1999) Harvard Jean Monnet Working Papers, No 7/99, available at: *http://www.law.harvard.edu/ programs/JeanMonnet/papers/papers99.html*

This chapter aims to explore the 'appropriate' role for the Union in anti-discrimination law through an overview of existing national legislation and, more importantly, the traditions, philosophies and policies these laws represent. These will be compared with the Article 13 Directives in order to analyse the extent to which the existing national legal regimes have informed and shaped the Directives, as well as the degree to which the Directives will in turn provoke revision and reform of national laws and policies. Clearly, the confines of a single chapter can only aim to identify some key points of convergence and divergence, and this chapter does not seek to provide a comprehensive analysis of each Member State's law and policy. Moreover, in order to find a common point of reference, an emphasis has been placed on national laws on discrimination in employment—this being the area where national laws are already most developed, as well as the shared element of the Framework and Racial Equality Directives.

I. Sources of anti-discrimination law

Before proceeding to the analysis of Member States' laws, it is necessary to consider the sources of protection against discrimination. Non-discrimination norms exist at a number of levels; international, European, national and subnational. Previously, certain Member States have relied on ratified instruments of international law to provide legal protection for individuals. For example, Greece has no specific anti-discrimination law covering racial discrimination, but it has ratified the International Convention on the Elimination of Racial Discrimination, which may be invoked by an individual in the national courts.[3] Alternatively, constitutional prohibitions on discrimination have been used as substitutes to specific laws. For instance, whilst Portugal has not adopted specific legislation on racism in workplace, the constitutional guarantees to equality apply to all persons resident on the territory,[4] and these specifically cover non-discrimination on grounds of race in the workplace.[5]

---

[3] Commission, 'Legal Instruments to Combat Racism and Xenophobia' (Luxembourg: OOPEC, 1992) 33.

[4] 'Toutes les dispositions constitutionnelles sur les droits, libertés et garanties sont en principe aussi applicables aux étrangers, qui jouissent, de ce fait, de droits de prestation reconnus par la Constitution' Art 15, see M Palma Carlos, 'La prévention du racisme sur les lieux de travail au Portugal' Working Paper No WP/95/40/FR (Dublin: European Foundation for the Improvement of Living and Working Conditions, 1995) 23–24.

[5] Art 59: ibid 25.

Nonetheless, the first identifiable impact of the Directives on Member States' legal traditions will be in requiring more specific legislative protection than that conferred by either international instruments or constitutional guarantees. This is based on the need to ensure the effectiveness and accessibility of the rights for individuals. Irrespective of the legal theory, empirical evidence suggests that individuals find it difficult in practice to rely on international law as a source of protection against discrimination.[6] Similarly, constitutional requirements on equality may be described as useful legal weapons in the fight against discrimination, but not necessarily sufficient instruments to provide comprehensive protection and to address the particular case of discrimination in the workplace. Forbes and Meade point out that all Member States have believed it necessary to supplement the constitutional guarantees to equality with specific legislation in respect of gender equality.[7] Indeed, the Court of Justice has required this. In *Commission v Greece*, the Court rejected arguments that general constitutional provisions could constitute sufficient implementation of Community law on equal pay for women and men:

Even if the provisions of the Greek Constitution are directly applicable, the relevant special Greek rules do not satisfy the requirements laid down by the case-law of the Court according to which the principles of legal certainty and the protection of individuals require an unequivocal wording which would give the persons concerned a clear and precise understanding of their rights and obligations and would enable the courts to ensure that those rights and obligations are observed.[8]

Based on these principles, it is reasonable to conclude that Member States will be required to implement the Directives through specific and detailed legislation. Therefore, this chapter will focus on the presence or absence in the Member States of such legislative provisions.

In examining the Member States' existing legal provisions, it may be said that there are, broadly speaking, three levels of legal protection. These will be termed 'equality laws', 'anti-discrimination laws', and an 'absence of any

---

[6] For example, on Italy, the Commission has noted that international human rights norms may be invoked in domestic legal proceedings, but 'there are an extremely limited number of court decisions applying international norms on racism or discrimination': Commission (n 3 above) 32.

[7] I Forbes and G Meade, *Measure for Measure: a comparative analysis of measures to combat racial discrimination in the Member Countries of the European Community* Equal Opportunities Study Group, University of Southampton, Research Series No 1 (London: Department of Employment, 1992) 13.

[8] Case C–187/98 *Commission v Greece* [1999] ECR I–7713, para 54. See also Case C–162/99 *Commission v Italy* [2001] ECR I–541.

specific legal provision'. Whilst the latter is more or less self-explanatory, the first two categories need additional clarification.

In the majority of Member States, one finds the existence of *anti-discrimination* laws. These may be summarised as largely a set of negative obligations, focusing on actions that employers must refrain from, as opposed to the imposition of positive duties on employers to act in favour of equal opportunities. Thus, there is a focus on providing a legal remedy for individuals in the face of manifest discrimination, but much less attention to the need to identify and challenge the discriminatory structures in the labour market which may perpetuate disadvantage for vulnerable groups. The legislation is founded on the notion of individual litigants enforcing non-discrimination through recourse to the legal protection provided by the law. Therefore, the major legal questions which arise concern issues such as the definition of discrimination, access to justice, the nature of the judicial process, the burden of proof, protection from victimisation and remedies.

In practice, individuals face a wide range of barriers to litigation, such as costs (financial and emotional), information and awareness, and legal procedures. As discussed in Chapter 2, this model possesses serious deficiencies in terms of the effective enforcement of equal treatment.[9] In contrast, states with *equality* laws have recognised the limits of an anti-discrimination strategy dependent on individual litigants and have responded principally in two directions. First, institutional provision has been made to support individual litigants, with a view to rendering more effective and accessible the right to non-discrimination. Second, measures have been adopted which break the link with the individual plaintiff, thereby focusing on collective mechanisms to combat discrimination. This frequently manifests itself in the adoption of certain forms of positive action. Such measures include making public procurement contracts conditional on firms meeting equality requirements (contract compliance), monitoring the workforce for its gender/ethnic/religious profile, and targeting advertisements at groups currently underrepresented in the workforce.[10]

Clearly, there are Member States that fall between the three categories. This chapter is not so much concerned with making an argument about the

---

[9] J Blom, B Fitzpatrick, J Gregory, R Knegt and U O'Hare, *The Utilisation of Sex Equality Litigation in the Member States of the European Community* V/782/96-EN (Brussels: Report to the Equal Opportunities Unit of DG V, 1995).

[10] The best existing example of such an equality law regime in the European Union probably exists in Northern Ireland, in relation to religious discrimination. See the Fair Employment and Treatment (Northern Ireland) Order 1998, No 3162 (NI 21).

categorisation of legal regimes, but rather simply seeks to employ these titles as a useful means of presenting the pattern of national legislation.

II. Equality law regimes

Within the category of equality law regimes, a difference may be made between those states with 'comprehensive' equality laws, and those with 'mixed-level' equality laws. In the former category, one finds the Netherlands, Ireland and Sweden, where laws exist which favour equal opportunities on grounds of both race and sexual orientation. In the latter group, there is the UK, Belgium and Italy. These are referred to as 'mixed-level' equality law regimes as they are characterised by a relatively high level of protection against racial discrimination, but the absence of any specific legislative protection against sexual orientation discrimination. What binds all these states together though, is the presence in their equality legislation of proactive measures that go beyond a simple ban on discrimination. Principally, these are:

—thorough legal prohibitions on direct and indirect discrimination, including harassment and victimisation;
—the existence of independent bodies to assist victims;
—provision for the use of positive action.

(a) Comprehensive equality law regimes

(i) The Netherlands

Anti-discrimination law in the Netherlands has developed incrementally.[11] An amendment in 1991 added sexual orientation to Article 429quater of the Penal Code, which already prohibited, *inter alia*, racial discrimination 'in the performance of a public office, a profession or a business'.[12] Furthermore, by virtue of the Civil Code, Article 1401, it is possible to bring an action in civil law for any unlawful act; therefore, the prohibition of discrimination in criminal law also created the possibility of bringing a civil action against such

---

[11] See further, P Rodrigues, 'Racial discrimination and the law in the Netherlands' (1994) 20 *New Community* 381.

[12] K Waaldijk, 'The legal situation in the Member States' in A Clapham and K Waaldijk (eds), *Homosexuality: a European Community issue—essays on lesbian and gay rights in European law and policy* (Dordrecht: Martinus Nijhoff, 1993) 106.

discrimination. Nonetheless, the law proved difficult to use in practice,[13] and a lengthy debate ensued on providing a specific civil law foundation for anti-discrimination norms.

In September 1994, the Netherlands adopted the General Equal Treatment Act. Section 1 of the Act forbids any direct or indirect discrimination 'between persons on the grounds of religion, belief, political opinion, race, sex, nationality, heterosexual or homosexual orientation or civil status.'[14] (Notably, disability and age are not included in this list, although draft legislation has been submitted on both grounds of discrimination.[15]) Harassment on any of the grounds covered in section 1 has been held to be contrary to the Act.[16] The law applies to both the public and the private sectors, and in all aspects of the employment relationship, including education and training prior to or during the course of employment.[17] Moreover, it extends to the provision of goods and services, including education, housing, social services, healthcare and cultural affairs.[18]

A number of general exceptions are provided for in the Act, including where 'racial appearance is a determining factor';[19] where the measure is designed to 'place women or persons belonging to a particular ethnic or cultural minority group in a privileged position in order to eliminate or reduce *de facto* inequalities and the discrimination is reasonably appropriate to that aim';[20] and 'legal relations within religious communities and independent sections thereof and within other associations of a spiritual nature'.[21] Specific exceptions in relation to the ban on discrimination in employment include: 'the freedom of an institution founded on religious or ideological principles to impose requirements which, having regard to the institution's purpose, are necessary for the fulfilment of the duties attached to a post; such requirements may not lead to discrimination on the sole grounds of political opinion, race, sex, nationality, heterosexual or homosexual orientation or civil status.'[22] This clearly covers similar contours to the religious organisation exception in the Framework Directive, Article 4(2). In the several cases that

---

[13] M Gras and F Bovenkerk, 'Preventing racism at the workplace: the Netherlands' Working Paper No WP/95/49/EN (Dublin: European Foundation for the Improvement of Living and Working Conditions, 1995) 30.

[14] Available at: http://www.cgb.nl/act_frameset.html

[15] See further, See L Waddington, 'Tweede-generatie richtlijnen Gelijke Behandeling: de nieuwe Richtlijn inzake gelijke behandeling ongeacht ras of etnische afstamming en de Kaderrichtlijn gelijke behandeling in arbeid en beroep' (2000) 12 Sociaal Recht 357.

[16] Commissie Gelijke Behandeling, *Annual Report 1997* (Utrecht: Commissie Gelijke Behandeling, 1998) 13.

[17] s 5.   [18] s 7(1).   [19] s 2(4).   [20] s 2(3).   [21] s 3.   [22] s 5(2)(a).

have arisen concerning an employment requirement of a specific religious affiliation, the employer has generally been held to be within the law.[23] Section 5(6) contains a significant exception for 'discrimination on grounds of civil status in relation to pension provision'. This provides a legal defence to employers restricting pension schemes to married partnerships, a practice also accommodated in the Framework Directive by virtue of Recital 22. However, the discriminatory effects of such an exception in Dutch law are considerably ameliorated by the fact that same-sex marriage is now possible in the Netherlands, albeit only since 1 April 2001.

The main focus for positive action has been the 1994 Act for the Promotion of Proportional Labour Participation of Non-Nationals,[24] which requires all employers with more than 35 employees to monitor the ethnic profile of their workforce and to draw up plans for the creation of a proportional workforce. This is supplemented by a requirement to release these figures on an annual basis. The Act did not enjoy a particularly successful introduction. Opposition persisted, mainly from employers, but also tacitly from certain trade unions.[25] A principled antagonism to ethnic monitoring, based on its similarities to racial classifications employed during the Second World War, seems to lie at the heart of the problem.[26] Indeed, by the end of 1996, just 26 per cent of companies presented the information required and only 12 per cent had a specific policy on the employment of ethnic minorities.[27] The law was subsequently amended in 1998 to make the reporting requirements less bureaucratic and more easily enforced through civil law penalties.[28] Nonetheless, subsequent research continues to reveal poor compliance with this law.[29] More generally, there has been a considerable amount of experimentation with positive action policies. For example, a 1991 survey recorded that nearly 20 per cent of all local authorities were using positive action, including a limited use of contract compliance. Eighty-two per cent had used schemes where preference was given for ethnic minorities, where job applicants had equal qualifications.[30] In

---

[23] Commissie Gelijke Behandeling (n 16 above) 28.

[24] Wet Bevordering Evenredige Arbeidsdeelname Allochtonen.

[25] F Glastra, P Schedler and E Kats, 'Employment equity policies in Canada and the Netherlands: enhancing minority employment between public controversy and market initiative' (1998) 26 *Policy and Politics* 163, 169.

[26] ibid 170.   [27] ibid.   [28] ibid 171.

[29] European Monitoring Centre on Racism and Xenophobia (EUMC), *Diversity and equality for Europe—annual report 1999* (Vienna: EUMC, 2000) 40.

[30] M Gras and F Bovenkerk, 'Preventing racism at the workplace: the Netherlands' Working Paper No WP/95/49/EN (Dublin: European Foundation for the Improvement of Living and Working Conditions, 1995) 39–40.

the future, such schemes may be vulnerable to legal challenge as unlawful discrimination. Similar measures to promote gender equality have been the subject of litigation before the Court of Justice. The settled case law now indicates that preferential treatment programmes must not give an automatic and unconditional priority to persons from the under-represented group.[31]

The main innovation of the Equal Treatment Act was the creation of an Equal Treatment Commission, the *Commissie Gelijke Behandeling* (CGB).[32] Any individual may submit a written complaint of unlawful discrimination to the CGB. Alternatively, a trade union or a pressure group may submit a complaint on behalf of an individual, or where the pressure group was founded to promote the interests of the groups covered by the Equal Treatment Act, then they are entitled to file complaints to the CGB independently of any individual.[33] Where the CGB decides that it can process the complaint, it will hold an investigation, following which it makes a determination as to whether or not the Equal Treatment law was violated. Whilst its determinations are not legally binding, in practice its decisions are 'usually accepted and carried out'.[34] In any case, where decisions are not complied with it remains open for the complainant to bring a court action against the employer. Interestingly, the Netherlands was the only Member State to propose that an equal treatment body should also be provided for in the Framework Directive.[35]

Alongside the CGB, since 1985, the *Landelijk Bureau Racismebestrijding* (LBR) has existed as an independent organisation funded by the Ministry of Justice to combat racial discrimination. It does not enjoy any specific legal powers, but it does provide advice to individuals, and may choose to bring or support legal cases on a strategic basis.[36] The LBR also assists a network of around 40 anti-discrimination agencies throughout the Netherlands, to

---

[31] See Case C–450/93 *Kalanke v Freie Hansestadt Bremen* [1995] ECR I–3069; Case C–409/95 *Marschall v Land Nordrhein-Westfalen* [1997] ECR I–6363; Case C–158/97 *Badeck v Hessischer Ministerpräsident* [2000] ECR I–1875; Case C–407/98 *Abrahamsson and Anderson v Fogelqvist* [2000] ECR I–5539.

[32] See J Blom, 'The Dutch Equal Treatment Commission' (1995) 24 ILJ 84.

[33] Commissie Gelijke Behandeling, *Equal treatment: a constitutional right* (Utrecht: Commissie Gelijke Behandeling, 1995).

[34] ibid.

[35] EU Council, 'Outcome of Proceedings of the Social Questions Working Party on 21/22 February 2000' No 6435/00, Brussels, 1 March 2000, n 26.

[36] I Forbes and G Meade, *Measure for Measure: a comparative analysis of measures to combat racial discrimination in the Member Countries of the European Community* Equal Opportunities Study Group, University of Southampton, Research Series No 1 (London: Department of Employment, 1992) 58.

which individuals may bring complaints. These receive approximately 2,000 complaints each year.[37] The agencies seek to facilitate conciliation between the two parties but, failing that, they will pass the case to the CGB for a determination.[38]

Enforcement appears to remain a problem. Gras and Bovenkerk concluded their 1995 overview with the following comments: 'victims of discrimination are often insufficiently acquainted with the legal proceedings . . . an active prosecution policy is lacking . . . the onus of proof is with the plaintiff, and demonstrating the occurrence of discrimination is very difficult'.[39] With regard to positive action, they argue that 'many plans and initiatives have been developed, but these have been largely without any tangible effects'.[40] Nonetheless, the Netherlands would appear to have a very accessible system of legal remedies for discrimination. In 1997, the CGB reported that it received 813 complaints, resulting in 171 decisions, with over 50 per cent finding unlawful discrimination.[41] About 30 per cent of all decisions concerned racial, religious or nationality discrimination. The majority of decisions continue to relate to sex discrimination, and just seven decisions addressed sexual orientation discrimination.

(ii) Ireland

New legislation revolutionising employment equality law in Ireland was finally adopted in 1998 and came into effect on 18 October 1999.[42] The Employment Equality Act 1998 is relatively similar to the Dutch Equal Treatment Act, most especially in the institutional arrangements. Section 6 forbids direct and indirect discrimination in all aspects of the employment relationship on grounds of gender, marital status, family status, sexual orientation, religious belief, age, disability, race, and membership of the Traveller community. Furthermore, harassment in the workplace on any of these grounds is also forbidden and the employer is placed under a duty to take all

---

[37] P Rodrigues, 'The Dutch experience of enforcement agencies: current issues in Dutch anti-discrimination law' in M MacEwen (ed), *Anti-discrimination law enforcement: a comparative perspective* (Aldershot: Ashgate, 1997) 54.

[38] Migration News Sheet, November 1996, 14.

[39] M Gras and F Bovenkerk, 'Preventing racism at the workplace: the Netherlands' Working Paper No WP/95/49/EN (Dublin: European Foundation for the Improvement of Living and Working Conditions, 1995) 47.

[40] ibid 45. See also Rodrigues (n 37 above) 61.

[41] Commissie Gelijke Behandeling, *Annual Report 1997* (Utrecht: Commissie Gelijke Behandeling, 1998) 8.

[42] L Buckley, 'Employment Equality Act 1998 (Ireland)' (2000) 29 ILJ 273.

reasonable steps to ensure a harassment-free workplace.[43] The legislation applies equally to the public and private sectors,[44] including trade unions, professional associations and employment agencies.[45] It has since been complemented by the Equal Status Act 2000, which prohibits discrimination on the same grounds, but in the areas of goods and services, accommodation and education.

A variety of exceptions are provided for in the Employment Equality Act 1998. Pensions are excluded from the definition of remuneration,[46] which will not be compatible with either of the Article 13 Directives. A number of exceptions relate to discrimination on the ground of sexual orientation. First, section 16(5) states 'nothing in this Act shall be construed as requiring an employer to recruit, retain in employment or promote an individual if the employer is aware, on the basis of a criminal conviction of the individual or other reliable information, that the individual engages, or has a propensity to engage, in any form of sexual behaviour which is unlawful'. This provision seems designed to ensure that discrimination against paedophiles is not forbidden by the Act, and it finds a shadow in the Framework Directive, Article 2(5). However, the generous terms of s 16(5) may be wider than the Directive will permit.

Section 34 provides a series of amendments aimed at protecting employment benefits that are related to marriage—for example, a bonus to an employee who is getting married, or benefits provided in respect of employees' spouses. Again, the Framework Directive, Recital 22 is aimed at protecting this type of behaviour from challenge as indirect sexual orientation discrimination and should ensure this aspect of Irish law remains permissible.

Finally, as in the Netherlands, the sensitive issue of the freedom of religious organisations proved to be one of the most controversial aspects of the whole legislation.[47] After lengthy debate and revision, s 37 states:

(1) A religious, educational or medical institution which is under the direction or control of a body established for religious purposes or whose objectives include the provision of services in an environment which promotes certain religious values shall not be taken to discriminate against a person . . . if—

(a) it gives more favourable treatment, on the religious ground, to an employee or a prospective employee over that person where it is reasonable to do so in order to maintain the religious ethos of the institution, or

---

[43] s 23 covers sexual harassment and s 32 addresses harassment on all other grounds.

[44] s 8.   [45] s 13.   [46] ss 2(1) and 13.

[47] S Mullally, 'Mainstreaming equality in Ireland: a fair and inclusive accommodation?' (2001) 21 Legal Studies 99, 103.

(b) it takes action which is reasonably necessary to prevent an employee or a prospective employee from undermining the religious ethos of the institution.

A key issue for the Irish Government was ensuring that the Framework Directive did not impinge on this carefully crafted provision of the Employment Equality Act. Indeed, according to press reports, it was instrumental in ensuring the addition of the second paragraph to Article 4(2) of the Directive (good faith and loyalty requirements), which deals with the same concerns protected in s 37(1)(b) of the Act.[48]

Positive action is expressly permitted in the Act on grounds of gender,[49] but elsewhere it is only allowed in respect of persons over the age of 50, people with disabilities and members of the Traveller community.[50] This provision seems rather limited, as there is no legislative protection for positive action schemes for ethnic minorities outside the Traveller community. Nevertheless, the Racial Equality Directive will not require any change in the status quo here.

As in the Netherlands, Irish law creates separate institutions for adjudication on individual complaints on the one hand, and the promotion of equality on the other. With regard to individual enforcement, individuals must first submit complaints to the Office of the Director of Equality Investigations (ODEI), which has strong powers of investigation, and may issue binding decisions, including compensation of up to two years' pay where there is a finding of unlawful discrimination.[51] The first decision under the Act finding discrimination on a ground other than gender was on 29 December 2000. In *Equality Authority v Ryanair*,[52] an airline which advertised for a 'young and dynamic professional' was fined €10,158 for unlawful age discrimination and ordered to complete a 'comprehensive review of its equal opportunities policies' within six months.

Alongside the ODEI, the Act created the Equality Authority. This is charged with the promotion of equal opportunities and may draw up statutory codes of practice.[53] Moreover, the Authority enjoys the power to invite businesses to carry out equality reviews and to introduce equality action

---

[48] 'Churches lobbied on EU Directive', Irish Times, 19 October 2000.   [49] s 24.

[50] s 33.

[51] See generally Pt VII of the Act. The Director may also order any person to take a specified course of action to avoid future discrimination. The obligation to proceed first with the Director's office does not apply to cases of gender discrimination or discriminatory dismissals. Finally, it should be noted that higher levels of compensation are available in respect of gender discrimination claims (s 82).

[52] DEC-E/2000/14, available at *http://www.odei.ie/*   [53] s 56.

plans.[54] Ultimately, businesses can be the subject of a court order compelling compliance with these action plans.[55] Moreover, the Authority also has the power to refer alleged cases of discrimination to the ODEI in its own name.[56] The Authority has received complaints on all of the discrimination grounds except for family status, with harassment emerging as a key issue 'across the age, race, disability, sexual orientation and Traveller grounds'.[57] The ODEI dealt with 59 employment discrimination cases in 1999, but this rose to 139 in 2000.[58]

(iii) Sweden

Unlike the Netherlands and Ireland, in Sweden a separate institutional framework exists for racial and sexual orientation discrimination. In 1986, the office of Discrimination Ombudsman (DO) was created, and charged with the task of preventing the occurrence of racial discrimination, providing advice to individuals, and promoting good relations between different ethnic groups.[59] However, the law still did not actually prohibit racial discrimination in employment, a step that was taken only after much debate in 1994.[60] In 1999, this law was further amended and strengthened,[61] and at the same time a law prohibiting discrimination in working life because of sexual orientation was adopted.[62] Significantly, this creates an Ombudsman against Discrimination because of Sexual Orientation (HomO); Ombudsmen also exist in relation to gender and disability discrimination.

Although there are separate laws on racial and sexual orientation discrimination, there is a certain degree of overlap. Direct discrimination is forbidden, but is subject to a general exception where 'the treatment is justified with regard to an idealistic or other special interest which is clearly more important'.[63] The breadth of this exception does not appear to be compatible with either Directive. In contrast, indirect discrimination is defined in terms comparable to the Directive—both laws refer to behaviour that is 'particularly

---

[54] ss 69–70.   [55] s 72.   [56] s 85.

[57] Equality News, autumn 2000, 3. Available at: *http://www.equality.ie/publications.shtml*

[58] 'Complaints submitted to equality body up 1,700%', Irish Times, 28 July 2001.

[59] M Soininen and M Graham, 'Persuasion contra legislation: preventing racism at the workplace: Sweden', Working Paper No WP/95/53/EN (Dublin: European Foundation for the Improvement of Living and Working Conditions, 1995) 23.

[60] It should be noted though that public sector employees were already protected against discrimination on the basis of the guarantees of non-discrimination in the Constitution (ibid 18).

[61] Law 1999: 130 on measures against ethnic discrimination in working life. Available at: *www.do.se*

[62] Law 1999: 133. Available at: *www.homo.se*   [63] Law 1999: 133, s 3; Law 1999: 130, s 8.

disfavourable' to persons of a particular ethnic background or sexual orientation.[64] Discrimination is forbidden in recruitment, promotion, training, pay, working conditions and termination of the employment contract.[65] Victimisation and harassment are expressly prohibited.[66] Moreover, where it comes to the attention of the employer that an employee considers themselves to have been harassed on a prohibited ground, the employer is under a duty to investigate and take such measures as are reasonably necessary to prevent harassment in the future.

Whilst the above elements are common to both laws, the law on ethnic discrimination goes further in s 4 which imposes a duty to promote ethnic diversity: 'within the framework of her or his activities an employer shall carry out a goal-oriented work in order to actively promote ethnic diversity in working life.' Section 5 specifies that this requires employers to make reasonable accommodations 'to ensure that the working conditions are suitable for employees without regard to their ethnic background'. The importance of this part of the law lies in the shift away from a negative duty not to discriminate towards a positive duty to promote ethnic diversity in the workplace, coupled with an implicit concept of reasonable accommodation.

Individuals who feel they have been discriminated against may approach directly the DO or HomO. The primary goal of both Ombudsmen is to facilitate voluntary compliance by the employer.[67] If this fails, the relevant trade union has priority to pursue the case, and the Ombudsman may only bring the litigation 'if the union refrains from doing so'.[68] This institutional balance is reflected in the Racial Equality Directive, where the right of equal treatment bodies to assist individuals is 'without prejudice' to the legal standing conferred on associations and organisations to bring cases on behalf of individuals.[69]

It is difficult to make any assessment at this stage of the effectiveness of the laws adopted in 1999. The HomO has recorded two cases of sexual orientation harassment in August 2000 where an out of court settlement was reached awarding compensation to the complainants.[70] The DO's office has recorded a significant increase in complaints since the 1999 law reform; whereas 121 complaints were received in 1998, 184 were received in 1999.[71]

---

[64] Law 1999: 133, s 4; Law 1999: 130, s 9.
[65] Law 1999: 133, s 5; Law 1999: 130, s 10.
[66] Law 1999: 133, ss 7 and 8; Law 1999: 130, ss 12 and 13.
[67] Law 1999: 133, s 16; Law 1999: 130, s 22.
[68] Law 1999: 133, s 25; Law 1999: 130, s 38.
[69] Framework Directive, Art 13(2).   [70] See *http://www.homo.se*
[71] EUMC, *Diversity and equality for Europe—annual report 1999* (Vienna: EUMC, 2000) 42.

(b) Mixed-level equality regimes

(i) United Kingdom

UK law is notable for the significant differences in the level of protection accorded to different grounds of discrimination. Racial discrimination in employment was first forbidden in Great Britain in 1968, four years earlier than any other Member State. Eight years later, this legislation was substantially revised and strengthened with the enactment of the Race Relations Act 1976 (RRA).[72] In 1997, this legislation was extended to Northern Ireland.[73] The RRA 1976 forbids direct or indirect discrimination on 'racial grounds',[74] and 'racial grounds' is defined as on the basis of 'colour, race, nationality, or ethnic or national origins'.[75] The ban on discrimination includes recruitment, the terms and conditions of employment, and the termination of employment.[76] Subsequent case law has held that the terms of the Act also prohibit racial harassment in the workplace.[77] The Act applies to the public and the private sectors, with a number of limited exemptions.[78] The RRA 1976 also applied to goods, services and facilities, housing and education. However, the Race Relations (Amendment) Act 2000 extended the ban on discrimination to all functions of public authorities.[79] Moreover, this covers 'any person certain of whose functions are functions of a public nature';[80] for example, this would apply to a private company running a prison.[81] The Amendment Act also introduces a positive duty on specified public authorities to have due regard to the need to eliminate unlawful discrimination and promote equality of opportunity and good race relations in carrying out their functions.[82] Any individual who believes that they have been subject to unlawful discrimination in the workplace may bring an action before an

---

[72] For an overview of the context in which the legislation was adopted, see Z Layton-Henry, *The Politics of Immigration: immigration, 'race' and 'race' relations in post-war Britain* (Oxford: Blackwell, 1992).

[73] Race Relations (Northern Ireland) Order 1997, No 869 (NI 6).   [74] s 1.   [75] s 3.

[76] s 4.

[77] For example, *Tower Boot Co v Jones* [1997] IRLR 168 CA. See L Buckley, 'Vicarious Liability and Employment Discrimination' (1997) 26 ILJ 158.

[78] These include employment in a private household (s 4(3)), or where race is a 'genuine occupational qualification'; eg the provision of welfare services for a particular racial or ethnic group (s 5).

[79] RRA as amended, s 19B(1).   [80] RRA as amended, s 19B(2)(a).

[81] Commission for Racial Equality, 'Strengthening the Race Relations Act' (London: CRE, 2000).

[82] RRA as amended, s 71(1).

employment tribunal for compensation. Since 1994, there has been no monetary limit on the amount of compensation the tribunal may award.[83]

What distinguished the 1976 legislation was the establishment of the
Commission for Racial Equality (CRE).[84] The CRE is charged with the
elimination of discrimination, the promotion of equality of opportunity and
good ethnic relations, and keeping the legislation under review.[85] It provides
advice and assistance to individuals, and may provide legal representation
where the case raises an issue of principle or where it would be unreasonable
to expect the complainant to deal with the issue independently.[86] In addition
to its support of individuals, it also may bring legal proceedings in cases of
persistent discrimination, and it may conduct formal investigations into
organisations, firms or areas of economic activity where unlawful discrimination is suspected.[87]

The Act foresees a variety of positive action measures, principally in training schemes, which may be restricted to the members of a particular racial
group.[88] These may be provided by employers or training bodies and may be
either general, non-vocational courses, or vocational training for sectors
where the racial group in question is under-represented. Employers are also
entitled to provide special training courses for existing employees, and to
restrict this to members of a particular racial group that is currently under-
represented in the workforce. Finally, employers are permitted to encourage
members of a particular racial group to apply for jobs where they are under-
represented. Beyond these forms of positive action which are specifically provided for in the legislation, the CRE recommends that employers monitor
the ethnic profile of their workforce, and consider setting goals and time-
tables for bringing about a change in the ethnic composition of the workforce
for groups which are currently under-represented.[89]

Despite the range of measures taken to combat racial discrimination in the
RRA 1976, significant problems remain. In 1998, the CRE recommended a
series of revisions to the Act, in particular to strengthen the definition of
indirect discrimination and to place more obligations on employers in

---

[83] C Bourne and J Whitmore, *Race and sex discrimination* (London: Sweet & Maxwell, 2nd edn,
1993) 57.

[84] In Northern Ireland, the functions of CRE are exercised by the Equality Commission, since
1999.

[85] s 43.   [86] s 66.   [87] s 48.   [88] ss 35–38.

[89] J Wrench and D Owen, 'Preventing racism at the workplace: the UK national report'
Working Paper No WP/95/50/EN (Dublin: European Foundation for the Improvement of
Living and Working Conditions, 1995) 35.

respect of positive action.[90] The European Commission against Racism and Intolerance (ECRI) also identified problems with the RRA in its 2001 report. In particular, it highlighted the need for express provision on shifting the burden of proof.[91] Whilst the Racial Equality Directive will require some of these changes to the RRA, it will not place any new obligations on the UK with regard to positive action.

The RRA remains an instrument which, compared to other EU jurisdictions, is relatively well used by individual litigants. Between April 1999 and March 2000, 11,000 persons approached the CRE for advice about bringing legal proceedings.[92] The CRE recorded 1,001 cases on racial discrimination before employment tribunals and courts in 1999.[93] However, the average compensation award in racial discrimination cases in 1999 was £9,948.[94]

In sharp contrast to this picture, no legislative protection exists against sexual orientation discrimination. Litigants have tried various strategies in recent years to challenge this form of discrimination through reliance on unfair dismissal laws,[95] sex discrimination laws[96] and general human rights law.[97] Most cases have been unsuccessful, however, there are signs that this is changing. In particular, in *Smith and Grady v UK*, and *Lustig-Prean and Beckett v UK*,[98] the Court of Human Rights held the UK ban on lesbians and gay men in the military to be in breach of ECHR, Article 8 on the right to respect for private life. As the Convention has been incorporated into UK domestic law since October 2000 (by virtue of the Human Rights Act 1998) there may be

---

[90]   CRE, 'Reform of the Race Relations Act 1976' (London: CRE, 1998).

[91]   ECRI, 'Second report on the UK' CRI (2001) 6 (Strasbourg: Council of Europe, 2001) 10.

[92]   Equal Opportunities Review (Jan/Feb 2001) 'CRE cannot act alone' No 95, 4.   [93]   ibid 5.

[94]   Equal Opportunities Review (Sept/Oct 2000) 'Compensation awards '99' No 93.

[95]   Employment Rights Act 1996. Examples of cases where challenges to sexual orientation-based dismissals have failed include: *Saunders v Scottish National Camp Association* [1980] IRLR 174; *Wiseman v Salford CC* [1981] IRLR 202; *Nottinghamshire CC v Bowley* [1978] IRLR 252 EAT; *Boychuk v HJ Symons Holdings Ltd.* [1977] IRLR 395; *Gardiner v Newport County Borough Council* [1974] IRLR 262. See further, R Cohen, S O'Byrne and P Maxwell, 'Employment discrimination based on sexual orientation: the American, Canadian and UK responses' (1999) 17 Law and Inequality: a journal of theory and practice 1.

[96]   Case C–249/96 *Grant v South-West Trains* [1998] ECR I–636; *Smith v Gardner Merchant Ltd* [1998] All ER CA; *Governing Body of Mayfield Secondary School v Pearce* [2000] IRLR 548; *Pearce v Governing Body of Mayfield School* [2001] IRLR 669; *Advocate General for Scotland v MacDonald* [2001] IRLR 431, Scottish Court of Session.

[97]   *R v Ministry of Defence, ex p Smith and other appeals* [1996] 1 All ER 257, CA.

[98]   *Lustig-Prean and Beckett v UK* (2000) 29 EHRR 548; *Smith and Grady v UK* (2000) 29 EHRR 493.

possibilities to rely on the Convention to challenge certain forms of sexual orientation discrimination, at least in public sector employment.[99]

Against this picture of relatively weak legal protection, the public sector has been at the forefront of developing proactive policies to prevent sexual orientation discrimination. For example, in 1995, 90 per cent of Metropolitan authorities stated that their equal opportunities policies expressly included lesbians and gay men.[100] Furthermore, it is in the UK that one finds some of the only examples of positive action policies for lesbians and gay men. For example, South Yorkshire Police and Sussex Police have advertised vacancies in the gay press, and specifically welcomed applications from gay persons, so as to improve police relations with the gay community.[101]

Finally, it should be noted that in Northern Ireland, all public authorities are under a duty in carrying out their functions to:

have due regard to the need to promote equality of opportunity—(a) between persons of different religious belief, political opinion, racial group, age, marital status or sexual orientation; (b) between men and women generally; (c) between persons with a disability and persons without; and (d) between persons with dependants and persons without.[102]

The scope of this duty would include the employment functions of public authorities.

(ii) Belgium

The situation in Belgium shares certain similarities with that in the UK. The legal framework in respect of racial discrimination is well developed, whereas measures addressing sexual orientation discrimination are more recent. However, in the wake of the Article 13 Directives, the Belgian Government has now proposed moving towards an integrated equality law regime.

An Act for the suppression of racism was adopted on 30 July 1981, but it was only in April 1994 that this was amended to include a prohibition on employment discrimination. Article 2a of the 1994 Act forbids discrimination on grounds of race, colour, descent, national or ethnic origins, and

---

[99] See further, N Bamforth, 'Sexual orientation discrimination after *Grant v South-West Trains*' (2000) 63 MLR 694.

[100] Equal Opportunities Review (July/Aug 1997) 'Equality for lesbians and gay men in the workplace', No 74, 20, 22.

[101] ibid 27.

[102] Northern Ireland Act 1998, s 75. See further B Fitzpatrick, 'The Fair Employment and Equal Treatment (Northern Ireland) Order 1998, The Northern Ireland Act 1998' (1999) 28 ILJ 336.

nationality. This applies to recruitment, execution of the contract of employment, training and dismissal.[103] The definition of 'discrimination' provided in the law would appear to cover indirect discrimination.[104] Trade unions and employers' associations are allowed to assist plaintiffs, as are registered associations with a vocation to combat discrimination (albeit after a period of five years' existence).[105] This aspect of Belgian law bears a clear resemblance to the legal standing provisions in the Directives.[106] However, unlike in the UK, the Netherlands, Ireland or Sweden, citizenship remains a significant barrier to employment in the public sector. This is exacerbated by the very limited possibilities for naturalisation in Belgian law. Forbes and Meade conclude that many ordinary occupations, which are located in the public sector, remain closed to even second and third generation immigrants due to the citizenship requirement.[107]

Notwithstanding these remarks, the law is strengthened by the existence of the Centre pour l'Egalité des Chances et la Lutte contre le Racisme, which was created within the Prime Minister's Office in 1993. The Centre combines both the function of a policy advisory service with the provision of direct assistance to individual victims of discrimination through its complaints office. Moreover, the Centre also enjoys the right to be a party to legal proceedings under the 1981 law against racism; thus, it may provide practical legal support to individual plaintiffs.[108] In 1999, the Centre received 919 complaints, demonstrating the important role it plays in providing an access point for victims of discrimination.[109] The largest group of complaints relates to discrimination at the workplace.[110] Nonetheless, significant problems remain regarding enforcement. In particular, the reliance on criminal

[103] A Martens, 'La prévention du racisme sur les lieux de travail en Belgique' Working Paper No WP/95/39/FR (Dublin: European Foundation for the Improvement of Living and Working Conditions, 1995) 39.

[104] The 1994 amendment of the law defines discrimination as 'toute distinction, exclusion, restriction ou préférence ayant ou pouvant avoir pour but *ou pour effect* de détruire, de compromettre ou limiter la reconnaissance, la jouissance ou l'exercise, dans des conditions d'égalité, des droits de l'homme et des libertés fondamentales' (ibid 38; emphasis added).

[105] I Forbes and G Meade, *Measure for Measure: a comparative analysis of measures to combat racial discrimination in the Member Countries of the European Community* Equal Opportunities Study Group, University of Southampton, Research Series No 1 (London: Department of Employment, 1992) 28.

[106] Framework Directive, Art 9(2); Racial Equality Directive, Art 7(2).

[107] Forbes and Meade (n 105 above) 26.

[108] J Wrench, *Preventing racism at the workplace—a report on 16 European countries* (Dublin: European Foundation for the Improvement of Living and Working Conditions, 1996) 73.

[109] EUMC, *Diversity and equality for Europe—annual report 1999* (Vienna: EUMC, 2000) 18.

[110] ECRI, 'Second report on Belgium' CRI (2000) 2 (Strasbourg: Council of Europe, 2000) 9.

law sanctions has been regarded as unsatisfactory, in part because the standard of proof is often difficult to achieve, but also because the available remedies are rather inflexible and at times inappropriate.[111]

In contrast, law on sexual orientation discrimination remains embryonic. In 1999, the social partners agreed to add disability and sexual orientation to the list of prohibited discrimination grounds in Collective Agreement 38 on the recruitment and selection of workers.[112] This was subsequently made generally binding by a Royal Decree.[113] Furthermore, in December 2000 the Belgian Government proposed to amend the law on racial discrimination to extend its protection to a wider range of discriminatory grounds, including disability, age, sexual orientation, and religious or philosophical convictions.[114] The competence of the Centre will be extended to include all these new discriminatory grounds; therefore, this proposal is an early example of the Article 13 Directives having a 'levelling-up' impact. Moreover, enforcing the anti-discrimination laws will be added to the aims of the Labour Inspectorate.[115]

(iii) Italy[116]

Legislation to forbid racism in the workplace has been in place in Italy since Article 13 of Law 903/1977[117] amended Article 15 of Law 300/1970[118] to extend its coverage to '*discriminazione politica, religiosa, razziale, di lingua o di*

---

[111] Centre pour l'Egalité des chances et la Lutte contre le Racisme, 'Discrimination à l'embauche de personnes de nationalité ou d'origine étrangère—synthèse' (Bruxelles: Centre pour l'Egalité des chances et la Lutte contre le Racisme, 1998) 2. Also, J Costa-Lascoux, 'Equality and non-discrimination: ethnic minorities and racial discrimination' in Council of Europe (ed), *Rights of persons deprived of their liberty—equality and non-discrimination* (NP Engel, 1997) 285.

[112] J Jacqmain, 'Belgium' in S Prechal and A Masselot, *Bulletin Legal Issues in Equality*, No 1/2000 (Brussels: Commission, 2000) 38.

[113] Arrêté royal du 31 août 1999 rendant obligatoire la convention collective de travail no 38quater du 14 juillet 1999, conclue au sein du Conseil national du Travail, modifiant la convention collective de travail no 38 du 6 décembre 1983 concernant le recrutement et la sélection de travailleurs, modifiée par les conventions collectives de travail no 38bis du 29 octobre 1991 et no 38ter du 17 juillet 1998, Moniteur Belge, 21.9.1999.

[114] Communiqué, 6 December 2000, 'Lutte contre le racisme'. Available from: *http://faits.fgov.be*

[115] 'La loi va traquer toutes les discriminations', Le Soir, 8 December 2000.

[116] Special thanks to Stefano Fabeni for generous assistance in completing this section.

[117] L 9 dicembre 1977, n 903—Parità di trattamento tra uomini e donne in materia di lavoro (reproduced in R Scognamiglio, *Codice di diritto del lavoro—annotato con la giurisprudenza—1° Parte Generale, Tomo 1, Disciplina Legislativa* (Bologna: Zanichelli, 2nd edn, 1980) 243.

[118] L 20 maggio 1970, n 300—Norme sulla tutela della libertà sindacale e dell'attività sindacale nei luoghi di lavoro e norme sul collocamento (GU n 131, 27-5-1970, 3404).

sesso'. Article 15 specifies that workers shall not be subject to, *inter alia*, discrimination in dismissals, the assignation of tasks, transfers, or disciplinary measures. Complaints may be brought to the Labour Inspectorate, but the problems surrounding proof mean that it is difficult to establish discrimination, and there have been only a small number of cases brought pursuant to this law.[119] The more relevant legal provisions appear to be those in immigration law, particularly where these provide for equal working conditions between Italian and immigrant workers. Campani *et al* note that Law 943/1986 established the principle of equality of opportunity between national and non-national workers, including equal treatment in the workplace.[120] These provisions were further strengthened by the adoption of the 'Martelli Law' (No 39/1990), which sought, *inter alia*, to grant rights to equal pay and working conditions to migrant workers.[121]

This variety of legal sources for protection against racial discrimination has now been superseded to some extent by the 'Napolitano–Turco' immigration law adopted in March 1998.[122] Law 40/1998 is principally concerned with rules regarding entry and residence, but within this framework an important set of new anti-discrimination norms can be found. Article 41(1)[123] forbids direct and indirect[124] discrimination in the provision of goods and services, access to employment, housing, training, and social services on the basis of race, religion, ethnicity or nationality. Paragraph 2(e) clarifies that this prohibition applies to any discriminatory act or behaviour by an employer. Finally, Article 41(3) establishes that this ban on racial

[119]   Forbes and Meade (n 105 above) 52.

[120]   G Campani, F Carchedi, G Mottura and E Pugliese, 'La prévention des formes de discrimination et de racisme dans les lieux de travail en Italie', Working Paper No WP/95/47/FR (Dublin: European Foundation for the Improvement of Living and Working Conditions, 1995) 20. Article 1 of L 30 dicembre 1986, n 943 (GU n 8, 12-1-87) states 'La Repubblica italiana . . . garantisce a tutti i lavoratori extracomunitari legalmente residenti nel suo territorio e alle loro famiglie parità di trattomento e piena uguaglianza di diritti rispetto ai lavoratori italiani'.

[121]   E Vasta, 'Rights and Racism in a new country of immigration: the Italian case' in J Solomos and J Wrench (eds), *Racism and Migration in Western Europe* (Oxford: Berg, 1993) 88.

[122]   L 6 marzo 1998, n 40 Disciplina dell'immigrazione e norme sulla condizione dello straniero (GU n 59, 12-3-98). The law is often referred to by the name of its ministerial sponsers, Giorgio Napolitano and Livia Turco.

[123]   The law has now been reproduced in the 'Testo unico delle disposizioni concernenti l'immigrazione e norme sulla condizione dello straniero'. Although the content remains the same, Art 41 becomes Art 43 and Art 42 becomes Art 44.

[124]   Indirect discrimination is defined as every prejudicial treatment following from the adoption of criteria which disadvantage a significant proportion of the workers of a determined race, ethnic or linguistic group, religion or citizenship, provided that these requirements are not essential to the development of the business.

discrimination extends to all individuals, whether Italian, EU nationals or third country nationals.

Article 42 establishes a special procedure allowing an action in civil law against discrimination, but with protective provisions designed to ensure that these are quicker and less expensive than normal civil actions. Where a judge finds discriminatory behaviour, he or she may order an end to this behaviour and any other measure suitable for removing the effects of the discrimination.[125] Significantly, Article 42(9) provides that statistical evidence is admissible in support of a claim of discrimination, and Article 42(10) allows for trade unions to bring a complaint where the discrimination is of a collective character.

Beyond the ban on discrimination, Law 40/1998 also proves to be quite innovative in a range of measures to improve enforcement of the law. The most interesting of these is Article 42(11) which provides that where a firm has been found guilty of discrimination in its acts or behaviour, the public administration and other local bodies may exclude such a firm for up to two years from access to financial or credit assistance schemes and competing for public procurement contracts. This is clearly one of the few examples in the EU of a legislative basis for contract compliance. With regard to enforcement agencies, Article 42(12) requires the regional authorities, in collaboration with the provincial and communal authorities and immigrants' organisations, to establish observation, information and legal assistance centres which shall help victims of discrimination based on race, ethnicity, nationality or religion. These centres are to be complemented by the creation of a committee for integration policy at the national level, drawing together ministerial representatives and policy experts.[126] This shall prepare an annual report on integration policy with proposals to the government on a range of subjects, including actions against racism.[127]

The first report of this Committee confirmed the challenge facing the Italian authorities in translating the law into practice. It recorded that convictions for racism were 'numerically insignificant'.[128] Moreover, the EU Monitoring Centre on Racism has noted that few of the legal assistance centres foreseen in the law have actually been established.[129] The underlying difficulties are great. As Vasta points out, many immigrants' employment depends on their illegal status; employers want cheap and flexible labour, and

---

[125] Art 42.   [126] Art 44.   [127] Art 44(2).

[128] Cited in EUMC, *Diversity and equality for Europe—annual report 1999* (Vienna: EUMC, 2000) 23.

[129] ibid 63.

workers that regularise risk dismissal.[130] Lo Faro comments that the position of immigrants in the Italian labour market is characterised by a systematic marginalisation.[131] Access to the civil service is also very difficult as this requires Italian or EU nationality, but the majority of migrants are third country nationals.[132]

There are no specific provisions on sexual orientation discrimination in Italian law, although general provisions of labour law may provide a certain level of protection.[133] The law on dismissal from employment appears to provide the greatest support, with Biagini *et al* reporting that all cases where sexual orientation was the reason for dismissal have been found to be contrary to the law governing the termination of employment.[134] There have been various proposals in the past to introduce an explicit ban on sexual orientation discrimination, although none have yet been adopted.[135] For example, in 1999, a new anti-discrimination law to forbid discrimination on a wide range of grounds, including all the EC Treaty, Article 13 grounds was submitted,[136] but this was never adopted by the Parliament. In June 2001, new proposals to forbid sexual orientation discrimination were once again submitted by various Parliamentary deputies.[137]

(c) Equality law regimes: a review

Taking an overview of these six cases, two principal features emerge. First, it is noticeable that enforcement remains one of the paramount challenges, irrespective of the form of the law. Establishing sufficient proof emerged as a recurrent problem for those individuals who have the courage to make a complaint. In all the states under examination, these difficulties have

---

[130] Vasta (n 121 above) 95.

[131] A Lo Faro, 'Immigrazione, lavoro, cittadinanza' (1997) 76 Giornale di diritto del lavoro e di relazioni industriali 536, 552.

[132] Vasta (n 121 above) 90.

[133] S Fabeni, 'I diritti civili degli omosessuali. Profili di diritto comparato' Tesi di Laurea (Torino: Università degli Studi di Torino, 1998) 358. Menzione argues existing laws on sexual discrimination could be applied to cases of discrimination on grounds of sexual orientation: E Menzione, *Manuale dei diritti degli omosessuali* (Bologna: Libreria di Babilonia, 1996) 54.

[134] E Biagini, G Bertozzo and M Ravaioli, 'Italy' in N Beger, K Krickler, J Lewis and M Wuch (eds), *Equality for Lesbians and Gay Men: a relevant issue in the civil and social dialogue* (Brussels: ILGA-Europe, 1998) 66.

[135] Fabeni (n 133 above) 359.

[136] 'Sanzioni penali a chi discrimina: arriva la legge', La Repubblica, 8 October 1999.

[137] See Proposta di legge, Norme contro la discriminazione motivata dall'orientamento sessuale: D'iniziativa dei deputati De Simone, Vendola, Pisapia, Mascia, Deiana, 11 June 2001. An alternative proposal on the same theme has also been submitted in June 2001 by Deputy Grillini.

prompted the creation of institutional structures to provide proactive assistance to victims of discrimination. Significantly, these institutions are shaped
by the national context and legal tradition within which they are located. For
example, the Swedish discrimination ombudsmen fit with the traditional role
and importance of ombudsmen in Scandinavian legal systems,[138] whereas the
UK has an established preference for 'group-specific' agencies.[139] The
Article 13 Directives clearly reflect the experience at the national level that
specific measures on enforcement are necessary to ensure the law is effective.
At the same time, the Directives will not confront the diversity in national
practice on the form and balance of institutional support. The Directives
provide scope for intervention by both associations and (in the case of the
Racial Equality Directive) an equal treatment body. It is significant that
Belgium, one of the first states to commence implementation of the
Directives, has chosen to extend the remit of its equal treatment body to all
Article 13 grounds, even though this is not required by the Framework
Directive. If other Member States choose to adopt a horizontal approach to
the implementation of the Directives—that is, equivalent protection for all
grounds—then the Racial Equality Directive may provide considerable
spillover benefits for the other discriminatory grounds.

As a second interim conclusion, it should be noted that some states have
chosen to move beyond general measures to assist individual complainants
and towards the institution of positive action schemes. On the whole, it must
be said that these are still relatively weak. In most cases, positive action is permitted, but not required. The Netherlands provides the only example of a
state-wide attempt to impose a duty to take proactive measures, in the form
of ethnic monitoring and business equality plans. Yet, the difficulties that
have been encountered in introducing such measures suggest this is a sensitive field where many employers and even trade unions remain to be con-
vinced of the benefits of such action. Against this picture, there were some
examples of innovative positive action schemes, such as the UK provision for
training schemes limited to members of ethnic minority communities, or
preference schemes in Dutch local authorities where job candidates are
equally qualified. Again, the tone of the Directives accords with the national
traditions—permitting, not obliging positive action. At the same time, gender equality case law from the Court of Justice has placed certain limits on the

---

[138] Interview: MaLou Lindholm MEP, Brussels, 16.10.97.

[139] For example, the Equal Opportunities Commission, or the Disability Rights Commission.
Against this, it should be noted that the separate equality agencies in Northern Ireland have been
merged into a common 'Equality Commission'.

scope for positive action that, if applied to the Article 13 Directives, could also curtail Member States' freedom in this area.[140] Indeed, for this reason the UK negotiated a specific exception in the Framework Directive to protect its quota scheme to boost Catholic participation in the Northern Ireland police service.[141] Finally, the influence of existing national practice is also evident in the exceptions to the ban on discrimination—for example, the exceptions in the Framework Directive pertaining to religious employers or partners' benefits are a reflection of exceptions already entrenched in national statutes.

III. Anti-discrimination law regimes

The states in this category may be distinguished from the previous group of states by the absence of any institutional support to individual litigants, and a lack of experimentation with positive action as a means to combat discrimination. Whilst these states share the basic characteristic of having forbidden discrimination in law, they remain divided by strong differences in experience and practice. First, these states are, as with the previous group, stratified between those with a comprehensive ban on discrimination (that is, covering both racial and sexual orientation discrimination), and those with only a 'mixed-level' anti-discrimination law—in all cases this implies that racial discrimination in employment is forbidden, but sexual orientation discrimination is not. Beyond this basic difference, several patterns emerge across the Member States.

(a) *Comprehensive anti-discrimination law regimes*

(i) Denmark

In 1996, Denmark adopted a wide-ranging ban on discrimination in the labour market.[142] Section 1(1) forbids both direct and indirect discrimination on grounds of 'race, colour, religion, political belief, sexual orientation

---

[140] See n 31 above.   [141] Framework Directive, Art 15(1).

[142] Lov om forbud mod forskelsbehandling på arbejdsmarkedet mv; 12 juni 1996, Lovtidende Afdeling, No 459, 2526-2527. Many thanks to Kim Jensen of LBL for supplying me with an English translation of the law. See also, S Jensen, 'La reconnaissance des préférences sexuelles: le modèle scandinave' in D Borrillo (ed), *Homosexualités et droit* (Paris: Presses Universitaires de France, 1998).

or national, social or ethnic origin'. Discrimination is prohibited in all aspects of employment, including education and training.[143] Access to the public sector for third country nationals is not a significant problem as there are relatively few major distinctions drawn between citizens and other non-Danish residents.[144] The most controversial exception to the ban on discrimination is with regard to religious organisations. Section 6(1) provides that the provisions forbidding discrimination 'shall not apply to an employer whose enterprise has the express object of promoting a particular political or religious opinion, unless this is in conflict with European Community law'. Whilst this is a broader exception than the Framework Directive permits, the final clause indicates that the Directive will take precedence.

With regard to positive action, s 9(2) states that:

this Act shall be without prejudice to measures being introduced by virtue of other legislation, by virtue of provisions having their legal basis in other legislation or otherwise by means of public initiatives, with a view to promoting employment opportunities for persons of a particular race, colour, religion, political opinion, sexual orientation or national, social or ethnic origin.

On the one hand, this does not exclude any particular group from positive action measures, unlike the provisions in the Netherlands and Ireland. On the other, positive action appears to be only protected when taken by the public sector, or under state authority—a very significant restriction. Indeed, a Commission report from 2000 recorded no case law under this provision.[145] Furthermore, s 4 of the law forbids employers from requesting, collecting or obtaining data on, *inter alia*, the ethnic origin of employees or prospective employees, thereby prohibiting any form of ethnic monitoring.

No institution has been established in Denmark to assist individual plaintiffs. In 1993, a Board of Ethnic Equality was created with a general responsibility to combat discrimination, but this is not empowered to deal with individual cases.[146] An Ombudsman exists but in 1996 there was no record of any cases concerning racism being brought before this institution.[147] This

---

[143] s 2.

[144] J Hjarnø, 'Preventing racism at the workplace: the Danish national report' Working Paper No WP/95/42/EN (Dublin: European Foundation for the Improvement of Living and Working Conditions, 1995) 5.

[145] Commission, 'Report on Member States' legal provisions to combat discrimination' (Luxembourg: OOPEC, 2000) 19.

[146] J Wrench, *Preventing racism—a report on 16 European countries* (Dublin: European Foundation for the Improvement of Living and Working Conditions, 1996) 75.

[147] ibid.

lack of institutional support for plaintiffs may be reflected in the fact that only five cases have been brought to court under the 1996 Act.[148] ECRI's recent report on Denmark concludes that the main difficulty lies in establishing proof, and that this is exacerbated by the prohibition in the Act on employers keeping records on the ethnic origins of employees.[149]

(ii)   France

Racial discrimination in employment has been unlawful in France since 1972. The Law of 1 July 1972 amended section 416-3 of the Penal Code which states that a criminal offence has been committed where an employer discriminates on grounds of membership of a 'specific racial group, nationality, race or religion' in recruitment or dismissal.[150] The Law of 4 August 1982 also amends the Labour Code to forbid any punishment or dismissal in employment because of 'origin, ethnicity, nationality or race'.[151] Nonetheless, there was no express ban on indirect discrimination, and there was a strong emphasis on demonstrating that the actions of the employer were specifically due to a person's race or ethnicity. Therefore, problems surrounding proof have been cited as one of the central weaknesses in French law.[152] By focusing on criminal sanctions, the law aims to punish more extreme violations of the law, which includes discrimination in employment, but more frequently racist words or threats. Indeed, in respect of employment discrimination, ECRI concluded the existing anti-discrimination provisions are 'virtually unused'.[153]

With regard to sexual orientation, the Penal Code, and the Criminal Code of Procedure, were amended in July 1985 to insert the word '*mœurs*' into most of the anti-discrimination provisions therein.[154] This was complemented by an amendment to the Labour Code in 1986, again to insert *mœurs* within the

---

[148]   ECRI, 'Second report on Denmark' CRI (2001) 4 (Strasbourg: Council of Europe, 2001) 8.

[149]   ibid.

[150]   I Forbes and G Meade, *Measure for Measure: a comparative analysis of measures to combat racial discrimination in the Member Countries of the European Community* Equal Opportunities Study Group, University of Southampton, Research Series No 1 (London: Department of Employment, 1992) 35.

[151]   ibid 36.

[152]   V De Rudder, M Tripier, F Vourc'h and V Simon, 'La prévention du racisme dans l'entreprise en France' Working Paper No WP/95/44/FR (Dublin: European Foundation for the Improvement of Living and Working Conditions, 1995) 21.

[153]   ECRI, 'Second report on France' CRI (2000) 31 (Strasbourg: Council of Europe, 2000) 15.

[154]   K Waaldijk, 'The legal situation in the Member States' in A Clapham and K Waaldjik (eds), *Homosexuality: a European Community issue—essays on lesbian and gay rights in European law and policy* (Dordrecht: Martinus Nijhoff, 1993) 79. Law No 85-772 of 25 July 1985, Penal Code Arts 187-1, 187-2, 416 and 416-1. Code of Criminal Procedure, Art 2-6.

relevant anti-discrimination provision.[155] 'Mœurs' may be defined as morals or habits: *un mode de vie*. This has been understood to include sexual orientation, as was held to be the case in a decision by the Cour de cassation from 1991.[156] In the case in question, the Fraternité Saint-Pie X had employed P as a sacristan since 1985. P was homosexual, but maintained his privacy and this was not known to either his employer, or to the vast majority of churchgoers. Following an indiscretion, his homosexuality came to the knowledge of the Fraternité and he was dismissed in June 1987. He challenged this dismissal as an unfair breach of contract and the Cour de cassation held that as the dismissal was based solely on his *mœurs*, it was contrary to the Labour Code, Article L 122-35.

Explicit protection against sexual orientation discrimination now exists in the Labour Code by virtue of Law No 2001-1066 of 16 November 2001 concerning the fight against discrimination.[156a] This law is clearly designed to implement both the Racial Equality and Framework Directives. Article L 122-45 forbidding employment discrimination is amended to add, *inter alia*, the terms 'orientation sexuelle', 'âge', 'état de santé' [state of health] and 'handicap'. This Article covers both direct and indirect discrimination, as well as providing for a shift in the burden of proof in discrimination cases.

The new law adds a further paragraph to the Labour Code, Article L 122-45-1. This provides legal standing for trade unions and organisations working against any of the forms of discrimination mentioned in Article L 122-45, provided they have been established for at least five years. These organisations play a central role in the enforcement of the law, and provide advice and assistance to individuals.[157]

In recent years, there has been a growing debate on the effectiveness of the existing anti-discrimination law model in France.[158] In particular, there has been a focus on whether there is a need for greater support of individual litigants. A first step in this direction was the decision in 1999 to establish

---

[155] Waaldijk, (n 154 above) (as amended by Law No 86-76 of 17 January 1986). The Labour Code Art 122-35 provides that there should be no less favourable treatment of 'les salariés dans leur emploi ou leur travail (...) en raison (...) de leurs mœurs (...) de leurs opinions ou confessions (...), à capacité professionnelle égale'.

[156] *P . . . c. Association Fraternité Saint-Pie X*. (1991) II Juris classeur périodique, no 21724, 303.

[156a] [2001] JO 267/18311.

[157] For example, SOS Racisme or the Mouvement contre le racisme: C Lloyd, 'Race relations in Britain and France: problems of interpretation' in F Hawkins, A Dummett, C Lloyd, J Wrench and D Joly, *Special Seminar Series on 1992*, Research Paper in Ethnic Relations No 17 (Warwick: University of Warwick, 1991) 28. See the Code of Criminal Procedure, Art 2-6.

[158] A Hargreaves, 'Half-measures: anti-discrimination policy in France' (2000) 18 *French politics, culture and society* 83.

'commissions d'accès à la citoyenneté' (CODACs) in each *départment* to monitor and combat cases of racism. Hargreaves concludes that the impact of the CODACs has not been substantial.[159] Law 2001-1066 includes a variety of measures to enhance enforcement. The investigative powers of the Labour Inspectorate in discrimination cases are increased.[160] In addition, a free national telephone advice service is established in order to assist victims of racial discrimination.[161]

Finally, it is important to note that positive action is not permitted in France. The fundamental principles that underpin the French approach to the integration of immigrant communities focus on equality for citizens and assimilation, rather than the recognition of specific minority groups. Positive action is perceived as reinforcing the separation of ethnic groups, even leading to ghettoisation.[162] In particular, measures such as race-specific training schemes, such as exist in the UK, would be a breach of anti-discrimination law in France.

(iii) Luxembourg

The legal situation in Luxembourg is comparable to that in France. On 19 July 1997, Luxembourg prohibited discrimination on a wide range of grounds, including race and sexual orientation, through an amendment to the Penal Code, Article 454.[163] Discrimination is expressly forbidden in recruitment and dismissal decisions.[164] It is less obvious whether all the terms and conditions within employment are comprehensively covered by this law, but Article 455(6) states that it is unlawful to '*sanctionner*' (punish) someone in a discriminatory fashion in the course of employment. This potentially covers a variety of discriminatory actions, such as non-promotion. The law does not, though, explicitly forbid remuneration discrimination, nor does it

---

[159] A Hargreaves, 'Half-measures: anti-discrimination policy in France' (2000) 18 *French politics, culture and society* 83

[160] Amendment to Labour Code, Art L 611-9.   [161] Law 2001-1066, Art 9.

[162] Lloyd (n 157 above) 21.

[163] Loi du 19 juillet 1997 complétant le code pénal en modifiant l'incrimination du racisme et en portant incrimination du révisionnisme et d'autres agissements fondés sur des discriminations illégales (Journal Officiel du Grand-Duché de Luxembourg, A-No 54, 1680, 7 août 1997). Art 454, as amended, states that: 'constitue une discrimination toute distinction opérée entre les personnes physiques à raison de leur origine, de leur couleur de peau, de leur sexe, de leur orientation sexuelle, de leur situation de famille, de leur état de santé, de leur handicap, de leurs mœurs, de leurs opinions politiques ou philosophiques, de leurs activités syndicales, de leur appartenance ou de leur non appartenance, vrai ou supposées, à une ethnie, une national, une race ou une religion déterminée.'

[164] Art 455(6).

clarify if indirect discrimination is unlawful. The law applies to both the public and the private sector, and carries a penalty of eight days' to two years' imprisonment, and €248 to €24,789 in fines. As in France, no equality agency exists, but Article VI of the law makes provision for civil organisations to bring anti-discrimination cases, where the case relates to their basic objectives, such as anti-racism, or the promotion of human rights. Such organisations may not bring cases if the individual concerned objects. This law had still not been used by the end of 1999.[165]

(iv) Finland

In Finland, the Penal Code was amended in April 1995. Chapter 47, s 3 states:

any employer or representative acting for an employer who, without good reason, discriminates against a jobseeker when advertising a vacancy or recruiting staff or against an employee:
1) on grounds of race, national or ethnic origin, colour, language, gender, age, relations, sexual preference or state of health; or
2) on grounds of religion, political opinion, political or industrial activity or a comparable circumstance,
shall be sentenced for work discrimination to a fine or up to six months' imprisonment.[166]

The definition of 'discrimination' may be criticised as being rather weak. In particular, it would seem that any act of discrimination is open to justification on grounds that the employer had 'good reason'. There is no reference to indirect discrimination or harassment in the workplace. Protection against discrimination may also be found under the Employment Contracts Act, which requires an employer to treat workers equally 'without any unwarranted discrimination on the basis of, among other grounds, his or her origin'.[167] The Employment Contracts Act No 55/2001 extends the list of discriminatory grounds that are specified to include, *inter alia*, 'sexual preferences'.[168]

No specific institution exists for dealing with individual complaints of discrimination.[169] Nonetheless, the Ombudsman for Aliens is one possible

---

[165] EUMC, *Diversity and equality for Europe—annual report 1999* (Vienna: EUMC, 2000) 39.

[166] Law of 21 April 1995/578, cited in R Hiltunen, 'Finland' in N Beger, K Krickler, J Lewis and M Wuch (eds), *Equality for Lesbians and Gay Men: a relevant issue in the civil and social dialogue* (Brussels: ILGA-Europe, 1998) 43.

[167] Commission, 'Report on Member States' legal provisions to combat discrimination' (Luxembourg: OOPEC, 2000) 33.

[168] S Mayne and S Malyon, *Employment law in Europe* (London: Butterworths, 2001) 298.

[169] E Ekholm and M Pitkänen, 'Preventing racism at the workplace: Finland—report on the ethnic minorities and migrants in the Finnish labour market' Working Paper No WP/95/52/EN

mechanism through which issues of racism could be raised. In 1999 it was reported that this office will have its remit extended to include racial discrimination and be renamed the Ombudsman against Ethnic Discrimination.[170] It should also be noted that the Labour Inspectorate monitors compliance with the Contracts of Employment Act.[171] In 1998, the police recorded 319 racist crimes, but it is not clear what proportion of these related to employment.[172]

(v) Spain

Article 14 of the Constitution states that 'Spaniards are equal before the law and no discrimination whatsoever may prevail on account of birth, race, sex, religion, opinion or any other personal or social condition or circumstance'.[173] This applies to the actions of the public sector. Moreover, the last clause, 'personal or social condition or circumstance' has been held to cover sexual orientation in a number of instances,[174] and provides an additional layer of protection against employment discrimination, including sexual orientation harassment in the workplace.[175]

In the private sector, Law No 8 of 1980 requires that 'as a party to an employment relationship a worker shall have the right: (c) to freedom from discrimination, when seeking employment or after having found employment, on grounds of . . . race, social circumstances, religious or political ideas'.[176] These legal provisions were supplemented in 1995 by an amendment to the Penal Code to forbid many categories of discrimination.[177] Article 314 in the Title on 'offences against the rights of workers' prohibits discrimination in both the public and the private sectors of employment on grounds of, *inter alia*, race or ethnicity, and sexual orientation.[178] Breach of

(Dublin: European Foundation for the Improvement of Living and Working Conditions, 1995) 29–30.

[170] EUMC (n 165 above) 68.   [171] Commission (n 167 above) 34.

[172] EUMC (n 165 above) 28.

[173] I Forbes and G Meade, *Measure for Measure: a comparative analysis of measures to combat racial discrimination in the Member Countries of the European Community* Equal Opportunities Study Group, University of Southampton, Research Series No 1 (London: Department of Employment, 1992) 66.

[174] C Lestón, 'Spain' in N Beger, K Krickler, J Lewis and M Wuch (eds), *Equality for Lesbians and Gay Men: a relevant issue in the civil and social dialogue* (Brussels: ILGA-Europe, 1998) 79.

[175] Information kindly supplied by César Lestón.

[176] s 4(2); Forbes and Meade (n 173 above) 67.

[177] Ley Organica, 23 noviembre 1995, no 10/1995, Codigo Penal Texto.

[178] 'Los que produzcan una grave discriminacíon en el empleo, público o privado, contra alguna persona por razón de su ideología, religión o creencias, su pertenencia a una etnia, raza o nacíon,

this article will require reparation for the economic damage caused, with the possibility of imprisonment from six months to two years.

Complaints of discrimination in the private labour market may be brought to the Labour Inspectorate, or directly to the civil courts. In the public sector, complaints may be made to the *Defensor del Pueblo* (People's Advocate), who is responsible for monitoring standards in public administration.[179] Nonetheless, the effectiveness of this legislation may be called into question. In the public sector, nationality of an EU Member State is a prerequisite for employment; thus, most resident ethnic minorities are excluded.[180] In the private sector, ethnic minorities are highly marginalised. Cachón notes that many migrant workers are undocumented, and consequently, they 'cannot make formal complaints or take legal actions, since this would be risky and detrimental for them'.[181] As a result, these individuals end up in very low paid work, with poor working conditions and no social security protection.

(b) Mixed-level anti-discrimination law regimes

(i) Portugal

Migration from former Portuguese colonies has existed since the 1960s; thus, the ethnic minority population is considerably more settled than in other southern European states, and many possess Portuguese citizenship.[182] Constitutional guarantees to equality apply to all persons resident on the territory,[183] and these specifically cover non-discrimination on grounds of race in the workplace.[184] Furthermore, unlike in most EU Member States, the

se sexo, orientacíon sexual, situacíon familiar, enfermedad o minusvalía, po ostentar la representacíon legal o sindical de los trabajadores, por el parentesco con otros traabajadores de la empresa o por el uso de alguna de las lenguas oficiales dentro del Estado español, y no restablezcan la situacíon de igualdad ante la Ley tras requerimiento o sancíon administrativa, reparando los daños económicos que se hayan derivado, serán castigados con la pena de prisión de seis meses a dos años o multa de seis a doce meses.'

[179] Forbes and Meade (n 173 above) 68.

[180] L Cachón, 'Preventing racism at the workplace: Spain' Working Paper No WP/95/41/EN (Dublin: European Foundation for the Improvement of Living and Working Conditions, 1995) 27.

[181] ibid 40.

[182] M Palma Carlos, 'La prévention du racisme sur les lieux de travail au Portugal' Working Paper No WP/95/40/FR (Dublin: European Foundation for the Improvement of Living and Working Conditions, 1995) 1.

[183] Art 15: ibid 23. 'Toutes les dispositions constitutionnelles sur les droits, libertés et garanties sont en principe aussi applicables aux étrangers, qui jouissent, de ce fait, de droits de prestation reconnus par la Constitution' (ibid 24).

[184] Art 59: ibid 25.

constitutional requirements bind both public and private bodies.[185] Moreover, in 1999 a new anti-discrimination law was adopted, forbidding racism in various areas, including the labour market, health and education.[186] This law also established an Advisory Committee for Equality and against Racial Discrimination, although this does not have responsibility for individual complaints.[187] In practice, there have been very few cases. Moreover, ethnic minorities are still disproportionately located in unstable occupations, with poor working conditions.[188] Palma Carlos concludes that the weak labour market position of these individuals, combined with their low awareness of their rights, goes a long way to explaining the lack of recourse to the law.[189]

In respect of sexual orientation discrimination, no specific provisions exist, but the constitution would appear to provide a possible defence to discriminatory dismissal. Article 53 states that 'security in employment shall be guaranteed to workers and dismissals without just cause or for political or ideological reasons shall be prohibited'.[190] Whilst Article 13 of the constitution on the principle of equality does not expressly include sexual orientation, it states that 'no person shall be privileged, favoured, disadvantaged, deprived of any right or freed from any duty because of his sex . . . or social condition'.

(ii) Germany

The anti-discrimination provisions in German law are relatively weak. No rule specifically forbids sexual orientation discrimination, and the guarantees against racial discrimination are often undermined in practice by legal forms of discrimination based on nationality.

The Works Constitution Act 1972, Article 75 places an obligation on employers and Works Councils to ensure there is no discrimination on grounds of, *inter alia*, 'race, creed, nationality, origin'.[191] Sexual orientation is not mentioned in the Act, but it is an open-ended equality guarantee.[192]

---

[185] Art 18.

[186] Law 134/99: EUMC, *Diversity and equality for Europe—annual report 1999* (Vienna: EUMC, 2000) 66.

[187] ibid.   [188] Palma Carlos (n 182 above) 4.   [189] ibid 43.

[190] T Martins de Oliveira, *Equality in law between men and women in the European Community—Portugal* (London: Martinus Nijhoff, 1995).

[191] I Forbes and G Meade, *Measure for Measure: a comparative analysis of measures to combat racial discrimination in the Member Countries of the European Community* Equal Opportunities Study Group, University of Southampton, Research Series No 1 (London: Department of Employment, 1992) 41.

[192] P Skidmore, 'Improving the position of lesbians and gay men at work: a German case study', forthcoming.

Individuals who feel they have been unfairly treated may pursue their complaint through either the Works Council or the administrative courts.[193] However, this provision does not apply to the public sector, nor does it cover job applicants.[194] Moreover, it is not applicable to 'religious communities and their charitable or educational institutions, whatever their legal form'.[195] Implementation of the anti-discrimination norms depends heavily on the attitude of the Works Council.[196] The Commissioner for Foreigners has made clear the practical obstacles facing ethnic minorities: 'migrants who have suffered discrimination and wish to claim damages are often impeded in doing so by their lack of knowledge of the legal situation—not least because their rights are not expressly anchored in law—and in many cases by the difficulty of furnishing evidence'.[197]

Despite being well established, ethnic minorities in Germany often still face a 'guestworker' mentality, and it is only recently that there is a growing acceptance that these minorities are permanent residents.[198] This has been reinforced by historically limited opportunities for naturalisation and the entrenched system of employment preference for German (and EU) nationals. Access to the public sector is dependent on possession of EU nationality, and private sector work can also be problematic. As a result, migrants are concentrated: 'in jobs with few opportunities for cooperation and communication, high levels of stress or health impairment, monotony, shift work, piece-work, poor opportunities for qualification and promotion, and a high risk of dismissal and/or unemployment'.[199]

Despite the absence of specific rules against sexual orientation discrimination, there is at least one recorded case of an individual successfully challenging a dismissal due to homosexuality, through reliance on unfair dismissal

---

[193] Forbes and Meade (n 191 above) 42.

[194] Anon, 'Preventing racism at the workplace: Germany' Working Paper No WP/95/43/EN (Dublin: European Foundation for the Improvement of Living and Working Conditions, 1995) 42.

[195] Commission, 'Report on Member States' legal provisions to combat discrimination' (Luxembourg: OOPEC, 2000) 20.

[196] Research into migrant workers has indicated that many migrants do not have full confidence in works councils to represent their interests. This may reflect the fact that in 1990 only 4% of the members of works councils were of migrant origin, yet such workers accounted for 8% of the labour force (Anon, n 194 above).

[197] The Federal Government's Commissioner for Foreigners' Affairs, 'Report by the Federal Government's Commissioner for Foreigners' Affairs on the situation of foreigners in the Federal Republic of Germany in 1993' (Berlin: The Federal Government's Commissioner for Foreigners' Affairs, 1994) 74.

[198] ibid 87.   [199] ibid 31.

laws.[200] However, Skidmore highlights that the protection which unfair dismissal law may confer is considerably weaker in respect of religious employers. This is given a wide definition in Germany and it is estimated to encompass over 600,000 employees in areas such as hospitals and residential care facilities run with a religious ethos. These employers are given much greater discretion and previous case law has accepted homosexuality as a justifiable reason for dismissal by such an employer.[201] This context helps explain the support from Germany for a specific exception for religious employers in the Framework Directive.[202]

IV. States without any specific anti-discrimination legislation

Greece and Austria are the only Member States that do not possess specific legal provisions on either racial or sexual orientation discrimination in employment. On the one hand, the social context of migration in Greece and Austria differs greatly. The pattern of irregular migration seen in Italy and Spain is also witnessed in Greece, whereas the situation in Austria is comparable to that in Germany, with its legacy of 'guestworkers'. On the other hand, the legal situation in Austria and Greece is actually rather similar, to the extent that nationality requirements actively discriminate against many ethnic minorities.

(i) Austria

In Austria, nationality is difficult to acquire, yet it is a condition for public sector employment. In the private sector, third country national workers may vote for the Works Council, but may not be elected to it.[203] Furthermore, when

---

[200] European Current Law Year Book (1995) No 1472, 632. Judgment of the Bundesarbeitsgericht (2 AZR 617/93, June 23, 1994) [1994] DB 2190. See further, Skidmore (n 192 above).

[201] Skidmore (n 192 above).

[202] EU Council, 'Outcome of proceedings of the Working Party on Social Questions on 13 June 2000' No 9423/00, Brussels, 20 June 2000, n 20.

[203] A Gächter, 'Preventing racism at the workplace: Austria' Working Paper No WP/95/51/EN (Dublin: European Foundation for the Improvement of Living and Working Conditions, 1995) VII. There is a proposal now to allow third country nationals to be elected to Works Councils: ECRI, 'Second report on Austria' CRI (2001) 3 (Strasbourg: Council of Europe, 2001) 13.

reducing their workforce, employers are obliged to give priority to non-nationals in redundancies.[204] Also crucial is the fact that 'regardless of the length of residence, the right to reside in Austria is tied to the ability to generate sufficient *per capita* income'.[205] Most foreign workers are only entitled to around thirty weeks' unemployment benefit, after which they must be self-sufficient, or risk losing their residency rights.[206] This creates a situation where employees are highly dependent on their employer, and vulnerable to exploitation. Gächter argues it produces a 'systematic allocation [of ethnic minorities] to the worst occupations without upward mobility in time to better jobs'.[207] On Austria, Wrench concludes 'the legal discrimination operating against migrant workers through national policy is so comprehensive that it overshadows any discrimination which might operate at the informal level'.[208]

No general legislative protection exists in relation to sexual orientation discrimination. However, dismissal based on sexual orientation would appear to be contrary to unfair dismissal laws.[209]

(ii) Greece

Whilst there is legislation on racism, this does not prohibit discrimination in employment.[210] In legal theory, Greek law would permit reliance on the provisions of International Convention on the Elimination of Racial Discrimination in a court action, but the absence of any case law means this remains only a hypothetical possibility.[211] In practice, a large number of ethnic minorities in Greece are undocumented and consequently without rights.[212] They face difficult working conditions, low pay and great job insecurity.[213] The high level of institutionalised discrimination exacerbates the

---

[204] ECRI (n 203 above).   [205] Gächter (n 203 above).   [206] ibid 23.   [207] ibid.

[208] J Wrench, *Preventing racism at the workplace—a report on 16 European countries* (Dublin: European Foundation for the Improvement of Living and Working Conditions, 1996) 35.

[209] Commission, 'Termination of employment relationships—the legal situation in the Member States of the European Union' (Luxembourg: OOPEC, 1997) 23.

[210] Law 927/1979. See further, ECRI, 'Second report on Greece' CRI (2000) 32 (Strasbourg: Council of Europe, 2000) 7.

[211] I Forbes and G Meade, *Measure for measure: a comparative analysis of measures to combat racial discrimination in the Member Countries of the European Community* Equal Opportunities Study Group, University of Southampton, Research Series No 1 (London: Department of Employment, 1992) 46.

[212] R Fakiolas, 'Preventing racism at the workplace: Greece' Working Paper No WP/95/45/EN (Dublin: European Foundation for the Improvement of Living and Working Conditions, 1995) VI.

[213] EU Council, 'Report on the Greek round table held in Athens on 18 January 1995' No 4687/95 RAXEN 7, Brussels, 3 February 1995, 10.

disadvantage experienced in the private labour market. The public sector and certain professions remain closed to non-EU nationals, even including lawyers, doctors, dentists and midwives.[214] One positive development is the creation of an Ombudsman's Office in 1997 that, although having a general remit to protect citizens' rights, has also been able to provide assistance to migrant workers facing discrimination.[215]

There is also an absence of any legislative protection in relation to sexual orientation discrimination. Batsioulas states that the issue has not been discussed extensively in Greece, but that there have been reports of incidents of dismissal and harassment due to sexual orientation.[216]

V. Convergence and divergence

The aim of this chapter was to gain a better understanding of the *appropriate* role for the European Union in anti-discrimination law, based on an analysis of existing laws at the national level. Bringing together the wide range of material presented, a number of observations and conclusions may be made. Perhaps the most immediate trend to note is the increasing openness of the Member States in recent years to revising existing anti-discrimination statutes, or introducing new measures altogether. Between 1994 and 2000, new measures on racial and/or sexual orientation discrimination in employment were adopted in eleven of the fifteen Member States, as presented in Table 6.1 below. Above all, this evidence of a favourable environment for anti-discrimination law helps explain the relative ease with which the Article 13 Directives were adopted. Before turning to the identification of the most general trends, it is worth first looking further at the specific situation regarding racial and sexual orientation discrimination respectively.

(a)   Racial discrimination

Even from this brief study, it is evident that qualitative differences exist between the Member States in their legal traditions in respect of combating

---

[214] Commission, 'Legal Instruments to Combat Racism and Xenophobia' (Luxembourg: OOPEC, 1992) 14.

[215] ECRI (n 210 above) 8.

[216] A Batsioulas, 'Greece' in N Beger, K Krickler, J Lewis and M Wuch (eds), *Equality for Lesbians and Gay Men: a relevant issue in the civil and social dialogue* (Brussels: ILGA-Europe, 1998) 58.

Table 6.1 Legislative initiatives in the EU Member States on racial and/or sexual orientation discrimination in employment, 1994–2000

Year in which the legislation entered into force	Adoption of new legislation on racial and/or sexual orientation discrimination in employment
1994	Belgium, Sweden, the Netherlands
1995	Finland, Spain
1996	Denmark
1997	Luxembourg, United Kingdom
1998	Italy
1999	Ireland, Sweden, Portugal
2000	Belgium

racism. In particular, the nature of the problem and the areas where action is most needed differ. One can identify broadly three challenging issues in terms of equal access and equal treatment for ethnic minorities in the labour market.

First, there is the question of *undocumented migrants*, and the overlapping issue of work in the *clandestine economy*. This particularly concerns the southern European states, such as Spain, Italy and Greece. The development of significant levels of immigration to these states, combined with the reality that most of these new migrants arrive in an irregular legal situation, creates distinct issues regarding anti-discrimination law. Nonetheless, irregular migration continues at varying levels throughout the Member States, therefore, it would be an error to regard this as exclusively the concern of southern states. On the one hand, the situation of undocumented workers is especially difficult as they are highly vulnerable to exploitative working conditions and cannot have recourse to the law because of their residential status.[217] On the other hand, both illegal and legal migrants are found in the informal sector of the economy, where again the nature of the situation prevents recourse to the law. Clearly, this is not purely a question for anti-discrimination law, but also raises important questions relating to immigration law. How to provide effective guarantees against racism for these individuals, whilst at the same time resolving their precarious residential status presents a difficult challenge

[217] ECRI (n 210 above) 10.

to the Member States. In this respect, Law 40/1998 from Italy provides an interesting example of how regularising the entry and residence of migrants may also be combined with new measures to confront racism. The rights conferred by the Racial Equality Directive in principle apply to any person present in the Union and therefore include undocumented workers, but flanking measures in EU immigration policy will be needed to make the Directive meaningful for such individuals.

The second issue that can be highlighted is the question of *nationality discrimination*. In all states, citizens enjoy more legal entitlements than third country nationals.[218] However, the extent of the privileges of citizenship varies considerably. For example, several Member States, including France, Italy, Greece, Germany and Austria, require most public sector workers to possess EU citizenship. Yet, when such policies coincide with a restrictive policy on naturalisation, many permanently resident ethnic minorities find themselves systematically excluded from a large section of the labour market. Paradoxically, the Member States where naturalisation is most available, such as the Netherlands and Sweden, are also those where nationality is of lesser consequence, at least for participation in the labour market. In essence, it is a question of finding the equilibrium between the retention of the right to make legitimate distinctions based on citizenship, whilst avoiding legal forms of institutionalised discrimination. This is an especially sensitive issue, as it touches directly on an area that has traditionally been one of the central prerogatives of the nation-state. Furthermore, the perspectives of the Member States here are rooted in deep-seated 'philosophical concepts of citizenship'[219] that are likely to prove difficult to reconcile.

Predictably, the Racial Equality Directive avoids any potential clash with Member States' traditions on the rights of citizens. Article 3(2) excludes difference of treatment based on nationality from the scope of the Directive and this will be a major impediment to third country nationals seeking to challenge discrimination. Importantly, the Commission has since proposed extending rights to equal treatment to third country nationals who are long-term residents in the European Union.[220] The draft Directive provides that persons legally residing in a Member State for five years would be entitled to

---

[218] A Lo Faro, 'Immigrazione, lavoro, cittadinanza' (1997) 76 Giornale di diritto del lavoro e di relazioni industriali 536, 552.

[219] Commission, 'Communication from the Commission to the Council and the European Parliament on Immigration and Asylum Policy' COM (94) 23, 35.

[220] Commission, 'Proposal for a Council Directive concerning the status of third country nationals who are long-term residents' COM (2001) 127.

the status of a 'long-term resident'. This would then confer an entitlement to 'equal treatment with nationals' in various areas including employment, education, recognition of qualifications, social protection, healthcare, access to goods and services, and housing.[221] If adopted, this Directive would provide a vital complement to the Racial Equality Directive. However, it will confront very different national traditions that pose a serious challenge to finding unanimity within the Council.

If the issues discussed above may be regarded as 'external' factors in racial discrimination law, then one must also be conscious of the range of 'internal' legal problems that need to be addressed. The problem of *proof* appears to be the most common barrier to challenging discriminatory practices. A 1992 report to the Commission concluded: 'numerous legal measures have been and are being taken by European countries, particularly in regard to racial discrimination. Nonetheless, there remains discrimination in law and in practice, while remedies often prove inadequate due to procedural barriers, problems of proof and lack of resources'.[222]

Moreover, to the extent that legislation has been successfully enforced, it has not prevented the perpetuation of ethnic minority disadvantage in the labour market, especially in respect of unemployment.[223] There is also considerable evidence that the penalisation of overt discrimination merely gives way to more covert forms of discrimination, which are much more difficult to detect and prevent.[224]

One of the strongest and most innovative features of the Racial Equality Directive is its willingness to engage directly with the problems of enforcement. This seems an obvious area where EU intervention is appropriate. In contrast to the highly contested terrains of citizenship and the rights of undocumented migrants, the Union clearly has a legitimate interest in ensuring that any norms it agrees are effectively enforced. To this end, a variety of measures have been adopted to help prevent the Directive remaining silent on the statute book—for example, the requirement to create equal treatment bodies, the extension of legal standing to NGOs, provision for a shift in the burden of proof, and the obligation on Member States to provide effective sanctions. Whilst these form a constructive contribution, it would be rash to assume that they will solve enforcement difficulties. Underlying the problems

---

[221] Art 12: ibid. [222] Commission n 214 above 18.

[223] H Lutz, 'Migrant women, racism and the Dutch labour market' in J Solomos and J Wrench (eds), *Racism and Migration in Western Europe* (Oxford: Berg, 1993).

[224] J Wrench and J Solomos, 'The politics and processes of racial discrimination in Britain' in J Solomos and J Wrench (eds), *Racism and Migration in Western Europe* (Oxford: Berg, 1993) 164.

experienced with enforcement at the national level is the burden placed on the individuals who bring complaints. Even with the most effective systems of individual enforcement, there are likely to remain situations where individual litigation is extremely difficult. For example, if an employer does not publicly advertise vacancies, but instead recruits through informal mechanisms, then it may be possible to exclude potential ethnic minority employees without any *individual* being aware of the denial of equal opportunity. Alternatively, in a dispersed workforce, as may be the case for groups of teleworkers who operate principally from their own home, it would be very difficult for an individual worker to discover if they were being treated less favourably than other workers. Tackling such forms of unequal treatment depends on the existence of collective enforcement mechanisms that do not rely exclusively on the existence of a specific individual complainant. For example, the Irish Equality Authority can require firms to conduct equality business reviews and to establish equality action plans, with these commitments ultimately being enforceable in law.

The Racial Equality Directive is more ambiguous on collective enforcement procedures. It does not oblige Member States to give associations the right to bring litigation in their own name, and it talks generally about equal treatment bodies conducting 'independent surveys concerning discrimination', in contrast to the Commission's original proposal for the bodies to have the right to commence 'investigations'.[225] This undoubtedly reflects the general experience of the Member States in anti-discrimination law, which is mainly based around enforcement by individuals.

Positive actions schemes are another response to the limits of individual litigation. Yet, the picture is very patchy in the Member States; indeed, in some states—most especially France—there are strong objections to this approach. Similarly, ethnic monitoring policies are very divisive within the Member States. In this light, the Racial Equality Directive may be appropriate in adopting a permissive stance towards positive action or ethnic monitoring without obliging states to pursue these measures.

(b) Sexual orientation

At first sight, it is evident that existing legislative protection against sexual orientation discrimination lags a long way behind that in relation to racial discrimination. However, it is also clear that this is a rapidly changing situation. Perhaps the most significant fact is the high degree of overlap between

---

[225] Commission, 'Proposal for a Council Directive implementing the principle of equal treatment between persons irrespective of racial or ethnic origin' COM (1999) 566, 19.

recent anti-discrimination provisions on race, and those on sexual orientation. In the Netherlands, Ireland, Denmark, Finland, Spain, Luxembourg and France, the ban on sexual orientation discrimination forms part of a legal provision that simultaneously prohibits racial discrimination. A picture emerges where sexual orientation manages to be included in the context of a general equality law, but often lacks sufficient political support to form the basis for an exclusive legislative act. (In this respect, the 1999 Swedish law creating a specific Ombudsman on sexual orientation discrimination is quite exceptional.) Experience at the EU level has been similar: first, where sexual orientation was included in EC Treaty, Article 13 on the coat-tails of a general anti-discrimination clause; and second, with the inclusion of sexual orientation in the general Framework Directive.

Even where discrimination has been forbidden in national law, this is rarely an absolute ban, but normally it is subject to a number of qualifications. This is again reflected in the Framework Directive, which is distinguished from the Racial Equality Directive by the variety of general and specific exceptions permitted to the ban on discrimination. At the national level, the fact that the exceptions to the ban on sexual orientation discrimination are common to several Member States indicates a significant degree of comparability between the different laws. The most sensitive issue by far is religion. The legislative acts in Ireland, the Netherlands and Denmark all provide a specific exemption for religious employers, and this issue has also arisen in France and Germany. Its sensitivity is reflected in the difficult compromise negotiated in the Framework Directive, Article 4(2).

Beyond the question of religious employers, at least two other issues are commonly exempted from non-discrimination requirements: recognition of same-sex partners and positive action. With regard to the former, Member States seem reluctant to accept that recognition of the right to non-discrimination in the workplace implies the recognition of same-sex partners. To some extent, it is tenuous to separate these issues as non-recognition of one's partner does lead to discrimination, most especially in the area of remuneration, as was exemplified in the cases of *Grant v South-West Trains*[226] and *D and Sweden v Council*.[227] Against this, the consequences of recognising partners in the workplace would be potentially far-reaching, as this would then bring into question discrimination in social welfare benefits between same-sex and married and unmarried opposite-sex couples, as well as more

---

[226] C–249/96 [1998] ECR I–621.
[227] Cases C–122/99P and C–125/99 [2001] ECR I–4319.

fundamentally the need for state recognition of non-marital partnerships. The Framework Directive, Recital 22 reflects the reluctance of the Member States to engage with the wider issues and a desire to curtail the scope of the Directive to sexual orientation discrimination against individuals, rather than individuals and their partners. Nonetheless, Recital 22 is not a total exception, but rather it indicates to the courts a possible justification for indirect discrimination against same-sex couples in workplace benefits. As such, there is valuable space for the gradual emergence of more rigorous standards.

With respect to positive action, no Member State has specific provisions requiring such a course of action by employers. Naturally, certain forms of positive action would be inappropriate in relation to sexual orientation discrimination. In particular, workforce monitoring would not be a suitable mechanism for a variety of reasons, such as concerns over confidentiality, or the difficulty in establishing what a 'proportionate representation' of lesbians or gay men would be.[228] Nonetheless, other forms of positive action, such as proactive recruitment in sectors where lesbians and gay men have been traditionally rejected, are possible. The most obvious examples would be the armed forces and law enforcement agencies. Once again, the Directive leaves a welcome degree of flexibility to the Member States to adapt their policies to local circumstances.

Finally, it must be noted that even where protection is available, litigation levels remain very low, in both absolute and comparative terms. This is most likely a reflection of the fundamental difficulty with sexual orientation discrimination cases. In order to obtain redress, individual litigants may be compelled to make public aspects of their private life, and for many persons this might be regarded as imposing a higher personal cost than the original act of discrimination.[229] This being the case, there is a special need to complement individual protection against sexual orientation discrimination with alternative, collective enforcement methods. However, the Framework Directive is particularly weak in this area, neither permitting independent actions by relevant organisations, nor providing for institutional support in the form of an equal treatment body.

---

[228] 'Equality for lesbians and gay men in the workplace' (July/Aug 1997) 74 *Equal Opportunities Rev* 20, 23.

[229] A Clapham and J Weiler, 'Human dignity shall be inviolable: the human rights of gays and lesbians in the EC legal order' (1992) III(2) Collected Courses in the Academy of European Law 237, 251.

(c) Models of anti-discrimination law

Despite the diversity of the national legal provisions, certain *patterns* emerge which tend to group together different Member States.[230] First, one can point to a well-developed concept of laws favouring the realisation of equal opportunities in the UK, Ireland and the Netherlands. Detailed legislation forbids discrimination in employment and this is reinforced by the existence of equal treatment bodies, designed to facilitate the use of the legislation by individual claimants. Furthermore, there is often explicit provision for positive action. Arguably, the laws in these Member States reflect a significant influence from practices in North America, both the USA and Canada.[231]

In contrast to this approach, the French anti-discrimination regime is grounded in a rejection of the concept of minorities, and focuses on the provision of individual rights. Whereas the influence of this French model is quite evident in Luxembourg, in Belgium one finds a mixture of elements drawn from both the French and the Dutch perspectives, notwithstanding the different philosophies that underpin each state's legislative framework. A frequent argument is made to the effect that the French system is incompatible with the 'Dutch–Anglo–American' approach.[232] Lloyd challenges this position as based more on caricature than on reality.[233] Whilst undoubted differences do exist between the underlying philosophies of law, the practical solutions adopted may often be rather similar. For example, the French system places considerable importance on enforcement of the law through NGOs. This implies some recognition of a group dimension to the problem.[234] Alternatively, whilst positive action is often cited as an illustration of the supposed gulf between the two systems, in practice its use has not been central to the promotion of equality in either the UK or the Netherlands. The central element has remained individual complaints. The Racial Equality Directive strikes a balance between institutional and NGO-based enforcement, as well as leaving open thorny questions such as positive action.

---

[230] K Waaldijk, 'Standard sequences in the legal recognition of homosexuality' (1994) 4 *Australasian Gay and Lesbian L Rev* 50, 51.

[231] S Small, 'Unravelling racialised relations in the United States of America and the United States of Europe' in J Solomos and J Wrench (eds), *Racism and Migration in Western Europe* (Oxford: Berg, 1993) 235. On the influence of Canada, see J Wrench, *Preventing racism at the workplace—a report on 16 European countries* (Dublin: European Foundation for the Improvement of Living and Working Conditions, 1996) 163.

[232] C Lloyd, 'Concepts, models and anti-racist strategies in Britain and France' (1991) 18 *New Community* 63, 65.

[233] ibid 66.   [234] ibid.

Denmark and Sweden provide a further alternative. In both cases, legislation against discrimination in access to goods and services, or in respect of incitement to hatred, has been in place for some time.[235] Nonetheless, employment discrimination has only been forbidden relatively recently. The reticence that has marked the adoption of laws on employment discrimination reflects the more general reluctance of the state to intervene in the field of labour market regulation. Soininen and Graham note that 'in Sweden, it is the labour market partners . . . who play an important role in the formulation and implementation of labour market policies. . . . This extends to the formulation and implementation of immigration policies, including the regulation of immigration and anti-discrimination policies'.[236]

Neilsen suggests that one may speak of a 'Nordic model' of labour law, which is characterised by a strong emphasis on collective labour law, determined by the Social Partners, and a low emphasis on individual rights guaranteed on a statutory basis.[237] Thus, the absence (until more recent times) of statutory protection against racial or sexual orientation discrimination is not so much indicative of the Danish or Swedish record on these two issues, but merely reflects the overall framework of domestic labour law. This tradition is also evident in the terms of the Danish 1996 anti-discrimination law. Section 1(2) provides that 'this Act shall not be applicable to the extent that similar protection from discrimination follows from a collective agreement'. In the same vein, the scope for enforcement of the Directives via collective agreements was a key issue for the Danish government in the legislative negotiations.[238]

---

[235] In Denmark, incitement laws in respect of racism, and laws forbidding racial discrimination in commercial activities were introduced in 1971 (J Hjarnø, 'Preventing racism at the workplace: the Danish national report' Working Paper No WP/95/42/EN (Dublin: European Foundation for the Improvement of Living and Working Conditions, 1995) 30). These were amended in 1987 to add sexual orientation: S Jensen, 'Denmark' in N Beger, K Krickler, J Lewis and M Wuch (eds), *Equality for Lesbians and Gay Men: a relevant issue in the civil and social dialogue* (Brussels: ILGA-Europe, 1998) 38. In Sweden, the existing bans on incitement and discrimination in commercial activities in respect of racial discrimination were extended to cover sexual orientation discrimination also in 1987: B Skolander, 'Sweden' in N Beger, K Krickler, J Lewis and M Wuch (eds), *Equality for Lesbians and Gay Men: a relevant issue in the civil and social dialogue* (Brussels: ILGA-Europe, 1998) 81.

[236] M Soininen and M Graham, 'Persuasion contra legislation: preventing racism at the workplace: Sweden' Working Paper No WP/95/53/EN (Dublin: European Foundation for the Improvement of Living and Working Conditions, 1995) 16.

[237] R Neilsen, *Equality in law between men and women in the European Community—Denmark* (London: Martinus Nijhoff, 1995) 3.

[238] EU Council, 'Outcome of proceedings of the Social Questions Working Party on 14 March 2000' No 6942/00, Brussels, 31 March 2000, n 51; EU Council, 'Outcome of proceedings of the Social Questions Working Party on 14 and 28 March 2000' No 6941/00, Brussels, 31 March 2000, n 48.

In relation to the southern states (Portugal, Spain, Italy and Greece) and the German-speaking states (Germany and Austria), both in the fields of racial and sexual orientation discrimination there was little evidence of a significant body of case law. The legal guarantees were generally not as strong as in some of the northern states, particularly in relation to sexual orientation. In fact, Spain is the only one of these states to have explicitly prohibited sexual orientation discrimination in the workplace. Where legislation did exist, it did not appear to have been particularly successful in its implementation and enforcement. Again, this reveals differences in national legal traditions: 'legal rules, effective in some systems, are nothing but experiments in others, subject to unpredictable responses from social rules'.[239] For these states, the Directives do represent a genuine change in the existing legal tradition and culture. In particular, the requirement in the Racial Equality Directive for equal treatment bodies guarantees institutional reform and innovation. This demonstrates the interaction between national legal traditions and European norms. Whilst the Directives in many ways reflect and respect the established approaches in the states with 'equality law regimes', for other states where existing law is much weaker and less well defined, the Directives will be central to the forging of an anti-discrimination legal tradition.

Examining the legal competence conferred on the Union by EC Treaty, Article 13 provides us with some guidance on the scope for developing EU anti-discrimination law. However, the material presented in this chapter suggests that more may be gleaned from an examination of the blend of existing national legal traditions and cultures. For example, a requirement on all businesses to monitor the ethnicity of their workforce would certainly be within the legal competence of the European Union, but it seems inappropriate at this stage because of the strong differences of opinion between and within Member States on the suitability of this instrument. Alternatively, obliging Member States to take positive action for ethnic minority communities under-represented in the labour market would be within the legal competence of the Union, but again this is a policy choice where the Member States are characterised by divergence rather than convergence. The Directives represent a careful negotiation of the diverse national legal traditions, while at the same time promoting the progressive development of national law towards stronger protection against discrimination. As such, the Directives do not reflect any single model of anti-discrimination law and they provide a

---

[239] S Sciarra, 'Labour law—a bridge between public services and citizenship rights' in M Freedland and S Sciarra, *Public services and citizenship in European law—public and labour law perspectives* (Oxford: Clarendon Press, 1998) 189.

significant range of discretion for Member States to locate the minimum rights required within their own national context. Clearly, too much national discretion risks undermining the very content of the rights being conferred. This is a criticism that can certainly be levelled at aspects of the Framework Directive—for example, the general exception to the ban on discrimination in Article 2(5) or the open-ended possibilities to justify age discrimination in Article 6. Moreover, respecting national difference is controversial where this strikes at the heart of the effectiveness of the instrument. For instance, the exclusion of nationality discrimination from both Directives and the protection for marital benefits in the Framework Directive provide protection for some of the most common forms of discriminatory treatment in the workplace. Nonetheless, the Directives have negotiated an upward trend in national law that will produce quite significant changes in the legal regime in most of the Member States. Moreover, by introducing a Europeanisation of anti-discrimination law and policy, the Directives open a dialogue between the Member States on the correct law and policy mix. As Member States will share a common legislative foundation, more useful comparisons can be yielded in the future on the relative effectiveness and accessibility of the law. Such debate and dialogue ultimately may be more crucial to policy development than the boundaries of legal competence explored in Chapter 5.

7

The Transformation of EU Anti-Discrimination Law

The changes that have taken place in EU anti-discrimination law are plain to see, but the long-term significance of these developments to European social policy in general is less clear. At the outset of this book, Chapter 1 identified the two poles of European social policy—a market integration model, and a social citizenship model. Having surveyed the evolution of EU anti-discrimination law, it seems appropriate to return to the initial theoretical framework to consider how the new legal initiatives may reposition European social policy. The second part of this chapter looks further at the reasons that help explain the transformation of the role of the European Union in regulating discrimination. In particular, the impact of the European Employment Strategy, converging national legal traditions and the contribution of European civil society are analysed. Finally, this chapter examines the nature of the new anti-discrimination law. Whilst the Directives provide a key legal foundation, are these isolated measures, or part of a new European policy framework on anti-discrimination? In this light, it is appropriate to examine the potential for future development of the EU's role in this field.

I. Escape from the market? European social policy after Article 13

Chapter 1 introduced the two dominant paradigms between which European social policy operates. First, there is the 'market integration model', which foresees a social policy defined by, and dependent on, the needs of economic integration. Common standards in the social sphere are only agreed to the

extent necessary to avoid certain Member States gaining an unfair competitive advantage through social deregulation. The alternative vision of
European social policy makes fundamental rights the cornerstone of legal
integration. There is a vision of the Union as a supranational guarantor of
fundamental rights, which in turn is expected to foster a stronger relationship
between the EU and its citizens.[1] In this fashion, fundamental rights could
legitimise European integration through the promotion of a real sense of
European citizenship and identity.[2]

The history of European social policy demonstrates that whilst the market
integration model has undergone some mutation, it remains very present.
There have been periodic attempts to develop a more autonomous social policy, such as the 1976 social action programme, or the 1989 Social Charter, but
these have largely failed to bring about the radical transformation so often
requested by, *inter alia*, trade unions, civil society and academic opinion. It is
tempting to see the EU Charter of Fundamental Rights as opening another
doorway to an independent and vibrant social policy. The significance of the
Charter is clearly enhanced by its high profile status; unlike the 1989 Charter,
it is a general initiative of EU constitutional law, rather than a limited attempt
to re-launch a specific policy. Moreover, one of the key virtues of the Charter
is the equation of social rights with civil, political and economic rights.
Nonetheless, the frailty of the Charter's legal character places immediate
question marks over the direct value of its contribution. These are reinforced
by the careful twinning of the Charter to the existing limits on EU competence imposed by the Treaties.[3] Given that the Treaties themselves reflect the
economic orientation of European integration, then the space for implementation and enforcement of many of the social rights in the Charter is drasti-
cally curtailed.[4]

Even if the dynamics of market integration remain highly persuasive in
determining the direction of European social policy, it would be churlish
to deny the signs of progress. A steady trickle of new social law instruments
have emerged in recent years, across diverse fields. For example, workplace

---

[1] The 1995 Comité des Sages on social rights argued that the 'inclusion of civic and social rights
in the Treaties would help . . . prevent Europe from being perceived as a bureaucracy assembled by
technocratic elites far removed from daily concerns': Commission, 'For a Europe of civic and social
rights—Report by the Comité des Sages' (Luxembourg: OOPEC, 1996) 26.

[2] C Barnard, 'P v S: kite flying or a new constitutional approach' in A Dashwood and S O'Leary,
The principle of equal treatment in European Community law (London: Sweet & Maxwell, 1997) 66.

[3] Arts 51 and 52 [2000] OJ C364/1.

[4] K Lenaerts and E de Smijter, 'A "Bill of Rights" for the European Union' (2001) 38 CML Rev
273, 288.

consultation rights have been significantly advanced,[5] alongside progress in the protection of atypical forms of employment.[6] Moreover, as has been shown, concrete steps forward have been made in combating discrimination. Certainly, these measures are not without a market integration foundation. Discrimination creates obstacles to cross-border transactions and unhindered free movement. This is most visible in respect of the cross-border dissemination of racist publications,[7] or the barriers emerging from the growing divergence of national laws on the legal recognition of non-marital partnerships.[8] Ironically, however, the Article 13 Directives are not directly concerned with either of these examples of discrimination creating distortions within the internal market. On the contrary, the primary focus of the Directives is discrimination between individuals in the labour market (and beyond), most instances of which will have no connection to cross-border trade or the migration of workers. Therefore, whilst the Directives do not contradict the objectives of market integration, they are not central to this project.

In response, there is a temptation to assume that the Directives reflect a new golden era of citizenship-based social policy; a body of social law founded on the guarantee of fundamental human rights. The Directives can easily be placed within the wider aims of the social citizenship model—building links between the Union and the individual citizen. Certainly, they make a valuable contribution in promoting a more sophisticated understanding of the diversity of the European populace. The process of implementing the Directives should also heighten awareness of the relevance and potential impact of the European Union within communities that have previously had little stake in European integration.[9]

---

[5] Directive 2001/86/EC of 8 October 2001 supplementing the Statute for a European company with regard to the involvement of employees [2001] OJ L294/22. Political agreement on the Directive on informing and consulting employees was reached in the Council on 11 June 2001 (Press Release, 2357th meeting of the Employment and Social Policy Council, Luxembourg, Doc 9397/01, Presse 225).

[6] Council Directive (EC) 1999/70 of 28 June 1999 concerning the framework agreement on fixed-term work concluded by ETUC, UNICE and CEEP [1999] OJ L175/43; and Council Directive (EC) 97/81 of 15 December 1997 concerning the Framework Agreement on part-time work concluded by UNICE, CEEP and the ETUC [1998] OJ L14/9.

[7] For an example, see P Rodrigues, 'The Dutch experience of enforcement agencies: current issues in Dutch anti-discrimination law' in M MacEwen (ed), *Anti-discrimination law enforcement: a comparative perspective* (Aldershot: Ashgate, 1997) 61.

[8] This diversity has been noted by the Court: Cases C–122/99P and C–125/99P *D and Sweden v Council* [2001] ECR I–4319, para 50.

[9] J King, 'Ethnic minorities and multilateral European institutions' in A Hargreaves and J Leaman (eds), *Racism, Ethnicity and Politics in Contemporary Europe* (Aldershot: Edward Elgar, 1995) 181.

At the same time, the capacity of the Directives to enhance citizenship, and hence public interest and commitment to the Union, should not be overstated. In certain Member States, the benefits conferred by the Directives may be relatively subtle. Where national law already guarantees comparatively high protection against discrimination—for example in the Netherlands and Ireland—then the impact of the Directives may be much less visible to individuals than in states where protection is weak or non-existent, such as Greece or Austria. Weiler highlights the diminishing returns in guaranteeing human rights.[10] New rights are most meaningful where they provide concrete and substantial added value to the pre-existing situation.

Nonetheless, the Directives provide concrete assistance in fleshing out the thin body of citizens' rights in EU law. Together with the *acquis* on gender and nationality discrimination, the Union is carving out a key role in protecting citizens against all forms of discrimination. This is also reflected in the prominence of 'equality' within the EU Charter on Fundamental Rights.[11] The underlying concept of citizenship, however, is blurred around the edges. Whereas the EC Treaty construction of Union citizenship is focused on nationals of the Member States,[12] the citizenship rights in the Directives apply to all persons on Union territory. Yet, this picture can be illusory given the exclusion of protection from discrimination based on possession of third country nationality.[13] The waters are muddied further in the Charter. Most of the rights conferred apply generally to 'everyone', or in the negative, 'no one'. Moreover, certain prerogatives of Union citizens (by virtue of the EC Treaty provisions) are extended by the Charter to all residents—for example, the right to petition the Parliament or to make a complaint to the EU Ombudsman.[14] In contrast, other provisions are limited to Union citizens,[15] or legally resident third country nationals.[16] Finally, an evolving body of rights for various categories of third country nationals is emerging as the Union constructs the Area of Freedom, Justice and Security, pursuant to EC Treaty, Title IV.[17] This

---

[10] J Weiler, *The Constitution of Europe—'Do the new clothes have an emperor?' and other esssays in European integration* (Cambridge: Cambridge University Press, 1999) 334.

[11] Chapter III, Arts 20–26 [2000] OJ C364/1.   [12] EC Treaty, Art 17.

[13] Framework and Racial Equality Directives, Art 3(2).   [14] Arts 44 and 43 respectively.

[15] For example, Art 15(2): 'every citizen of the Union has the freedom to seek employment, to work, to exercise the right of establishment and to provide services in any Member State.'

[16] Art 15(3): 'nationals of third countries who are authorised to work in the territories of the Member States are entitled to working conditions equivalent to those of citizens of the Union.'

[17] For an overview of the initiatives being taken, see Commission, 'Scoreboard to review progress on the creation of an area of "Freedom, Security and Justice" in the European Union' COM (2000) 167 final/2.

complex picture presents a fuzzy image of Union citizenship. Whilst nationals of the Member States are clearly in pole position, an intermediate body of rights—a form of quasi-citizenship[18]—is developing for those third country nationals who are long-term and permanently resident in the Union.

If there is a lack of clarity surrounding the boundaries of citizenship, this uncertainty is also reflected in the ongoing dilemma between market and social citizenship. The Racial Equality Directive is particularly important here, representing a bold step by the Union into the regulation of areas of social policy mainly reserved to national discretion. In contrast, the citizen actor within the Framework Directive is the familiar market citizen, and any spillover effects in social welfare or family law are deliberately excluded.[19] Although the Racial Equality Directive steps outside the confines of participation in the market, the considerable ambiguity surrounding the material scope of the Directive and the competence conferred by EC Treaty, Article 13 makes it difficult to predict its full impact. A very narrow reading of EU competence and the Directive could confine it to the cross-border, private sector delivery of services such as health and education[20]—an interpretation that would reinforce the centrality of market citizenship. However, there is real space for a more imaginative and progressive reading of the Directive, which may be informed by the emphasis on social rights also present in the EU Charter. Above all, there is an evident need for greater information on the range of legal instruments and policies that already exist in the Member States to combat racial discrimination in areas such as health, education and social security. It is not difficult to see how the Directive can be applied to individual cases of discrimination in these areas: for example, where a child is refused a place at a particular school because of her ethnic origin. Yet, promoting equality in education raises more fundamental policy issues, such as the representation of ethnic diversity within the curriculum.[21] It is less obvious how such issues can be confronted through the boundaries of the Racial Equality Directive.[22] The ability of the Union to meet these challenges will reveal its capacity to move from market to social citizenship.

---

[18] N Reich, 'Union citizenship—metaphor or source of rights?' (2001) 7 ELJ 4, 18.

[19] Framework Directive, Art 3(3) and Recital 22.

[20] G de Búrca, 'The drafting of the European Union Charter of Fundamental Rights' (2001) 26 ELR 126, 135.

[21] M Laflèche, 'Racial equality standards in education' in NICEM, *Human rights and racial equality conference report* (Belfast: Northern Ireland Council for Ethnic Minorities, 1998) 28.

[22] The dialogue with NGOs (Art 12) and the 'surveys' and 'reports' (Art 13) which the equal treatment body can undertake seem relevant starting points.

II. Explaining the new anti-discrimination law

As discussed above, Article 13 and the Directives reconfigure European social policy towards a greater emphasis on the social citizenship approach, without abandoning altogether the market-making focus of earlier periods. Logically, the next question arising is how to account for this shift. Many different factors have had a part to play, but this section concentrates on three underlying themes that seem especially relevant. First, the emergence of a new approach to social policy centred on the European Employment Strategy. Second, the convergence of national law on combating discrimination, and third, the growing role being played by European civil society.

(a) The open method of co-ordination: a third way?

Over a period of around five years, there has been a fundamental shift in EU social policy away from a focus on market *integration*, in favour of emphasising market *participation*.[23] There have been a number of strategic influences guiding this change. First, the persistently high levels of unemployment experienced during the 1990s confirmed that simply completing the internal market was not going to deliver sufficient economic growth and competitiveness.[24] Moreover, the costs of these high levels of unemployment were placing great strain on national finances, especially when these were confronted with the added pressure of meeting the single currency convergence criteria.[25] A second factor, which has become increasingly dominant, is the pending impact of demographic change. The ageing European population profile acts as a double-edged sword. On one side, it will significantly reduce the economically active proportion of the population, thereby diminishing contributions to public finances and risking the emergence of labour shortages.[26] On the other side, an ageing population will place greater demands on social protection systems, especially healthcare.[27]

---

[23]   J Kenner, 'Employment and macroeconomics in the EC Treaty: a legal and political symbiosis?' (2000) 7 Maastricht J of Eur and Comparative L 375, 396.

[24]   ibid 377.

[25]   E Szyszczak, 'The evolving European employment strategy' in J Shaw (ed), *Social law and policy in an evolving European Union* (Oxford: Hart Publishing, 2000) 199.

[26]   Commission, 'Towards a Europe for all ages—promoting prosperity and intergenerational solidarity' COM (1999) 221, 7.

[27]   ibid 18.

The primary response to these European trends has been a new policy focus on increasing participation in the labour market. The European Social Agenda agreed by the European Council in December 2000 states: 'the ultimate goal is, on the basis of the statistics available, to bring the employment rate (which currently stands at an average of 61%) up to a level which is as near as possible to 70% by 2010 and to increase the proportion of working women (currently an average of 51%) to over 60% by 2010'.[28]

A new methodology for implementing European employment policy has also evolved. The Treaty of Amsterdam inserted a new chapter on employment in the EC Treaty,[29] which provided for the co-ordination of national and European policies. The dominant characteristic of the new approach is the 'open method of coordination'.[30] In employment policy, this has centred on the agreement of an annual set of European guidelines.[31] Member States then report on their implementation of these guidelines in annual national action plans, permitting the emergence of a system of 'peer review'.[32] Moreover, this technique has since been exported to the co-ordination of social protection polices and policies on social inclusion.[33]

How does this impact on anti-discrimination law and policy? First of all, the European employment strategy has undoubtedly breathed new life into European social policy. Whilst the co-ordination of national policies is built around essentially soft law instruments, as well as persuasion via new processes of dialogue and exchange,[34] it has allowed European policy intervention in aspects of social policy hitherto strictly 'off-limits' for the Union.[35] Moreover, the pervasive influence of the market integration model has been diminished in this new social policy context. The stress placed on enhancing labour market participation cuts through the market integration/social citizenship theoretical divide. European social policy is extending beyond the limits of market integration, yet the new initiatives are not really geared towards the guarantee of fundamental social rights (although this may be a consequence).

Crucially, anti-discrimination law has a key location within this brand of social policy. Discrimination is an obvious barrier to market participation and

---

[28] European Social Agenda approved by the Nice European Council meeting on 7, 8 and 9 December 2000 [2001] OJ C157/4.

[29] Title VIII.

[30] Presidency Conclusions, Stockholm European Council, 23–24 March 2001, para 2.

[31] EC Treaty, Article 128.   [32] Szyszczak (n 25 above) 213.

[33] See European Social Agenda approved by the Nice European Council meeting on 7, 8 and 9 December 2000 [2001] OJ C157/4, sections III and IV.

[34] E Szyszczak, 'Social Policy' (2001) 50 ICLQ 175, 176.   [35] Szyszczak (n 25 above) 203.

from the outset one of the four pillars of the Employment Guidelines has been equal opportunities for women. Since then, there has been a growing acceptance that raising participation in the labour market must also tackle the barriers faced by key groups such as people with disabilities, ethnic minorities, and most especially older persons.[36] More recently, there has been a greater acknowledgement of the role that migrant labour from outside the Union will play in combating labour shortages in specific areas.[37] Combating racism has emerged as crucial to ensuring the labour market participation of existing ethnic minority communities within the Union,[38] as well as attracting, in particular, highly skilled migrant workers from outside the Union.

Certain European labour lawyers have expressed reservations about the preference for soft law instruments within this new model of social policy; Sciarra speaks graphically of the emergence of 'a new and vague category of non-rights'.[39] In the area of anti-discrimination law, however, the European Employment Strategy dovetailed with Article 13 and reinforced the relevance of combating all forms of discrimination to wider Union social and economic policy objectives.

(b) Converging national legal traditions

A second supporting factor that has certainly helped facilitate Article 13 and the Directives is evidence of converging national provisions in anti-discrimination law. As illustrated in Chapter 6, national anti-discrimination law remains quite diverse. To some extent, the differences in national discrimination laws reflect the general patterns of labour law traditions. For example, in 1989, the Commission stated its view that there were essentially three labour law families within the Community.[40] The largest of these was the Romano–Germanic

---

[36] Council Resolution on the 1999 employment guidelines [1999] OJ C69/2, Guidelines 4, 6 and 9. Note also the emphasis on facilitating the participation of older workers in the labour market in Council Recommendation of 19 January 2001 on the implementation of Member States' employment policies [2001] OJ L22/27.

[37] Commission, 'Communication on a Community immigration policy' COM (2000) 757, 25. See also Guidelines 6 and 7, Council Decision (EC) 2001/63 of 19 January 2001 on Guidelines for Member States' employment policies for the year 2001 [2001] OJ L22/18.

[38] For example, see recommendations on the Netherlands, Council Recommendation of 19 January 2001 on the implementation of Member States' employment policies [2001] OJ L22/27.

[39] S Sciarra, 'The employment title in the Amsterdam Treaty. A multi-language legal discourse' in D O'Keeffe and P Twomey (eds), *Legal issues of the Amsterdam Treaty* (Oxford: Hart Publishing, 1999) 170.

[40] Commission, 'Comparative study on rules governing working conditions in the Member States—a synopsis' SEC (89) 1137.

system, which covers the majority of the continental European states, and is characterised by comprehensive labour market regulation with central state direction. An alternative to this dominant (if internally diverse) model, was the Nordic system of labour law, founded on regulation through collective agreements between the Social Partners, with a minimal role for direct state intervention. Finally, the British–Irish system is characterised as one of low state regulation, combined with relatively weak collective mechanisms, thereby producing a more *laissez-faire* system of industrial relations.[41] Although this approach is slightly dated, in respect of anti-discrimination law, a number of similar legal families can be identified.[42]

The Nordic group is quite evident in anti-discrimination law and is characterised by the absence of a tradition of the state providing individual rights to non-discrimination through national legislation. Where individual rights have been dealt with, this is through collective agreements.[43] There are, however, signs that this model is undergoing a transformation. EU law in the field of sexual equality has already required the creation of statutory individual rights to non-discrimination, contrary to the traditional approach. Indeed, in *Commission v Denmark*,[44] the Court of Justice held that collective agreements alone would only be a satisfactory means of implementing Directives where these guarantee to all workers the rights contained in the original EU legislation.[45] (In practice, this tends to require implementing legislation to ensure that rights are extended to non-unionised labour.) The shift towards individual rights is evident from the fact that Sweden, Denmark and Finland have all now adopted legislation to forbid, *inter alia*, racial and sexual orientation discrimination. Whilst these legislative changes occurred at a similar time, their nature varies considerably. The Swedish legislation is distinguished by the role assigned to the Ombudsmen, albeit with deference to trade union intervention. Although Denmark and Finland did not immediately replicate this

---

[41] See further, B Fitzpatrick, 'Community Social Policy after Maastricht' (1992) 21 ILJ 199; J Due, J Steen Madsen and C Strøby Jensen, 'The Social Dimension: convergence or diversification of industrial relations in the single European market?' (1991) 22 *Industrial Relations J* 85.

[42] It should be noted that whilst the models proposed are mainly designed in reference to the examination of national laws on racial and sexual orientation discrimination, in many instances the comments are also valid for other areas of anti-discrimination law.

[43] R Neilsen, *Equality in law between men and women in the European Community—Denmark* (London: Martinus Nijhoff, 1995) 3–6.

[44] Case 143/83 *Commission v Denmark* [1985] ECR 427.

[45] See also, Case 235/84 *Commission v Italy* [1986] ECR 2291, where the AG went even further, stating that 'a Directive cannot be implemented by collective bargaining unless they are given the force of law by legislation' (2295).

approach, creating such Ombudsmen is already underway in Finland[46] and is being actively considered in Denmark.[47]

Another cluster of states centres on the UK, Ireland and the Netherlands. The laws of these states are characterised by an emphasis on individual complaint mechanisms, alongside the existence of specialist equality bodies to assist individuals. Less substantial, but also significant, are the measures to challenge structural discrimination, such as the limited forms of positive action. Litigation levels are considerably higher than in other Member States, reflecting the relative accessibility of the anti-discrimination mechanisms, which are located primarily in the civil law.[48] In addition, the Irish and Dutch legislation provides a very broad level of protection against many kinds of discrimination. Interestingly, there are now signs within the UK of a shift in favour of this 'multiple discrimination' approach.[49]

The model of a 'Romano–Germanic' legal family is difficult to sustain with reference to anti-discrimination law. As already indicated, the Netherlands is more similar to the UK and Ireland in its approach to anti-discrimination law. Moreover, substantial differences exist between the remaining states that seem too great to allow for their location in a single legal family. Arguably, there are (at least) three clusters present: France, Luxembourg and Belgium; Germany and Austria; and a Southern Europe grouping.

The legal regimes in France, Luxembourg and Belgium share three dominant characteristics. First, a relatively broad prohibition on discrimination. Second, the legal provisions are located within the Penal Code, and are thus subject to criminal law procedures. Third, relevant NGOs enjoy legal standing to bring litigation in their own name. In Belgium, this is complemented by the Centre pour l'égalité des chances et la lutte contre le racisme

---

[46] EUMC, *Diversity and equality for Europe—annual report 1999* (Vienna: EUMC, 2000) 68.

[47] ibid 55.

[48] This also holds true in respect of sex discrimination laws in these states: J Blom, B Fitzpatrick, J Gregory, R Knegt and U O'Hare, *The Utilisation of Sex Equality Litigation in the Member States of the European Community* Doc V/782/96-EN (Brussels: Report to the Equal Opportunities Unit of DG V, 1995) 9–11. See also C Kilpatrick, 'Community or communities of courts in European integration? Sex equality dialogues between UK courts and the ECJ' (1998) 14 ELJ 121, 133.

[49] B Hepple, M Choussey and T Choudhury, *Equality: a new framework—report of the independent review of the enforcement of UK anti-discrimination legislation* (Oxford: Hart Publishing, 2000); Office of the First Minister and Deputy First Minister of Northern Ireland, 'Promoting equality of opportunity—a Single Equality Bill for Northern Ireland—initial consultation by Office of the First Minister and Deputy First Minister', May 2001, available at *http://www.ofmdfmni.gov.uk/equality/*

which acts as an institutional focal point for individuals. As noted in Chapter 6, France is actively debating the establishment of such an agency.[50]

Germany and Austria are characterised by weak anti-discrimination law in the areas of race and sexual orientation. In contrast, it is worth highlighting that in both Germany and Austria, there exists a considerably stronger institutional framework in respect of gender discrimination. For example, in Germany, many of the Länder have established 'equality ombudswomen' at the state and local level, and even for specific public agencies.[51] Moreover, the experimentation with positive action by the different Länder is well known as a result of the *Kalanke*, *Marschall* and *Badeck* cases.[52] In Austria, Equal Opportunities Officers exist to assist individual complainants, and the Equal Opportunities Commission, prior to court proceedings, can decide individual cases.[53]

Finally, a rather loose Southern Europe group may be proposed, comprising Greece, Italy, Portugal, and Spain. In these states, one generally finds a minimal level of protection against discrimination in the workplace, but weak mechanisms for the implementation of this legislation, reflected in the very low levels of litigation. The main institution responsible for enforcing equality law is the Labour Inspectorate; Blom *et al* conclude that 'there is virtually no evidence of successful pursuit of equality issues by labour inspectors in these Member States'.[54] Whilst these comments pertain to sexual discrimination law, they are equally valid in respect of racial discrimination. With the exception of Spain, sexual orientation discrimination is not prohibited by law in this group.

There is, then, no shortage of different models through which the legal traditions of the Member States can be analysed. These models provide useful instruments for identifying the alternative approaches to anti-discrimination law. They permit one to rise above the minutiae of national regulations and to examine the broader picture. Nevertheless, as a general criticism, models are necessarily limited in their utility precisely because they tend to obscure subtle differences between states, and thereby deny the true complexity of the situation. The danger of stereotyping is particularly great. Whether or not

---

[50] A Hargreaves, 'Half-measures: anti-discrimination policy in France' (2000) 18 *French politics, culture and society* 83.

[51] Blom *et al* (n 48 above) 6.

[52] Case C–450/93 *Kalanke v Freie Hansestadt Bremen* [1995] ECR I–3069; Case C–405/95 *Marschall v Land Nordrhein-Westfalen* [1997] ECR I–6363; Case C–158/97 *Badeck v Hessischer Ministerpräsident* [2000] ECR I–1875.

[53] See further S Mayne and S Malyon, *Employment law in Europe* (London: Butterworths, 2001) 35.

[54] Blom *et al* (n 48 above) 29.

models are employed, the variety in Member States' legal traditions on both racial and sexual orientation discrimination is evident. This diversity helps both to explain the progress made so far, as well as the limitations experienced.

First, it is possible to see a steady convergence in national law during the 1990s, with a majority of states choosing to revise and extend their national legislation, often embracing the grounds addressed in Article 13. Furthermore, the effectiveness of anti-discrimination law has been given greater prominence as Member States acknowledge the limited impact of older legislation that was rarely used. The trend towards institutional assistance for litigants is evident and this is reflected in the Racial Equality Directive. In contrast, in those areas where national law remains very limited and quite disparate, progress has been more difficult. For example, both Directives are relatively silent on the role for positive action in national anti-discrimination policies. Alternatively, the highly flexible provisions on age discrimination in the Framework Directive are more comprehensible when viewed against the paucity of national law in this area.[55] National legal convergence does not, by itself, explain the intervention of EU law. Paradoxically, national legal divergence is a greater reason for intervention when viewed through the lens of the internal market. However, converging trends undoubtedly facilitate agreement on common European legal norms.

(c) *The role of European civil society*

Finally, it would be an error to overlook the dynamic role organisations and associations have played in raising the profile of discrimination issues within EU law and policy discourses. This reflects a more general increase in lobbying the EU institutions in the post-internal market period.[56] Nonetheless, the political and often geographic distance of the institutions from grassroots activism, combined with the enormous difficulties involved in simultaneously altering opinion across the fifteen Member States calls into question the true significance of cross-border NGOs.

The experience in relation to sexual equality policy suggests that European pressure groups are significant, but not a fundamental prerequisite to policy development. Indeed, the equal opportunities legislation of the 1970s was developed largely in the absence of a European lobbying network. Several authors suggest that the presence of a group of committed individuals working

---

[55] See Commission, 'Report on Member States' legal provisions to combat discrimination' (Luxembourg: OOPEC, 2000).

[56] A Dummett, 'Europe? Which Europe?' (1991) 18 *New Community* 167, 171.

for the advancement of women within the Commission was the main source propelling the policy forward.[57] Certainly, the Commission is in a pivotal position to influence policy development through its control of the legislative agenda. In addition, its ability to provide (and withdraw) funding from NGOs allows it to exert a considerable amount of influence. Yet, civil society associations remain important through their role in shaping opinion.[58] Even in equal opportunities, Hoskyns notes that 'the political environment created by the vigour of the women's movement should be seen as providing at least part of the explanation for the continued expansion of the EC level women's policy'.[59]

Pressure groups may thus be characterised as a necessary, if not sufficient, precondition to the development of policy. In the 1990s, the Commission provided financial assistance to support the creation of institutionalised cross-border pressure groups, including the European Women's Lobby, the European Disability Forum[60] and the European Migrant's Forum. The relationship between the Commission and these organisations may be characterised as one of dual dependency.[61] On the one hand, the organisations depend on the Commission for their financial resources and for their position as quasi-official representatives of European NGOs. On the other, the Commission is dependent on the organisations to provide them with information and, perhaps more importantly, to confer a degree of democratic legitimacy on policy initiatives. Geddes comments that this is a 'fairly standard model of supranational interest cooption followed by the Commission across a range of policy areas designed to add a veneer of legitimacy to policy development'.[62]

Nonetheless, the relationship is uneasy as the Commission can rarely fulfil the objectives (and expectations) of the associations involved. European

[57] Hoskyns states a key influence in sex equality policy was 'the existence of committed individuals, mainly women, either in the EC institutions, or doing work for them—lone women': C Hoskyns, *Integrating Gender—Women, Law and Politics in the European Union* (London: Verso, 1996) 83. See also B Hepple, 'Equality and Discrimination' in P Davies, A Lyon-Caen, S Sciarra, and S Simitis, *European Community Labour Law: Principles and Perspectives. Liber Amicorum Lord Wedderburn* (Oxford: Clarendon Press, 1997) 243.

[58] A Geddes, 'The representation of "migrant's interests" in the European Union' (1998) 24 *J of Ethnic and Migration Studies* 695, 697.

[59] Hoskyns (n 57 above) 97.

[60] See further, L Waddington, *Disability, employment and the European Community* (Antwerpen: Maklu, 1995) 125.

[61] D Lehmkuhl, *The importance of small differences: the impact of European integration on the associations in the German and Dutch road haulage industries* PhD thesis (Florence: European University Institute, 1998) 24.

[62] Geddes (n 58 above) 707.

NGOs can be caught between the need to maintain credibility with grass-roots activists who demand a critical stance towards the institutions, and the need to avoid alienating the Commission through making 'unrealistic' demands. In this context, the Migrants' Forum has been a notable failure.[63] Its 'official' nature made many national NGOs wary of participation and it failed to acquire the necessary representative status to act as a source of legitimacy.[64]

In the fields under examination, the Starting Line Group is a persuasive example of an NGO having a genuine impact on the EU policy agenda, through its tactic of producing draft legislative proposals as opposed to general recommendations.[65] Evidence of the high-level recognition of this organisation may be seen from the fact that the European Parliament has expressly endorsed its proposals on various occasions.[66] In contrast to the well-developed European lobby on racism, historically there have been few organisations working on lesbian and gay rights at the EU level. The main organisation involved has been the European region of the International Lesbian and Gay Association, ILGA-Europe. Although constrained by limited resources, it has established itself as the main interlocutor for the EU institutions on lesbian and gay issues.

Whilst sexual equality law developed in a 'top-down' nature, this seems less true in respect of race and sexual orientation discrimination law. The advances in these areas have been preceded by persistent pressure from the voluntary sector. At the same time, it must be recognised that these groups tend to depend on both the Commission and the Parliament to allow them to make progress towards achieving their goals. The Parliament provides an important voice for the concerns of pressure groups, through articulating their demands in reports and resolutions.[67] The role of the Commission is

[63] For more detail on its turbulent history, see G Danese, 'Trans-national collective action of migrants in Europe: the case of migrants in Italy and Spain' (1998) 24 *J of Ethnic and Migration Studies* 715.

[64] J King, 'Ethnic minorities and multilateral European institutions' in A Hargreaves and J Leamas (eds), *Racism, Ethnicity and Politics in Contemporary Europe* (Aldershot: Edward Elgar, 1995) 190.

[65] See further, C Gearty, 'The internal and external "other" in the Union legal order: racism, religious intolerance and xenophobia in Europe' in P Alston, M Bustelo and J Heenan (eds), *The European Union and Human Rights* (Oxford: Oxford University Press, 1999) 350–355.

[66] Resolution on racism and xenophobia [1993] OJ C342/19; Resolution on racism, xenophobia and anti-Semitism [1994] OJ C323/154; Resolution on the communication from the Commission 'An action plan against racism' [1999] OJ C98/491.

[67] Waddington (n 60 above) 98 reaches similar conclusions in respect of disability discrimination.

more directly connected to resources. Nonetheless, the importance attached by the institutions to the input of NGOs is revealed in the Article 13 Action Programme. This provides for the 'core funding' of a limited number of European NGOs in the areas covered by Article 13.[68] Clearly, these groups have few sanctions with which to cajole the Council (in particular) into supporting their recommendations. However, the Union's need to forge better links with individuals provides NGOs with a strategic role and influence that may be greater than their formal powers would suggest.

III. A new anti-discrimination policy framework?

The adoption of the Directives provides a strong foundation for EU policy on combating discrimination. Nonetheless, both Chapters 3 and 4 noted the relative isolation in which they are located. This is less true for combating racism, where various EU-funded initiatives have previously existed.[69] The Article 13 Action Programme clearly aims to 'fill out' the policy space surrounding the Directives, and this objective is also supported by the Equal programme which aims 'to promote new means of combating all forms of discrimination and inequalities in connection with the labour market'.[70] (The priority attached to enhancing labour market participation is once again confirmed if one compares the budget for Equal (€2,847 million[71]) with that for the Action Programme (€98.4 million).[72]) Despite the contribution these programmes will doubtless make, the construction of an overall policy framework on combating discrimination demands further work.[73] Crucially, the challenge of mainstreaming equality norms into all aspects of EU law and

---

[68] Council Decision (EC) 2000/750 of 27 November 2000, Annex, establishing a Community action programme to combat discrimination (2001 to 2006) [2000] OJ L303/23.

[69] Commission, 'Commission report on the implementation of the action plan on racism—mainstreaming the fight against racism', January 2000. Available at: http://europa.eu.int/comm/employment_social/fundamri/eu_racism/main_en.htm

[70] Commission, 'Communication from the Commission to the Member States establishing the guidelines for the Community initiative Equal concerning transnational cooperation to promote new means of combating all forms of discrimination and inequalities in connection with the labour market [2000] OJ C127/2, para 3.

[71] ibid para 67.

[72] Council Decision (EC) 2000/750, Art 10 of 27 November 2000 establishing a Community action programme to combat discrimination (2001 to 2006) [2000] OJ L303/23.

[73] D Borrillo, 'L'orientation sexuelle en Europe—esquisse d'une politique publique anti-discriminatoire' (July–August 2000) *Le Temps Modernes* 263, 278.

policy remains open. First, it is essential that other law and policy initiatives do not contradict or diminish the measures being taken under the auspices of Article 13. For example, there has been constant criticism of the Union's policies on immigration and asylum for the potentially negative effects of these measures on relations between different ethnic groups in the EU.[74] Second, there is a need to mobilise positively other policies in order to advance equal opportunities.

Traditionally, the main legal guarantee of non-discrimination throughout EU law has been the fundamental rights case law of the Court of Justice.[75] Notwithstanding its non-binding nature, the Charter of Fundamental Rights provides a significant step forward in clarifying the content of the rights recognised by the European Union. For instance, Article 21(1) of the Charter resolves any lingering doubts as to whether the principle of equal treatment includes non-discrimination on the ground of sexual orientation. Indeed, in its judgment in *D and Sweden v Council*, the Court of Justice implicitly acknowledges the existence of this principle, albeit in the context of a finding that this principle had not been violated.[76] Yet, even if the content of the rights guaranteed by the Court is becoming clearer, this judicial principle alone cannot guarantee equal opportunities throughout EU law and policy.

First, as with any litigation-based mechanism, the guarantee is *reactive* rather than *proactive*. Therefore, the Court normally intervenes only when the right has already been breached, and even here it depends on the willingness of an individual with the requisite legal standing to pursue such an action. The absence of any litigation in the history of the Court concerning racial discrimination in EU law demonstrates how issues can be neglected merely because no suitable litigation has been forthcoming.[77]

Second, even after the Charter, ambiguity continues to surround the interpretation and application of certain rights it confers. *D and Sweden v Council* exemplifies the difficulties here. On the one hand, the Advocate-General relied on the Charter as a defence against the argument that there should be equal treatment for same-sex and opposite-sex couples. Indeed, he used the

---

[74] A Geddes, 'Immigrants, ethnic minorities and the European Union's democratic deficit' (1995) 33 *J of Common Market Studies* 197, 207.

[75] See further ch 1 above.

[76] 'as regards infringement of the principle of equal treatment of officials irrespective of their sexual orientation, it is clear that it is not the sex of the partner which determines whether the household allowance is granted, but the legal nature of the ties between the official and the partner' (Cases C–122/99P and C–125/99P [2001] ECR I–4319, para 47).

[77] D Curtin and M Geurts, 'Race discrimination and the European Union Anno 1996: from rhetoric to legal remedy?' (1996) 14 *Netherlands Q of Human Rights* 147, 153.

Charter (and its explanatory memorandum) to diminish persuasive arguments based on case law from the European Court of Human Rights that stressed the importance of non-discrimination on grounds of sexual orientation.[78] In contrast, the Court adopted a highly formalistic approach to exclude analysis of these sensitive issues. An exploration of the substance of the right to private and family life in relation to registered partnerships was avoided by finding that there had been no interference with the right in the first place.[79]

The underlying message which emerges from both *D and Sweden v Council* and *Grant v South-West Trains* is the reluctance of the Court to take the lead on morally sensitive questions relating to the definition of 'the family'.[80] In both cases, the Court points to the EU legislature as the body responsible for changing the status quo.[81] Despite the questionable decisions in both *D* and *Grant*, the Court is right to place the spotlight on the legislative organs. The issue of unmarried partners goes well beyond equal pay (which was the key issue in both *D* and *Grant*). Most obviously, it extends into free movement rights and the definition of family members.[82] This is also a prevalent issue within the Union's emerging body of immigration and asylum law.[83] Reference to 'family members' also arises in other, more diverse EU legal instruments. For example, Directive (EEC) 86/613 on equal treatment of self-employed women and men applies to self-employed workers and 'their spouses'.[84] It would be unsatisfactory, as well as unrealistic, to rely simply on the Court to deal with the equal treatment issues arising in all of these diverse areas. Instead, mainstreaming equality norms—in this case equal treatment irrespective of sexual orientation—places a duty on the EU institutions to respond in a proactive manner to questions such as same-sex partners and their place within EU law. To date, there is little evidence that the Union is willing to tackle this issue directly. The Framework Directive quietly aims to protect workplace benefits for married couples through Recital 22. Within

---

[78] Opinion of A-G Mischo, para 97.

[79] Cases C–122/99P and C–125/99P *D and Sweden v Council* [2001] ECR I–4319, para 60.

[80] This continues the pattern established in Case C–59/85 *Reed v Netherlands* [1986] ECR 1283.

[81] *D and Sweden v Council* (n 79 above) para 38; Case C–249/96 *Grant v South-West Trains* [1998] ECR I–621, 651.

[82] Reg (EEC) 1612/68 [1968] OJ Spec Ed (II) 475, Art 10.

[83] See in particular, Commission, 'Proposal for a Directive on the right to family reunification' COM (1999) 638, Art 5.

[84] Council Dir (EEC) 86/613, Art 2 of 11 December 1986 on the application of the principle of equal treatment between men and women engaged in an activity, including agriculture, in a self-employed capacity, and on the protection of self-employed women during pregnancy and motherhood [1986] OJ L359/56.

its proposals on immigration, asylum and free movement law, the Commission has favoured an approach based on formal equal treatment.[85] Therefore, EU or non-EU migrants will be entitled to recognition of their unmarried partners (same-sex or opposite-sex) for the purposes of immigration law only if they are present in states where national law treats unmarried partnerships as corresponding to married partnerships. Whilst this would be a step forward, ironically it would not confront the major obstacle to free movement, which exists when unmarried couples with legal recognition of their partnership in their Member State of origin wish to move to another Member State where there is no legal recognition of unmarried partnerships.

Mainstreaming is also required to protect against inadvertent or unanticipated negative effects on equal opportunities as a result of EU law and policy. This can be illustrated by reference to an example from free movement law. As part of the completion of the internal market, the rules governing the mutual recognition of qualifications acquired in the Union have been considerably enhanced.[86] No rules, however, exist regarding the recognition of qualifications obtained by third country nationals *in the EU*,[87] or qualifications obtained *in third countries*, irrespective of the nationality of the holder.

The greater problem is the non-recognition of qualifications acquired in a third country. For instance, in *Tawil-Albertini*,[88] a French national who gained a qualification in dentistry from Lebanon had this recognised as satisfactory by three different Member States—Belgium, the UK and Ireland. Nonetheless, the Court decided that the relevant legislation on the mutual recognition of qualifications[89] did not oblige France to recognise the Lebanese qualification, irrespective of the actions of other Member States.[90]

---

[85] For example, Commission, 'Proposal for a Directive on the right to family reunification' COM (1999) 638; Commission, 'Proposal for a European Parliament and Council Directive on the right of citizens of the Union and their family members to move and reside freelyw ithin the territory of the Member States' COM (2001) 257.

[86] Council Dir (EEC) 89/48 on mutual recognition of higher education diplomas [1989] OJ L19/16; Council Dir (EEC) 92/51 on mutual recognition of qualifications [1992] OJ L209/29.

[87] P Craig and G de Búrca, *The evolution of EU law* (2nd edn, Oxford: Oxford University Press, 1999) 743–44. In 1999, the Commission proposed that in certain circumstances third country nationals should be entitled to equal treatment with EU citizens in respect of the mutual recognition of qualifications obtained in the EU: Commission, 'Proposal for a Directive of the European Parliament and of the Council on the posting of workers who are third country nationals for the provision of cross-border services; proposal for a Council Directive extending the freedom to provide cross-border services to third country nationals established within the Community' COM (1999) 3.

[88] Case C–154/93 *Tawil-Albertini v Ministre des Affaires Sociales* [1994] ECR I–451.

[89] Dir (EEC) 78/686 on recognition of dental qualifications OJ [1978] L 233/1.

[90] [1994] ECR I–451, 463.

Recently, the Court has adopted a more flexible approach. In *Hocsman*, the applicant was (at the relevant time for the proceedings) a Spanish national who had obtained a medical diploma in Argentina, which was subsequently recognised by Spain. However, he was later refused authorisation to practise medicine in France, albeit after several years spent already working there. The Court held that the French authorities were obliged to take into consideration 'all the diplomas, certificates and other evidence of formal qualifications of the person concerned and his relevant experience'.[91]

The mutual recognition of qualifications within the European Union does not, by itself, place ethnic minorities at any disadvantage. Yet, the failure of the Member States to establish parallel schemes for qualifications from third countries is likely to place ethnic minorities at a particular disadvantage in the labour market.[92] Whilst clearly this is a complex issue, a first step would be to consider qualifications from countries such as Turkey, Morocco or Algeria, as these are major countries of origin for ethnic minorities in the Union, and institutional relationships already are in place with these states through the association agreements.

Partnership rights and recognition of third country qualifications are merely two examples of the potential for mainstreaming to inform the creation of an overall anti-discrimination policy framework in all aspects of EU law and policy. In recent years, the Commission has embraced the language of mainstreaming. It is a well-established discourse within EU gender equality policy and it has been introduced in relation to policies on combating racism and disability discrimination.[93] Nevertheless, by definition, for mainstreaming equality to be truly effective there must be mechanisms to ensure that equality considerations are systematically taken into account in the formulation, administration and evaluation of all policies.[94] In the absence of clear procedures there is a risk that mainstreaming becomes haphazard and variable, depending on the issue and/or the individuals involved. There is some evidence that this is currently the experience within EU law making.

---

[91] Case C–238/98 *Hocsman v Ministre de l'Emploi et de la Solidarité* [2000] ECR I–6623, para 35.

[92] E Szyszczak, 'Race Discrimination: the limits of market equality?' in B Hepple and E Syzszczak (eds), *Discrimination: the limits of the law* (London: Mansell, 1992) 127.

[93] Commission, 'Commission report on the implementation of the action plan on racism— mainstreaming the fight against racism', January 2000. Available at: http://europa.eu.int/ comm/employment_social/fundanvi/eu_racism/mais_en.htm; Commission, 'Mainstreaming disability within EU employment and social policy' DGV services working paper, 1999. Available at: http://europa.eu.int/comm/dgs/employment_social/key_en.htm

[94] S Mullally, 'Mainstreaming equality in Ireland: a fair and inclusive accommodation?' (2001) 21 Legal Studies 99, 110.

For example, Chapter 4 noted the rise and fall of the practice of including anti-discrimination clauses in legislative proposals from DG Employment and Social Affairs.

Various possibilities for how mainstreaming might be more effectively achieved are already emerging at the national level. For example, the Northern Ireland Act 1998, s 75 imposed on all public authorities a statutory duty to have 'due regard' to equality of opportunity on nine different grounds, including all the Article 13 grounds. All public authorities are then obliged to submit reports on action taken to the Equality Commission in Northern Ireland.[95] Alternatively, the British Race Relations Act 1976 (as amended), s 71(1) imposes a duty on specified public authorities to have due regard to the need to eliminate racial discrimination and to promote equality of opportunity. The Commission for Racial Equality monitors this duty and it can serve a 'compliance notice' where it is satisfied that the duty is not being complied with.[96] This notice can subsequently be enforced by Court order.[97] Without suggesting that either of these relatively recent innovations should be directly transposed to the EU institutional framework, they provide examples of the options available, and the need for the Union to find instruments through which equality norms can be woven into all areas of law and policy.

IV. The next steps for Article 13

In this final section, it is appropriate to look ahead briefly and consider the future implementation of Article 13. Naturally, the effective implementation of the two Directives already adopted must form a central element of future anti-discrimination policy. Nonetheless, further legislative interventions are already anticipated. In June 2001, the Council reached political agreement on a Directive amending the Equal Treatment Directive to incorporate many of the elements present in the Article 13 Directives.[98] The European Social Agenda commits the Commission to submitting a further Directive extending the principle of equal treatment between women and men to areas outside

---

[95] S Mullally, 'Mainstreaming equality in Ireland: a fair and inclusive accommodation?' (2001) 21 Legal Studies 113. The precise mechanism is set out in the Northern Ireland Act 1998, Sch 9, reproduced in *Equal Opportunities Rev*, No 83, January/February 1999.

[96] Race Relations Act 1976 (as amended), s 71D.   [97] s 71E(2).

[98] Press release, 2357th meeting of the Employment and Social Policy Council, Luxembourg, Doc 9397/01, Presse 225.

employment.[99] Moreover, the Commission has indicated its intention to submit a specific Directive on disability discrimination in 2003.[100] Therefore, it is clear that alongside the implementation of the Directives already adopted, a rolling programme of new anti-discrimination law is at least promised.

The key issue which future legislation must confront is the equality hierarchy within EU law. In a very clear sense, one of the foundational objectives of Article 13 was to move away from the pre-existing hierarchical structure. The inherent contradiction of a system of anti-discrimination law which itself discriminates in the degree of legal protection afforded was one of the underlying weaknesses of EU anti-discrimination law prior to Article 13; there was no obvious justification for the privileged position of discrimination based on gender and EU nationality. On various occasions since Article 13's inception, the institutions have used the rhetoric of equal treatment within anti-discrimination law. In July 1999, the Commission provided funding for projects designed to be 'preparatory measures aimed at combating and preventing discrimination in accordance with Article 13 of the Treaty'.[101] This initiative was distinguished by 'a new horizontal approach to combating discrimination as opposed to the target-group specific approach of the past'.[102] This spirit also informs the Action Programme which declares that 'the different forms of discrimination cannot be ranked: all are equally intolerable'.[103]

Irrespective of these statements, the reality of the Directives adopted is a reinforcement of the equality hierarchy, not its diminution or disappearance. The prohibition of discrimination on grounds of racial or ethnic origin attracts stronger enforcement mechanisms, as well as a wider material scope. Within the Framework Directive, clear distinctions are drawn between the different discriminatory grounds in terms of the exceptions applicable and the implementation period. Is this new hierarchy defensible? A recurrent argument is the need for specificity in discrimination law. Different grounds of discrimination have peculiar features and the law needs to be tailored in response. For example, (non-) recognition of partners is an issue that primarily arises in respect of sexual orientation discrimination and in order to be

[99] European Social Agenda approved by the Nice European Council meeting on 7, 8 and 9 December 2000 [2001] OJ C157/4.

[100] L Waddington, 'Article 13 EC: setting priorities in the proposal for a horizontal employment Directive' (2000) 29 ILJ 176, 181.

[101] Commission, 'Call for proposals, VP/1999/016' [1999] OJ C191/14.

[102] ibid para II(1).

[103] Council Decision (EC) 2000/750 of 27 November 2000 establishing a Community action programme to combat discrimination (2001 to 2006) [2000] OJ L303/23, Recital 5.

clear the law may need to address this individually. Alternatively, the situation of pregnant workers is manifestly linked to gender discrimination and hence, to be most effective, gender equality law requires special provisions in this area. Consequently, there is a risk that where legislation attempts to encompass all grounds of discrimination it ends up either mired in complexity or it is diluted by its generality.

Yet, equal protection against discrimination does not imply identical provision. It is important that this discussion is not confused with the debate over whether to have a single equality law and/or single equality bodies. This is one instance where the principle of subsidiarity provides a relatively clear indication that discretion should be left to national authorities as to whether equality provisions and institutions should be horizontal (all grounds) or vertical (ground-specific). Single equality laws can have internal hierarchies, and single equality bodies can have internal priorities. Conversely, different statutes and different bodies do not, by themselves, prevent equal protection standards across various discriminatory grounds.

Some flexibility within the law to accommodate the peculiarities of each of the grounds of discrimination is only to be expected (and sometimes welcomed). However, it is a mistake to regard this as a justification for fundamentally different levels of protection. The key issues generating an equality hierarchy in EU anti-discrimination law relate to the material scope of the ban on discrimination, the permitted exceptions and the enforcement procedures available. It is difficult to understand why victims of sexual and/or racial discrimination require institutional assistance under EU law, whilst victims of other forms of discrimination do not. Joke Swiebel, one of the Parliament's rapporteurs on the Framework Directive, stressed that even if the material scope of the Directives differed, there should not be a divergence in the 'level of protection' that applied.[104] Similarly, the application of the ban on racial and ethnic discrimination to areas outside employment does not seem to reflect specific facets of these forms of discrimination, but simply the political will in the Council.

The persistence of the equality hierarchy is an issue that poses two essential problems for the Union. First, EU law remains weak in dealing with multiple discrimination. Again, there has been rhetorical recognition of overlapping forms of discrimination. For instance, the preambles of both Directives refer to the need to promote equality between women and men in

---

[104] Parliament, 'Report by the Committee on Employment and Social Affairs on the proposal for a Council Directive establishing a general framework for equal treatment in employment and occupation' [Mann/Swiebel] A5-264/2000, 50.

the implementation of the Directives 'especially since women are often the victims of multiple discrimination'.[105] Yet, the relatively simple example of a German woman of Turkish origin who faces harassment because of her gender, ethnic origin and religion poses considerable difficulties for EU law. If the harassment occurs in employment, all dimensions are prohibited, but institutional support is only required in respect of the gender and ethnic harassment.[106] If the harassment occurs in the provision of services, then only ethnic harassment is prohibited. An effective strategy against multiple discrimination requires much greater coordination of anti-discrimination law and more equality in the level of protection available.

Second, at a more general level, the potential for anti-discrimination law to confer an enhanced commitment to the Union on the part of individuals could be undermined if there is a perception that 'some are more equal than others'.[107] The social citizenship model identifies the guarantee of fundamental rights as a key mechanism for the EU to connect with individuals and thereby to build a sense of trust and loyalty within the public towards European integration.[108] For example, if lesbians and gay men in Italy are aware that they have gained protection against discrimination in employment because of European Union law, and that their national government was unlikely otherwise to adopt such measures, then their perception of the Union may be improved. At its most basic, they may consider the European Union is a good thing as it is addressing issues important to their everyday lives. This potentially positive sentiment must, however, be balanced against the possibly negative signals which arise if individuals perceive that their concerns are being treated less seriously, or with less urgency, than those of other groups. For example, if associations representing older people feel that age discrimination is not being given the same priority as other forms of discrimination by the EU, then any beneficial sentiment for the Union generated by the Framework Directive may be diminished or cancelled out. Of course individuals' attitudes to the European Union are produced by a complex mix of factors and not the simplistic cause and effect outlined above. Yet, as one influence in a much wider picture, the hierarchical structure of anti-discrimination law does suggest a different level of commitment from the

[105] Racial Equality Dir, Recital 14; Framework Dir, Recital 3.

[106] This assumes the successful adoption of the amendment to the Equal Treatment Directive.

[107] L Flynn, 'The implications of Article 13 EC—after Amsterdam, will some forms of discrimination be more equal than others? (1999) 36 CML Rev 1127.

[108] J Weiler, *The Constitution of Europe—'Do the new clothes have an emperor?' and other esssays in European integration* (Cambridge: Cambridge University Press, 1999) 334.

Union to different forms of discrimination. The negative side-effects of this impression should not be entirely ignored.

Although equal protection may be a desirable long-term objective, political exigencies may not make this feasible in the short term. Issues such as third country nationals' access to public sector employment or workplace benefits for unmarried partners remain sensitive. There is a temptation for the Union to keep these issues off the agenda—areas where differences of opinion are too broad to allow for current progress. A more constructive response, however, may be to focus on intermediate solutions. In the past, soft law often provided a means to maintain policy momentum, even when binding legislation remained a distant possibility.[109] In highly controversial areas, non-binding instruments could indicate standards to be aimed at, encouraging employers and Member States to reflect on existing practices.[110]

At the same time, certain lessons can be learnt from the experience of earlier forms of soft law. First, it should be in the form of recognised Community instruments, such as recommendations and opinions.[111] The proliferation of measures, such as memoranda, conclusions, resolutions and declarations, has not proven especially constructive or effective, as the status of these instruments is quite vague.[112] Moreover, the official instruments set down in the EC Treaty can be expected to carry greater weight before national and European courts.[113] This also tends to ensure a more constructive input from bodies such as the Parliament, whereas conclusions and declarations from the Council often appear with little or no prior consultation.

Second, these instruments tend to be at their most effective when they build on pre-existing, binding Community law measures.[114] For instance, the Recommendation on dignity at work[115] provided a flexible set of standards

---

[109] S Sciarra, 'European Social Policy and Labour Law—Challenges and Perspectives' (1995) IV(I) Collected Courses of the Academy of European Law 301, 340.

[110] K Wellens and G Borchardt, 'Soft law in European Community law' (1989) 14 ELR 267, 310–311.

[111] EC Treaty, Art 249.

[112] J Kenner, 'EC Labour Law: the Softly Softly Approach' (1995) 14 Intl J of Comparative Labour L and Industrial Relations 307, 311.

[113] Case C–322/88 *Grimaldi v Fonds des maladies professionnelles* [1989] ECR 4407, para 18. Also, J Snyder, 'The effectiveness of European Community law: institutions, processes, tools and techniques' (1993) 56 MLR 19, 33.

[114] J Kenner, 'Citizenship and fundamental rights: reshaping the European social model' in J Kenner (ed), *Trends in European social policy. Essays in memory of Malcolm Mead* (Aldershot, Dartmouth, 1995) 45.

[115] Commission Recommendation on the dignity of women and men at work [1992] OJ L49/1.

against which judicial bodies could assess the behaviour of employers, as well as providing an indication that sexual harassment should be regarded as sexual discrimination contrary to Community law.[116] In contrast, Waddington notes how the Commission's guideline on the employment of disabled people,[117] which was not reinforced by binding law, had little discernible impact on national legal developments.[118]

Third, there needs to be an indication that the Member States take the non-binding instrument seriously and are prepared to reconsider national practice as a result. A practical expression of this can be the inclusion of a requirement for Member States to produce periodic reports on how they are implementing the soft law measure. The deletion of such a requirement from the 1990 Council Resolution on racism and xenophobia[119] illustrated that the Member States had little intention of putting the rhetoric of the resolution into practice—as was subsequently borne out by experience. Overall, soft law might become more effective if it was used with less frequency, but with a greater intensity of obligations.

Positively, a place for complementary legal instruments has already been carved out within the Directives. Both instruments ascribe a role to the Social Partners in forging 'collective agreements, codes of conduct' and 'agreements laying down anti-discrimination rules'.[120] Yet, in the broader fields covered by the Racial Equality Directive, the Social Partners are not necessarily the most appropriate actors. For example, patients' associations or students' groups should clearly be involved in elaborating norms for the implementation of non-discrimination requirements in the areas of health and education. Soft law measures in these spheres seem especially essential. The Union has limited experience in regulating matters such as health, education and housing. The Racial Equality Directive leaves a blurred picture of the rights it confers in these areas. Therefore, it would be valuable guidance for the Union to elaborate in more detail how equal treatment should be ensured in these fields. More generally, the potential application of the open method of co-ordination to anti-discrimination policies should be considered. This was endorsed in 1999 by the European Parliament Employment

---

[116] See further, J Gregory, 'Sexual Harassment—making the best use of European law' (1995) 2 *Eur J of Women's Studies* 421.

[117] Council Recommendation [1986] OJ L225/43.

[118] L Waddington, *Disability, employment and the European Community* (Antwerpen: Maklu, 1995) 107–108.

[119] Council Resolution on the fight against racism and xenophobia [1990] OJ C157/1.

[120] Racial Equality Directive, Art 11; Framework Directive, Art 13.

and Social Affairs Committee,[121] which recommended periodic reports in a similar model to the European Employment Strategy. Such an approach could lay the foundation for coordinating policy development in areas such as positive action or contract compliance, matters currently left completely open to Member State discretion.

V. Concluding remarks

The advent of Article 13 has ushered in a new period in EU anti-discrimination law. The Directives already adopted should make a valuable contribution to protecting the human rights of individuals, removing barriers to participation in the labour market as well as facilitating free movement. Yet, as the EU expands its legal reach into areas hitherto within the national domain, caution should be exercised when confronting established legal traditions, in all their diversity. A careful balance needs to be secured between raising the threshold of fundamental rights in EU law, while respecting certain choices in national law reflecting different socio-legal cultures. The input of the Union seems likely to be at its most constructive where it concentrates on ensuring that once legislation is adopted, this will be fully and effectively implemented. Moreover, if it is to retain credibility, both with the Member States and with its citizens, the Union must clearly and convincingly 'lead by example'.[122] A rigorous commitment to respect for the principle of equality throughout EU law and policy, as well as in the Union's own practices as an employer, is naturally a starting point as the Union works towards the transformation of anti-discrimination law.

---

[121] Parliament, 'Working Document: a framework for action on non-discrimination at EU level based on Art 13 of the Amsterdam Treaty' [Ojala and Hughes] PE 229.570/fin, 25 March 1999.

[122] A Cassese, C Lalumière, P Leuprecht and M Robinson, *Leading by example: a human rights agenda for the European Union for the Year 2000. Agenda of the Comité des Sages and final project report* (Florence, European University Institute, 1998).

Annex 1

Council Directive (EC) 2000/43 of 29 June 2000 implementing the principle of equal treatment between persons irrespective of racial or ethnic origin

Official Journal L 180/22, 19 July 2000.

THE COUNCIL OF THE EUROPEAN UNION,
Having regard to the Treaty establishing the European Community and in particular Article 13 thereof,
Having regard to the proposal from the Commission,[1]
Having regard to the opinion of the European Parliament,[2]
Having regard to the opinion of the Economic and Social Committee,[3]
Having regard to the opinion of the Committee of the Regions,[4]
Whereas:

(1) The Treaty on European Union marks a new stage in the process of creating an ever closer union among the peoples of Europe.

(2) In accordance with Article 6 of the Treaty on European Union, the European Union is founded on the principles of liberty, democracy, respect for human rights and fundamental freedoms, and the rule of law, principles which are common to the Member States, and should respect fundamental rights as guaranteed by the European Convention for the Protection of Human Rights and Fundamental Freedoms and as they result from the constitutional traditions common to the Member States, as general principles of Community Law.

(3) The right to equality before the law and protection against discrimination for all persons constitutes a universal right recognised by the Universal Declaration of Human Rights, the United Nations Convention on the Elimination of all forms

---

[1] Not yet published in the Official Journal.
[2] Opinion delivered on 18 May 2000 (not yet published in the Official Journal).
[3] Opinion delivered on 12 April 2000 (not yet published in the Official Journal).
[4] Opinion delivered on 31 May 2000 (not yet published in the Official Journal).

of Discrimination Against Women, the International Convention on the Elimination of all forms of Racial Discrimination and the United Nations Covenants on Civil and Political Rights and on Economic, Social and Cultural Rights and by the European Convention for the Protection of Human Rights and Fundamental Freedoms, to which all Member States are signatories.

(4) It is important to respect such fundamental rights and freedoms, including the right to freedom of association. It is also important, in the context of the access to and provision of goods and services, to respect the protection of private and family life and transactions carried out in this context.

(5) The European Parliament has adopted a number of Resolutions on the fight against racism in the European Union.

(6) The European Union rejects theories which attempt to determine the existence of separate human races. The use of the term 'racial origin' in this Directive does not imply an acceptance of such theories.

(7) The European Council in Tampere, on 15 and 16 October 1999, invited the Commission to come forward as soon as possible with proposals implementing Article 13 of the EC Treaty as regards the fight against racism and xenophobia.

(8) The Employment Guidelines 2000 agreed by the European Council in Helsinki, on 10 and 11 December 1999, stress the need to foster conditions for a socially inclusive labour market by formulating a coherent set of policies aimed at combating discrimination against groups such as ethnic minorities.

(9) Discrimination based on racial or ethnic origin may undermine the achievement of the objectives of the EC Treaty, in particular the attainment of a high level of employment and of social protection, the raising of the standard of living and quality of life, economic and social cohesion and solidarity. It may also undermine the objective of developing the European Union as an area of freedom, security and justice.

(10) The Commission presented a communication on racism, xenophobia and anti-Semitism in December 1995.

(11) The Council adopted on 15 July 1996 Joint Action (96/443/JHA) concerning action to combat racism and xenophobia[5] under which the Member States undertake to ensure effective judicial cooperation in respect of offences based on racist or xenophobic behaviour.

(12) To ensure the development of democratic and tolerant societies which allow the participation of all persons irrespective of racial or ethnic origin, specific action in the field of discrimination based on racial or ethnic origin should go beyond access to employed and self-employed activities and cover areas such as education, social protection including social security and healthcare, social advantages and access to and supply of goods and services.

(13) To this end, any direct or indirect discrimination based on racial or ethnic origin as regards the areas covered by this Directive should be prohibited throughout

[5] [1996] OJ L185/5.

the Community. This prohibition of discrimination should also apply to nationals of third countries, but does not cover differences of treatment based on nationality and is without prejudice to provisions governing the entry and residence of third-country nationals and their access to employment and to occupation.

(14) In implementing the principle of equal treatment irrespective of racial or ethnic origin, the Community should, in accordance with Article 3(2) of the EC Treaty, aim to eliminate inequalities, and to promote equality between men and women, especially since women are often the victims of multiple discrimination.

(15) The appreciation of the facts from which it may be inferred that there has been direct or indirect discrimination is a matter for national judicial or other competent bodies, in accordance with rules of national law or practice. Such rules may provide in particular for indirect discrimination to be established by any means including on the basis of statistical evidence.

(16) It is important to protect all natural persons against discrimination on grounds of racial or ethnic origin. Member States should also provide, where appropriate and in accordance with their national traditions and practice, protection for legal persons where they suffer discrimination on grounds of the racial or ethnic origin of their members.

(17) The prohibition of discrimination should be without prejudice to the maintenance or adoption of measures intended to prevent or compensate for disadvantages suffered by a group of persons of a particular racial or ethnic origin, and such measures may permit organisations of persons of a particular racial or ethnic origin where their main object is the promotion of the special needs of those persons.

(18) In very limited circumstances, a difference of treatment may be justified where a characteristic related to racial or ethnic origin constitutes a genuine and determining occupational requirement, when the objective is legitimate and the requirement is proportionate. Such circumstances should be included in the information provided by the Member States to the Commission.

(19) Persons who have been subject to discrimination based on racial and ethnic origin should have adequate means of legal protection. To provide a more effective level of protection, associations or legal entities should also be empowered to engage, as the Member States so determine, either on behalf or in support of any victim, in proceedings, without prejudice to national rules of procedure concerning representation and defence before the courts.

(20) The effective implementation of the principle of equality requires adequate judicial protection against victimisation.

(21) The rules on the burden of proof must be adapted when there is a prima facie case of discrimination and, for the principle of equal treatment to be applied effectively, the burden of proof must shift back to the respondent when evidence of such discrimination is brought.

(22) Member States need not apply the rules on the burden of proof to proceedings in which it is for the court or other competent body to investigate the facts of the case. The procedures thus referred to are those in which the plaintiff is not required to prove the facts, which it is for the court or competent body to investigate.

(23) Member States should promote dialogue between the social partners and with non-governmental organisations to address different forms of discrimination and to combat them.

(24) Protection against discrimination based on racial or ethnic origin would itself be strengthened by the existence of a body or bodies in each Member State, with competence to analyse the problems involved, to study possible solutions and to provide concrete assistance for the victims.

(25) This Directive lays down minimum requirements, thus giving the Member States the option of introducing or maintaining more favourable provisions. The implementation of this Directive should not serve to justify any regression in relation to the situation which already prevails in each Member State.

(26) Member States should provide for effective, proportionate and dissuasive sanctions in case of breaches of the obligations under this Directive.

(27) The Member States may entrust management and labour, at their joint request, with the implementation of this Directive as regards provisions falling within the scope of collective agreements, provided that the Member States take all the necessary steps to ensure that they can at all times guarantee the results imposed by this Directive.

(28) In accordance with the principles of subsidiarity and proportionality as set out in Article 5 of the EC Treaty, the objective of this Directive, namely ensuring a common high level of protection against discrimination in all the Member States, cannot be sufficiently achieved by the Member States and can therefore, by reason of the scale and impact of the proposed action, be better achieved by the Community. This Directive does not go beyond what is necessary in order to achieve those objectives,

HAS ADOPTED THIS DIRECTIVE:

CHAPTER I
GENERAL PROVISIONS

Article 1: Purpose
The purpose of this Directive is to lay down a framework for combating discrimination on the grounds of racial or ethnic origin, with a view to putting into effect in the Member States the principle of equal treatment.

Article 2: Concept of discrimination
1. For the purposes of this Directive, the principle of equal treatment shall mean that there shall be no direct or indirect discrimination based on racial or ethnic origin.

2. For the purposes of paragraph 1:
    (a) direct discrimination shall be taken to occur where one person is treated less favourably than another is, has been or would be treated in a comparable situation on grounds of racial or ethnic origin;
    (b) indirect discrimination shall be taken to occur where an apparently neutral provision, criterion or practice would put persons of a racial or ethnic origin at a particular disadvantage compared with other persons, unless that provision, criterion or practice is objectively justified by a legitimate aim and the means of achieving that aim are appropriate and necessary.
3. Harassment shall be deemed to be discrimination within the meaning of paragraph 1, when an unwanted conduct related to racial or ethnic origin takes place with the purpose or effect of violating the dignity of a person and of creating an intimidating, hostile, degrading, humiliating or offensive environment. In this context, the concept of harassment may be defined in accordance with the national laws and practice of the Member States.
4. An instruction to discriminate against persons on grounds of racial or ethnic origin shall be deemed to be discrimination within the meaning of paragraph 1.

Article 3: Scope
1. Within the limits of the powers conferred upon the Community, this Directive shall apply to all persons, as regards both the public and private sectors, including public bodies, in relation to:
    (a) conditions for access to employment, to self-employment and to occupation, including selection criteria and recruitment conditions, whatever the branch of activity and at all levels of the professional hierarchy, including promotion;
    (b) access to all types and to all levels of vocational guidance, vocational training, advanced vocational training and retraining, including practical work experience;
    (c) employment and working conditions, including dismissals and pay;
    (d) membership of and involvement in an organisation of workers or employers, or any organisation whose members carry on a particular profession, including the benefits provided for by such organisations;
    (e) social protection, including social security and healthcare;
    (f) social advantages;
    (g) education;
    (h) access to and supply of goods and services which are available to the public, including housing.
2. This Directive does not cover difference of treatment based on nationality and is without prejudice to provisions and conditions relating to the entry into and residence of third-country nationals and stateless persons on the territory of Member States, and to any treatment which arises from the legal status of the third-country nationals and stateless persons concerned.

Article 4: Genuine and determining occupational requirements

Notwithstanding Article 2(1) and (2), Member States may provide that a difference of treatment which is based on a characteristic related to racial or ethnic origin shall not constitute discrimination where, by reason of the nature of the particular occupational activities concerned or of the context in which they are carried out, such a characteristic constitutes a genuine and determining occupational requirement, provided that the objective is legitimate and the requirement is proportionate.

Article 5: Positive action

With a view to ensuring full equality in practice, the principle of equal treatment shall not prevent any Member State from maintaining or adopting specific measures to prevent or compensate for disadvantages linked to racial or ethnic origin.

Article 6: Minimum requirements

1. Member States may introduce or maintain provisions which are more favourable to the protection of the principle of equal treatment than those laid down in this Directive.
2. The implementation of this Directive shall under no circumstances constitute grounds for a reduction in the level of protection against discrimination already afforded by Member States in the fields covered by this Directive.

CHAPTER II
REMEDIES AND ENFORCEMENT

Article 7: Defence of rights

1. Member States shall ensure that judicial and/or administrative procedures, including where they deem it appropriate conciliation procedures, for the enforcement of obligations under this Directive are available to all persons who consider themselves wronged by failure to apply the principle of equal treatment to them, even after the relationship in which the discrimination is alleged to have occurred has ended.
2. Member States shall ensure that associations, organisations or other legal entities, which have, in accordance with the criteria laid down by their national law, a legitimate interest in ensuring that the provisions of this Directive are complied with, may engage, either on behalf or in support of the complainant, with his or her approval, in any judicial and/or administrative procedure provided for the enforcement of obligations under this Directive.
3. Paragraphs 1 and 2 are without prejudice to national rules relating to time limits for bringing actions as regards the principle of equality of treatment.

Article 8: Burden of proof

1. Member States shall take such measures as are necessary, in accordance with their national judicial systems, to ensure that, when persons who consider themselves

wronged because the principle of equal treatment has not been applied to them establish, before a court or other competent authority, facts from which it may be presumed that there has been direct or indirect discrimination, it shall be for the respondent to prove that there has been no breach of the principle of equal treatment.

2. Paragraph 1 shall not prevent Member States from introducing rules of evidence which are more favourable to plaintiffs.
3. Paragraph 1 shall not apply to criminal procedures.
4. Paragraphs 1, 2 and 3 shall also apply to any proceedings brought in accordance with Article 7(2).
5. Member States need not apply paragraph 1 to proceedings in which it is for the court or competent body to investigate the facts of the case.

Article 9: Victimisation
Member States shall introduce into their national legal systems such measures as are necessary to protect individuals from any adverse treatment or adverse consequence as a reaction to a complaint or to proceedings aimed at enforcing compliance with the principle of equal treatment.

Article 10: Dissemination of information
Member States shall take care that the provisions adopted pursuant to this Directive, together with the relevant provisions already in force, are brought to the attention of the persons concerned by all appropriate means throughout their territory.

Article 11: Social dialogue
1. Member States shall, in accordance with national traditions and practice, take adequate measures to promote the social dialogue between the two sides of industry with a view to fostering equal treatment, including through the monitoring of workplace practices, collective agreements, codes of conduct, research or exchange of experiences and good practices.
2. Where consistent with national traditions and practice, Member States shall encourage the two sides of the industry without prejudice to their autonomy to conclude, at the appropriate level, agreements laying down anti-discrimination rules in the fields referred to in Article 3 which fall within the scope of collective bargaining. These agreements shall respect the minimum requirements laid down by this Directive and the relevant national implementing measures.

Article 12: Dialogue with non-governmental organisations
Member States shall encourage dialogue with appropriate non-governmental organisations which have, in accordance with their national law and practice, a legitimate interest in contributing to the fight against discrimination on grounds of racial and ethnic origin with a view to promoting the principle of equal treatment.

CHAPTER III
BODIES FOR THE PROMOTION OF EQUAL TREATMENT

Article 13

1. Member States shall designate a body or bodies for the promotion of equal treatment of all persons without discrimination on the grounds of racial or ethnic origin. These bodies may form part of agencies charged at national level with the defence of human rights or the safeguard of individuals' rights.
2. Member States shall ensure that the competences of these bodies include:
   —without prejudice to the right of victims and of associations, organisations or other legal entities referred to in Article 7(2), providing independent assistance to victims of discrimination in pursuing their complaints about discrimination,
   —conducting independent surveys concerning discrimination,
   —publishing independent reports and making recommendations on any issue relating to such discrimination.

CHAPTER IV
FINAL PROVISIONS

Article 14: Compliance

Member States shall take the necessary measures to ensure that:

   (a) any laws, regulations and administrative provisions contrary to the principle of equal treatment are abolished;
   (b) any provisions contrary to the principle of equal treatment which are included in individual or collective contracts or agreements, internal rules of undertakings, rules governing profit-making or non-profit-making associations, and rules governing the independent professions and workers' and employers' organisations, are or may be declared, null and void or are amended.

Article 15: Sanctions

Member States shall lay down the rules on sanctions applicable to infringements of the national provisions adopted pursuant to this Directive and shall take all measures necessary to ensure that they are applied. The sanctions, which may comprise the payment of compensation to the victim, must be effective, proportionate and dissuasive. The Member States shall notify those provisions to the Commission by 19 July 2003 at the latest and shall notify it without delay of any subsequent amendment affecting them.

Article 16: Implementation

Member States shall adopt the laws, regulations and administrative provisions necessary to comply with this Directive by 19 July 2003 or may entrust management and labour, at their joint request, with the implementation of this Directive as regards provisions falling within the scope of collective agreements. In such cases, Member States shall ensure that by 19 July 2003, management and labour introduce the necessary measures by agreement, Member States being required to take any necessary measures to enable them at any time to be in a position to guarantee the results imposed by this Directive. They shall forthwith inform the Commission thereof.

When Member States adopt these measures, they shall contain a reference to this Directive or be accompanied by such a reference on the occasion of their official publication. The methods of making such a reference shall be laid down by the Member States.

Article 17: Report

1. Member States shall communicate to the Commission by 19 July 2005, and every five years thereafter, all the information necessary for the Commission to draw up a report to the European Parliament and the Council on the application of this Directive.
2. The Commission's report shall take into account, as appropriate, the views of the European Monitoring Centre on Racism and Xenophobia, as well as the viewpoints of the social partners and relevant non-governmental organisations. In accordance with the principle of gender mainstreaming, this report shall, inter alia, provide an assessment of the impact of the measures taken on women and men. In the light of the information received, this report shall include, if necessary, proposals to revise and update this Directive.

Article 18: Entry into force

This Directive shall enter into force on the day of its publication in the Official Journal of the European Communities.

Article 19: Addressees

This Directive is addressed to the Member States.

Done at Luxembourg, 29 June 2000.

For the Council
The President
M. Arcanjo

Annex 2

Council Directive (EC) 2000/78 of 27 November 2000 establishing a general framework for equal treatment in employment and occupation

Official Journal L 303/16, 2 December 2000.

THE COUNCIL OF THE EUROPEAN UNION,

Having regard to the Treaty establishing the European Community, and in particular Article 13 thereof,

Having regard to the proposal from the Commission,[1]

Having regard to the Opinion of the European Parliament,[2]

Having regard to the Opinion of the Economic and Social Committee,[3]

Having regard to the Opinion of the Committee of the Regions,[4]

Whereas:

(1) In accordance with Article 6 of the Treaty on European Union, the European Union is founded on the principles of liberty, democracy, respect for human rights and fundamental freedoms, and the rule of law, principles which are common to all Member States and it respects fundamental rights, as guaranteed by the European Convention for the Protection of Human Rights and Fundamental Freedoms and as they result from the constitutional traditions common to the Member States, as general principles of Community law.

(2) The principle of equal treatment between women and men is well established by an important body of Community law, in particular in Council Directive 76/207/EEC of 9 February 1976 on the implementation of the principle of equal treatment for men and women as regards access to employment, vocational training and promotion, and working conditions.[5]

---

[1] [2000] OJ C177E/42.

[2] Opinion delivered on 12 October 2000 (not yet published in the Official Journal).

[3] [2000] OJ C204/82.   [4] [2000] OJ C 226/1.   [5] [1976] OJ L39/40.

(3) In implementing the principle of equal treatment, the Community should, in accordance with Article 3(2) of the EC Treaty, aim to eliminate inequalities, and to promote equality between men and women, especially since women are often the victims of multiple discrimination.

(4) The right of all persons to equality before the law and protection against discrimination constitutes a universal right recognised by the Universal Declaration of Human Rights, the United Nations Convention on the Elimination of All Forms of Discrimination against Women, United Nations Covenants on Civil and Political Rights and on Economic, Social and Cultural Rights and by the European Convention for the Protection of Human Rights and Fundamental Freedoms, to which all Member States are signatories. Convention No 111 of the International Labour Organisation (ILO) prohibits discrimination in the field of employment and occupation.

(5) It is important to respect such fundamental rights and freedoms. This Directive does not prejudice freedom of association, including the right to establish unions with others and to join unions to defend one's interests.

(6) The Community Charter of the Fundamental Social Rights of Workers recognises the importance of combating every form of discrimination, including the need to take appropriate action for the social and economic integration of elderly and disabled people.

(7) The EC Treaty includes among its objectives the promotion of coordination between employment policies of the Member States. To this end, a new employment chapter was incorporated in the EC Treaty as a means of developing a coordinated European strategy for employment to promote a skilled, trained and adaptable workforce.

(8) The Employment Guidelines for 2000 agreed by the European Council at Helsinki on 10 and 11 December 1999 stress the need to foster a labour market favourable to social integration by formulating a coherent set of policies aimed at combating discrimination against groups such as persons with disability. They also emphasise the need to pay particular attention to supporting older workers, in order to increase their participation in the labour force.

(9) Employment and occupation are key elements in guaranteeing equal opportunities for all and contribute strongly to the full participation of citizens in economic, cultural and social life and to realising their potential.

(10) On 29 June 2000 the Council adopted Directive 2000/43/EC[6] implementing the principle of equal treatment between persons irrespective of racial or ethnic origin. That Directive already provides protection against such discrimination in the field of employment and occupation.

(11) Discrimination based on religion or belief, disability, age or sexual orientation may undermine the achievement of the objectives of the EC Treaty, in particular the attainment of a high level of employment and social protection, raising

---

[6] [2000] OJ L180/22.

the standard of living and the quality of life, economic and social cohesion and solidarity, and the free movement of persons.

(12) To this end, any direct or indirect discrimination based on religion or belief, disability, age or sexual orientation as regards the areas covered by this Directive should be prohibited throughout the Community. This prohibition of discrimination should also apply to nationals of third countries but does not cover differences of treatment based on nationality and is without prejudice to provisions governing the entry and residence of third-country nationals and their access to employment and occupation.

(13) This Directive does not apply to social security and social protection schemes whose benefits are not treated as income within the meaning given to that term for the purpose of applying Article 141 of the EC Treaty, nor to any kind of payment by the State aimed at providing access to employment or maintaining employment.

(14) This Directive shall be without prejudice to national provisions laying down retirement ages.

(15) The appreciation of the facts from which it may be inferred that there has been direct or indirect discrimination is a matter for national judicial or other competent bodies, in accordance with rules of national law or practice. Such rules may provide, in particular, for indirect discrimination to be established by any means including on the basis of statistical evidence.

(16) The provision of measures to accommodate the needs of disabled people at the workplace plays an important role in combating discrimination on grounds of disability.

(17) This Directive does not require the recruitment, promotion, maintenance in employment or training of an individual who is not competent, capable and available to perform the essential functions of the post concerned or to undergo the relevant training, without prejudice to the obligation to provide reasonable accommodation for people with disabilities.

(18) This Directive does not require, in particular, the armed forces and the police, prison or emergency services to recruit or maintain in employment persons who do not have the required capacity to carry out the range of functions that they may be called upon to perform with regard to the legitimate objective of preserving the operational capacity of those services.

(19) Moreover, in order that the Member States may continue to safeguard the combat effectiveness of their armed forces, they may choose not to apply the provisions of this Directive concerning disability and age to all or part of their armed forces. The Member States which make that choice must define the scope of that derogation.

(20) Appropriate measures should be provided, i.e. effective and practical measures to adapt the workplace to the disability, for example adapting premises and equipment, patterns of working time, the distribution of tasks or the provision of training or integration resources.

(21) To determine whether the measures in question give rise to a disproportionate burden, account should be taken in particular of the financial and other costs entailed, the scale and financial resources of the organisation or undertaking and the possibility of obtaining public funding or any other assistance.

(22) This Directive is without prejudice to national laws on marital status and the benefits dependent thereon.

(23) In very limited circumstances, a difference of treatment may be justified where a characteristic related to religion or belief, disability, age or sexual orientation constitutes a genuine and determining occupational requirement, when the objective is legitimate and the requirement is proportionate. Such circumstances should be included in the information provided by the Member States to the Commission.

(24) The European Union in its Declaration No 11 on the status of churches and non-confessional organisations, annexed to the Final Act of the Amsterdam Treaty, has explicitly recognised that it respects and does not prejudice the status under national law of churches and religious associations or communities in the Member States and that it equally respects the status of philosophical and non-confessional organisations. With this in view, Member States may maintain or lay down specific provisions on genuine, legitimate and justified occupational requirements which might be required for carrying out an occupational activity.

(25) The prohibition of age discrimination is an essential part of meeting the aims set out in the Employment Guidelines and encouraging diversity in the workforce. However, differences in treatment in connection with age may be justified under certain circumstances and therefore require specific provisions which may vary in accordance with the situation in Member States. It is therefore essential to distinguish between differences in treatment which are justified, in particular by legitimate employment policy, labour market and vocational training objectives, and discrimination which must be prohibited.

(26) The prohibition of discrimination should be without prejudice to the maintenance or adoption of measures intended to prevent or compensate for disadvantages suffered by a group of persons of a particular religion or belief, disability, age or sexual orientation, and such measures may permit organisations of persons of a particular religion or belief, disability, age or sexual orientation where their main object is the promotion of the special needs of those persons.

(27) In its Recommendation 86/379/EEC of 24 July 1986 on the employment of disabled people in the Community,[7] the Council established a guideline framework setting out examples of positive action to promote the employment and training of disabled people, and in its Resolution of 17 June 1999 on equal employment opportunities for people with disabilities,[8] affirmed the importance of giving specific attention inter alia to recruitment, retention, training and lifelong learning with regard to disabled persons.

---

[7] [1986] OJ L225/43.   [8] [1999] OJ C186/3.

(28) This Directive lays down minimum requirements, thus giving the Member States the option of introducing or maintaining more favourable provisions. The implementation of this Directive should not serve to justify any regression in relation to the situation which already prevails in each Member State.

(29) Persons who have been subject to discrimination based on religion or belief, disability, age or sexual orientation should have adequate means of legal protection. To provide a more effective level of protection, associations or legal entities should also be empowered to engage in proceedings, as the Member States so determine, either on behalf or in support of any victim, without prejudice to national rules of procedure concerning representation and defence before the courts.

(30) The effective implementation of the principle of equality requires adequate judicial protection against victimisation.

(31) The rules on the burden of proof must be adapted when there is a prima facie case of discrimination and, for the principle of equal treatment to be applied effectively, the burden of proof must shift back to the respondent when evidence of such discrimination is brought. However, it is not for the respondent to prove that the plaintiff adheres to a particular religion or belief, has a particular disability, is of a particular age or has a particular sexual orientation.

(32) Member States need not apply the rules on the burden of proof to proceedings in which it is for the court or other competent body to investigate the facts of the case. The procedures thus referred to are those in which the plaintiff is not required to prove the facts, which it is for the court or competent body to investigate.

(33) Member States should promote dialogue between the social partners and, within the framework of national practice, with non-governmental organisations to address different forms of discrimination at the workplace and to combat them.

(34) The need to promote peace and reconciliation between the major communities in Northern Ireland necessitates the incorporation of particular provisions into this Directive.

(35) Member States should provide for effective, proportionate and dissuasive sanctions in case of breaches of the obligations under this Directive.

(36) Member States may entrust the social partners, at their joint request, with the implementation of this Directive, as regards the provisions concerning collective agreements, provided they take any necessary steps to ensure that they are at all times able to guarantee the results required by this Directive.

(37) In accordance with the principle of subsidiarity set out in Article 5 of the EC Treaty, the objective of this Directive, namely the creation within the Community of a level playing-field as regards equality in employment and occupation, cannot be sufficiently achieved by the Member States and can therefore, by reason of the scale and impact of the action, be better achieved at Community level. In accordance with the principle of proportionality, as set out in that Article, this Directive does not go beyond what is necessary in order to achieve that objective,

HAS ADOPTED THIS DIRECTIVE:

CHAPTER I
GENERAL PROVISIONS

Article 1: Purpose
The purpose of this Directive is to lay down a general framework for combating discrimination on the grounds of religion or belief, disability, age or sexual orientation as regards employment and occupation, with a view to putting into effect in the Member States the principle of equal treatment.

Article 2: Concept of discrimination
1. For the purposes of this Directive, the 'principle of equal treatment' shall mean that there shall be no direct or indirect discrimination whatsoever on any of the grounds referred to in Article 1.
2. For the purposes of paragraph 1:
   (a) direct discrimination shall be taken to occur where one person is treated less favourably than another is, has been or would be treated in a comparable situation, on any of the grounds referred to in Article 1;
   (b) indirect discrimination shall be taken to occur where an apparently neutral provision, criterion or practice would put persons having a particular religion or belief, a particular disability, a particular age, or a particular sexual orientation at a particular disadvantage compared with other persons unless:
      (i) that provision, criterion or practice is objectively justified by a legitimate aim and the means of achieving that aim are appropriate and necessary, or
      (ii) as regards persons with a particular disability, the employer or any person or organisation to whom this Directive applies, is obliged, under national legislation, to take appropriate measures in line with the principles contained in Article 5 in order to eliminate disadvantages entailed by such provision, criterion or practice.
3. Harassment shall be deemed to be a form of discrimination within the meaning of paragraph 1, when unwanted conduct related to any of the grounds referred to in Article 1 takes place with the purpose or effect of violating the dignity of a person and of creating an intimidating, hostile, degrading, humiliating or offensive environment. In this context, the concept of harassment may be defined in accordance with the national laws and practice of the Member States.
4. An instruction to discriminate against persons on any of the grounds referred to in Article 1 shall be deemed to be discrimination within the meaning of paragraph 1.
5. This Directive shall be without prejudice to measures laid down by national law which, in a democratic society, are necessary for public security, for the maintenance of public order and the prevention of criminal offences, for the protection of health and for the protection of the rights and freedoms of others.

Article 3: Scope
1. Within the limits of the areas of competence conferred on the Community, this Directive shall apply to all persons, as regards both the public and private sectors, including public bodies, in relation to:
   (a) conditions for access to employment, to self-employment or to occupation, including selection criteria and recruitment conditions, whatever the branch of activity and at all levels of the professional hierarchy, including promotion;
   (b) access to all types and to all levels of vocational guidance, vocational training, advanced vocational training and retraining, including practical work experience;
   (c) employment and working conditions, including dismissals and pay;
   (d) membership of, and involvement in, an organisation of workers or employers, or any organisation whose members carry on a particular profession, including the benefits provided for by such organisations.
2. This Directive does not cover differences of treatment based on nationality and is without prejudice to provisions and conditions relating to the entry into and residence of third-country nationals and stateless persons in the territory of Member States, and to any treatment which arises from the legal status of the third-country nationals and stateless persons concerned.
3. This Directive does not apply to payments of any kind made by state schemes or similar, including state social security or social protection schemes.
4. Member States may provide that this Directive, in so far as it relates to discrimination on the grounds of disability and age, shall not apply to the armed forces.

Article 4: Occupational requirements
1. Notwithstanding Article 2(1) and (2), Member States may provide that a difference of treatment which is based on a characteristic related to any of the grounds referred to in Article 1 shall not constitute discrimination where, by reason of the nature of the particular occupational activities concerned or of the context in which they are carried out, such a characteristic constitutes a genuine and determining occupational requirement, provided that the objective is legitimate and the requirement is proportionate.
2. Member States may maintain national legislation in force at the date of adoption of this Directive or provide for future legislation incorporating national practices existing at the date of adoption of this Directive pursuant to which, in the case of occupational activities within churches and other public or private organisations the ethos of which is based on religion or belief, a difference of treatment based on a person's religion or belief shall not constitute discrimination where, by reason of the nature of these activities or of the context in which they are carried out, a person's religion or belief constitute a genuine, legitimate and justified occupational requirement, having regard to the organisation's ethos. This difference of treatment shall be implemented taking account of Member States' constitutional

provisions and principles, as well as the general principles of Community law, and should not justify discrimination on another ground.

Provided that its provisions are otherwise complied with, this Directive shall thus not prejudice the right of churches and other public or private organisations, the ethos of which is based on religion or belief, acting in conformity with national constitutions and laws, to require individuals working for them to act in good faith and with loyalty to the organisation's ethos.

Article 5: Reasonable accommodation for disabled persons

In order to guarantee compliance with the principle of equal treatment in relation to persons with disabilities, reasonable accommodation shall be provided. This means that employers shall take appropriate measures, where needed in a particular case, to enable a person with a disability to have access to, participate in, or advance in employment, or to undergo training, unless such measures would impose a disproportionate burden on the employer. This burden shall not be disproportionate when it is sufficiently remedied by measures existing within the framework of the disability policy of the Member State concerned.

Article 6: Justification of differences of treatment on grounds of age

1. Notwithstanding Article 2(2), Member States may provide that differences of treatment on grounds of age shall not constitute discrimination, if, within the context of national law, they are objectively and reasonably justified by a legitimate aim, including legitimate employment policy, labour market and vocational training objectives, and if the means of achieving that aim are appropriate and necessary.

    Such differences of treatment may include, among others:

    (a) the setting of special conditions on access to employment and vocational training, employment and occupation, including dismissal and remuneration conditions, for young people, older workers and persons with caring responsibilities in order to promote their vocational integration or ensure their protection;

    (b) the fixing of minimum conditions of age, professional experience or seniority in service for access to employment or to certain advantages linked to employment;

    (c) the fixing of a maximum age for recruitment which is based on the training requirements of the post in question or the need for a reasonable period of employment before retirement.

2. Notwithstanding Article 2(2), Member States may provide that the fixing for occupational social security schemes of ages for admission or entitlement to retirement or invalidity benefits, including the fixing under those schemes of different ages for employees or groups or categories of employees, and the use, in the context of such schemes, of age criteria in actuarial calculations, does not constitute

discrimination on the grounds of age, provided this does not result in discrimination on the grounds of sex.

Article 7: Positive action

1. With a view to ensuring full equality in practice, the principle of equal treatment shall not prevent any Member State from maintaining or adopting specific measures to prevent or compensate for disadvantages linked to any of the grounds referred to in Article 1.

2. With regard to disabled persons, the principle of equal treatment shall be without prejudice to the right of Member States to maintain or adopt provisions on the protection of health and safety at work or to measures aimed at creating or maintaining provisions or facilities for safeguarding or promoting their integration into the working environment.

Article 8: Minimum requirements

1. Member States may introduce or maintain provisions which are more favourable to the protection of the principle of equal treatment than those laid down in this Directive.

2. The implementation of this Directive shall under no circumstances constitute grounds for a reduction in the level of protection against discrimination already afforded by Member States in the fields covered by this Directive.

CHAPTER II
REMEDIES AND ENFORCEMENT

Article 9: Defence of rights

1. Member States shall ensure that judicial and/or administrative procedures, including where they deem it appropriate conciliation procedures, for the enforcement of obligations under this Directive are available to all persons who consider themselves wronged by failure to apply the principle of equal treatment to them, even after the relationship in which the discrimination is alleged to have occurred has ended.

2. Member States shall ensure that associations, organisations or other legal entities which have, in accordance with the criteria laid down by their national law, a legitimate interest in ensuring that the provisions of this Directive are complied with, may engage, either on behalf or in support of the complainant, with his or her approval, in any judicial and/or administrative procedure provided for the enforcement of obligations under this Directive.

3. Paragraphs 1 and 2 are without prejudice to national rules relating to time limits for bringing actions as regards the principle of equality of treatment.

Article 10: Burden of proof

1. Member States shall take such measures as are necessary, in accordance with their national judicial systems, to ensure that, when persons who consider themselves

wronged because the principle of equal treatment has not been applied to them establish, before a court or other competent authority, facts from which it may be presumed that there has been direct or indirect discrimination, it shall be for the respondent to prove that there has been no breach of the principle of equal treatment.

2. Paragraph 1 shall not prevent Member States from introducing rules of evidence which are more favourable to plaintiffs.
3. Paragraph 1 shall not apply to criminal procedures.
4. Paragraphs 1, 2 and 3 shall also apply to any legal proceedings commenced in accordance with Article 9(2).
5. Member States need not apply paragraph 1 to proceedings in which it is for the court or competent body to investigate the facts of the case.

Article 11: Victimisation

Member States shall introduce into their national legal systems such measures as are necessary to protect employees against dismissal or other adverse treatment by the employer as a reaction to a complaint within the undertaking or to any legal proceedings aimed at enforcing compliance with the principle of equal treatment.

Article 12: Dissemination of information

Member States shall take care that the provisions adopted pursuant to this Directive, together with the relevant provisions already in force in this field, are brought to the attention of the persons concerned by all appropriate means, for example at the workplace, throughout their territory.

Article 13: Social dialogue

1. Member States shall, in accordance with their national traditions and practice, take adequate measures to promote dialogue between the social partners with a view to fostering equal treatment, including through the monitoring of workplace practices, collective agreements, codes of conduct and through research or exchange of experiences and good practices.
2. Where consistent with their national traditions and practice, Member States shall encourage the social partners, without prejudice to their autonomy, to conclude at the appropriate level agreements laying down anti-discrimination rules in the fields referred to in Article 3 which fall within the scope of collective bargaining. These agreements shall respect the minimum requirements laid down by this Directive and by the relevant national implementing measures.

Article 14: Dialogue with non-governmental organisations

Member States shall encourage dialogue with appropriate non-governmental organisations which have, in accordance with their national law and practice, a legitimate interest in contributing to the fight against discrimination on any of the grounds referred to in Article 1 with a view to promoting the principle of equal treatment.

CHAPTER III
PARTICULAR PROVISIONS

Article 15: Northern Ireland

1. In order to tackle the under-representation of one of the major religious commun-ities in the police service of Northern Ireland, differences in treatment regarding recruitment into that service, including its support staff, shall not constitute dis-crimination insofar as those differences in treatment are expressly authorised by national legislation.

2. In order to maintain a balance of opportunity in employment for teachers in Northern Ireland while furthering the reconciliation of historical divisions between the major religious communities there, the provisions on religion or belief in this Directive shall not apply to the recruitment of teachers in schools in Northern Ireland in so far as this is expressly authorised by national legislation.

CHAPTER IV
FINAL PROVISIONS

Article 16: Compliance

Member States shall take the necessary measures to ensure that:

  (a) any laws, regulations and administrative provisions contrary to the principle of equal treatment are abolished;

  (b) any provisions contrary to the principle of equal treatment which are includ-ed in contracts or collective agreements, internal rules of undertakings or rules governing the independent occupations and professions and workers' and employers' organisations are, or may be, declared null and void or are amended.

Article 17: Sanctions

Member States shall lay down the rules on sanctions applicable to infringements of the national provisions adopted pursuant to this Directive and shall take all measures necessary to ensure that they are applied. The sanctions, which may comprise the payment of compensation to the victim, must be effective, proportionate and dissua-sive. Member States shall notify those provisions to the Commission by 2 December 2003 at the latest and shall notify it without delay of any subsequent amendment affecting them.

Article 18: Implementation

Member States shall adopt the laws, regulations and administrative provisions neces-sary to comply with this Directive by 2 December 2003 at the latest or may entrust the social partners, at their joint request, with the implementation of this Directive as regards provisions concerning collective agreements. In such cases, Member States shall ensure that, no later than 2 December 2003, the social partners introduce the necessary measures by agreement, the Member States concerned being required to take any necessary measures to enable them at any time to be in a position to guarantee the results imposed by this Directive. They shall forthwith inform the Commission thereof.

In order to take account of particular conditions, Member States may, if necessary, have an additional period of 3 years from 2 December 2003, that is to say a total of 6 years, to implement the provisions of this Directive on age and disability discrimination. In that event they shall inform the Commission forthwith. Any Member State which chooses to use this additional period shall report annually to the Commission on the steps it is taking to tackle age and disability discrimination and on the progress it is making towards implementation. The Commission shall report annually to the Council.

When Member States adopt these measures, they shall contain a reference to this Directive or be accompanied by such reference on the occasion of their official publication. The methods of making such reference shall be laid down by Member States.

Article 19: Report
1. Member States shall communicate to the Commission, by 2 December 2005 at the latest and every five years thereafter, all the information necessary for the Commission to draw up a report to the European Parliament and the Council on the application of this Directive.
2. The Commission's report shall take into account, as appropriate, the viewpoints of the social partners and relevant non-governmental organisations. In accordance with the principle of gender mainstreaming, this report shall, inter alia, provide an assessment of the impact of the measures taken on women and men. In the light of the information received, this report shall include, if necessary, proposals to revise and update this Directive.

Article 20: Entry into force
This Directive shall enter into force on the day of its publication in the Official Journal of the European Communities.

Article 21: Addressees
This Directive is addressed to the Member States.

Done at Brussels, 27 November 2000.

For the Council
The President
É. Guigou

BIBLIOGRAPHY

I. European Union official documentation

(i) Commission

'Social Action Programme' EC Bull Supplement, 2/74.

Proposal for a Council Directive concerning the approximation of the legislation of the Member States in order to combat illegal migration and illegal employment [1978] OJ C97/9

'Guidelines for a Community Policy on Migration' COM (85) 48.

'Communication from the Commission to the Council on the fight against racism and xenophobia' [1988] OJ C214/32.

'Report on the implementation in the Member States of Directive 77/486/EEC on the education of the children of migrant workers' COM (88) 787.

'Comparative study on rules governing working conditions in the Member States—a synopsis' SEC (89) 1137.

'Communication from the Commission concerning its action programme relating to the implementation of the Community Charter of Fundamental Social Rights for Workers' COM (89) 586.

'Explanatory Memorandum on the proposals for Directives concerning certain employment relationships' COM (90) 228.

'Legal Instruments to Combat Racism and Xenophobia' (Luxembourg: OOPEC, 1992).

'Green Paper: European Social Policy—Options for the Union' COM (93) 551.

'Communication on immigration and asylum policy' COM (94) 23.

'European Social Policy—a way forward for the Union: a White Paper' COM (94) 333.

'Contributions to the preparatory work for the White Paper on European social policy' Social Europe 2/94.

'Proposal for a Council Directive on the right of third country nationals to travel in the Community' COM (95) 346.

'Communication from the Commission on racism, xenophobia and anti-semitism and Proposal for a Council Decision designating 1997 European Year against Racism' COM (95) 653.

'Proposal for a Council Directive on the framework agreement on parental leave concluded by UNICE, CEEP, and the ETUC' COM (96) 26.

'Consultation of management and labour on the prevention of sexual harassment at work' COM (96) 373.

'Proposal for a Council Regulation (EC) establishing a European Monitoring Centre for Racism and Xenophobia' COM (96) 615.

'Communication on illegal and harmful content on the Internet' COM (96) 487.

'For a Europe of civic and social rights—Report by the Comité des Sages' (Luxembourg: OOPEC, 1996).

'Annual Report from the Commission: Equal Opportunities for Women and Men in the European Union 1996' COM (96) 650 (published 12 February 1997).

'Proposal for a Council Act establishing the Convention on rules for the admission of third country nationals to the Member States' COM (97) 387.

'Proposal for a Council Regulation (EC) amending Regulation (EEC) 1408/71 as regards its extension to nationals of third countries' COM (97) 561.

'Termination of employment relationships—the legal situation in the Member States of the European Union' (Luxembourg: OOPEC, 1997).

'The European institutions in the fight against racism: selected texts' (Luxembourg: OOPEC, 1997).

'An action plan against racism' COM (1998) 183.

'Towards an Area of Freedom, Security and Justice' COM (1998) 459.

'Proposal for a Council Directive establishing a general framework for informing and consulting employees in the European Community' COM (1998) 612.

'Proposal for a European Parliament and Council Regulation amending Council Regulation (EEC) No. 1612/68 on freedom of movement for workers within the Community' [1998] OJ C344/9.

'Racism and xenophobia in Europe, Eurobarometer Opinion Poll No 47.1' (Luxembourg: OOPEC, 1998).

'Employment in Europe 1997—analysis of key issues' (Luxembourg: OOPEC, 1998).

'From guidelines to action: the national action plans for employment' (Luxembourg: OOPEC, 1998).

'Proposal for a Directive of the European Parliament and of the Council on the posting of workers who are third country nationals for the provision of cross-border services; proposal for a Council Directive extending the freedom to provide cross-border services to third country nationals established within the Community' COM (1999) 3.

'Towards a Europe for all ages—promoting prosperity and intergenerational solidarity' COM (1999) 221.

'Countering racism, xenophobia and anti-semitism in the candidate countries' COM (1999) 256.

'Communication on certain Community measures to combat discrimination' COM (1999) 564.

'Proposal for a Council Directive establishing a general framework for equal treatment in employment and occupation' COM (1999) 565.

'Proposal for a Council Directive implementing the principle of equal treatment between persons irrespective of racial or ethnic origin' COM (1999) 566.

'Proposal for a Council Decision establishing a Community Action Programme to combat discrimination 2001–2006' COM (1999) 567.

'Proposal for a Council Directive on the right to family reunification' COM (1999) 638.

'Call for proposals, VP/1999/016' [1999] OJ C191/14.

'Mainstreaming disability within EU employment and social policy' DGV services working paper, 1999. Available at: http://europa.eu.int/comm/dgs/employment_social/key_en.htm

'Affirming fundamental rights in the European Union—time to act' Report of the expert group on fundamental rights (Luxembourg: OOPEC, 1999).

'Report on the activities of the European Monitoring Centre on Racism and Xenophobia' COM (2000) 265.

'Amended proposal for a Council Directive implementing the principle of equal treatment between persons irrespective racial or ethnic origin' COM (2000) 328.

'Proposal for a Directive of the European Parliament and of the Council amending Council Directive 76/207/EEC on the implementation of the principle of equal treatment for men and women as regards access to employment, vocational training and promotion, and working conditions' COM (2000) 334.

'Communication on a Community immigration policy' COM (2000) 757.

'Creating a safer information society by improving the security of information infrastructures and combating computer-related crime' COM (2000) 890.

'Communication establishing the guidelines for the Community initiative Equal concerning transnational cooperation to promote new forms of combating all forms of discrimination and inequalities in connection with the labour market' [2000] OJ C127/2.

'Report on Member States' legal provisions to combat discrimination' (Luxembourg: OOPEC, 2000).

'Report on the implementation of the action plan against racism—mainstreaming the fight against racism', January 2000. Available at:
http://europa.eu.int/comm/employment_social/fundamri/eu_racism/main_en.htm

'Scoreboard to review progress on the creation of an Area of "Freedom, Security and Justice" in the European Union' COM (2000) 167 final/2.

'Proposal for a Council Directive concerning the status of third country nationals who are long-term residents' COM (2001) 127.

'Proposal for a European Parliament and Council Directive on the right of citizens of the Union and their family members to move and reside freely within the territory of the Member States' COM (2001) 257.

(b) Council

'Report on the Greek round table held in Athens on 18 January 1995' No 4687/95 RAXEN 7, Brussels, 3 February 1995.

'Reflection Group report and other references for documentary purposes' (Brussels: General Secretariat of the Council of the European Union, 1995).

Consultative Commission on Racism and Xenophobia, 'Final Report' Ref 6906/1/95 Rev 1 Limite RAXEN 24 (Brussels: General Secretariat of the Council of the European Union, 1995).

Conference of the representatives of governments of the Member States, 'European Union Today and Tomorrow—adapting the European Union for the benefit of its peoples and preparing it for the future', CONF/2500/96, 5 December 1996.

'Note de Comité K.4 au Coreper' Doc 7808/1/98 REV 1, Brussels, 29 April 1998.

'Outcome of Proceedings of the Social Questions Working Party on 21/22 February 2000' No 6435/00, Brussels, 1 March 2000.

'Outcome of proceedings of the Social Questions Working Party on 14 March 2000' No 6942/00, Brussels, 31 March 2000.

'Outcome of proceedings of the Social Questions Working Party on 10 May 2000' Doc 8454/00, Brussels, 16 May 2000.

'Outcome of proceedings of the Working Party on Social Questions on 13 June 2000' No 9423/00, Brussels, 20 June 2000.

(c) Parliament

'Report of the Committee on Political Affairs on human rights in the Soviet Union' [Bethell] A1-1364/82.

'Report for the Committee on Social Affairs and Employment on sexual discrimination at the workplace' [Squarcialupi] A1-1358/83.

'Committee of Inquiry into the Rise of Fascism and Racism in Europe' (Luxembourg: OOPEC, 1985).

'Report of the Committee on Women's Rights on violence against women' A2-44/86.

'Report of the Political Affairs Committee on the Joint Declaration against Racism and Xenophobia and an action programme by the Council of Ministers' A2-261/88.

'Report of the Committee of Inquiry on Racism and Xenophobia' (Luxembourg, OOPEC, 1991).

'Report for the Committee on Internal Affairs and Citizens Rights on Equal Rights for Homosexuals and Lesbians in the European Community' [Roth] A3-28/94.

'Annual report of the Committee on Civil Liberties and Internal Affairs on respect for human rights in the European Union in 1994' [Esteban Martin] A4-223/96.

'Annual report on respect for human rights in the European Union (1995)' [Roth] A4-112/97.

'Report of the Committee on Civil Liberties and Internal Affairs on respect for human rights in the European Union (1996)' [Pailler] A4-34/98.

'Report of the Committee on Civil Liberties and Internal Affairs on respect for human rights in the European Union (1997)' [Schaffner] A4-468/98.

'Working Document: a framework for action on non-discrimination at EU level based on Art 13 of the Amsterdam Treaty' [Ojala and Hughes] PE 229.570/fin, 25 March 1999.

'Report by the Committee on Employment and Social Affairs on the proposal for a Council Directive establishing a general framework for equal treatment in employment and occupation' [Mann/Swiebel] A5-264/2000.

II. General bibliography

Allen, 'Article 13 and the search for equality in Europe: an overview' in Europaforum Wien (eds), *Anti-discrimination: the way forward* (Wien: Europaforum, 1999).

Anon, 'Preventing racism at the workplace: Germany' Working Paper No WP/95/43/EN (Dublin: European Foundation for the Improvement of Living and Working Conditions, 1995).

Armstrong, 'Legal integration: theorizing the legal dimension of European integration' (1998) 36 J of Common Market Studies 149.

Armstrong, 'Tales of the Community: sexual orientation discrimination and EU law' (1998) 20 J of Social Welfare and Family L 455.

Arnull, *The European Union and its Court of Justice* (Oxford: Oxford University Press, 1999).

Baldwin-Edwards, 'Immigration after 1992' (1991) 19 *Policy and Politics* 199.

Bamforth, *Sexuality, Morals and Justice* (London: Cassell, 1997).

Bamforth, 'Sexual orientation discrimination after *Grant v South-West Trains*' (2000) 63 MLR 694.

Barnard, 'A European litigation strategy: the case of the Equal Opportunities Commission' in Shaw and More (eds), *New Legal Dynamics of European Union* (Oxford: Clarendon Press, 1995).

Barnard, 'P v S: kite flying or a new constitutional approach' in Dashwood and O'Leary (eds), *The principle of equal treatment in European Community law* (London: Sweet & Maxwell, 1997).

Barnard, 'The United Kingdom, the "Social Chapter" and the Amsterdam Treaty' (1997) 26 ILJ 275.

Barnard, 'Some are more equal than others: the decision of the Court of Justice in *Grant v South-West Trains*' (1998) 1 Cambridge Ybk of Legal Studies 147.

Barnard, 'Article 13: through the looking glass of Union citizenship' in O'Keeffe and Twomey (eds), *Legal issues of the Amsterdam Treaty* (Oxford: Hart Publishng, 1999).

Barnard, 'Regulating competitive federalism in the European Union? The case of EU social policy' in Shaw (ed), *Social law and policy in an evolving European Union* (Oxford: Hart Publishing, 2000).

Barnard, *EC Employment Law* (2nd edn, Oxford: Oxford University Press, 2000).

Barnard and Hepple, 'Indirect discrimination: interpreting *Seymour-Smith*' (1999) 58 Cambridge LJ 399.

Batsioulas, 'Greece' in Beger, Krickler, Lewis and Wuch (eds), *Equality for Lesbians and Gay Men: a relevant issue in the civil and social dialogue* (Brussels: ILGA-Europe, 1998).

Beger, 'Queer readings of Europe: gender identity, sexual orientation and the (im)potency of rights politics at the European Court of Justice' (2000) 9 Social and Legal Studies 249.

Beger, Krickler, Lewis and Wuch (eds), *Equality for lesbians and gay men: a relevant issue in the civil and social dialogue* (Brussels: ILGA-Europe, 1998).

Bell, 'EU anti-discrimination policy: from equal opportunities between women and men to combating racism' LIBE 102 EN (Luxembourg: European Parliament, 1998).

Bell, 'Sexual Orientation and Anti-Discrimination Policy: the European Community' in Carver and Mottier (eds), *The Politics of Sexuality* (London: Routledge, 1998).

Bell, 'Shifting conceptions of sexual discrimination at the Court of Justice: from *P v S* to *Grant v SWT*' (1999) 5 Eur LJ 63.

Bell, 'The new Article 13 EC Treaty: a sound basis for European anti-discrimination law?' (1999) 6 Maastricht J of Eur and Comparative L 5.

Bell, 'Mainstreaming equality norms into European Union asylum law' (2001) 26 ELR 20.

Bell, 'Meeting the challenge? A comparison between the EU Racial Equality Directive and the Starting Line' in Chopin and Niessen (eds), *The Starting Line and the incorporation of the Racial Equality Directive into the national laws of the EU Member States and accession states* (London: Migration Policy Group and Commission for Racial Equality, 2001).

Bell and Waddington, 'The 1996 Intergovernmental conference and the prospects of a non-discrimination Treaty article' (1996) 25 ILJ 320.

Bennet, Erin and Harris, *Research on bioethics: AIDS—ethics, justice and European policy* (Luxembourg: OOPEC, 1998).

Bercusson, 'The European Community's Charter of Fundamental Social Rights of Workers' (1990) 53 MLR 624

Bercusson, 'The conceptualization of European Labour Law' (1995) 24 ILJ 3.

Bercusson, Deakin, Koistinen, Kravaritou, Mückenberger, Supiot and Veneziani, *A Manifesto for a Social Europe* (Brussels: European Trade Union Institute, 1996).

Bernard, 'What are the purposes of EC discrimination law?' in Dine and Watt (eds), *Discrimination Law—concepts, limitations, and justifications* (London: Longman, 1996).

Berthou and Masselot, 'La CJCE et les couples homosexuels' (1998) 12 Droit Social 1034.

Biagi, 'Fortune smiles on the Italian EU Presidency: talking half-seriously about the posted workers and parental leave directives' (1996) 12 Intl J of Comparative Labour Law and Industrial Relations 97.

Biagini, Bertozzo and Ravaioli, 'Italy' in Beger, Krickler, Lewis and Wuch (eds), *Equality for Lesbians and Gay Men: a relevant issue in the civil and social dialogue* (Brussels: ILGA-Europe, 1998).

Binnie, 'Invisible Europeans: sexual citizenship in the New Europe' (1997) 29 Environment and Planning A 237.

Blanpain, Hepple, Sciarra and Weiss, *Fundamental Social Rights: Proposals for the European Union* (Leuven: Peeters, 1996).

Blom, 'The Dutch Equal Treatment Commission' (1995) 24 ILJ 84.

Blom, Fitzpatrick, Gregory, Knegt and O'Hare, *The Utilisation of Sex Equality Litigation in the Member States of the European Community* V/782/96-EN (Report to the Equal Opportunities Unit of DG V, 1995).

Borrillo (ed), *Homosexualités et droit* (Paris: PUF, 1998).

Borrillo, 'L'homophobie dans le discours des jurists autour du débat sur l'union entre personnes de même sexe' in Tin and Pastre (eds), *Homosexualités, expression/ repression* (Paris: Stock, 1999).

Borrillo, 'L'orientation sexuelle en Europe—esquisse d'une politique publique antidiscriminatoire' (July/August 2000) *Le Temps Modernes* 263.

Borrillo, 'Sexual orientation and human rights in Europe' in Bhatia, O'Neill, Gael and Bendin (eds), *Peace, justice and freedom—human rights challenges in the new millennium* (Alberta: University of Alberta Press, 2000).

Borrillo, 'Le Pacte civil de solidarité: une reconnaissance timide des unions de même sexe' (2001) 3 Aktuelle Juristische Praxis 299.

Bourne and Whitmore, *Race and sex discrimination* (London: Sweet & Maxwell, 2nd edn, 1993).

Braibant, 'La Charte des droits fondamentaux' (2001) 1 Droit Social 69.

Bribosia, 'Liberté, sécurité et justice' (1998) *Revue du Marché Unique Européen* 27.

Buckley, 'Vicarious Liability and Employment Discrimination' (1997) 26 ILJ 158.

Buckley, 'Employment Equality Act 1998 (Ireland)' (2000) 29 ILJ 273.

Burrows, 'Sex and sexuality in the European Court' (1998) 14 Intl J of Comparative Labour L and Industrial Relations 153.

Butt-Philip, 'EU Immigration Policy: Phantom, Fantasy or Fact?' (1994) 17 *West European Politics* 168.

Cabral, 'Arrêt Grant' (1998) *Revue du Marché Unique Européen* 254.

Cachón, 'Preventing racism at the workplace: Spain' Working Paper No WP/95/41/EN (Dublin: European Foundation for the Improvement of Living and Working Conditions, 1995).

Campani, Carchedi, Mottura and Pugliese, 'La prévention des formes de discrimination et de racisme dans les lieux de travail en Italie', Working Paper No WP/95/47/FR (Dublin: European Foundation for the Improvement of Living and Working Conditions, 1995).

Campbell and Lardy, 'Discrimination against transsexuals in employment' (1996) 21 ELR 412.

Canor, 'Equality for lesbians and gay men in the European Community legal order' (2000) 7 Maastricht J of Eur and Comparative L 273.

Cassese, Lalumière, Leuprecht and Robinson, *Leading by example: a human rights agenda for the European Union for the Year 2000. Agenda of the Comité des Sages and final project report* (Florence: European University Institute, 1998).

Centre pour l'Egalité des chances et la Lutte contre le Racisme, 'Discrimination à l'embauche de personnes de nationalité ou d'origine étrangère—synthèse' (Bruxelles: Centre pour l'Egalité des chances et la Lutte contre le Racisme, 1998).

Cholewinski, *Migrant workers in international human rights law—their protection in countries of employment* (Oxford: Clarendon Press, 1997).

Chopin and Niessen (eds), *Proposals for legislative measures to combat racism and to promote equal rights in the European Union* (London: Commission for Racial Equality, 1998).

Christian Institute, 'European threat to religious freedom—a response to the European Union's Employment Directive' (London: Christian Institute, 2000).

Cirkel, 'Gleichheitsrechte im Gemeinschaftsrecht' (1998) 51 Neue Juristische Wochenschrift 3332.

Clapham and Waaldijk (eds), *Homosexuality: a European Community issue—essays on lesbian and gay rights in European law and policy* (Dordrecht: Martinus Nijhoff, 1993).

Clapham and Weiler, 'Human dignity shall be inviolable: the human rights of gays and lesbians in the EC legal order' (1992) III(2) Collected Courses in the Academy of European Law 237.

Cohen, O'Byrne and Maxwell, 'Employment discrimination based on sexual orientation: the American, Canadian and UK responses' (1999) 17 Law and Inequality: a journal of theory and practice 1.

Collins, *The European Communities—the social policy of the first phase. Volume 2 The European Economic Community 1958–72* (London: Martin Robertson, 1975).

Collins, 'EU Sexual Harassment Policy' in Elman (ed), *Sexual Politics and the European Union: the new Feminist Challenge* (Oxford: Berghahn Books, 1996).

Commissie Gelijke Behandeling, *Equal treatment: a constitutional right* (Utrecht: Commissie Gelijke Behandeling, 1995).

Commissie Gelijke Behandeling, *Annual Report 1997* (Utrecht: Commissie Gelijke Behandeling, 1998).

Commission for Racial Equality, 'Reform of the Race Relations Act 1976' (London: CRE, 1998).

Commission for Racial Equality, 'Strengthening the Race Relations Act' (London: CRE, 2000).

Connor, 'Community discrimination law: no right to equal treatment in employment in respect of same sex partner' (1998) 23 ELR 378.

Costa-Lascoux, 'Equality and non-discrimination: ethnic minorities and racial discrimination' in Council of Europe (ed), *Rights of persons deprived of their liberty—equality and non-discrimination* (NP Engel, 1997).

Council of Europe Press, *Human Rights in International Law—basic texts* (Strasbourg: Council of Europe, 1992).

Craig, *Privacy and employment law* (Oxford: Hart Publishing, 1999).

Craig and de Búrca, *EU law—text, cases and materials* (2nd edn, Oxford: Oxford University Press, 1998).

Cram, 'The European Commission as a multi-organization: social policy and IT policy in the European Union' (1994) 1 J of Eur Public Policy 195.

Crouch, 'Un commento al saggio di Simitis' (1997) 76 Giornale di diritto del lavoro e di relazioni industriali 643.

Crouch, 'Introduction' in Crouch (ed), *After the Euro: shaping institutions for governance in the wake of European monetary union* (Oxford: Oxford University Press, 2000).

Curtin and Geurts, 'Race discrimination and the European Union Anno 1996: from rhetoric to legal remedy?' (1996) 14 *Netherlands Q of Human Rights* 147.

Danese, 'Trans-national collective action of migrants in Europe: the case of migrants in Italy and Spain' (1998) 24 *J of Ethnic and Migration Studies* 715.

Davies, 'The Emergence of European Labour Law' in W McCarthy (ed), *Legal Interventions in Industrial Relations: Gains and Losses* (Oxford: Basil Blackwell, 1992).

Davies, 'Market integration and social policy in the Court of Justice' (1995) 24 ILJ 49.

de Búrca, 'Fundamental human rights and the reach of EC law' (1993) 13 OJLS 283.

de Búrca, 'The language of rights and European integration' in More and Shaw (eds), *New legal dynamics of European Union* (Oxford: Clarendon Press, 1995).

de Búrca, 'The quest for legitimacy in the European Union' (1996) 59 MLR 349.

de Búrca, 'The role of equality in European Community Law' in Dashwood and O'Leary (eds), *The principle of equal treatment in European Community law* (London: Sweet & Maxwell, 1997).

de Búrca, 'The principle of subsidiarity and the Court of Justice as an institutional actor' (1998) 36 J of Common Market Studies 217.

de Búrca, 'Reappraising subsidiarity's significance after Amsterdam' (1999) Harvard Jean Monnet Working Papers 7/99: *http://www.law.harvard.edu/programs/ JeanMonnet/papers/papers99.html*

de Búrca, 'The drafting of the European Union Charter of Fundamental Rights' (2001) 26 ELR 126.

de Rudder, Tripier, Vourc'h and Simon, 'La prévention du racisme dans l'entreprise en France' Working Paper No WP/95/44/FR (Dublin: European Foundation for the Improvement of Living and Working Conditions, 1995).

de Schutter and Weyembergh, 'Statutory cohabitation under Belgian law: a step towards same-sex marriage?' in Wintemute and Andenaes (eds), *Legal recognition of same sex partnerships—a study of national, European and international law* (Oxford: Hart Publishing, 2001).

de Witte, 'Community law and national constitutional values' (1991/2) Legal issues of Eur Integration 1.

de Witte, 'Protection of fundamental social rights in the European Union—the choice of the appropriate legal instrument' in Betten and MacDevitt (eds), *The protection of fundamental social rights in the European Union* (London: Kluwer Law International, 1996).

Deakin and Wilkinson, 'Rights vs Efficiency? The economic case for transnational labour standards' (1994) 23 ILJ 289.

Dehousse, 'Community competences: are there limits to growth? in R Dehousse (ed), *Europe after Maastricht: an ever closer union?* (Munich: Law Books in Europe, 1994).

Denys, 'Homosexuality: A Non-Issue in Community Law?' (1999) 24 ELR 419.

Department of Health, 'An investigation into conditional organ donation', 22 February 2000: available at: *http://www.doh.gov.uk/organdonation/*

Dickens, 'Anti-discrimination Legislation: exploring and explaining the impact on women's employment' in McCarthy (ed), *Legal Interventions in Industrial Relations: Gains and Losses* (Oxford: Basil Blackwell, 1992).

Docksey, The Principle of Equality between Men and Women as a Fundamental Right under Community Law' (1991) 20 ILJ 258.

Doherty, '*Bickel*—extending the boundaries of European citizenship' (1999) 8 Irish J of Eur L 70.

Dougan, 'The Equal Treatment Directive: retaliation, remedies and direct effect' (1999) 24 ELR 664.

Due, Steen Madsen and Strøby Jensen, 'The Social Dimension: convergence or diversification of industrial relations in the single European market?' (1991) 22 *Industrial Relations J* 85.

Dummett, 'Europe? Which Europe?' (1991) 18 *New Community* 167.

Dummett, 'Racial Equality and "1992"' (1991) 3 *Feminist Rev* 85.

Dummett, 'The Starting Line: A proposal for a draft Council Directive concerning the elimination of racial discrimination' (1994) 20 *New Community* 530.

Dustin and d'Orey, *A culture of suspicion—the impact of internal immigration controls* (London: Joint Council for the Welfare of Immigrants, Commission for Racial Equality and the Refugee Council, 1998).

Eatwell, 'Why are fascism and racism reviving in Western Europe?' (1994) 65 *Political Q* 313.

European Commission against Racism and Intolerance (ECRI), 'Second report on Belgium' CRI (2000) 2 (Strasbourg: Council of Europe, 2000).

ECRI, 'Second report on France' CRI (2000) 31 (Strasbourg: Council of Europe, 2000).

ECRI, 'Second report on Greece' CRI (2000) 32 (Strasbourg: Council of Europe, 2000).

ECRI, 'Second report on Austria' CRI (2001) 3 (Strasbourg: Council of Europe, 2001).

ECRI, 'Second report on Denmark' CRI (2001) 4 (Strasbourg: Council of Europe, 2001).

ECRI, 'Second report on the UK' CRI (2001) 6 (Strasbourg: Council of Europe, 2001).

Editorial, 'Are European values being hoovered away?' (1993) 30 CML Rev 445.

Editorial, 'The EU Charter of Fundamental Rights still under discussion' (2001) 38 CML Rev 1.

Ekholm and Pitkänen, 'Preventing racism at the workplace: Finland—report on the ethnic minorities and migrants in the Finnish labour market' Working Paper No WP/95/52/EN (Dublin: European Foundation for the Improvement of Living and Working Conditions, 1995).

Ellis, *European Community sexual equality law* (Oxford: Oxford University Press, 1991).

Ellis, *European Community sex equality law* (2nd edn, Oxford: Oxford University Press, 1998).

Elman, 'The limits of citizenship: migration, sex discrimination and same-sex partners in EU law' (2000) 38 J of Common Market Studies 729.

European Disability Forum, *Guide to the Amsterdam Treaty* (Brussels: EDF, 1998).

European Monitoring Centre on Racism and Xenophobia, *Diversity and equality for Europe—annual report 1999* (Vienna: EUMC, 2000).

Evans, 'Third-country nationals and the Treaty on European Union' (1994) 5 Eur J of Intl L 199.

Everson, 'The legacy of the market citizen' in Shaw and More (eds), *New legal dynamics of European Union* (Oxford: Clarendon Press, 1995).

Fabeni, 'I diritti civili degli omosessuali. Profili di diritto comparato' Tesi di Laurea (Torino: Università degli Studi di Torino, 1998).

Fair Employment Commission, *Fair Employment in Northern Ireland—Code of Practice* (Belfast: Department of Economic Development, 1989).

Fakiolas, 'Preventing racism at the workplace: Greece' Working Paper No WP/95/45/EN (Dublin: European Foundation for the Improvement of Living and Working Conditions, 1995).

The Federal Government's Commissioner for Foreigners' Affairs, 'Report by the Federal Government's Commissioner for Foreigners' Affairs on the situation of foreigners in the Federal Republic of Germany in 1993' (Berlin: The Federal Government's Commissioner for Foreigners' Affairs, 1994).

Fennelly, 'The Area of "Freedom, Security and Justice" and the European Court of Justice—a personal view' (2000) 49 ICLQ 1.

Fitzpatrick, 'Community Social Policy after Maastricht' (1992) 21 ILJ 199.

Fitzpatrick, 'Straining the definition of health and safety?' (1997) 26 ILJ 115.

Fitzpatrick, 'The Community's social policy: recent developments and remaining problems' in S Konstadinidis (ed), *A People's Europe: turning a concept into content* (Aldershot: Dartmouth, 1999).

Fitzpatrick, 'The Fair Employment and Equal Treatment (Northern Ireland) Order 1998, The Northern Ireland Act 1998' (1999) 28 ILJ 336.

Flynn, 'The implications of Article 13 EC—after Amsterdam, will some forms of discrimination be more equal than others?' (1999) 36 CML Rev 1127.

Forbes and Mead, *Measure for Measure: a comparative analysis of measures to combat racial discrimination in the Member Countries of the European Community* Equal Opportunities Study Group, University of Southampton, Research Series No 1 (London: Department of Employment, 1992).

Foreign and Commonwealth Office, *A Partnership of Nations* (London: HMSO, 1997).

Fredman, *Women and the law* (Oxford: Clarendon Press, 1997).

Fredman, 'Affirmative action and the Court of Justice: a critical analysis' in Shaw (ed), *Social law and policy in an evolving European Union* (Oxford: Hart Publishing, 2000).

Fredman, McCrudden and Freedland, 'An EU Charter of fundamental rights' (2000) PL 178.

Fries and Shaw, 'Citizenship of the Union: first steps in the European Court of Justice' (1998) 4 Eur PL 533.

Gächter, 'Preventing racism at the workplace: Austria' Working Paper No WP/95/51/EN (Dublin: European Foundation for the Improvement of Living and Working Conditions, 1995).

Gearty, 'The internal and external "Other" in the Union legal order: racism, religious intolerance and xenophobia in Europe' in P Alston with M Bustelo and J Heenan, *The EU and human rights* (Oxford: Oxford University Press, 1999).

Geddes, 'Immigrants, ethnic minorities and the European Union's democratic deficit' (1995) 33 J of Common Market Studies 197.

Geddes, 'The representation of "migrant's interests" in the European Union' (1998) 24 *J of Ethnic and Migration Studies* 695.

Geddes, *Immigration and European integration—towards Fortress Europe?* (Manchester: Manchester University Press, 2000).

George, *Politics and Policy in the European Community* (Oxford: Oxford University Press, 1991).

Gil Ibáñez, *The administrative supervision and enforcement of EC law: powers, procedures and limits* (Oxford: Hart Publishing, 1999).

Glastra, Schedler and Kats, 'Employment equity policies in Canada and the Netherlands: enhancing minority employment between public controversy and market initiative' (1998) 26 *Policy and Politics* 163.

GLEN and NEXUS Research Cooperative, *Poverty—lesbians and gay men. The economic and social effects of discrimination* (Dublin: Combat Poverty Agency, 1995).

Gori, 'Union citizenship and equal treatment: a way of improving Community educational rights?' (1999) 21 J of Social Welfare and Family L 405.

Gras and Bovenkerk, 'Preventing racism at the workplace: the Netherlands' Working Paper No WP/95/49/EN (Dublin: European Foundation for the Improvement of Living and Working Conditions, 1995).

Greco, 'Nuovi sviluppi in materia di tutela dei diritti fondamentali' (1999) Rivista italiana di diritto pubblico comunitario 1369.

Gregory, 'Sexual Harassment—making the best use of European law' (1995) 2 *Eur J of Women's Studies* 421.

Guiguet, 'Le droit communautaire et la reconnaissance des partenaires de même sexe' (1999) Cahiers de droit européen 537.

Guild, 'Race Discrimination and Community Law' (1993) 1 Migrantenrecht 6.

Guild, 'EC law and the means to combat racism and xenophobia' in Dashwood and O'Leary (eds), *The principle of equal treatment in European Community law* (London: Sweet & Maxwell, 1997).

Guild, 'The EC Directive on race discrimination: surprises, possibilities and limitations' (2000) 29 ILJ 416.

Guild, *Immigration Law in the European Community* (London: Kluwer Law International, 2001).

Guild, 'Free movement and same-sex relationships: existing EC law and Article 13 EC' in Wintemute and Andenaes (eds), *Legal recognition of same sex partnerships—a study of national, European and international law* (Oxford: Hart Publishing, 2001).

Guild with Niessen, *The developing immigration and asylum policies of the European Union—adopted Conventions, Resolutions, Recommendations, Decisions and Conclusions* (London: Kluwer Law International, 1996).

Hailbronner and Polakiewicz, 'Non-EC nationals in the European Community: the need for a coordinated approach' (1992) 3 Duke J of Intl L 49.

Hammar, *European immigration policy—a comparative study* (Cambridge: Cambridge University Press, 1985) 275.

Hargreaves, 'Half-measures: anti-discrimination policy in France' (2000) 18 *French politics, culture and society* 83.

Harrison, 'Using EC law to challenge sexual orientation discrimination at work' in Hervey and O'Keeffe (eds), *Sexual Equality in the European Union* (Chichester: John Wiley and Sons, 1996).

Hegarty and Keown, 'Hierarchies of discrimination: the political, legal and social prioritisation of the equality agenda in Northern Ireland' (1996) 15 *Equal Opportunities Intl* 1.

Heinze, *Sexual Orientation: a human right—an essay on international human rights law* (Dordrecht: Martinus Nijhoff, 1995).

Helfer and Miller, 'Sexual orientation and human rights: towards an United States and transnational jurisprudence' (1996) 9 Harvard Human Rights J 61.

Hepple, 'The Implementation of the Community Charter on Fundamental Social Rights' (1990) 53 MLR 643.

Hepple, 'Social Values and European Law' (1995) 48 CLP II: Collected Papers 39.

Hepple, 'Equality and Discrimination' in P Davies, A Lyon-Caen, S Sciarra, and S Simitis, *European Community Labour Law: Principles and Perspectives. Liber Amicorum Lord Wedderburn* (Oxford: Clarendon Press, 1997).

Hepple, Choussey and Choudhury, *Equality: a new framework—report of the independent review of the enforcement of UK anti-discrimination legislation* (Oxford: Hart Publishing, 2000).

Herman, 'The politics of law reform: lesbian and gay rights struggles in the 1990s' in Bristow and Wilson (eds), *Activating Theory: lesbian, gay, bisexual politics* (London: Lawrence and Wishart, 1993).

Hervey, 'Migrant workers and their families in the European Union: the pervasive market ideology of Community law' in Shaw and More, *New Legal Dynamics of European Union* (Oxford: Clarendon Press, 1995).

Hervey, 'Buy baby: the European Union and the regulation of human reproduction' (1998) 18 OJLS 207.

Hervey, 'Putting Europe's house in order: racism, race discrimination and xeno-phobia after the Treaty of Amsterdam' in O'Keeffe and Twomey (eds), *Legal issues of the Amsterdam Treaty* (Oxford: Hart Publishing, 1999).

Hervey, 'Social solidarity: a buttress against internal market law?' in Shaw (ed), *Social law and policy in an evolving European Union* (Oxford: Hart Publishing, 2000).

Hervey, 'Up in smoke? Community (anti) tobacco law and policy' (2001) 26 ELR 101.

Hervey and O'Keeffe, *Sex Equality in the European Union* (Chichester, John Wiley and Sons, 1996).

Hiltunen, 'Finland' in Beger, Krickler, Lewis and Wuch (eds), *Equality for Lesbians and Gay Men: a relevant issue in the civil and social dialogue* (Brussels: ILGA-Europe, 1998).

Hjarnø, 'Preventing racism at the workplace: the Danish national report' Working Paper No WP/95/42/EN (Dublin: European Foundation for the Improvement of Living and Working Conditions, 1995).

Home Office, 'Statistics on race and the criminal justice system' (London: Home Office, 2000).

Hoskyns, *Integrating Gender—Women, Law and Politics in the European Union* (London: Verso, 1996).

Idot, 'Homosexualité, droit communautaire, et Traité d'Amsterdam' (1998) 4 (April) Europe 3.

International Labour Organisation (ILO), *Social Aspects of European Economic Cooperation—report by a group of experts* (London: Staples Press, 1956).

ILO, *Equality in employment and occupation: report of the Committee of Experts on the application of Conventions and Recommendations* (Geneva: ILO, 1996).

ILO, *International Labour Conventions and Recommendations 1919–1951 Volume 1* (Geneva: ILO, 1996).

ILO, *International Labour Conventions and Recommendations 1952–1976 Volume 2* (Geneva: ILO, 1996).

ILO, 'Combatting discrimination against (im)migrant workers and ethnic minorities in the world of work' Information Bulletin No 5 (Geneva: ILO, 1998).

Jacqmain, 'Belgium' in Prechal and Masselot, *Bulletin Legal Issues in Equality*, No 1/2000 (Brussels: Commission, 2000).

James, 'Occupational health and safety' in Gold (ed), *The Social Dimension—Employment in the European Community* (2nd edn, London: Pinter Publishers, 1993).

JCWI, *Annual report and policy review* (London: JCWI, 1996).

Jensen, 'Denmark' in Beger, Krickler, Lewis and Wuch (eds), *Equality for Lesbians and Gay Men: a relevant issue in the civil and social dialogue* (Brussels: ILGA-Europe, 1998).

Jensen, 'La reconnaissance des préférences sexuelles: le modèle scandinave' in D Borrillo (ed), *Homosexualités et droit* (Paris: PUF, 1998).

Kahn-Freund, 'Labor law and social security' in Stein and Nicholson (eds), *American Enterprise in the European Common Market—A Legal Profile. Volume 1* (Michigan: Ann Arbor, 1960).

Kahn-Freund, 'On uses and misuse of comparative law' (1974) 37 MLR 1.

Kahn-Freund, 'The European Social Charter' in Jacobs (ed), *European law and the individual* (Oxford: North Holland Publishing, 1976).

Kenner, 'Citizenship and fundamental rights: reshaping the European social model' in Kenner (ed), *Trends in European social policy. Essays in memory of Malcolm Mead* (Aldershot: Dartmouth, 1995).

Kenner, 'EC Labour Law: the Softly Softly Approach' (1995) 14 Intl J of Comparative Labour L and Industrial Relations 307.

Kenner, 'Employment and macroeconomics in the EC Treaty: a legal and political symbiosis?' (2000) 7 Maastricht J of Eur and Comparative L 375.

Kilpatrick, 'Community or communities of courts in European integration? Sex equality dialogues between UK courts and the ECJ' (1998) 14 Eur LJ 121.

King, 'Ethnic minorities and multilateral European institutions' in Hargreaves and Leaman (eds), *Racism, Ethnicity and Politics in Contemporary Europe* (Aldershot: Edward Elgar, 1995).

Laflèche, 'Racial equality standards in education' in NICEM, *Human rights and racial equality conference report* (Belfast: Northern Ireland Council for Ethnic Minorities, 1998).

Lalement, 'France' in Beger, Krickler, Lewis and Wuch (eds), *Equality for lesbians and gay men: a relevant issue in the civil and social dialogue* (Brussels: ILGA-Europe, 1998).

Langrish, 'The Treaty of Amsterdam: Selected Highlights' (1998) 23 ELR 3.

Layton-Henry, *The Politics of Immigration: immigration, 'race' and 'race' relations in post-war Britain* (Oxford: Blackwell, 1992).

Lehmkuhl, *The importance of small differences: the impact of European integration on the associations in the German and Dutch road haulage industries* PhD thesis (Florence: European University Institute, 1998).

Leibfried and Pierson, 'Social policy—left to courts and markets?' in Wallace and Wallace (eds), *Policy-making in the European Union* (Oxford: Oxford University Press, 2000).

Lenaerts, 'Fundamental Rights to be included in a Community catalogue' (1991) 16 ELR 367.

Lenaerts and de Smijter, 'A "Bill of Rights" for the European Union' (2001) 38 CML Rev 273.

Lenaerts and van Nuffel, *Constitutional law of the European Union* (London: Sweet & Maxwell, 1999).

Lestón, 'Spain' in Beger, Krickler, Lewis and Wuch (eds), *Equality for Lesbians and Gay Men: a relevant issue in the civil and social dialogue* (Brussels: ILGA-Europe, 1998).

Lichtenberg, 'The rights of Turkish workers in Community Law' (1995) 24 ILJ 90.

Lloyd, 'Concepts, models and anti-racist strategies in Britain and France' (1991) 18 *New Community* 63.

Lloyd, 'Race relations in Britain and France: problems of interpretation' in Hawkins, Dummett, Lloyd, Wrench and Joly, *Special Seminar Series on 1992*, Research Paper in Ethnic Relations No 17 (Warwick: University of Warwick, 1991).

Lo Faro, 'Immigrazione, lavoro, cittadinanza' (1997) 76 Giornale di diritto del lavoro e di relazioni industriali 536.

Lo Faro, *Regulating Social Europe—reality and myth of collective bargaining in the EC legal order* (Oxford: Hart Publishing, 2000).

Lutz, 'Migrant women, racism and the Dutch labour market' in Solomos and Wrench (eds), *Racism and Migration in Western Europe* (Oxford: Berg, 1993).

Lyon-Caen, 'Subsidiarity' in Davies, Lyon-Caen, Sciarra and Simitis, *European Community Labour Law: Principles and Perspectives. Liber Amicorum Lord Wedderburn* (Oxford: Clarendon Press, 1997).

MacEwan, *Tackling racism in Europe: an examination of anti-discrimination law in practice* (Oxford: Berg Publishers, 1995).

Mancini and O'Leary, 'The new frontiers of sex equality law in the European Union' (1999) 24 ELR 331.

Martens, 'La prévention du racisme sur les lieux de travail en Belgique' Working Paper No WP/95/39/FR (Dublin: European Foundation for the Improvement of Living and Working Conditions, 1995).

Martins de Oliveira, *Equality in law between men and women in the European Community—Portugal* (London: Martinus Nijhoff, 1995).

Mattera, 'Civis europaeus sum—citoyennété européenne, droit de circulation et de séjour, applicabilité directe de l'Art. 8A du traité CE' (1998) Revue du marché unique européen 5.

Mayer, 'Ethnocentrism and the *Front National* vote in the 1988 French Presidential election' in Hargreaves and Leaman (eds), *Racism, Ethnicity and Politics in Contemporary Europe* (Aldershot: Edward Elgar, 1995).

Mayne and Malyon, *Employment law in Europe* (London: Butterworths, 2001).

McColgan, *Discrimination Law—text, cases and materials* (Oxford: Hart Publishing, 2000).

McCrudden, 'Racial Discrimination' in McCrudden and Chambers (eds), *Individual Rights and the Law in Britain* (Oxford: Clarendon Press, 1994).

McCrudden, *Mainstreaming fairness in the future governance of Northern Ireland* (Belfast: Committee on the Administration of Justice, 1998).

McGlynn, 'EC Sex Equality: towards a human rights foundation' in Hervey and O'Keeffe (eds), *Sex equality in the European Union* (Chichester: John Wiley and Sons, 1996).

Menzione, *Manuale dei diritti degli omosessuali* (Bologna: Libreria di Babilonia, 1996).

Milward, *The European rescue of the nation-state* (London: Routledge, 1992).

Monar and Bieber, *Citizenship and the Union* European Parliament Directorate-General for Research Working Paper; Legal Series W-5, 6-1995.

Monar, 'Justice and Home Affairs in the Treaty of Amsterdam: reform at the price of fragmentation' (1998) 23 ELR 320

More, 'The principle of equal treatment: from market unifier to fundamental right?' in Craig and de Búrca (eds), *The evolution of EU law* (Oxford: Oxford University Press, 1999).

Morgan (ed), *The Times Guide to the European Parliament* (London: Times Newspapers, 1994).

Mosley, 'The social dimension of European integration' (1990) 129 Intl Labour Rev 147.

Mullally, 'Mainstreaming equality in Ireland: a fair and inclusive accommodation?' (2001) 21 Legal Studies 99.

Neilsen, *Equality in law between men and women in the European Community—Denmark* (London: Martinus Nijhoff, 1995).

O'Leary, 'The principle of equal treatment on grounds of nationality in Article 6 EC. A lucrative source of rights for Member State nationals?' in Dashwood and O'Leary, *The principle of equal treatment in European Community law* (London: Sweet & Maxwell, 1997).

O'Leary, 'Employment and residence for Turkish workers and their families: analogies with the case-law of the Court of Justice on Art 48 EC' in Università di Bologna, Seminario Giuridico (ed), *Scritti in onore di Giuseppe Federico Mancini— Vol. II. Diritto dell'Unione Europea* (Milano: Giuffrè,1998).

O'Leary, 'Putting flesh on the bones of European Union citizenship' (1999) 24 ELR 68.

O'Neill, 'The choice of a legal basis: more than a number' (1994) 1 Irish J of Eur Law 44.

Office of the First Minister and Deputy First Minister of Northern Ireland, 'Promoting equality of opportunity—a Single Equality Bill for Northern Ireland—initial consultation by Office of the First Minister and Deputy First Minister', May 2001, available at *http://www.ofmdfmni.gov.uk/equality/*

Ogata, 'Refugees and asylum-seekers: a challenge to European immigration policy' in Ogata, Cohn-Bendit, Fortescue, Haddawi and Khalevinski, *Towards a European Immigration Policy* (Brussels: Philip Morris Institute for Public Policy Research, 1993).

Organisation for Economic Cooperation and Development, *Trade, Employment and Labour Standards: A study of core workers rights and international trade* (Paris: OECD, 1996).

Orloff, 'Gender and the social rights of citizenship: the comparative analysis of gender relations and welfare states' (1993) 58 *American Sociological Rev* 303.

Palma Carlos, 'La prévention du racisme sur les lieux de travail au Portugal' Working Paper No WP/95/40/FR (Dublin: European Foundation for the Improvement of Living and Working Conditions, 1995).

Palmer, *Less equal than others—a survey of lesbians and gay men at work* (London: Stonewall, 1993).

Parmar, 'Human rights and the constitutional dimensions of the Charter of Fundamental Rights of the European Union' Paper presented at the 18th Annual Graduate Student Conference, The Institute for the Study of Europe, Columbia University, 29 March 2001.

Peers, 'Towards Equality: Actual and Potential Rights of Third-Country Nationals in the European Union' (1996) 33 CML Rev 7.

Peers, 'Social security equality for Turkish nationals' (1999) 24 ELR 627.

Perico, 'Il Parlamento Europeo e i diritti degli omosessuali' (1994) 9/10 Aggiornamenti Sociali 593.

Pescatore, 'Nice—Aftermath' (2001) 38 CML Rev 265.

Plender, 'Competence, European Community law and nationals of non-member states' (1990) 39 ICLQ 599.

Poiares Maduro, 'Striking the elusive balance between economic freedom and social rights in the EU' in Alston, Bustelo and Heenan (eds), *The EU and human rights* (Oxford: Oxford University Press, 1999).

Praesidium, 'Text of the explanations relating to the complete text of the Charter as set out in CHARTE 4487/00 CONVENT 50' CHARTE 4473/00 CONVENT 49, 11 October 2000.

Prechal and Burrows, *Gender discrimination law of the European Community* (Aldershot, Dartmouth, 1990).

Purdy and Devine, 'Social Policy' in Artis and Lee (eds), *The Economics of the European Union—policy and analysis* (Oxford: Oxford University Press, 1994).

Reich, 'Union citizenship—metaphor or source of rights?' (2001) 7 Eur LJ 4.

Rodrigues, 'Racial discrimination and the law in the Netherlands' (1994) 20 *New Community* 381.

Rodrigues, 'The Dutch experience of enforcement agencies: current issues in Dutch anti-discrimination law' in MacEwen (ed), *Anti-discrimination law enforcement: a comparative perspective* (Aldershot: Ashgate, 1997).

Rose, *Diverse communities: the evolution of lesbian and gay politics in Ireland* (Cork: Cork University Press, 1994).

Rubenstein, *Report on the Problem of Sexual Harassment in the Member States of the European Community* (Luxembourg: OOPEC, 1988).

Salas, 'The stable unions law in Catalonia' in Wintemute and Andenaes (eds), *Legal recognition of same sex partnerships—a study of national, European and international law* (Oxford: Hart Publishing, 2001).

Sanglin-Grant and Schneider, *Moving on up? Racial equality and the corporate agenda. A study of FTSE 100 companies*, (London: The Runnymede Trust, 2000).

Saunders, 'Getting lesbian and gay issues on the international human rights agenda' (1996) 18 *Human Rights Q* 67.

Scappucci, 'Court of First Instance refuses to recognize Swedish 'Registered Partnership' rights and duties' (2000) 6 Eur Public L 355.

Schimmel and Heun, 'The legal situation of same-sex partnerships in Germany: an overview' in Wintemute and Andenaes (eds), *Legal recognition of same-sex partnerships—a study of national, European and international law* (Oxford: Hart Publishing, 2001).

Sciarra, 'European Social Policy and Labour Law—Challenges and Perspectives' (1995) IV(I) Collected Courses of the Academy of European Law 301.

Sciarra, 'Social Values and the Multiple Sources of European Social Law' (1995) 1 Eur LJ 60.

Sciarra, 'Labour law—a bridge between public services and citizenship rights' in Freedland and Sciarra, *Public services and citizenship in European law—public and labour law perspectives* (Oxford: Clarendon Press, 1998).

Sciarra, 'From Strasbourg to Amsterdam: prospects for the convergence of European social rights policy' in Alston, Bustelo and Heenan (eds), *The EU and human rights* (Oxford: Oxford University Press, 1999).

Sciarra, 'The employment title in the Amsterdam Treaty. A multi-language legal discourse' in O'Keeffe and Twomey (eds), *Legal issues of the Amsterdam Treaty* (Oxford: Hart Publishing, 1999).

Scognamiglio, *Codice di diritto del lavoro—annotato con la giurisprudenza—1° Parte Generale, Tomo 1, Disciplina Legislativa* (Bologna: Zanichelli, 2nd edn, 1980).

Shanks, *European Social Policy, Today and Tomorrow* (Oxford: Pergamon Press, 1977).

Shaw, 'The many pasts and futures of citizenship in the European Union' (1997) 22 ELR 554.

Shaw, 'The interpretation of European Union citizenship' (1998) 61 MLR 293.

Simitis, 'Dismantling or strengthening labour law: the case of the European Court of Justice' (1996) 2 Eur LJ 156.

Simmonds, 'The Concertation of Community Migration Policy' (1988) 25 CML Rev 177.

Skidmore, 'No gays in the military, Lawrence of Arabia need not apply' (1995) 24 ILJ 363.

Skidmore, 'Homosexuals have human rights too' (1996) 25 ILJ 63.

Skidmore, 'Can transsexuals suffer sex discrimination?' (1997) 19 J of Social Welfare and Family L 105.

Skidmore, 'The EC Framework Directive on Equal Treatment in Employment: towards a comprehensive Community anti-discrimination policy?' (2001) 30 ILJ 126.

Skidmore, 'Improving the position of lesbians and gay men at work: a German case study', forthcoming.

Skolander, 'Sweden' in Beger, Krickler, Lewis and Wuch (eds), *Equality for lesbians and gay men: a relevant issue in the civil and social dialogue* (Brussels: ILGA-Europe, 1998).

Small, 'Unravelling racialised relations in the United States of America and the United States of Europe' in Solomos and Wrench (eds), *Racism and Migration in Western Europe* (Oxford: Berg, 1993).

Snyder, 'The effectiveness of European Community law: institutions, processes, tools and techniques' (1993) 56 MLR 19.

Soininen and Graham, 'Persuasion contra legislation: preventing racism at the workplace: Sweden', Working Paper No WP/95/53/EN (Dublin: European Foundation for the Improvement of Living and Working Conditions, 1995).

Spencer, *States of Injustice—a guide to human rights and civil liberties in the European Union* (London: Pluto Press, 1995).

Spicker, 'The Principle of Subsidiarity and the Social Policy of the European Community' (1991) 1 J of Eur Social Policy 3.

Stychin, '*Grant*-ing rights: the politics of rights, sexuality and European Union' (2000) 51 Northern Ireland Legal Q 281.

Szyszczak, 'L'Espace Sociale Européenne: reality, dreams, or nightmares?' (1990) 33 German Ybk of Intl Law 284.

Szyszczak, 'Race Discrimination: the limits of market equality?' in Hepple and Syzszczak (eds), *Discrimination: the limits of the law* (London: Mansell, 1992).

Szyszczak, 'Building a European constitutional order: prospects for a general non-discrimination standard' in Dashwood and O'Leary (eds), *The principle of equal treatment in European Community law* (London: Sweet & Maxwell, 1997).

Szyszczak, 'The evolving European employment strategy' in Shaw (ed), *Social law and policy in an evolving European Union* (Oxford: Hart Publishing, 2000).

Szyszczak, *EC Labour Law* (Harlow: Longman, 2000).

Szyszczak, 'Social Policy' (2001) 50 ICLQ 175.

Teague and Grahl, '1992 and the emergence of a European industrial relations area' (1990) XIII Journal of Eur Integration 167.

Terrett, 'A bridge too far? Non-discrimination and homosexuality in European Community law' (1998) 4 Eur PL 487.

Thalhammer, Zucha, Enzenhofer, Salfinger and Ogris, 'Attitudes towards minority groups in the European Union' (Vienna: European Monitoring Centre on Racism and Xenophobia, 2001).

Thränhardt, *Europe—a new immigration continent. Policies and Politics in Comparative Perspective* (Hamburg: Lit, 1992).

Tobler, 'Europe: same-sex couples under the law of the EU' (2001) 3 Aktuelle Juristische Praxis 269.

United Nations High Commission for Refugees, *An overview of protection issues in Western Europe: legislative trends and positions taken* (Geneva: UNHCR, 1994).

Vaid, *Virtual equality: the mainstreaming of gay and lesbian liberation* (New York: Anchor Books, 1996).

Valentine, 'An equal place to work? Anti-lesbian discrimination and sexual citizenship in the European Union' in M García-Ramon and J Monk (eds) *Woman of the European Union—the politics of work and daily life* (London: Routledge, 1996).

Valiente, 'Sexual harassment in the workplace—equality policies in post-authoritarian Spain' in Carver and Mottier (eds), *The politics of sexuality—identity, gender, citizenship* (London, Routledge/ECPR Studies in European political science, 1998).

van der Klaauw, 'Amnesty Lobbies for Refugees' in Pedler and van Schendelen (eds), *Lobbying in the European Union—Companies, Trades Associations and Issue Groups* (Aldershot: Dartmouth Publishing, 1994).

Vasta, 'Rights and Racism in a new country of immigration: the Italian case' in Solomos and Wrench (eds), *Racism and Migration in Western Europe* (Oxford: Berg, 1993).

Vogel-Polsky, 'What future is there for a Social Europe after the Strasbourg summit?' (1990) 19 ILJ 65.

Waaldijk, 'The legal situation in the Member States' in A Clapham and K Waaldijk (eds), *Homosexuality: a European Community issue—essays on lesbian and gay rights in European law and policy* (Dordrecht: Martinus Nijhoff, 1993).

Waaldijk, 'Standard sequences in the legal recognition of homosexuality' (1994) 4 Australasian Gay and Lesbian L Rev 50.

Waaldijk, 'Free Movement of Same-Sex Partners' (1996) 3 Maastricht J of Eur and Comparative L 271.

Waddington, *Disability, employment and the European Community* (Antwerpen: Maklu, 1995).

Waddington, 'Testing the limits of the EC Treaty Article on Non-discrimination' (1999) 28 ILJ 133.

Waddington, 'Throwing some light on Article 13 EC Treaty' (1999) 6 Maastricht J of Eur and Comparative L 1.

Waddington, 'Article 13 EC: setting priorities in the proposal for a horizontal employment Directive' (2000) 20 ILJ 176.

Waddington, 'Tweede-generatie richtlijnen Gelijke Behandeling: de nieuwe Richtlijn inzake gelijke behandeling ongeacht ras of etnische afstamming en de Kaderrichtlijn gelijke behandeling in arbeid en beroep' (2000) 12 Sociaal Recht 357.

Waddington and Bell, 'More Equal than Others: Distinguishing European Union Equality Directives' (2001) 38 CML Rev 587.

Weatherill, *EC Consumer law and policy* (London: Longman, 1997).

Webber, 'From ethnocentrism to Euro-racism' (1991) 32 *Race and Class* 11.

Wedderburn, 'Labour standards, global markets and labour laws in Europe' in W Sengenberger and D Campbell (eds), *International labour standards and economic interdependence* (Geneva: International Institute for Labour Studies, 1994).

Wedderburn, *Labour Law and Freedom: Further Essays in Labour Law* (London: Lawrence and Wishart, 1995).

Weiler, 'Thou shalt not oppress a stranger: on the judicial protection of the human rights of non-EC nationals—a critique' (1992) 3 Eur J of Intl L 65.

Weiler, 'Fundamental rights and fundamental boundaries: on standards and values in the protection of human rights' in Neuwahl and Rosas (eds), *The European Union and human rights* (London: Martinus Nijhoff, 1995).

Weiler, *The Constitution of Europe—'Do the new clothes have an emperor?' and other essays on European integration* (Cambridge: Cambridge University Press, 1999).

Wellens and Borchardt, 'Soft law in European Community law' (1989) 14 ELR 267.

Whittle, 'Disability discrimination and the Amsterdam Treaty' (1998) 23 ELR 50.

Whittle, 'Disability rights after Amsterdam: the way forward' (2000) European Human Rights L Rev 33.

Whittle, 'The concept of disability discrimination and its legal construction', Paper presented at the workshop *Discrimination and affirmative action on the labour market—legal perspectives*, organised by Swedish National Institute for Working Life, 6–7 November 2000, Brussels.

Wintemute, 'Sexual Orientation Discrimination' in McCrudden and Chambers (eds), *Individual Rights and the Law in Britain* (Oxford: Clarendon Press, 1994).

Wintemute, Sexual Orientation and Human Rights—the United States Constitution, the European Convention and the Canadian Charter (Oxford: Clarendon Press, 1995).

Wintemute, 'Recognising new kinds of direct sex discrimination: Transsexualism, Sexual Orientation and Dress Codes' (1997) 60 MLR 334.

Wintemute, 'Libertés et droit fondamentaux des personnes gays, lesbiennes et bisexuelles en Europe' in Borrillo (ed), *Homosexualités et droit* (Paris: Presses Universitaires de France, 1998).

Wintemute and Andenaes (eds), *Legal recognition of same sex partnerships—a study of national, European and international law* (Oxford: Hart Publishing, 2001).

Wrench and Owen, 'Preventing racism at the workplace: the UK national report' Working Paper No WP/95/50/EN (Dublin: European Foundation for the Improvement of Living and Working Conditions, 1995).

Wrench, *Preventing racism at the workplace—a report on 16 European countries* (Dublin: European Foundation for the Improvement of Living and Working Conditions, 1996).

Wrench, *European Compendium of Good Practice for the Prevention of Racism at the Workplace* (Luxembourg: OOPEC, 1997).

Wrench and Solomos, 'The politics and processes of racial discrimination in Britain' in Solomos and Wrench (eds), *Racism and Migration in Western Europe* (Oxford: Berg, 1993).

INDEX

Printed in the United Kingdom
by Lightning Source UK Ltd.
135064UK00007B/233/A